Beowulf
and
The Fight at Finnsburh
A Bibliography

Beowulf

and

The Fight at Finnsburh

A Bibliography

Donald K. Fry
State University of New York
Stony Brook

Published for the Bibliographical Society
of the University of Virginia

The University Press of Virginia
Charlottesville

THE UNIVERSITY PRESS OF VIRGINIA

Copyright © 1969 by the Rector and Visitors
of the University of Virginia

First published 1969

Standard Book Number: 8139-0268-1
Library of Congress Catalog Card Number: 70-94760
Printed in the United States of America

For Fredson Bowers
winedryhten

Preface

THIS project originated in my dissatisfaction with existing bibliographies of *Beowulf* and *The Fight at Finnsburh*, which lack comprehensiveness, accuracy, and a useful system of classification. It was begun five years ago as a first step toward a dissertation on *Beowulf* and formulaic structures and largely completed before I decided to write on *Judith* instead. Although it was then in card form, it proved so useful in routine research work that publication seemed desirable.

No bibliography is ever finished, no catalog of 2280 items ever lacks inaccuracies, and no system of classification totally succeeds. Because of these limitations, a periodical note listing corrections and reclassifications is planned in a year or so; therefore, notice of errors or misclassifications is solicited from readers. Supplements or revised editions listing works omitted or published later are also contemplated. To aid this continuing effort, I would greatly appreciate notices of books and reviews, as well as offprints of articles. My address is available in the MLA directory.

I have accumulated many debts which I am pleased to acknowledge here. I wish to thank all those friends who looked up obscure references in remote places, especially Mark Kimble, David Hamilton, David Bevington, Ed Kessler, Allen Macduff, Charles Long, and Lee Piepho. I am grateful to the staff of Alderman Library at the University of Virginia, particularly Mr. Kenneth Stubbs and Miss Helena Koiner. Various colleagues have helped with suggestions and criticism, including Fredson Bowers, Lester Beaurline, Elizabeth Day, Bob Kellogg, Bruce Rosenberg, and Carol Wolf. Many persons, too numerous to mention, have kindly responded to my requests for clarifications of their published works.

The University of Virginia Faculty Research Committee provided a grant during the summer of 1967, for which I am most grateful. Of course, I must thank the Bibliographical Society of the University of Virginia for subsidizing this expensive volume.

Most of all, I wish to thank Mr. David Thelen, who has served as my research assistant for two years. His conscientiousness, accuracy, enthusiasm, versatility, and knack for serendipity have immensely improved this volume.

D. K. F.

Charlottesville, Virginia

Contents

Introduction

THE purpose of this volume is to provide a tool by which research scholars and students may quickly and accurately determine what previous scholarship can be brought to bear on specific literary and linguistic problems concerning *Beowulf* and *The Fight at Finnsburh*. This objective demands a useful system of classification and various modes of information access. Most scholarship defies simple classification, since any given work may deal with several subjects, for example, with diction, textual problems, religious interpretation, and historical backgrounds. The usual approach of previous bibliographers has been to list an item under some extremely wide category, such as R. W. Chambers's section 8: "Questions of literary history, date and authorship: *Beowulf* in the light of history, archaeology, heroic legend, mythology and folklore," with occasional cross references. Such a broad scope is meaningless for practical purposes, particularly if the article has an uninformative title, such as "Zum *Beowulf*."

This bibliography utilizes multiple classifications within the entries themselves, so that the reader may evaluate the potential usefulness of a work on the basis of its title, subject classifications, compiler's remarks, reviews, and the like. Item [412] (brackets indicate entry numbers) is a good example:

> 412   CREED, ROBERT PAYSON. "The Making of an Anglo–Saxon Poem." *ELH*, 26 (1959), 445–54. (dct, for, tec; 356–59) Replies by Fry [591], Greenfield [669], Lawrence [1186], and Stevick [2012].
> Review: R. M. Wilson, *YWES*, 40 (1959), 60

From this entry the scholar learns that the article deals with diction (dct), formulaic characteristics (for), narrative technique (tec), and lines 356–59 of *Beowulf*. He can also consult each of the four cross-referenced entries and a review. From all this information, plus the title of the article, he can decide whether or not he needs to see it. Publication data are provided in case he does.

Access to this information comes in any one of three ways: by direct approach, through indexes, or by browsing. If the title and author are known, the researcher may turn directly to the entry. Or, if he knows the subject (or subjects), he may find the article by means of the subject indices (some entries including line numbers are also indexed.) These same indexes may be used to compile a list of every work ever written on any given subject. Finally, simple browsing through the entries may turn up items of interest for further exploration. I have found that titles themselves spark trains of productive thought.

At first glance the format of the entries may seem formidable, but the system once mastered is simple to use. The first information given is the author's name, and the entries are arranged alphabetically by name, with anonymous entries [24–28] in sequence under *anon*. In each author's section entries are arranged alphabetically by title, disregarding articles such as *the* or *das*. Untitled entries follow the titled, in order of source of publication. Next comes publication data, in the *PMLA* format with some modifications. Subject classifications enclosed in parentheses follow, with line numbers treated placed after a semicolon: e.g., (dct, for, tec; 356–59). The subject codes are phonetic and easily memorized in a few moments; *the categories are meant to be suggestive rather than restrictive*. Then, where necessary, compiler's remarks are added for clarification and cross references. Reviews of the item conclude the entry. In the case of multiple editions or appearances, each is treated as a subentry, with its own remarks, reviews, and occasionally additional classifications.

Every work published before July 1967 which deals with *Beowulf* or *Finnsburh* in any useful and significant way, regardless of quality, is included. Mere mentions are not listed unless they are early (before 1850) or by important literary figures, e.g., by Sir Walter Scott [1885]. I have made no effort to exhaust anthologies, minor literary histories, general encyclopedias, or dictionaries. Some reviews are of sufficient significance as to deserve subject classifications; these are listed as separate entries, with appropriate cross references under the work they review. Derivative works, such as poems, plays, and novels, are included but not analyzed by subject, although they are indexed.

Abbreviations

Dania	*Dania (Tidsskrift for Folkemål og Folkeminder)*
DDABAU	*Doctoral Dissertations Accepted by American Universities*
DLZ	*Deutsche Literaturzeitung*
DS	*Danske Studier*
DUJ	*Durham University Journal*
DVLG	*Deutsche Vierteljahrsschrift für Literaturwissenschaft und Geistesgeschichte*
EA	*Etudes Anglaises*
E&S	*Essays and Studies by Members of the English Association*
E&S, UCPE	*Essays and Studies, University of California Publications in English*
EdL	*Etudes de Lettres* (Université de Lausanne)
EETS	*Early English Text Society*
EGS	*English and Germanic Studies*
EHR	*English Historical Review*
ELH	*ELH* (sometimes listed as *Journal of English Literary History*)
ELN	*English Language Notes*
English	*English* (London)
EPS	*English Philological Studies*
ES	*English Studies*
ESt	*Englische Studien*
EST	*English Studies Today*
FT	*Finsk-Tidskrift*
FuF	*Forschungen und Fortschritte*
GDM	*Gads Danske Magazin* (formerly *Danske Tidsskrift*)
GGA	*Göttingische gelehrte Anzeigen*
GM	*Gentleman's Magazine*
GR	*Germanic Review*
GRM	*Germanisch-romanische Monatsschrift*
Hist Zs	*Historische Zeitschrift*
HZM	*Handelingen van de Zuidnederlandse Maatschappij voor Taal-en Letterkunde en Geschiedenis*
IALR	*International Anthropological and Linguistic Review*
IEY	*Iowa English Yearbook*
IF	*Indogermanische Forschungen*
JAF	*Journal of American Folklore*
JEGP	*Journal of English and Germanic Philology*
JHI	*Journal of the History of Ideas*
JRSAI	*Journal of the Royal Society of Antiquaries of Ireland*
KN	*Kwartalnik Neofilologiczny* (Warsaw)
KVHAA	*Kungl. Vitterhets Historie och Antikivitets Akademiens Handlingar. Filol. -filos. serien*
L&L	*Life and Letters*
LB	*Leuvense Bijdragen*

LGRP or *Litbl*	*Literaturblatt für germanische und romanische Philologie*
LitCbl	*Literarisches Centralblatt*
LM	*Language Monographs*
LRNYEP	*Literary Review, New York Evening Post*
LSE	*Lund Studies in English*
LUA	*Lunds Universitets Årsskrift*
MA	*Le Moyen Âge*
MAE	*Medium Ævum*
MArc	*Medieval Archaeology*
MLN	*Modern Language Notes*
MLQ	*Modern Language Quarterly*
MLR	*Modern Language Review*
MMPMR	*Münchener Museum für Philologie des Mittelalters und der Renaissance*
MP	*Modern Philology*
N&Q	*Notes and Queries*
NAR	*North American Review*
NB	*Namn och Bygd*
NJKA	*Neue Jahrbücher für das klassische Altertum*
NM	*Neuphilologische Mitteilungen*
NMs	*Neuphilologische Monatsschrift*
NRs	*Neue Rundschau*
NS	*Die Neueren Sprachen*
NSM	*Nuovi Studi Medievali*
NT	*Nordisk Tidskrift*
NTF	*Nordisk Tidskrift för Filologi*
NTVKI	*Nordisk Tidskrift för Vetenskap, Konst och Industri*
NYHTB	*New York Herald Tribune Books*
NYTBR	*New York Times Book Review*
OM	*Oxford Magazine*
PBA	*Proceedings of the British Academy*
PLPLS-LHS	*Proceedings of the Leeds Philosoph. and Lit. Society, Lit. and Hist. Section*
PMASAL	*Papers of the Michigan Academy of Science, Arts, and Letters*
PMLA	*PMLA (Publications of the Modern Language Association)*
PQ	*Philological Quarterly*
Q&F	*Quellen und Forschungen*
QFSK	*Quellen und Forschungen zur Sprach- und Kulturgeschichte der Germanischen Völker*
QJS	*Quarterly Journal of Speech*
RAA	*Revue Anglo-Américaine*
RBPH	*Revue Belge de Philologie et d'Histoire*
RC	*Revue Critique*
RES	*Review of English Studies*

RG	*Revue Germanique*
RL	*Reallexikon der germanischen Altertumskunde*, ed. by J. Hoops
RLV	*Revue des Langues Vivantes* (Brussels)
Saga-Book	*Saga-Book* (Viking Society for Northern Research)
SAQ	*South Atlantic Quarterly*
SELJ	*Studies in English Literature* (English Literary Society of Japan, University of Tokyo)
SEP	*Studien zur englischen Philologie* (often called *Morsbachs Studien*)
SGG	*Studia Germanica Gandensia*
SIL	*Studies in Linguistics*
SN	*Studia Neophilologica*
SÖAW	*Sitzungsberichte der Österreichischen Akademie der Wissenschaften in Wien. Phil.-hist. Klasse*
SP	*Studies in Philology*
SPAW	*Sitzungsberichte der Preussischen Akademie der Wissenschaften. Phil.-hist. Klasse*
Sprache	*Die Sprache* (Vienna)
SR	*Sewanee Review*
SRL	*Saturday Review* (London)
SS	*Scandinavian Studies*
SSLSN	*Skrifter utgivna av Svenska Litteratursällskapet. Studier i Nordisk Filologi*
SSN	*Scandinavian Studies and Notes*
TCAAS	*Transactions of the Connecticut Academy of Arts and Sciences*
THSC	*Transactions of the Honorable Society of Cymmrodorion*
TLS	*Times* (London) *Literary Supplement*
TNTL	*Tijdschr. voor Ned. Taal- en Letterkunde* (Leiden)
TPP	*Tidskrift for Philologi og Paedagogik*
TPS	*Transactions of the Philological Society*
TR	*La Table Ronde*
TRSL	*Transactions of the Royal Society of Literature* (London)
TSL	*Tennessee Studies in Literature*
TSLL	*Texas Studies in Language and Literature*
UCPE	*University of California Studies in English*
UKPHS	*University of Kansas Publications, Humanistic Studies*
UMSE	*University of Mississippi Studies in English*
UTQ	*University of Toronto Quarterly*
UUA	*Uppsala Universitets Årsskrift*
UWSLL	*University of Wisconsin Studies in Language and Literature*
VSLA	*Vetenskaps-societeten i Lund Årsbok*
WR	*Westminster Review*
WSt	*Word Study*
YBVS	*Year Book of the Viking Society*

YR	*Yale Review*
YSE	*Yale Studies in English*
YWES	*Year's Work in English Studies*
YWMLS	*Year's Work in Modern Language Studies*
ZAA	*Zeitschrift für Anglistik und Amerikanistik (East Berlin)*
ZDA	*Zeitschrift für Deutsches Altertum und Deutsche Literatur*
ZDP	*Zeitschrift für Deutsche Philologie (Berlin-Bielefeld-München)*
ZFDG	*Zeitschrift für Deutsche Geschichtswissenschaft*
ZOG	*Zeitschrift für die österreichischen Gymnasien*
ZVS	*Zeitschrift für Vergleichende Sprachforschung*

COLLECTIONS:

Baugh	*Studies in Medieval Literature in Honor of Professor Albert Croll Baugh*, ed. by M. Leach. Philadelphia, 1961
Behaghel	*Germanische Philologie: Ergebnisse und Aufgaben: Festschrift für O. Behaghel*, ed. by A. Goetze, W. Horn, and F. Maurer. Heidelberg, 1934
Brodeur	*Studies in Old English Literature in Honor of Arthur G. Brodeur*, ed. by S. B. Greenfield. Eugene, Ore., 1963
Brown	*Essays and Studies in Honor of Carleton Brown.* N.Y., 1940
Collitz	*Studies in Honor of Hermann Collitz.* Baltimore, 1930
Curry	*Essays in Honor of Walter Clyde Curry.* Nashville, 1954
Deutschbein	*Englische Kultur in sprachwissenschaftlicher Deutung: Festschrift für Max Deutschbein*, ed. by W. Schmidt. Leipzig, 1936
Dickins	*The Anglo–Saxons: Studies in Some Aspects of Their History and Culture Presented to Bruce Dickins*, ed. by P. Clemoes. London, 1959
Ehrismann	*Vom Werden des deutschen Geistes: Festgabe Gustav Ehrismann.* Berlin and Leipzig, 1925
Fischer	*Festschrift für Walther Fischer, zu seinem 70. Geburtstag.* Heidelberg, 1959
Flasdieck	*Britannica: Festschrift für Hermann Flasdieck*, ed. by W. Iser and H. Schabram. Heidelberg, 1960
Förster	*Britannica: Max Förster, zum sechzigsten Geburtstage.* Leipzig, 1929
French	*Essays in Literary History Presented to J. Milton French*, ed. by R. Kirk and C. F. Main. New Brunswick, N.J., 1960
Furnivall	*An English Miscellany Presented to Dr. Furnivall.* Oxford, 1901
Hammerich	*Festgabe für L. L. Hammerich: Aus Anlass seines siebzigsten Geburtstages.* Copenhagen, 1962
Hart	*Studies in Language and Literature in Celebration of the Seventieth Birthday of James Morgan Hart.* N.Y., 1909

Hübner	Festschrift für Walter Hübner, ed. by D. Riesner and H. Gneuss. Berlin, 1964
Jespersen	A Grammatical Miscellany Offered to Otto Jespersen on His 70th Birthday. London and Copenhagen, 1930
Kittredge	Anniversary Papers by Colleagues and Pupils of George Lyman Kittredge. Boston and London, 1913
Klaeber	Studies in English Philology: A Miscellany in Honor of Frederick Klaeber, ed. by K. Malone and M. B. Ruud. Minneapolis, 1929
Krause	?Festschrift für K. E. Krause. Rostock, 1890
Liebermann	Texte und Forschungen zur englischen Kulturgeschichte: Festgabe für Felix Liebermann zum 20. Juli 1921. Halle, 1921
Luick	Neusprachliche Studien: Festgabe für Karl Luick. Supplement to Die Neueren Sprachen (1925)
Magoun	Franciplegius: Medieval and Linguistic Studies in Honor of Francis Peabody Magoun, Jr., ed. by J. B. Bessinger and R. P. Creed. N.Y., 1965
Malone	Philologica: The Malone Anniversary Studies, ed. by T. A. Kirby and H. B. Woolf. Baltimore, 1949
Manly	The Manly Anniversary Studies in Language and Literature. Chicago, 1923
Moneta	?P. Moneta, zum 40 jähr. Dienstjub. Vienna, 1892
Morsbach	Festschrift für Lorenz Morsbach. Halle a.S., 1913
Mossé	Mélanges de linguistique et de philologie: Fernand Mossé in memoriam. Paris, 1959
Nakayama	Essays in English and American Literature: In Commemoration of Professor Takejaro Nakayama's Sixty-first Birthday. Tokyo, 1961
Otsuka	Studies in English Grammar and Linguistics: A Miscellany in Honour of Takanobu Otsuka, ed. by K. Araki, T. Egawa, T. Oyama, and M. Yasui. Tokyo, 1958
PGrdr	Grundriss der germanischen Philologie, ed. by Hermann Paul
Sapori	Studi in onore di Armando Sapori. Milan, 1957
Schade	Festschrift zum siebzigsten Geburtstag Oskar Schade. Königsberg, 1896
Schlaugh	Studies in Language and Literature in Honor of Margaret Schlaugh. Warsaw, 1966
SHL&CS	Studies in Heroic Legend and Current Speech, ed. by S. Einarsson and N. E. Eliason. Copenhagen 1959
SHOEL	Studies in the History of Old English Literature, by Kenneth Sisam. Oxford, 1953 [1963]
Sievers	Germanica: Eduard Sievers zum 75. Geburtstage. Halle, 1925

Smith	*Early English and Norse Studies Presented to Hugh Smith in Honour of His Sixtieth Birthday*, ed. by A. Brown and P. Foote. London, 1963
Spira	*Festschrift zum 75. Geburtstag von Theodor Spira*, ed. by H. Viebrock and W. Erzgräber. Heidelberg, 1961
Spitzer	*Studia Philologica et Litteraria in Honorem Leo Spitzer*, ed. by A. G. Hatcher and K. L. Selig. Bern, 1958
Taylor	*Humaniora: Essays in Literature, Folklore, Bibliography, Honoring Archer Taylor on His Seventieth Birthday*, ed. by W. D. Hand and G. O. Ault. Locust Valley, N.Y., 1960
Tegnér	*Studier Tillägnade Esaias Tegnér.* Lund, 1918
Tolkien	*English and Medieval Studies Presented to J. R. R. Tolkien on the Occasion of His Seventieth Birthday*, ed. by N. Davis and C. L. Wrenn. London, 1962
12BP	*Twelve "Beowulf" Papers, 1940–1960, with Additional Comments.* Neuchatel, 1962. [166]
Viëtor	*Festschrift Wilhelm Viëtor.* Supplement to *Die Neueren Sprachen* (1910)
Wessén	*Festskrift tillägnade Elias Wessén.* Lund, 1954
Wolff	*Festschrift für Ludwig Wolff zum 70. Geburtstag.* Neumünster, 1962

SUBJECT CLASSIFICATIONS

alg	Allegory (as opposed to symbolism)
ana	Analogues (as opposed to sources)
arc	Archaeology
bbl	Bibliography
chr	Characters and characterization
com	Composition (includes author, date, place of origin)
dct	Diction (as opposed to individual word studies)
edt	Edition (includes partial editions and printings from other editions)
epc	Epic characteristics
Fep	Finnsburh episode (*Beowulf* 1063–1159a)
Fnb	*Fight at Finnsburh*
for	Oral-formulaic characteristics (after Magoun [1306])
gen	General treatment
hst	History (historical backgrounds in the poem and of the poet)
img	Imagery
inf	Influence (*of* the poem as opposed to *on* the poem)
int	Interpretation (except religious, symbolic, or allegorical)
ken	Kennings

lng   Linguistics (includes etymology)
mns   Manuscript (Cotton Vitellius A. XV [226])
mth   Mythology (folklore, pagan religious beliefs, and legends)
mtr   Meter (includes rhythm and alliteration)
nam   Names (proper and place names)
nts   Notes (notes to specific lines)
par   Paraphrase (as opposed to translation)
ref   Reference (concordance, pedagogy, any apparatus with the exception of notes, glossaries, and name indexes)
rel   Religion (Christian backgrounds and interpretations)
rht   Rhetoric
sch   Scholarship (reviews of research, studies of scholars)
smb   Symbolism (as opposed to allegory)
src   Source (sources of the poem)
stl   Style (miscellaneous stylistic studies)
str   Structure
tec   Technique (narrative technique)
thm   Themes (excluding oral-formulaic "themes")
trl   Translation (as opposed to paraphrase; discussions of methods of translation are labeled "about trl")
txt   Textual
unt   Unity
var   Variation
wrd   Words (studies of individual words as opposed to diction in general)

MISCELLANEOUS TERMS

Anz.   Anzeiger
?   Doubtful entry
<   Originates from
†   Unnumbered item

The Bibliography

1   AARSLEFF, Hans. *The Study of Language in England, 1780–1860.* Princeton, 1967. (lng, sch)

2   ABBOTT, Wilbur Cortez. "Hrothulf." *MLN*, 19 (1904), 122–25. (chr, hst, int, txt; 1163–66, 1181–88) Reply by Klaeber [1042].

3   ACKERMAN, Robert W. *Backgrounds to Medieval English Literature.* New York, Toronto, 1966: Random House paperback SLL-7. (Fnb, gen)

4   ADAMS, John F. *Beowulf: Analytic Notes and Review.* N.Y., 1965: Study Master Outline 101. (gen)

5   ADDY, Sidney Oldall. "The '*stapol*' in *Beowulf*: Hall and Chambers." *N&Q*, 152 (1927), 363–65. (hst, wrd; 926, 2718)
Review: M. Daunt, *YWES*, 8 (1927), 84

6   ALBERTSON, Clinton. "Anglo–Saxon Literature and Western Culture." *Thought*, 33 (1958), 93–116. (hst)

6.1 ——. *Anglo-Saxon Saints and Heroes.* N.Y., 1967. (com, hst)

7   ALFRED, William. *Beowulf.* In *Medieval Epics.* New York, 1963: Modern Library Giant ML-G87. pp. 1–83. (gen, trl)
Trans. into English prose, based on Klaeber [1026] and Wrenn [2244].
Reviews:
    1   G. F. Jones, *Speculum*, 39 (1964), 191–92
    2   R. M. Wilson, *YWES*, 44 (1963), 70–71

8   ALSTON, R. C. *An Introduction to Old English.* Evanston, Ill., and Elmsford, N.Y., 1962. (edt, nts; 1–52, 194–228, 1518–90)

9   AMIRA, Karl von. "Recht." *PGrdr*, IIb (1889), 35–200. (hst)
2d ed., III (1900), 51–222
3d ed., separately, [Strasbourg?], 1913

10   AMIS, Kingsley. "Anglo-Saxon Platitudes." *Spectator*, 198 (1957), 445. (gen) Review of Wright [2251]

10.1 ——. "Beowulf." In his *Case of Samples: Poems 1946–1956.* N.Y., 1957. p. 14. (poem)

11   ANDERSON, George Kulmer. *"Beowulf*, Chaucer, and Their Backgrounds." In Lewis Leary, ed., *Contemporary Literary Scholarship: A Critical Review.* N.Y., 1958. pp. 25–52. (sch)

12   ——. *The Literature of the Anglo–Saxons.* London, Princeton, 1949. (ana, bbl, chr, com, Fnb, gen, hst, mns, src, str, trl) Translates into English prose *Bwf* 418–24, 544–58, 559–67, 710–90, 853–74, 1071–74, 1114–17, 1357–77, 1724–68, 2247–66, 2444–62, 2732–43, 3020–27, 3178–82, and *Fnb* 2–9, 31–36.
Reviews:
   1   *CE*, 11 (1949–50), 174
   2   *TLS*, 25 Aug. 1950, p. 535
   3   E. V. K. Dobbie, *GR*, 25 (1950), 128–31
   4   N. E. Eliason, *MLN*, 66 (1951), 493–96
   5   A. Macdonald, *MLR*, 46 (1951), 471–73
   6   K. Malone, *JEGP*, 49 (1950), 243–45
   7   F. Mossé, *EA*, 5 (1952), 71
   8   D. Whitelock, *RES*, 4 (1953), 149–50
   9   R. M. Wilson, *YWES*, 30 (1949), 38–39
   10 H. B. Woolf, *ES*, 32 (1951), 223–25
Repr. N.Y., 1962
Review: R. M. Wilson, *YWES*, 43 (1962), 54

13   ——. *Old and Middle English Literature from the Beginnings to 1485.* Oxford, 1950. (bbl, gen)
Review: R. M. Wilson, *YWES*, 31 (1950), 44
Repr. N.Y., 1962: Collier paperback 04815

14   ——. "Old English Literature." In John H. Fisher, ed., *The Medieval Literature of Western Europe: A Review of Research, Mainly 1930–1960.* London, N.Y., 1966. pp. 35–71. (bbl, sch)
Review: *TLS*, 10 Nov. 1966, p. 1025

15   ANDERSON, L. F. *The Anglo–Saxon Scop.* University of Toronto Studies, Philological Series, 1. Toronto, 1903. (dct, hst, mtr)
Review: A. Heusler, *AfdA*, 31 (1908), 113–15

16   ANDERSON, Marjorie, and WILLIAMS, Blanche Colton. *Old English Handbook.* Boston, 1935. (edt; 491–661, 1345–76, 2669–2711)
Review: *TLS*, 12 Sept. 1936, p. 567

17   ANDREW, Samuel Ogden. *The Old English Alliterative Measure.* Croydon, 1931. (mtr)
Reviews:
   1   A. Brandl, *Archiv*, 161 (1932), 145–46

2   K. Brunner, *Beibl*, 44 (1933), 71–73
3   D. E. M. Clarke, *YWES*, 12 (1931), 60–62
4   J. R. Hulbert, *MP*, 29 (1932), 376–77
5   K. Malone, *JEGP*, 31 (1932), 639
6   S. Potter, *RES*, 9 (1933), 85–87

18   ——. *Postscript on "Beowulf."* Cambridge, 1948. (lng, mns, mtr, rht, stl)   Sequel to Andrew [21].
Reviews:
1   *N&Q*, 193 (1948), 373–74
2   K. Malone, *ES*, 32 (1951), 116–19
3   F. Mossé, *BSLP*, 45 (1951), 170–71
4   R. M. Wilson, *YWES*, 29 (1948), 60
5   C. L. Wrenn, *RES*, 1 (1950), 353–56

19   ——. "Relative and Demonstrative Pronouns in Old English." *Language*, 12 (1936), 283–93. (lng)

20   ——. "Some Principles of Old English Word Order." *MAE*, 3 (1934), 167–88. (lng)
Review: M. Serjeantson, *YWES*, 15 (1934), 78

21   ——. *Syntax and Style in Old English.* Cambridge, 1940. (lng, stl)   Andrew [18] is a sequel.
Reviews:
1   *TLS*, 14 Dec. 1940, p. 635
2   G. N. Garmonsway, *YWES*, 21 (1940), 42–43
3   H. Larsen, *JEGP*, 41 (1942), 85–88
4   A. Macdonald, *RES*, 17 (1941), 499–501
5   H. Meroney, *MP*, 39 (1946), 99–100 [2102]
6   S. Potter, *MLR*, 36 (1941), 252–55
7   G. V. Smithers, *MAE*, 12 (1943), 104–6

22   ——. "Three Textual Cruxes in *Beowulf*." *MAE*, 8 (1939), 205–7. (int, txt; 648–49, 1379, 3066–74b)
Review: G. N. Garmonsway, *YWES*, 20 (1939), 30–31

†   ANDREWS, A. E., see [1559].

23   ANGUS, Joseph. "Romance of *Beowulf*, (written) about 500." In his *Handbook of Specimens of English Literature.* London, [1872]. pp. 1–2. (gen)

24   ANON. "Beowulf." In *Chambers's Encyclopedia* (1875), II, 41–42. (gen)

25   ANON. "O monstro de Caim." *Epopéia*, 30 (1955), 3–20. (par)   Comic book, supposedly trans. from *Il Vittorioso* (?) of Rome.   Text in Portuguese, described and trans. by Magoun [1299].

26   ANON. "The Study of Words in *Beowulf*." *Word Study*, 7 (1931), 1. (lng, wrd)

27   ANON. (Untitled review of Thorkelin [2080]) *Dansk Lit-teratur-Tidende*, 1815, pp. 401–32, 437–46, 461–62. (trl, txt) Partial translation into Danish.

28   ANON. (Untitled review of Thorkelin [2080]) *Iduna*, 7 (1817), 133–59. (trl) Partial translation into Swedish.

29   ANSCOMBE, Alfred. "Beowulf in High-Dutch Saga." *N&Q*, 132 (1915), 133–34. (ana, nam)

30   ——. "Hama in the *Beowulf*." *N&Q*, 146 (1924), 112–13. (lng, nam, txt, wrd; 1198)

31   ——. "Hrethel the Great in Arthurian Romance." *N&Q*, 145 (1923), 327–28. (epc, nam) Attacks Chambers [307].

†   ANSON, W. S. W., see [2159].

32   ARBMAN, Erik Holger; ERICSSON, Mann; LINDQVIST, Sune; and LUNDBERG, Oskar. "Vendil in Uppland and the *Beowulf* Poem." In their *Vendel i Fynd och Forskning: Skrift med Anledning av Vendelmonumentets Tillkomst*. Uppsala, 1938. pp. 77–97. (arc, hst).
Review: C. L. Wrenn, *YWES*, 19 (1938), 40

33   ARMS, George W.; KIRBY, John P.; LOCKE, Louis G.; and WHITESELL, J. Edwin. "Beowulf." *Explicator*, 6 (1942), 1. (int; 736b–38b)

34   ARNDT, O. *Über die altgermanische epische Sprache*. Pader-born, 1877. (dct, epc, stl)

?35   ARNHEIM, J. "Über das Beowulflied." *Bericht der Jacob-son'schen Schule zu Seesen*, (1867–71). (par) Popular para-phrase in German.

36   ARNOLD, Thomas. *Beowulf: A Heroic Poem of the Eighth Century, with a Translation, Notes, and Appendix*. London, 1876. (com, edt, Fnb, hst, lng, mns, mtr, nam, nts, trl) Literal English prose, based on Thorpe [2084] and Grein [675]. Reviews:
      1   *Athenaeum*, 1877, II, 862–63
      2   *LitCbl*, 1877, no. 20
      3   J. M. Garnett, *AJPhil*, 1 (1880), 90–91
      4   H. Sweet, *Academy*, 10 (1876), 588c–89a
      5   R. Wülker, *Anglia*, 1 (1877), 177–86 [2265]
      6   ——, *LitCbl*, 1877, pp. 665–66

37   ——. *English Literature, 596–1832 (From the "Encyclopedia Britannica")*. N.Y., 1879. (com, gen, rel)

38   ——. *A Manual of English Literature*. London, 1862. (gen) 2d ed., 1870; 3d ed., 1873; Boston, 1876; 4th ed., London, 1877; 5th ed., Boston, 1880; 6th ed., 1882; 7th ed., 1896; 8th ed., 1898; 9th ed., London, N.Y., 1899

39 ———. *Notes on "Beowulf."* London, N.Y., 1898. (ana, gen)
Reviews:
    1 J. M. Garnett, *AJPhil*, 20 (1899), 442–44
    2 W. H. Hulme, *MLN*, 15 (1900), 23–26
    3 G. Sarrazin, *ESt*, 28 (1900), 410–18

40 ARON, Albert William. "Traces of Matriarchy in Germanic Hero-Lore." *Univ. of Wisconsin Studies in Language and Literature*, 9 (1920), esp. pp. 46–51. (hst)
Reviews:
    1 H. H. Bender, *AJPhil*, 42 (1921), 286–87
    2 T. P. Cross, *MP*, 18 (1921), 679–80

41 ASHDOWN, Margaret. "*Beowulf:* ll. 1543 ff." *MLR*, 25 (1930), 78. (int, txt, wrd; 1543–45)
Review: M. Daunt, *YWES*, 11 (1930), 55

42 ATKINS, J. W. H. *English Literary Criticism: The Medieval Phase.* Cambridge, 1943. (com, gen)
Repr. London, 1952

43 AUDEN, W. H. "A Short Ode to a Philologist." In *Tolkien*, pp. 11–12. (poem)

44 AURNER, Nellie Slayton. *An Analysis of the Interpretations of the Finnsburg Documents.* Univ. of Iowa Monographs, Humanistic Studies, 1, part 6. Iowa City, 1917. (bbl, Fnb, hst, int)

45 ———. *Hengest: A Study in Early English Hero Legend.* Univ. of Iowa Humanistic Studies, 2, part 1. Iowa City, 1921. (epc, Fnb, mth, nam)
Reviews:
    1 A. Heusler, *AfdA*, 42 (1923), 180–81
    2 F. Klaeber, *Archiv*, 144 (1922), 278
    3 F. Liebermann, *Beibl*, 35 (1924), 65–67

46 AXON, William Edward Armitage. "A Reference to the Evil Eye in *Beowulf.*" *TSRL*, 1899. (mth)

47 AYRES, Harry Morgan. *Beowulf, A Paraphrase.* Williamsport, Pa., 1933. (Fnb, hst, par) English prose on a saga model.
Reviews:
    1 *American Mercury*, 30 (1933), xx
    2 K. M., *MLN*, 49 (1934), 208

48 ———. "The Tragedy of Hengest in *Beowulf.*" *JEGP*, 16 (1917), 282–95. (epc, Fnb, int, nam; Fep)

49 AZARIAS (Brother). *The Development of English Literature: Old English Period.* N.Y., 1879. (gen)
2d ed., 1879.
Review: R. Wülker, *Anglia*, 4 Anz. (1881), 3–13
3d ed., 1890.

50   BACHLECHNER, Joseph von. "Eomâer und Heming (Hamlac)." *Germania*, 1 (1856), 297–303, 455–61. (hst)

51   ——. "Die Merovinge im *Beowulf.*" *ZDA*, 7 (1849), 524–26. (hst, int; 2921)

52   BÄCK, Hilding. *The Synonyms for "Child," "Boy," "Girl," in Old English: An Etymological-semasiological Investigation.* Lund Studies in English, 2. Lund 1934. (lng, wrd)
Review: M. Serjeantson, *YWES*, 15 (1934), 79

53   BAESECKE, George. *Vor- und Frühgeschichte des deutschen Schrifttums.* Vol. I, *Vorgeschichte.* Halle, 1940. (gen)

– 54   BAIRD, Joseph Lee. "Grendel the Exile." *NM*, 67 (1966), 375–81. (chr, dct, img)

55   ——. "The Rhetorical Strategies of the *Beowulf* Poet." Unpub. Ph.D. diss., Univ. of Kentucky, 1966. (rht)

56   ——. "Uses of Ignorance: *Beowulf* 435, 2330." *N&Q*, 212 (1967), 6–8. (chr, tec; 435, 2330)

57   BALL, Christopher J. E. "*Beowulf* 987." *Archiv*, 201 (1964), 43–46. (txt; 987).
Review: R. M. Wilson, *YWES*, 45 (1964), 60

58   ——. "Incge Beow. 2577." *Anglia*, 78 (1960), 403–10. (mth, txt; 2577)
Review: R. M. Wilson, *YWES*, 41 (1960), 55

59   BANNING, Adolf. *Die epischen Formeln im "Bêowulf."* Part 1: "Die verbalen Synonyma." Marburg diss., 1886. (dct, epc, var)

60   BARNES, Richard. "Horse Colors in Anglo–Saxon Poetry." *PQ*, 39 (1960), 510–12. (wrd)
Review: R. M. Wilson, *YWES*, 41 (1960), 55

61   BARNOUW, Adriaan J. "Nochmals zum ags. Gebrauch des Artikels." *Archiv*, 117 (1906), 366–67. (lng)

62   ——. *Textkritische Untersuchungen nach dem Gebrauch des bestimmten Artikels und des schwachen Adjektivs in der altenglischen Poesie.* Leiden, 1902. (lng, txt; 987ff, 1151–52, 2524ff)
Reviews:
    1   G. Binz, *ZDP*, 36 (1904), 269–74
    2   E. A. Kock, *ESt*, 32 (1903), 228–29
    3   L. L. Schücking, *GGA*, 167 (1905), II, 730–40 [1863]

63   BARTELS, Arthur. *Rechtsaltertümer in der ags. Dichtung.* Kiel diss., 1913. (hst)

64   BARTLETT, Adeline Courtney. *The Larger Rhetorical Patterns in Anglo–Saxon Poetry.* Columbia Univ. Studies in English and Comparative Literature, no. 122. N.Y., 1935. Cited as diss. in *DDABAU*, 1935–36, no. 3, 82, Columbia Univ., 1936. (rht, stl, str, tec)

Reviews:
  1 D. E. M. Clarke, *YWES*, 16 (1935), 71–73
  2 A. E. DuBois, *MLN*, 52 (1937), 132–33

65 BARTO, P. S. "The *Schwanritter-Sceaf* Myth in *Perceval le Gallois*." *JEGP*, 19 (1920), 190–200. (ana, mth)

† BASHE, Edwin J., see [794].

66 BASKERVILL, William Malone; and HARRISON, James A. *Anglo–Saxon Reader*. N.Y., 1898. (edt; 499–594, 791–836)
  2d ed., 1901, with John L. Hall.

67 BÄSSLER, Ferdinand. "*Beowulf*," "*Wieland der Schmied*," *und die Ravennaschlacht: Für die Jugend und das Volk*. Berlin, 1852. (par, rel) German paraphrase.
  2d ed., 1875.
  Review: F. Klaeber, *JEGP*, 5 (1903–5), 118

68 BASU, Nitish K. *History of English Literature from the Beginnings to Chaucer*. Calcutta, 1961. (gen)

69 BATCHELOR, C. C. "The Style of the *Béowulf:* A Study of the Composition of the Poem." *Speculum*, 12 (1937), 330–42. (com, dct, rel, stl, tec)

70 BATEMAN, J. *Ten Years Digging in Celtic and Saxon Grave Hills*. London, 1861. (arc)

71 BATESON, F. W., ed. *The Cambridge Bibliography of English Literature*. Cambridge, 1940; Suppl., 1957. Vol. I, pp. 63–68; Vol. V, pp. 63–70. (bbl)

72 BAUGH, Albert Croll. *Beowulf*. In A. C. Baugh and George William McClelland, eds., *Century Types of English Literature, Chronologically Arranged*. N.Y., 1925. pp. 4–43. (trl) English prose.
  Repr. in their *English Literature: A Period Anthology*. N.Y., 1954

73 BAUM, Paull Franklin. "The *Beowulf* Poet." *PQ*, 39 (1960), 389–99. (com, src, stl)
  Review: R. M. Wilson, *YWES*, 41 (1960), 53–54
  Repr. in Nicholson [1560], 353–65

74 ——. "The Character of Anglo–Saxon Verse." *MP*, 28 (1930–31), 143–56. (mtr)
  Review: M. Daunt, *YWES*, 11 (1930), 56

75 ——. "The Meter of the *Beowulf*." *MP*, 46 (1948–49), 73–91, 145–62. (mtr)
  Review: R. M. Wilson, *YWES*, 30 (1949), 41–42

76 Item canceled.

† BEACH, Mr., see [2272].

77   BEARE, W. *"Pollicis Ictus*, the Saturnian, and *Beowulf."*
      CP, 50 (1955), 89–97. (ana, mtr)

78   BEATY, John O. "The Echo-Word in *Beowulf* with a Note
      on the *Finnsburg Fragment."* *PMLA*, 49 (1934), 365–73.
      (chr, dct, Fnb, int, ken, rht, stl; *Fnb* 16, 33)
      Review: M. Serjeantson, *YWES*, 15 (1934), 66

79   ——. *Swords in the Dawn: A Story of the First Englishmen.*
      N.Y., 1937; London, 1938. (Fnb) Novel about Finnsburh.

80   BEHRE, Frank. *The Subjunctive in Old English Poetry.* Göte-
      borg, 1934. (lng)
      Review: M. Serjeantson, *YWES*, 15 (1934), 76–77

81   BELDEN, H. M. *"Beowulf* 62, Once More." *MLN*, 33
      (1918), 123–24. (int, txt; 62)

82   ——. "Onela the Scylding and Ali the Bold." *MLN*, 28
      (1913), 149–53. (ana, int, nam)

83   ——. "Scyld Scefing and Huck Finn." *MLN*, 33 (1918),
      315. (ana, chr)

84   BENARY, W. "Zum Beowulf-Grendelsage." *Archiv*, 130
      (1913), 154–55. (mth, nam) Concerns Grändelsmôr in
      Siebenbürgen.

85   BENEDETTI, A. *La canzone di "Beowulf," poema epico anglo-
      sassone del VI secolo: Versione italiana, con introduzione e note.*
      Palermo, 1916. (gen, nts, trl)

86   BENHAM, Allen Rogers. *English Literature from "Widsith" to
      the Death of Chaucer: A Source Book.* New Haven, 1916. (bbl,
      gen)

87   BENNETT, William H. "A West Norse-Frisian-Kentish
      Parallel." *IALR*, 1 (1953), 71–80. (ana, hst, lng, nam)
      On the Jutes.

88   BENNING, Helmut Anton. *"Welt" und "Mensch" in der
      altenglischen Dichtung: Bedeutungsgeschichtliche Untersuchung zum
      germanischaltenglischen Wortschatz.* *BEP*, 44. Münster diss.,
      1961. (dct, lng, wrd)
      Reviews:
        1 A. C. Bouman, *ES*, 43 (1962), 498–501
        2 A. Campbell, *RES*, 14 (1963), 99
        3 B. Carstensen, *NS*, 71 (1963), 283–84
        4 K. Grinda, *Anglia*, 79 (1962), 451–57
        5 C. A. Ladd, *N&Q*, 207 (1962), 395–96
        6 J. Rosier, *JEGP*, 61 (1962), 631–33
        7 R. M. Wilson, *YWES*, 42 (1963), 56
        8 C. L. Wrenn, *MAE*, 31 (1962), 140–41

†   BENTINCK-SMITH, M. G., see [951].

89   BEPLER, Helen I. "Sensory Impressions in *Beowulf*." Noted in *Abstracts of Theses, Univ. of Pittsburgh Bulletin*, 11 (1935), 313–14. (img)

90   BERENDSOHN, Walter A. "Altgermanische Heldendichtung." *NJKA*, 35 (1915), 633–48. (hst, mth)

91   ——. "Drei Schichten dichterischer Gestaltung im *Beowulf*-Epos." *MMPMR*, 2 (1913), 1–32. (com, str)

92   ——. "Die Gelage am Dänenhof zu Ehren Beowulfs." *MMPMR*, 3 (1914), 31–55. (ana, com, str)

93   ——. "Healfdenes Vater." *ANF*, 50 (1934), 148–56. (chr, hst, mth)
     Review: M. Serjeantson, *YWES*, 15 (1934), 62–63

94   ——. "*Hrólfssaga Kraka* und *Beowulf*-Epos." In *Niederdeutsche Studien: Festschrift für Conrad Borchling*. Neumünster, 1932. pp. 328–37. (ana, com, hst, mth)

95   ——. "Sind die Skyldinge und Skilfinge im *Beowulf* hunnische und herulische Könige?" *C&M*, 7 (1945), 114–37. (hst, nam)

96   ——. "Stilkritik am *Beowulf*-Epos." *ANF*, 54 (1939), 235–37. (com, stl)

97   ——. *Zur Vorgeschichte des "Beowulf."* Copenhagen, 1935. (com, src, stl, str)   Foreword by Otto Jespersen.
     Reviews:
         1   *TLS*, 19 Sept. 1935, p. 580
         2   A. Brandl, *Archiv*, 175 (1939), 228
         3   W. F. Bryan, *MLN*, 52 (1937), 374–78
         4   E. A. Kock, *ANF*, 53 (1937), 105–8
         5   K. Malone, *ES*, 19 (1937), 24–26
         6   F. Mossé, *RG*, 27 (1936), 399
         7   F. Norman, *MLR*, 31 (1936), 414–15
         8   E. A. Philippson, *GR*, 11 (1936), 294–96
         9   L. L. Schücking, *AfdA*, 55 (1936), 117–21
        10   L. Stettner, *GRM*, 24 (1936), 232–33
        11   G. Turville-Petre, *YWMLS*, 8 (1936–37), 235
        12   J. de Vries, *Neophil*, 21 (1936), 212–19
        13   C. L. Wrenn, *RES*, 13 (1937), 464–67

98   BERRY, Francis. "The Modernity of *Beowulf*." *L&L*, 53 (April 1947), 19–26. (gen, hst, mns, smb) Discusses Bone's translation [151].

99   ——. "A Suppressed 'Aposiopesis' in the *Fight at Finnsburg*." *N&Q*, 199 (1954), 186–87. (Fnb, int, rht, stl, tec; 1174, 3150–55)
     Review: R. M. Wilson, *YWES*, 35 (1954), 40

100   BESSAI, Frank. "Comitatus and Exile in Old English Poetry." *Culture*, 25 (1964), 130–44. (hst, thm)

101   BESSINGER, Jess Balsor, Jr. *"Beowulf* and the Harp at Sutton Hoo." *UTQ*, 27 (1958), 148–68. (ana, for, hst, mtr, smb)

102   ——. *"Beowulf, Caedmon's Hymn* and Other Old English Poems Read in Old English." Caedmon LP Record TC 1161 (1962). (gen, trl) Description and translation of text on jacket; reads 1–125, 195–225, 702–852, 3137–82, in Pope's system of metrics [1662], from Magoun text [1296].

103   ——. "The Sutton Hoo Ship-Burial: A Chronological Bibliography, Part Two." *Speculum*, 33 (1958), 515–22. (arc, bbl) Part 1 is Magoun [1311].
       Review: R. M. Wilson, *YWES*, 39 (1958), 70

 †   ——, see also [1296]

104   BEVIS, Richard W. *"Beowulf:* A Restoration." *ELN*, 2 (1965), 165–68. (epc, int, txt, 1541, 2094)

105   BIESE, A. *Die Entwicklung des Naturgefühls im Mittelalter und in der Neuzeit.* Leipzig, 1887. (img, thm)
       Trans. into English as *The Development of Feeling for Nature in the Middle Ages.* London, 1905. Repr., N.Y., 1963.

106   BINZ, Gustav. "Zeugnisse zur germanischen Sage in England." *Beitr*, 20 (1895), 141–223. (ana, Fnb, hst, mth, nam)

107   ——. (Untitled review of Trautmann [2107]) *Beibl*, 14 (1903), 358–60. (lng, txt)

108   ——. (Untitled review of Ries [1710]) *Beibl*, 22 (1911), 65–78 (lng)

109   ——. (Untitled review of Panzer [1618]) *Beibl*, 24 (1913), 321–27. (ana, mth)

110   ——. (Untitled review of Trautmann [2109]) *ZDP*, 37 (1905), 529–36. (Fnb, int, nam, txt, wrd; 1066–69)

 †   BIRCH, Walter de Gray, see [991].

111   BJÖRKMAN, Erik. "Bedwig in den westsächsischen Genealogien." *Beibl*, 30 (1919), 23–25. (chr, hst, mth, nam)

112   ——. *"Béovulf."* In Henrik Schück, ed., *Varldslitteraturen i urval och öfversättning.* Stockholm, 1902. pp. 463–74. (com, src, trl) Translates 2207–3182 into Swedish prose; introd. by Schück.

113   ——. "Bēow, Bēaw und Bēowulf." *ESt*, 52 (1918), 145–93. (mth, nam)

114   ——. "*Bēowulf* och Sveriges historia." *NT*, 1917, pp. 161–79. (chr, hst, nam)

115   ——. "Beowulfforskning och mytologi." *FT*, 84 (1918), 250–71. (mth)

116   ——. "*Haeðcyn* und *Hákon*." *ESt*, 54 (1920), 24–34. (ana, chr, hst, mth, nam)

117   ——. *Nordische Personennamen in England in alt- und frühmittelenglischer Zeit: ein Beitrag zur Englischen Namenkunde. SEP* 37. Halle a.S., 1910. (hst, mth, nam)

118   ——. "Scedeland, Scedenig." *NB*, 6 (1918), 162–68. (hst, nam) Answer to Lindroth [1257]; answers by Lindroth [1258–59].

119   ——. "Skialf och Skilfing." *NB*, 7 (1919), 163–81. (hst, nam) Ed. by Eilert Ekwall with a note on Björkman's work.

120   ——. "Sköldungaättens mytiska stamfäder." *NT*, 1918, pp. 163–82. (chr, hst, mth)

121   ——. *Studien über die Eigennamen im "Beowulf." SEP* 58. Halle a.S., 1920. (hst, mth, nam)
       Reviews:
       1   G. Binz, *LGRP*, 42 (1921), 173–74
       2   G. Neckel, *Archiv*, 148 (1925), 156
       3   W. Preusler, *LitCbl*, 73 (1922), 75
       4   F. R. Schroder, *GRM*, 9 (1921), 122

122   ——. "Über den Namen der Jüten." *ESt*, 39 (1908), 356–61. (hst, nam)

123   ——. "Zu altenglisch *Eote*, *Yte*, usw., dänischen *Jyder*, 'Jüten.'" *Beibl*, 28 (1917), 275–80. (hst, nam)

124   ——. "Zu einigen Namen im *Bēowulf*: Breca, Brondingas, Wealhþēo(w)." *Beibl*, 30 (1919), 170–80. (hst, mth, nam)

125   ——. (Untitled review of Heyne/Schücking [815]) *Beibl*, 30 (1919), 180–81. (int, lng, txt)

126   BLACKBURN, F. A. "The Christian Coloring in the *Beowulf*." *PMLA*, 12 (1897), 205–25. (com, rel, str)
       Rcpr. in Nicholson [1560], pp. 1–21

127   ——. "Note on Beowulf 1591–1617." *MP*, 9 (1911–12), 555–66. (int, mns, txt) Refuted by Chambers [312].

128   BLAIR, Peter Hunter. *An Introduction to Anglo–Saxon England*. Cambridge, 1956. (arc, com, Fnb, hst, mns, trl) Translates 721b–27, 1357b–61a, 1372b–76a into alliterative verse.
       Reviews:
       1   *TLS*, 3 March 1956, p. 66
       2   C. Brinton, *NYHTB*, 25 Dec. 1960, p. 32
       3   B. Colgrave, *RES*, 8 (1957), 422–24

    4 R. Cramp, *MAE*, 26 (1957), 117–20

    5 R. H. C. Davis, *EHR*, 72 (1957), 488–89

    6 ——, *History*, 42 (1957), 48–49

    7 M.M. Dubois, *EA*, 10 (1957), 145–46

    8 M. L. W. Laistner, *AHR*, 61 (1955–56), 939–40

    9 T. J. Oleson, *Speculum*, 31 (1956), 488–90

   10 D. M. Stenton, *Antiquity*, 31 (1957), 105–6

Repr. 1959; Cambridge paperback 1960

129   BLAKE, N. F. "The Heremod Digressions in *Beowulf*." *JEGP*, 51 (1962), 278–87. (chr, hst, mth, str, tec, txt, wrd; 898–915, 1709–23)

Review: R. M. Wilson, *YWES*, 43 (1962), 57

130   BLISS, Alan J. *The Metre of "Beowulf."* Oxford, 1958. (lng, mtr) See Clemons [343] and Willard [2217].

Reviews:

    1 K. Hansen, *ZAA*, 8 (1960), 77–80

    2 W. P. Lehmann, *JEGP*, 59 (1960), 137–42

    3 E. G. Stanley, *EPS*, 8 (1963), 47–53

    4 R. M. Wilson, *YWES*, 39 (1958), 70–71

    5 C. L. Wrenn, *RES*, 11 (1960), 414–16

 †   BLOMFIELD, Joan, see TURVILLE–PETRE, Mrs.

131   BLOOMFIELD, Morton W. "*Beowulf* and Christian Allegory: An Interpretation of Unferth." *Traditio*, 7 (1951), 410–15. (alg, chr, rel, smb)

Repr. in Nicholson [1560], pp. 155–64

132   ——. "Patristics and Old English Literature: Notes on Some Poems." *CL*, 14 (1962), 36–43. (int, rel, txt; 2330)

Review: R. M. Wilson, *YWES*, 43 (1962), 54–55

Also in *Brodeur*, pp. 36–44, and repr. in Nicholson [1560], pp. 367–72

133   BOBERG, Inger M. "Er Skjoldungerne Hunnerkinger?" *APS*, 18 (1945), 257–67. (hst)

134   ——. "Die Sage von Vermund und Uffe." *APS*, 16 (1942–43), 129–57. (ana)

135   BODE, Wilhelm. *Die Kenningar in der angelsächsischen Dichtung mit Ausblicken auf andere Litteraturen.* Strasbourg diss., Darmstadt and Leipzig, 1886. (dct, img, ken, stl, var)

Reviews:

    1 F. Bischoff, *Archiv*, 79 (1887), 115–16

    2 A. Brandl, *DLZ*, 8 (1887), 897–98

    3 F. B. Gummere, *MLN*, 2 (1887), 17–19 [725]

    4 F. Kluge, *ESt*, 10 (1887), 117

    5 R. M. Meyer, *AfdA*, 13 (1887), 136–38

136 BOEHLER, Maria. *Die altenglischen Frauennamen.* Berlin, 1930. (epc, nam)
Review: M. Daunt, *YWES*, 11 (1930), 63–64

137 BOEHMER, George H. "Prehistoric Naval Architecture of the North of Europe." *Report of the U.S. National Museum, under the Direction of the Smithsonian Institution* (1891), pp. 527–647. (hst)

138 BOER, Richard Constant. *Die altenglische Heldendichtung.* I. *Béowulf.* Halle a.S., 1912. (ana, com, mtr, sch)
Reviews:

    1 A. J. Barnouw, *Museum*, 21 (1913), 53–58

    2 W. E. Berendsohn, *Litbl*, 35 (1914), 152–54

    3 R. Dyboski, *Allgemeines Literaturblatt*, 22 (1913), 497–99

    4 R. Imelmann, *DLZ*, 34 (1913), 1062–66 [938]

    5 H. Jantzen, *Zeitschrift für Neusprachlichen Unterricht*, 13 (1914), 546–47

139 ———. "Die Béowulfsage. I. Mythische Reconstructionen; II. Historische Untersuchung der Überlieferung." *ANF*, 19 (1902), 19–88. (ana, hst, mth)
Review: *DLZ*, 23 (1902), 1956

140 ———. "Eene episode uit den *Beowulf.*" *Handelingen van het 3de Nederlandsche Philologen Congres* (1903), pp. 84–94. (hst; 1934)

141 ———. "Finnsage und Nibelungensage." *ZDA*, 47 (1903–4), 125–60. (ana, Fnb, mth, txt; Fep)

142 ———. *Die Sagen von Ermanerich und Dietrich von Bern.* Halle a.S., 1910. Esp. pp. 181–84. (ana, hst)

143 ———. *Studiën over de Metrik van het Alliteratievers.* Amsterdam, 1916. (mtr)

144 ———. "Studier over Skjoldungedigtningen." *Aarbøger for Nordisk Oldkyndighed og Historie*, 3 (1922), 133–266. (epc, hst, mth, stl) Reply by La Cour [395].

145 ———. *Untersuchungen über den Ursprung und die Entwicklung der Nibelungensage.* Halle a.S, 1909. Vol. III, chap. iv. (ana, mth) On Sigemund.

146 ———. "Zur *Grettissaga.*" *ZDP*, 30 (1898), 53–71. (epc, mth)

147 ———. (Untitled review of Chambers [307]) *ES*, 5 (1923), 105–18. (ana, mth) Reply by Chambers [310].

148 BOGNITZ, Alfred. *Doppelt-steigende Alliterationsverse (Sievers' Typus B) im Angelsächsischen.* Berlin diss., 1920. (mtr)

149   BOHLEN, Adolf. *Zusammengehörige Wortgruppen, getrennt durch Cäsur oder Versschluss, in der angelsächsischen Epik.* Berlin diss., 1908. (mtr)
Reviews:
   1   R. Dittes, *Beibl*, 20 (1909), 199–202
   2   A. Kroder, *ESt*, 40 (1908–9), 90

150   BOLTE, Johannes, and POLÍVKA, Georg. *Anmerkungen zu den Kinder und Hausmärchen der Brüder Grimm.* Leipzig, 1913–32. Vol. II (1915), pp. 297–318. (ana, mth)

150.1   BOND, George. "Links between *Beowulf* and Mercian History." *SP*, 40 (1943), 481–93. (com, hst, nam)
Review: D. Whitelock, *YWES*, 24 (1943), 31

151   BONE, Gavin. *Beowulf, in Modern Verse with an Essay and Pictures.* Oxford, 1945. (trl)
Reviews:
   1   M. Daunt, *YWES*, 26 (1945), 39
   2   L. Stone, *L&L*, 49 (1946), 232
   3   H. B. Woolf, *MLN*, 62 (1947), 143–44

152   BONGARTZ, J. "*Beowulf* als Schullektüre." *NMs*, 6 (1935), 396–414. (com, thm)   Answer by Schmidt [1808].

153   BONJOUR, Adrien. "Beowulf and Heardred." *ES*, 32 (1951), 193–200. (chr, epc, hst; 2200–6)
Repr. in *12BP*, pp. 67–76

154   ——. "*Beowulf* and the Beasts of Battle." *PMLA*, 72 (1957), 563–73. (for, img, smb, tec, thm)
Review: R. M. Wilson, *YWES*, 38 (1957), 75
Repr. in *12BP*, pp. 135–46 with additional commentary on pp. 147–49

155   ——. "*Beowulf* and the Snares of Literary Criticism." *EA*, 10 (1957), 30–36. (str, unt)   Answer to Van Meurs [2135], which attacked his [159].
Review: R. M. Wilson, *YWES*, 38 (1957), 74
Repr. in *12BP*, pp. 121–28 with additional commentary on pp. 129–33

156   ——. "*Beowulf* et le démon de l'analogie." In *12BP*, pp. 173–89. (alg, ana, img, rel, smb)   Answer to McNamee [1532].
Review: R. M. Wilson, *YWES*, 43 (1962), 56

157   ——. "*Beowulf* et l'épopée anglo–saxonne." *TR*, no. 132 (1958), 140–51. (com, for, gen, int, smb, tec)
Review: R. M. Wilson, *YWES*, 39 (1958), 71

158   ——. "The *Beowulf* Poet and the Tragic Muse." In *Brodeur*, pp. 129–35. (int, rel)
Review: R. M. Wilson, *YWES*, 44 (1963), 73

159   ——. *The Digressions in "Beowulf."* MAE Monographs, 5.
Oxford, 1950. (hst, str, tec, unt; Fep)   Answered by
Malone [1362] and Van Meurs [2135].
Reviews:
      1 G. Bonnard, *EdL*, June 1952, pp. 22–24
      2 C. Brady, *MLN*, 70 (1955), 521–24
      3 K. Malone, *Speculum*, 26 (1951), 148–50 [1407]
      4 G. Storms, *ES*, 33 (1952), 124–26
      5 R. M. Wilson, *MLR*, 46 (1951), 300
      6 ——, *YWES*, 31 (1950), 45–46
      7 H. B. Woolf, *MLQ*, 15 (1954), 182
Repr. 1965

160   ——. "Grendel's Dam and the Composition of *Beowulf*."
ES, 30 (1949), 113–24. (com, src, str, tec)
Review: R. M. Wilson, *YWES*, 30 (1949), 41
Repr. in *12BP*, pp. 29–42 with additional commentary on
pp. 43–50

161   ——. "Monsters Crouching and Critics Rampant: Or the
Beowulf Dragon Debated." *PMLA*, 68 (1953), 304–12.
(smb, str, unt) Defends Tolkien [2095] against attack by
Gang [603].
Review: R. M. Wilson, *YWES*, 34 (1953), 48
Repr. in *12BP*, pp. 97–106 with additional commentary on
pp. 107–13

162   ——. "On Sea Images in *Beowulf*." *JEGP*, 54 (1955), 111–
15. (dct, img, var, wrd)
Review: R. M. Wilson, *YWES*, 36 (1955), 61–62
Repr. in *12BP*, pp. 115–19

163   ——. "Poésie héroique du moyen age et critique littéraire."
Romania, 78 (1957), 243–55. (for, sch)
Review: R. M. Wilson, *YWES*, 38 (1957), 74
Repr. in *12BP*, pp. 151–64 with additional commentary on
pp. 165–72

164   ——. "The Problem of Dæghrefn." *JEGP*, 51 (1952),
355–59. (chr, epc, int, src)
Review: R. M. Wilson, *YWES*, 33 (1952), 40
Repr. in *12BP*, pp. 77–82 with additional commentary on
pp. 83–88

165   ——. "The Technique of Parallel Descriptions in *Beowulf*."
RES, n.s. 2 (1951), 1–10. (str, tec)
Repr. in *12BP*, pp. 51–62 with additional commentary on
pp. 63–65

166   ——. *Twelve "Beowulf" Papers, 1940–1960, with Additional
Comments.* Neuchatel, 1962. (bbl) Includes Bonjour [153–
56, 160–65, 167, and 169].

Reviews:

  1   D. Allen, *MAE*, 34 (1965), 177–78
  2   A. Crépin, *EA*, 16 (1963), 175–77
  3   B. Mitchell, *RES*, 15 (1964), 306–7
  4   G. Storms, *ES*, 47 (1966), 135–40
  5   L. Whitbread, *Anglia*, 81 (1963), 230–31
  6   R. M. Wilson, *YWES*, 43 (1962), 55–56

167   ——. "The Use of Anticipation in *Beowulf*." *RES*, 16 (1940), 290–99. (stl, tec, thm)
Review: G. N. Garmonsway, *YWES*, 21 (1940), 37
Repr. in *12BP*, pp. 11–20 with additional commentary on pp. 21–28

168   ——. "Weohstan's Slaying of Eanmund (*Beowulf* 2611–2625)." *ESt*, 27 (1946), 14–19. (epc, int, txt; 2611–25)

169   ——. "Young Beowulf's Inglorious Period." *Anglia*, 70 (1952), 339–44. (chr, epc, int) Attacks Malone [1362].
Review: R. M. Wilson, *YWES*, 33 (1952), 40
Repr. in *12BP*, pp. 89–93 with additional commentary on pp. 94–96

170   BONSER, Wilfrid. *An Anglo–Saxon and Celtic Bibliography (450–1087)*. 2 vols. Berkeley and Los Angeles, Oxford, 1957. (bbl)
Reviews:

  1   *TLS*, 13 Dec. 1957, p. 764
  2   C. W. Dunn, *MLN*, 75 (1960), 704–7
  3   R. J. Schoeck, *Speculum*, 33 (1958), 267–68
  4   F. T. Wainwright, *EHR*, 73 (1958), 466–69
  5   R. M. Wilson, *YWES*, 38 (1957), 71

171   BORGES, Jorge Luis. "The Art of Fiction, XXXIX (An Interview by Ronald Christ)." *Paris Review*, 40 (1967), 116–64. (epc)

172   ——. "Compositión escrita en un ejemplar de la gesta de *Beowulf*." In his *Antología personal*. Buenos Aires, 1961. p. 187. (poem)
Trans. with foreword by Anthony Kerrigan in *A Personal Anthology*. New York, 1967.

173   BOTKINE, L. *Beowulf: Analyse historique et géographique*. Paris and Le Havre, 1876. (hst) Replaced by the introd. to his [174].
Review: K. Körner, *ESt*, 1 (1877), 495–96

174   ——. *Beowulf, Épopée anglo–saxonne*. Traduite en francais pour la première fois, d'après le texte original. Le Havre, 1877. (hst, mtr, nts, trl) Partial translation into French prose, based on the Heyne [815] text.

Review: K. Körner, *ESt*, 2 (1879), 248–51 [1129]

175   BOUMAN, A. C. "Beowulf's Song of Sorrow." In *Mossé*,
pp. 41–43. (ana; 2444–62) Parallels David and Absolom.
Review: R. M. Wilson, *YWES*, 40 (1959), 61

176   ——. "Een Drietal Etymologieën: *Aibr, Eolete, Garsecg.*"
Neophilologus, 35 (1951), 238–41. (hst, lng, wrd; 223b–26a)

177   ——. "The Heroes of the *Fight at Finnsburh.*" *APS*, 10
(1935–36), 130–44. (epc, Fnb, hst, int, mth, nam, rel, txt;
1071–75, 1141, 1145)

178   ——. "The Old English Poems *The Wife's Lament* and *The
Husband's Message.*" In his *Patterns in Old English and Old
Icelandic Literature.* Leidse Germanistische en Anglistische
Reeks I. Leiden, 1962. pp. 41–91. (chr, Fnb, src; 874–
900)
Reviews:
       1   A. M. Arent, *MP*, 62 (1964), 155–58
       2   N. F. Blake, *MAE*, 32 (1963), 86–87
       3   S. Einarsson, *JEGP*, 62 (1963), 674–76
       4   R. Kellogg, *Speculum*, 39 (1964), 497–99

179   BOUTERWEK, Karl Wilhelm. "Das Beowulflied: Eine
Vorlesung." *Germania*, 1 (1856), 385–418. (gen, rel)

180   ——. *Caedmon's des Angelsachsen biblische Dichtungen.* Gütersloh, 1854. Vol. I, pp. c–cxvii. (edt, hst, lng, mth, rel; 15,
21) Edits lines 1–52, 102–14.

181   ——. "Zur Kritik des Beowulfliedes." *ZDA*, 11 (1859),
59–113. (int, lng, nam, sch, txt, wrd)

182   BOWRA, Cecil Maurice. *Heroic Poetry.* London, 1952.
(epc, Fnb, gen, stl, tec)
Reviews:
       1   F. Y. Thompson, *YWES*, 33 (1952), 7
       2   R. M. Wilson, *ibid.*, 37–38
Repr. 1961, 1964

183   BRACHER, Frederick George. "Understatement in Anglo-
Saxon Poetry." Unpub. Ph.D. diss., Univ. of California,
Berkeley, 1934. *DDABAU*, 1933–34, no. 1, 80. (rht, stl)
See his [184]

184   ——. "Understatement in Old English Poetry." *PMLA*,
52 (1937), 915–34. (rht, stl) From his [183].

185   BRADLEY, Henry. "*Beowulf.*" *Encyclopedia Britannica.*
11th ed., London, 1910. Vol. III, pp. 758–61. (gen)
14th ed., Vol. III, pp. 424–26.

186   ——. "The Numbered Sections in Old English Poetical
MSS." *PBA*, 7 (1915–16), 165–87. (mns)

187   BRADY, Caroline. *The Legends of Ermanaric.* Berkeley and
       Los Angeles, 1943. (ana, com, hst)
       Reviews:
           1 R. Girvan, *MLR*, 39 (1944), 403–4
           2 K. Malone, *JEGP*, 43 (1944), 449–53
           3 ——, *MLN*, 59 (1944), 185–88
           4 S. Rypins, *MLQ*, 6 (1945), 225–26
           5 P. W. Souers, *Speculum*, 20 (1945), 502–7
           6 E. Wahlgren, *CFQ*, 3 (1944), 248–50
           7 D. Whitelock, *YWES*, 24 (1943), 34–35

188   ——. "The Synonyms for 'Sea' in *Beowulf*." In *Studies in
       Honor of Albert Morey Sturtevant.* Univ. of Kansas Pub.,
       Humanistic Studies, no. 29. Lawrence, 1952. pp. 24–46.
       (dct, ken, wrd)   Continued by Woodward [2232].

†   BRANDES, H. B. C., see [991].

189   BRANDL, Alois. "Die Angelsächsische Literatur." *PGrdr*,
       II. 2d ed., Strasbourg, 1901–9. pp. 983–1024. (bbl, dct,
       epc, Fnb, gen, hst, int, lng, mth, sch, src, str)
       Reviews:
           1 F. Brie, *Archiv*, 119 (1907), 217
           2 W. W. Lawrence, *MLN*, 24 (1909), 149–53
           3 R. Wülker, *Beibl*, 20 (1909), 1–9
       Separate issue as *Geschichte der alteng. Literatur.* Strasbourg,
       1908.
       3d ed., 1911.

189.1 ——. "Beowulf und die Merowinger." In *Klaeber*, pp.
       182–88. (com, hst, int; 2920–21)   Expanded by his [190].

190   ——. *Ibid.* *SPAW*, 1929, pp. 207–11. (com, hst, int;
       2920–21)   Expansion of his [189.1].
       Review: M. Daunt, *YWES*, 10 (1929), 87–88
       Repr. in his *Forschungen und Charakteristiken.* Berlin, 1936

191   ——. "*Beowulf*-Epos und Aeneis in systematischer
       Vergleichung." *Archiv*, 171 (1937), 161–73. (ana, com, epc,
       hst, smb)
       Review: D. E. M. Clarke, *YWES*, 18 (1937), 55

192   ——. "Das Beowulfepos und die mercische Königskrisis um
       700." *FuF*, 12 (1936), 165–68. (com, hst)
       Review: G. Linke, *Archiv*, 170 (1936), 140
       Repr. in English: "The *Beowulf* Epic and the Crisis in the
       Mercian Dynasty about the year A.D. 700." *Research and
       Progress*, 2 (1936), 195–203

193   ——. "Einige Tatsachen betreffend Scyld Scefing." In
       Jespersen, pp. 31–37. (lng, mth, nam, rel, thm)
       Review: M. Daunt, *YWES*, 11 (1930), 61

194   ———. "Die Entstehungsgeschichte des Beowulfepos." Un-
       pub. lecture, summarized in *SPAW*, 1907, p. 615. (com)

195   ———. "Hercules und Beowulf." *SPAW*, 1928, no. 14, 161–
       67. (ana)
       Review: M. Daunt, *YWES*, 9 (1928), 67–68
       Repr. in his *Forschungen und Charakteristiken*. Berlin, 1936

196   ———. "Der Saalkampf in Finns Burg." In *Förster*, pp. 23–
       25. (Fnb, trl, unt) Translates *Finnsburh* into German
       alliterative verse.
       Review: M. Daunt, *YWES*, 10 (1929), 84–85
       Repr. in his *Forschungen und Charakteristiken*. Berlin, 1936

197   ———. "Über den gegenwärtigen Stand der *Beowulf*-
       Forschung." *Archiv*, 108 (1902), 152–55. (gen, sch)
       Review of research.

198   ———. "Die Urstammtafel der englischen Könige." *SPAW*,
       1918, p. 5. (hst, mth, nam) Summary of his [199].

199   ———. "Die Urstammtafel der Westsachsen und das *Beowulf*-
       Epos." *Archiv*, 137 (1918), 6–24. (hst, mth, nam) Sum-
       marized in his [198].
       Repr. in his *Forschungen und Charakteristiken*. Berlin, 1936

?200   ———. *Zum ags. Gedicht "Traumgesicht vom Kreuze Christi."*
       Berlin Akademie Sitzungsbericht (1905). (lng)

201   ———. "Zur Entstehung der germanischen Heldensage,
       gesehen vom angelsächsischen Standpunkt." *Archiv*, 162
       (1933), 191–202. (ana, epc, src) Expands Schneider [1813].
       Review: D. E. M. Clarke, *YWES*, 14 (1933), 100

202   ———. "Zur Gotensage bei den Angelsachsen." *Archiv*, 120
       (1908), 1–8. (ana, hst)
       Repr. in his *Forschungen und Charakteristiken*. Berlin, 1936

203   ———. "Zur Vorgeschichte der *Weird Sisters* im 'Macbeth.'"
       In *Liebermann*, pp. 252–70. (ana)

204   ———. (Untitled note) *Archiv*, 123 (1909), 473. (mth)
       Reply to Lawrence [1205].

205   ———. (Untitled review of Panzer [1618]) *Archiv*, 126 (1911),
       231–35. (ana, mth)

206   ———. (Untitled review of Julius Goebel, ed., *Germanic Litera-
       ture and Culture*. N.Y., 1914–16) *Archiv*, 143 (1922), 289–90.
       (epc, mth, nam, rel)

207   ———. (Untitled review of Mohr [1459]) *Archiv*, 165 (1934),
       290. (ken, rel)

†   ———, see [222] and [225].

208   BRATE, Erik. "Betydelsen av ortnamnet Skälv." *NB*, 1
       (1913), 102–8. (nam) On "Scylfingas."

209   ——. "Sinfjatle." *SSLSN*, 14 (1923), 1–8. (gen, hst, lng)

210   BRENNER, Oscar. "Zur Verteilung der Reimstäbe in der
        alliterienden Langzeile." *Beitr*, 19 (1894), 462–66. (mtr)

211   ——. (Untitled review of Heyne [815]) *ESt*, 4 (1881),
        135–39. (lng, txt, wrd; 224) On "eoletes."

212   BRETT, Cyril. "Notes on passages of Old and Middle
        English." *MLR*, 14 (1919), 1–9. (int, lng, txt, wrd; 2385,
        2771ff, 2792ff, 2999ff, 3066ff)

213   BREWER, Derek Stanley. "Aspects of Nature and Words-
        worth." In his *Proteus: Studies in English Literature.* Tokyo,
        1958. pp. 156–97. (img, trl; 1365–76) Translates 1365–76
        into English prose.
        Review: T. S. Dorsch, *YWES*, 39 (1958), 18–19

214   BREWER, Ebenezer Cobham. "*Beowulf.*" In his *Reader's
        Handbook.* New ed., London, 1911. p. 111. (gen)

215   BRIGGS, William Dinsmore. "On Kemp Malone's *Literary
        History of Hamlet*, 1." *JEGP*, 24 (1925), 413–24. (hst, mth,
        nam, thm, txt; 1–62) Review of Malone [1353]

216   BRIGHT, James Wilson. *An Anglo–Saxon Reader.* N.Y.,
        1891. (gen, mtr)
        Repr. 1894, 1917.
        Rev. by James R. Hulbert, 1935; repr. 1959.

217   ——. "Anglo–Saxon *umbor* and *seld-guma.*" *MLN*, 31
        (1916), 82–84. (txt; 46, 249, 1187)

218   ——. "*Beowulf*, 489–490." *MLN*, 31 (1916), 217–23. (txt;
        489–90)

219   ——. "An Idiom of the Comparative in Anglo–Saxon."
        MLN, 27 (1912), 181–83. (dct, lng, txt, wrd; 69–70)

220   ——. "Notes on the *Beowulf.*" *MLN*, 10 (1895), 43–44.
        (txt; 30, 306, 386–87, 623, 737)

221   ——. "Proper Names in Old English Verse." *PMLA*, 14
        (1899), 347–68. (mtr, nam)

222   BRINK, Bernhard Aegidius Konrad Ten. "Altenglische
        Literatur." *PGrdr*, 1893, II, part 1, pp. 510–50. (chr, Fnb,
        int, mth, mtr, stl; Fep) Unfinished.
        Repr. in his [225].

223   ——; MARTIN, E.; and SCHMIDT, E. *Beowulf: Unter-
        suchungen.* QFSK 62, Strasbourg and London, 1888. (com,
        gen, lng, mns, mth, src, var)
        Reviews:
            1   R. Heinzel, *AfdA*, 15 (1889), 153–82 [775]
            2   E. Koeppel, *ZDP*, 23 (1891), 113–22
            3   K. Kraus, *DLZ*, 12 (1891), 1605–7, 1846; reply by
                Brink [224]

4   F. Liebermann, *Deut. Zeitschrift für Geschichtswissenschaft*, 2 (1889), 197–99

5   H. Möller, *ESt*, 13 (1889), 247–315 [1461]

6   S. Singer, *ZOG*, 40 (1889), 777

7   R. Wülker, *Anglia*, 11 (1889), 319–21

8   ——, *LitCbl*, 40 (1889), 251

224 ——. "Beowulfkritik und ABAB." *DLZ*, 13 (1892), 109–12. (mtr) Reply to Kraus, *DLZ*, 12 (1891), 1605–7, 1846, which is a review of Brink [223].

225 ——. *Geschichte der englischen Literatur.* Berlin, 1877–93. (com, Fnb, hst)
Review: R. Wülker, *Anglia*, 2 (1878), 199–214
Trans. of 1st ed., by Horace M. Kennedy. London and N.Y., 1883. pp. 23–31. Rev. ed., by Kennedy and Brink. London and N.Y., 1889. (chr, com, Fnb, hst, int, mth, mtr, stl, trl) English title: *History of English Literature (to Wyclif).* Translates 2596–2612, 2661–68, 2788–2816 into English.
2d ed. of Vol. I, rev. by Alois Brandl. Berlin, 1899. Incorporates Brink [222], pp. 431–78. (chr, Fnb, int, mth, mtr, stl; Fep).

226 BRITISH MUSEUM MANUSCRIPT COTTON VITELLIUS A.XV. Folios 129 (132)a to 198 (201)b. (mns) The unique manuscript of the poem, issued in facsimile by Zupitza [2278] and Malone [1371].

227 BRIX, Hans. "Bjarkemaalet." *Analyser og Problemer: Under søgelsor i den aldre danske Litteratur*, II. Copenhagen, 1935. pp. 5–32. (ana)
Reviews:
     1   M. Kristensen, *DS*, 32 (1935), 85–86
     2   P. V. Rubow, *DS*, 32 (1935), 79–85

228 BROCH, Ada. *Die Stellung der Frau in der angelsächsischen Poesie.* Zurich diss., 1902. (hst)

229 BRODEUR, Arthur Gilchrist. *The Art of "Beowulf."* Berkeley and Los Angeles, London, 1959. (dct, for, gen, int, rel, str, tec, var) Attacks Malone [1389]; attacked by Hardy [750].
Reviews:
     1   P. Bacquet, *EA*, 17 (1964), 66–68
     2   A. Bonjour, *ES*, 43 (1962), 501–4
     3   S. B. Greenfield, *CL*, 12 (1960), 73–78
     4   P. Hodgson, *MLR*, 55 (1960), 425–27
     5   B. V. Lindheim, *Anglia*, 78 (1960), 224–28
     6   K. Malone, *MLN*, 75 (1960), 347–53 [1404]
     7   J. C. McGalliard, *MP*, 59 (1962), 276–82 [1531]
     8   J. C. Pope, *Speculum*, 37 (1962), 411–17 [1664]

       9   M. H. Strang, *DUJ*, 22 (1961), 124–26

     10   J. Turville-Petre, *RES*, n.s. 11 (1960), 417–19

     11   R. M. Wilson, *YWES*, 40 (1959), 59–60

230   ——. "The Climax of the Finn Episode." *UCPE*, 3 (1943), 285–361. (Fnb, int, lng; Fep, 1142–44)
Review: D. Whitelock, *YWES*, 24 (1943), 31–32

231   ——. "Design and Motive in the Finn Episode." *E&S*, *UCPE*, 14 (1943), 1–42. (Fnb, hst, str, tec, thm; Fep)
Review: D. Whitelock, *YWES*, 24 (1943), 31–32

232   ——. "Design for Terror in the Purging of Heorot." *JEGP*, 53 (1954), 503–13. (img, str, tec)
Review: R. M. Wilson, *YWES*, 35 (1954), 39–40

233   ——. "The Structure and Unity of *Beowulf*." *PMLA*, 68 (1953), 1183–95. (hst, str, thm, unt)
Review: R. M. Wilson, *YWES*, 34 (1953), 47

234   ——. (Untitled review of Sisam [1962]) *ELN*, 4 (1966), 133–35. (hst, int, smb, str, unt)

235   BRONSON, Elsie Straffin. "From *Beowulf* the Cleansing of Heorot." In Walter C. Bronson, ed., *English Poems: Old English and Middle English Periods*. Chicago, 1910. pp. 1–30, 343–44, 416. (bbl, nts, trl) Translates into English prose 189–498, 662–852, 1232–1650, 1787–1919, 2200–2820, 3120–82; based on Wyatt text [2267].

236   BROOKE, Christopher Nugent Lawrence. "The World of *Beowulf*." *History Today*, 13 (1963), 85–92. (arc, hst) Extract from his *Saxon and Norman Kings*. N.Y., 1963.

237   Item canceled.

238   BROOKE, Stopford A. *English Literature from the Beginnings to the Norman Conquest*. London and N.Y., 1898. (ana, com, epc, Fnb, mth, str, trl) Translates 32–42, 47–52, 211b–18, 221–24a, 237–51a, 1357b–76a, 2802–8, 2884–91, 3023b–27, 3114b–19, 3169–82 into alliterative English verse, based on Grein/Wülker [677].
Repr. 1899, 1908, 1912, 1919, 1921

239   ——. *History of Early English Literature*. 2 vols. London and N.Y., 1892. Vol. I, pp. 17–131. (chr, com, Fnb, gen, hst, img, mns, mth, nam, rel, str, trl) Partial translation into English alliterative verse, based on Grein/Wülker [677].
Reviews:

     1   O. Glöde, *ESt*, 22 (1896), 264–70

     2   C. F. McClumpha, *MLN*, 8 (1892), 27–29 [1528]

     3   R. Wülker, *Beibl*, 4 (1894), 170–76, 225–33

240   BROOKS, Kenneth R. *Andreas and the Fates of the Apostles*. Oxford, 1961. (ana, src)

Review: R. P. Creed, *Speculum*, 39 (1964), 499–501

241   BROWN, Anna Robertson. "The Battle with the Water-Sprite." *Poet Lore*, 2 (1890), 185–87. (trl, txt; 1493–1571) Translates 1493–1571 into English verse.

242   ——. "The Passing of Scyld." *Poet Lore*, 2 (1890), 133–34. (trl, txt; 26–53)   Translates 26–53 into English verse.

243   BROWN, Calvin S., Jr. "Beowulf's Arm-Lock." *PMLA*, 55 (1940), 621–27.   (ana, int; 748–49, 963–66, 1537–40, 2505–8)
Review: G. N. Garmonsway, *YWES*, 21 (1940), 36–37

244   ——. "On Reading *Beowulf*." *SR*, 50 (1942), 78–86. (epc, int)

245   BROWN, Carleton Fairchild. "*Beowulf*, 1080–1106." *MLN*, 34 (1919), 181–83. (int, txt; 1080–1106)

246   ——. "*Beowulf* and the *Blickling Homilies*, and Some Textual Notes." *PMLA*, 53 (1938), 905–16.   (ana, txt; 303–4, 403b, 457, 987, 1106, 1147–53, 1174, 1247b, 1357ff, 1372a, 1399, 1465–69, 2251b–54, 2525–26, 2556b–60, 2589)
Review: C. L. Wrenn, *YWES*, 19 (1938), 51–52

247   ——. "*Poculum Mortis* in Old English." *Speculum*, 15 (1940), 389–99. (dct, img, wrd; 769)
Review: G. N. Garmonsway, *YWES*, 21 (1940), 40–41

248   BROWN, Gerard Baldwin. *The Arts and Crafts of Our Teutonic Forefathers.* Edinburgh and Chicago, 1911. (hst)

249   ——. *Saxon Art and Industry in the Pagan Period.* Vols. III and IV in his *Arts in Early England.* London, 1915. (hst)

250   BRUCE-MITFORD, Rupert Leo Scott. "The Sutton Hoo Ship-Burial." Appendix to R. H. Hodgkin's *History of the Anglo-Saxons.* 3d ed., Oxford, 1952. Vol. II, pp. 696–734, 750–56 [827]. (arc)

251   ——. *The Sutton Hoo Ship Burial: A Provisional Guide.* London, 1947. (arc)
Repr. 1951, 1952, 1954
Rev. 1956; repr. 1957, 1959, 1961

252   ——. "The Sutton Hoo Ship-Burial: Recent Theories and Some Comments on General Interpretation." *Proceedings of the Suffolk Institute of Archaeology*, 25 (1950 for 1949), 1–78. (arc)

253   ——. "Treasure Trove: A Note on Law and Practice." In his *Recent Archaeological Excavations in Britain.* London, 1956. pp. 297–301. (arc)
Repr. 1957

†   ——, see [1253].

254 BRUNNER, Karl. "Why was *Beowulf* Preserved?" *EA*, 7 (1954), 1–5. (epc, for, hst, mns, rel, smb, str, tec)
Review: R. M. Wilson, *YWES*, 35 (1954), 39

255 BRYAN, William Frank. "*AĒrgōd* in *Beowulf*, and Other Old English Compounds of *ĀEr*." *MP*, 28 (1930), 157–61. (lng; 130a, 989a, 1329a, 2342a, 2586a)
Review: M. Daunt, *YWES*, 11 (1930), 71

256 ——. "*Béowulf* Notes." *JEGP*, 19 (1920), 84–85. (lng, txt; 303–6, 532–34, 867–71)

257 ——. "Epithetic Compound Folk-Names in *Beowulf*." In *Klaeber*, pp. 120–34. (dct, hst, nam, stl; 383, 392, 530ff)
Review: M. Daunt, *YWES*, 30 (1949), 78

258 ——. "The Waegmundings–Swedes or Geats?" *MP*, 34 (1936), 113–18. (chr, hst, nam; 2490, 2606–8)
Review: M. Serjeantson, *YWES*, 17 (1936), 61–62

259 BRYANT, Frank E. "*Beowulf* 62." *MLN*, 19 (1904), 121–22. (chr, hst, int; 62)

259.1 ——. "*Beowulf*, 62, Again." *MLN*, 21 (1906), 143–45. (chr, hst, int; 62)

259.2 ——. "*Beowulf* 62." *MLN*, 22 (1907), 96. (chr, hst, int; 62)

† BRYHER, Winifred. *Beowulf: A Novel*. N.Y., 1956. No relation to the poem.

260 BRYNJULFSSON, Gisli. "Oldengelsk og Oldnordisk." *Antikvarisk Tidsskrift* (Copenhagen), 1852–54, pp. 81–143. (ana, chr)

261 BUCHLOCH, Paul G. "Unity and Intention in *Beowulf*." *English Studies Today*, 4 (1966), 99–120. (ana, com, Fnb, hst, mth, rel, str, tec, thm, unt)

262 BUCK, Janet Taylor. "Aspects of Thematic Organization of *Beowulf*." Unpub. Ph.D. diss, Yale Univ., 1959–60. (for, str)

263 BUCK, Katherine Margaret. "Water-Trolls." *TLS*, 16 May 1929, p. 403. (ana, mth) Reply to Chambers [309].

264 ——. (Untitled reply to Davies [447]) *TLS*, 14 Dec. 1935, p. 859. (ana, mth) Reply by Davies [446].
Review: D. E. M. Clarke, *YWES*, 16 (1935), 81

265 BUCKHURST, Helen Thérèse McMillan. "Terms and Phrases for the Sea in Old English Poetry." In *Klaeber*, 103–19. (dct, ken, thm, var, wrd)
Review: M. Daunt, *YWES*, 10 (1929), 77

266 BUDDE, Erich. *Die Bedeutung der Trinkritter in der Kultur der Angelsachsen*. Jena diss., 1906. (hst)

267 BUGGE, Sophus. "Die Heimat der Altnordischen Lieder von den Welsungen und den Nibelungen." *Beitr*, 22 (1897), 115–34. (ana, com; 2730–33)

268 ——. "Die Heimat der Altnordischen Lieder von den Welsungen und den Nibelungen, II." *Beitr*, 35 (1909), 240–71. (ana, hst, src)

269 ——. *Helge-Digtene i den aeldre Edda.* Copenhagen, 1896. (hst)
Rev. ed., trans. by William Henry Schofield, *The Home of the Eddic Poems with Especial Reference to the Helgi-Lays.* London, 1899.

270 ——. "Mundo und Sigmund." *Beitr*, 35 (1909), 262–67, 490–93. (ana, hst, mth)

271 ——, and OLRIK, Axel. "Røveren ved Gråsten og *Beowulf.*" *Dania*, 1 (1890–91), 233–45. (mth; 2231–71)

272 ——. "Spredte iagttagelser vedkommende de oldengelska digte om *Beowulf* og *Waldere.*" *TPP*, 8 (1868–69), 40–78, 287–307. (Fnb, txt)

273 ——. "Studien über das Beowulfepos." *Beitr*, 12 (1887), 1–112, 360–75. (Fnb, hst, int, mth, nam, txt; Fep)

274 ——. "Zum *Beowulf.*" *ZDP*, 4 (1873), 192–224. (Fnb, txt)

275 BÜLBRING, Karl. *Altenglisches Elementarbuch.* Heidelberg, 1902. (gen, lng)

276 BURCHFIELD, R. W. "*Beowulf* 219 'ymb an tid.'" *MLR*, 50 (1955), 484–85. (lng, txt, 219)
Review: R. M. Wilson, *YWES*, 36 (1955), 61

277 BURTON, Richard. "The Oldest English Lyric." *Poet-Lore*, 5 (1893), 57–67. (dct, gen, img, mtr, stl)

278 BUSH, J. D. "A Note on *Beowulf*, 1600–1605." *MLN*, 36 (1921), 251. (int, txt, wrd; 1600–1605)

279 BYERS, John R., Jr. "On the Decorating of Heorot." *PMLA*, 80 (1965), 299–300. (img, int; 991–92) Answers Rosier [1737].

280 ——. "A Possible Emendation of *Beowulf* 461b." *PQ*, 46 (1967), 125–28. (txt; 461b)

281 CABANISS, Allen. "*Beowulf* and the Liturgy." *JEGP*, 54 (1955), 195–201. (ana, rel, tec)
Review: R. M. Wilson, *YWES*, 36 (1955), 60
Repr. in Nicholson [1560], pp. 223–32

282 CAIN, A. M. "Myth in *Beowulf*." Unpub. Ph.D. diss., Aberdeen Univ., 1953–54. (mth)

283   CALDWELL, James Ralston. "The Origin of the Story of
       Bǫdvar-Bjarki." *ANF*, 55 (1939–40), 223–75. (ana, mth)

284   CALDWELL, Robert Atchison. "A Study of the Visualiza-
       tion in *Beowulf*." Unpub. thesis, Univ. of Colorado, 1932.
       Summary in *Abstracts of Theses, Univ. of Colorado*, 1932, p. 15.
       (img, int, stl)

285   CALLAWAY, Morgan, Jr. "The Appositive Participle in
       Anglo–Saxon." *PMLA*, 16 (1901), 141–360. (lng)

286   ——. *The Consecutive Subjunctive in Old English*. Boston and
       London, 1933. (lng)

287   ——. *The Temporal Subjunctive in Old English*. Austin, Tex.,
       1931. (lng)
       Review: D. E. M. Clarke, *YWES*, 12 (1931), 64–66

287.1 CAMPBELL, A. "The Old English Epic Style." In
       Tolkien, pp. 13–26. (ana, dct, epc, for, mtr, src; 653–54,
       1695–97, 2836–42)
       Review: R. M. Wilson, *YWES*, 43 (1962), 56

288   CANDELARIA, Frederick. "'Gársecg' in *Beowulf*." *ELN*,
       1 (1964), 243–44. (dct, int, txt, wrd; 49, 515, 537)
       Review: R. M. Wilson, *YWES*, 45 (1964), 60

289   CANNON, Charles Dale. "The Religion of the Anglo–
       Saxons." *UMSE*, 5 (1964), 15–33. (mth, rel, sch)

290   CARNEY, James. "The Irish Elements in *Beowulf*." In his
       Studies in Irish Literature and History. Dublin, 1955. pp. 77–
       128. (ana, com, src)
       Reviews:
            1   *TLS*, 29 March 1957, p. 188
            2   T. S. Dorsch, *YWES*, 37 (1956), 10
            3   R. S. Loomis, *MAE*, 26 (1957), 197–99

291   CARPENTER, Rhys. *Folk Tale, Fiction and Saga in the
       Homeric Epics*. Berkeley and Los Angeles, 1946. (ana, epc,
       mth)

292   CARR, Charles T. *Nominal Compounds in Germanic*. London,
       1939. (dct, epc, img, wrd)

293   CARTWRIGHT, Thomas. "Brave Beowulf." In *Every
       Child's Library*. London, 1908. (par) Paraphrase in
       English.

294   CASSIDY, Frederic G. "How Free Was the Anglo–Saxon
       Scop?" In *Magoun*, pp. 75–85. (dct, for, lng) Continues
       Gattiker [622] and O'Neil [1599].

295   ——. "Suggested Re-punctuation of a Passage in *Beowulf*."
       MLN, 50 (1935), 88–89. (int, txt; 746–49)
       Review: D. E. M. Clarke, *YWES*, 16 (1935), 83

296   CAWLEY, A. C. "Notes on Old English." *EGS*, 2 (1949), 75–80. (hst, wrd; 163–64, 1694–97)

297   CAWLEY, F. Stanton. "*Ivarr-Unferþ?*" *PMLA*, 45 (1930), 335–36. (ana, chr, nam)   Answer by Malone [1345], to which Cawley [298] replies.
      Review: M. Daunt, *YWES*, 11 (1930), 54

298   ——. (Untitled letter answering Malone [1345]) *PMLA*, 45 (1930), 628. (chr, hst)   Malone answers Cawley [297].

 †   CAZAMIAN, Louis, see [1215].

299   CECIONI, Cesare G. *Beowulf: Poema eroico anglosassone.* Bologne, 1959. (gen, nts, trl)   Trans. into Italian.

300   CHADWICK, Hector Munro. "Early National Poetry." In A. W. Ward and A. R. Waller, eds., *The Cambridge History of English Literature.* London and N.Y., 1907. Vol. I, pp. 21–44. (ana, com, Fnb, gen, hst, rel, src)
      Review: R. Wülker, *Beibl*, 19 (1909), 353–70

301   ——, and CHADWICK, Nora Kershaw. *The Growth of Literature.* Vol. I, *The Ancient Literatures of Europe.* Cambridge and N.Y., 1932. (ana, gen)
      Reviews:
          1   A. H. Krappe, *Speculum*, 8 (1933), 270–78
          2   K. Malone, *MLN*, 49 (1934), 348–49
          3   H. V. Routh, *RES*, 9 (1933), 209–13

302   ——. *The Heroic Age.* Cambridge, 1912. (epc, gen, hst)
      Reviews:
          1   R. W. Chambers, *ESt*, 48 (1914–15), 162–66
          2   A. Mawer, *MLR*, 8 (1913), 207–9.
      Pp. 47–56 repr. in Nicholson [1560], pp. 23–33

303   ——. *The Origin of the English Nation.* Cambridge, 1907. (hst, mth)
      Reviews:
          1   C. M. Andrews, *MLN*, 23 (1908), 261–62
          2   R. W. Chambers, *MLR*, 4 (1908–9), 262–66
          3   R. Huchon, *RG*, 3 (1908), 625–31
          4   G. Schütte, *ANF*, 25 (1909), 310–32

304   ——. *The Study of Anglo–Saxon.* Cambridge, 1941. (com, Fnb, gen, sch)
      Reviews:
          1   *TLS*, 14 June 1941, p. 291
          2   G. N. Garmonsway, *YWES*, 22 (1941), 43–44
          3   F. P. Magoun, *Speculum*, 20 (1945), 245–47
      2d ed., rev. with additions by Nora Kershaw Chadwick. Cambridge, 1955.

Reviews:
    1 H. Koziol, *Anglia*, 74 (1956), 240–41
    2 F. Mossé, *EA*, 9 (1956), 252
    3 R. M. Wilson, *YWES*, 36 (1955), 58

305   CHADWICK, Nora Kershaw. *Anglo–Saxon and Norse Poems*. Cambridge, 1922. (edt, trl)
Review: E. E. Wardale, *YWES*, 3 (1922), 25–27

306   ———. "The Monsters and *Beowulf*." In *Dickins*, pp. 171–203. (ana, com, hst, mth, wrd)
Review: R. M. Wilson, *YWES*, 40 (1959), 60

†   ———, see also [301] and [304].

307   CHAMBERS, Raymond Wilson. *Beowulf: An Introduction to the Study of the Poem with a Discussion of the Stories of Offa and Finn*. Cambridge, 1921. (ana, bbl, chr, com, epc, Fnb, hst, lng, mns, mth, nam, rel, sch, src, str) Attacked by Anscombe [31].
Reviews:
    1 *N&Q*, 141 (1921), 259
    2 *Observer*, 25 Sept. 1921.
    3 *TLS*, 12 Jan. 1922, p. 26
    4 R. C. Boer, *ES*, 5 (1923), 105–18 [147]
    5 E. Ekwall, *Beibl*, 33 (1922), 177–85 [518]
    6 B. Fehr, *ibid.*, 121–26
    7 E. Gosse, *Sunday Times*, 18 Sept. 1921, p. 17
    8 J. R. Hulbert, *MP*, 20 (1923), 436–37
    9 O. L. Jiriczek, *NS*, 31 (1923), 412–16
   10 A. Mawer, *MLR*, 18 (1923), 96–98
   11 R. J. Menner, *LRNYEP*, 20 Jan. 1923, p. 394
   12 H. R. Patch, *MLN*, 37 (1922), 418–27
 ?13 A. Ricci, *NSM*, I (1923)
   14 J. G. Robertson, *YBVS*, 1921, pp. 78–81
   15 F. Tupper, *JEGP*, 21 (1922), 680–84
   16 E. E. Wardale, *YWES*, 2 (1920–21), 33–35
2d ed., 1932
Reviews:
    1 *MAE*, 1 (1932), 229–31
    2 *N&Q*, 162 (1932), 467–68
    3 *TLS*, 15 Sept. 1932, p. 646
    4 D. E. M. Clarke, *YWES*, 12 (1931), 54–57
    5 W. Fischer, *Beibl*, 44 (1933), 332–35
    6 F. Klaeber, *MLR*, 27 (1932), 462–66
    7 K. Malone, *ES*, 14 (1932), 190–93
    8 F. Mossé, *RG*, 24 (1933), 49–52
    9 H. R. Patch, *Speculum*, 8 (1933), 278–79

    10 C. L. W [renn], *OM*, (20 Oct. 1932), 70

    11 ——, *RES*, 9 (1933), 204–9

3d ed., with supplement by C. L. Wrenn, 1959

Reviews:

    1 O. Funke, *ES*, 42 (1961), 95–98

    2 K. Malone, *N&Q*, 204 (1959), 342

    3 S. Potter, *RES*, 11 (1960), 306–7

    4 R. M. Wilson, *YWES*, 40 (1959), 59

Repr. 1963

308   ——. "*Beowulf* and the Heroic Age." Foreword to Strong [2031]. (com, gen, hst, rel)

Repr. as "*Beowulf* and the 'Heroic Age' in England" in his *Man's Unconquerable Mind*. London, 1939. pp. 53–69. Repr. 1939, 1952, 1955, 1964

309   ——. "*Beowulf* and Waterfall-Trolls." *TLS*, 9 May 1929, p. 383. (ana, mth) Answered by Buck [263].

310   ——. "Beowulf's Fight with Grendel, and Its Scandinavian Parallels." *ES*, 11 (1929), 81–100. (ana, mth) Reply to Boer [147].

Review: M. Daunt, *YWES*, 10 (1929), 88–89

311   ——. *England before the Norman Conquest*. London, 1926. (hst)

Review: M. Daunt, *YWES*, 7 (1926), 72

312   ——. "The 'Shifted Leaf' in *Beowulf*." *MLR*, 10 (1915), 37–41. (ana, int, mns, txt; 1591–1617) Refutes Blackburn [127].

313   ——. *Six Thirteenth Century Drawings Illustrating the Story of Offa and of Thryth (Drida) from MS Cotton Nero D. I*. London, 1912. (ana) Privately printed.

314   ——. "Some Sequences of Thought in Shakespeare and in the 147 Lines of 'Sir Thomas More.'" *MLR*, 26 (1931), 251–80. (ana) Answers Krappe [1140].

Repr. and expanded as "Shakespeare and the Play of *More*" in his *Man's Unconquerable Mind*. London, 1939. pp. 204–49. Repr. 1939, 1952, 1955, 1964

315   ——. *Widsith: A Study in Old English Historical Legend*. Cambridge, 1912. (Fnb, hst, nam)

Reviews:

    1 *Athenaeum*, 1912, I, 435

    2 *N&Q*, 125 (1912), 459

    3 W. A. Berendsohn, *LGRP*, 35 (1914), 384–86

    4 A. Brandl, *Archiv*, 129 (1912), 515–16

    5 B. Fehr, *Beibl*, 26 (1915), 289–95

    6 J. R. C. H[all], *YBVS*, 4 (1913), 38–39

7   R. Huchon, *RG*, 9 (1913), 94–96
8   R. Jordan, *ESt*, 45 (1912), 300–2
9   W. W. Lawrence, *MLN*, 28 (1913), 53–55
10   A. Mawer, *MLR*, 8 (1913), 118–21
11   A. Olrik, *NTF*, 4th ser., 1 (1912), 129–30
Repr. N.Y., 1965

316   ———. (Untitled translation of *Finnsburh*) In George Sampson, ed., *The Cambridge Book of Prose and Verse*. Cambridge, 1924. (trl of Fnb)
Reviews:
1   *N&Q*, 148 (1925), 72
2   G. H. Gerould, *Sat Rev*, 24 Oct. 1925, p. 239
3   K. Malone, *MLN*, 40 (1925), 320

†   ———, see [2268].

317   CHANEY, William A. "Grendel and the *Gifstol:* A Legal View of Monsters." *PMLA*, 77 (1962), 513–20. (chr, hst, int; 168–69)
Review: R. M. Wilson, *YWES*, 43 (1962), 57

318   CHAPMAN, Coolidge Otis. "*Beowulf* and *Apollonius of Tyre*." *MLN*, 46 (1931), 439–43. (ana, src)
Review: D. E. M. Clarke, *YWES*, 12 (1931), 72

319   CHAPMAN, Robert L. "Alas, Poor Grendel." *CE*, 17 (1956), 334–37. (chr, mth, rel, thm)

320   CHEFNEUX, Hélène. "Tapisserie de Bayeux." *Romania*, 55 (1934), 191–94. (ana, hst) See Dickins [471] and Paden [1612].
Review: D. Whitelock, *YWES*, 24 (1943), 33

321   CHILD, Clarence Griffin. "*Beowulf* 30, 53, 132[3], 2957." *MLN*, 21 (1906), 175–77, 198–200. (int, lng, mns, mtr, txt; 30, 53, 1323, 2957)

322   ———. "*Beowulf*" and the "*Finnesburh Fragment*." Boston and London, 1904: Riverside Literature Series 159. (Fnb, gen, nts, trl) Trans. into English prose.
Reviews:
1   *Nation*, 78 (1904), 477
2   A. Brandl, *Archiv*, 121 (1908), 473
3   J. H. G. Grattan, *MLR*, 3 (1908), 303–4
4   J. B. Henneman & L. W. Payne, *SR*, 12 (1904), 504–5
5   F. Klaeber, *Beibl*, 16 (1905), 225–27
6   T. Miller, *YBVS*, 1 (1909), 91–92
Repr. in Charles W. Jones, ed., *Medieval Literature in Translation*. N.Y., London, and Toronto, 1950. pp. 148–57. Lines 1251–1887 only.
Repr. 1952, 1955, 1957

323   ——. "Gummere's *Oldest English Epic*." *MLN*, 24 (1909), 253–54. (sch, about trl)   Review of Gummere [720], with answer by Gummere [724] and reply by Child [325].

324   ——. "Stapol = patronus." (Sp. *padron*, Port. *padrão*.)." *MLN*, 8 (1893), 252–53. (lng, wrd; 927)

325   ——. "Translation of Old English Verse." *MLN*, 25 (1910), 157–58. (about trl)   Reply to Gummere [724]; see Child [323].

†   CHRIST, Ronald, see [171].

326   CHURCH, Alfred John. "Beowulf." In his *Heroes of Chivalry and Romance*. London, 1898. pp. 3–60. (par) Selected English prose paraphrase, based on Kemble [989] and Earle [501].

327   CHURCH, Samuel Hardin. *Beowulf: A Poem*. N.Y., 1901. Poetic imitation using *Beowulf* material.

328   CLARAC, Pierre. "Beowulf." In his *Dictionnaire universel des lettres*. Paris, 1961. pp. 76–77. (gen)

329   CLARK, Donald Leman. "Rhetoric and the Literature of the English Middle Ages." *QJS*, 45 (1959), 19–28. (lng, rht, stl)

330   CLARK, George. "Beowulf and Bear's Son in the *Vishnu Purana*." *PQ*, 43 (1964), 125–30. (ana, mth)

331   ——. "Beowulf's Armor." *ELH*, 32 (1965), 409–41. (epc, img, tec, thm; 229–38, 240–50, 290–93, 303–6, 321–30, 333–36, 395–406, 677–85, 1282–87, 2029–31, 2059–60, 2556–65, 2964–81)

332   ——. "The Traveler Recognizes His Goal: A Theme in Anglo–Saxon Poetry." *JEGP*, 64 (1965), 645–59. (for, lng, str, tec)

333   CLARK, John Williams. *Early English: A Study of Old and Middle English*. London and Fairlawn, N.J., 1957. (lng, mtr; 1–3)
Reviews:
    1   M. W. Bloomfield, *AS*, 33 (1958), 198–99
    2   R. M. Wilson, *English*, 12 (1958–59), 18–19
Norton paperback N228, 1964.

334   CLARKE, Daisy Elizabeth Martin. "Beowulfiana." *MLR*, 29 (1934), 320–21. (ana, dct, img, ken; 760b, 984–85, 1357ff)
Review: M. Serjeantson, *YWES*, 15 (1934), 67

335   ——. *Culture in Early Anglo–Saxon England*. Baltimore and Oxford, 1947. (arc, hst)
Reviews:
    1   S. M. Kuhn, *JEGP*, 47 (1948), 414–15

2   R. M. Wilson, *YWES*, 28 (1947), 57–58

3   H. B. Woolf, *Speculum*, 23 (1948), 494–95

336   ——. "The Office of Thyle in *Beowulf.*" *RES*, 12 (1936), 61–66. (chr, mth)   Reply to Hübener [913].
Review: M. Serjeantson, *YWES*, 17 (1936), 60–61

337   ——. "Old English." *YWES*, 16 (1935), 66–90. (sch)

337.1   ——. *Ibid.*, 18 (1937), 54–65. (sch)

338   ——. "Old English Studies." *YWES*, 12 (1931), 54–80. (sch)

338.1   ——. *Ibid.*, 14 (1933), 73–102. (sch)

339   CLARKE, Mary G. *Sidelights on Teutonic History during the Migration Period.* Cambridge, 1911. (ana, arc, hst)
Reviews:
    1   R. W. Chambers, *ESt*, 48 (1914–15), 166–68
    2   B. Fehr, *Beibl*, 26 (1915), 19–20
    3   R. Imelmann, *DLZ*, 34 (1913), col. 1062–64
    4   A. Mawer, *MLR*, 7 (1912), 126–27

340   CLASSEN, Ernest. "O.E. 'Nicras' (*Beowulf*, 422, 575, 845, 1427)." *MLR*, 10 (1915), 85–86. (lng, wrd; 422, 575, 845, 1427)

341   ——. *On Vowel Alliteration in the Old Germanic Languages.* Univ. of Manchester Publications, Germanic Series, 1. Manchester, 1913. (mtr)
Reviews:
    1   E. Brate, *ANF*, 32 (1915), 125–28
    2   F. Klaeber, *Beibl*, 25 (1914), 164–66
    3   E. Noreen, *IF*, Anz., 33 (1914), 62–65

342   CLAUSEN, H. V. "Kong Hugleik." *DS*, 15 (1918), 137–49. (chr, hst)

343   CLEMONS, Elinor Diederich. "A Metrical Analysis of the Old English Poem *Exodus.*" Unpub. Ph.D. diss., Univ. of Texas, 1961. *DA*, 22 (1962), 3652. (mtr)   Comments on Bliss [130].

†   ——, see [2217].

344   COBB, George Willard. "The Subjunctive Mood in Old English Poetry." Unpub. Ph.D. diss., Johns Hopkins Univ., 1937. (lng)

345   COFFIN, Richard Neal. "*Beowulf* and Its Relationship to Norse and Finno-Ugric Beliefs and Narratives." Unpub. Ph.D. diss., Boston Univ., 1962. *DA*, 23 (1963), 1697. (ana, mth, src)

346   COHEN, Hennig. "*Beowulf*, 86–98." *Explicator*, 16 (1958), 40. (int, rel, unt; 86–98)

347   COHN, Martin. "Ist die Wortstellung ein brauchbares Kriterium für die Chronologie angelsächsischer Denkmäler?" *ESt*, 57 (1923), 321–29. (com, lng)   Reply to Hübener [918].

348   COLGRAVE, Bertram. "A Mexican Version of the 'Bear's Son' Folk Tale." *JAF*, 64 (1951), 409–13. (ana, mth)

349   ——. "Scūrheard." *MLR*, 32 (1937), 281. (int, txt, wrd; 1033a)
        Review: D. E. M. Clarke, *YWES*, 18 (1937), 55

350   COLLIER, William F. *History of English Literature in a Series of Biographical Sketches.* London, 1865. (gen)
        Repr. London and N.Y., 1880.
        Rev. ed., 1888.

351   COLLINDER, Björn. *"Beowulf" översatt i originalets versmått.* Stockholm, 1954. (trl)
        Review: A. S. C. Ross and E. G. Stanley, *EGS*, 6 (1960), 110–12

352   ——. "Beowulfskolier." In Wessén, pp. 16–25. (txt; 303b–6a, 1030–33a, 1114–18a, 1144–45, 2155–59, 2249–52a, 2255–57a, 3069–75, 3143–48a)

353   COLLINS, D. C. "The Kenning in Anglo–Saxon Poetry." *E&S*, 12 (1959), 1–17. (dct, ken)

 | COLLINS, Rowland L., see [1625].

354   COMSTOCK, Fanny A. "Beowulf." *Education*, 14 (1894), 334–48. (epc, gen)

355   CONYBEARE, John Josias. "The Battle of Finsborough." In *Brydges' British Bibliographer.* London, 1814. Vol. IV, pp. 261–67. (edt, Fnb, nts, trl)   Translates *Finnsburh* into Latin and English verse.

356   ——. *Illustrations of Anglo–Saxon Poetry.*   Ed. by William Daniel Conybeare. London, 1826. (edt, Fnb, mns, mtr, nts, par, trl, txt)   Collates *Beowulf* manuscript, translates selections into English blank verse, and paraphrases in Latin prose. Based on Thorkelin [2080] with 19 pages of textual corrections. Gives text of *Finnsburh* and translations into Latin and English. Corrections made to this ed. by Kemble [993].
        Reviews:
            1   *WM*, 7 (1828), 464–83
            2   H. Wheaton, *NAR*, 33 (1831), 326

357   ——. (Untitled letter to editor, dated 10 July 1817) *GM*, 87 (1817), part 2, 102–4. (mns, sch)   Praise for Turner [2125] and Thorkelin [2080].

† CONYBEARE, William Daniel, see [356].

358 COOK, Albert Stanburrough. "Aldhelm and the Source of *Beowulf* 2523." *MLN*, 40 (1925), 137–42. (com, src; 2523)

359 ——. "*Beowulf* 159–163." *MLN*, 40 (1925), 352–54. (ana, src; 159–63) Analogous to *Jeremiah* 13:16.

360 ——. "*Beowulf*, 704." *MLN*, 18 (1903), 160. (hst, int; ˏ 704a) Quotes a Mrs. Tweedie, *Through Finland in Carts* (N.Y., 1898), on elk-horn decoration.

361 ——. "*Beowulf* 1009." *MLN*, 9 (1894), 237–38. (ana; 1009)

362 ——. "*Beowulf* 1039 and the Greek ἀρχι—." *Speculum*, 3 (1928), 75–81. (ana, dct, src; 1039b)
Review: M. Daunt, *YWES*, 9 (1928), 71

363 ——. "*Beowulf*, 1422." *MLN*, 39 (1924), 77–82. (ana, com, mtr, src; 1422a)

364 ——. "Beowulfian and Odyssean Voyages." *TCAAS*, 28 (1926), 1–20. (ana)
Reviews:
    1 M. Daunt, *YWES*, 7 (1926), 54–57
    2 G. Hübener, *ESt*, 61 (1927), 290–92

365 ——. "The Beowulfian *maðelode*." *JEGP*, 25 (1926), 1–6. (ana, src)
Review: M. Daunt, *YWES*, 7 (1926), 54–57

366 ——. "Bitter Beer-Drinking." *MLN*, 40 (1925), 285–88. (ana, lng, wrd; 769) Cp. *Andreas*, lines 1528–35.

367 ——. *A Concordance to "Beowulf."* Halle, 1911. (ref)
Reviews:
    1 J. M. Garnett, *AJPhil*, 33 (1912), 86–87
    2 F. Klaeber, *JEGP*, 11 (1912), 277–79

368 ——. "Cynewulf's Part in Our *Beowulf*." *TCAAS*, 27 (1925), 385–406. (ana, com, src)
Reviews:
    1 S. J. Crawford, *MLR*, 22 (1927), 94–96
    2 G. Hübener, *ESt*, 61 (1927), 290–92

369 ——. *A First Book in Old English.* Boston, 1894. (edt, nts; 89–100)
2d ed., 1895; 3d ed., 1903

370 ——. "Greek Parallels to Certain Features of the *Beowulf*." *PQ*, 5 (1926), 226–34. (ana, stl)
Review: M. Daunt, *YWES*, 7 (1926), 54–57

371 ——. "Hellenic and Beowulfian Shields and Spears." *MLN*, 41 (1926), 360–63. (ana, hst, src)
Review: M. Daunt, *YWES*, 7 (1926), 54–57

372   ——. "An Irish Parallel to the *Beowulf* Story." *Archiv*, 103 (1899), 154–56. (ana, mth) Concerns "Patrick Kennedy's Legendary Fictions."

373   ——. "A Note on the *Beowulf*." *MLN*, 8 (1893), 59. (int, lng, thm; 572–73)

374   ——. "The Old English *Andreas* and Bishop Acca of Hexham." *TCAAS*, 26 (1924), 245–332. (ana, com, hst)
Reviews:
    1   E. Ekwall, *Beibl*, 36 (1925), 321–22
    2   H. M. Flasdieck, *ESt*, 61 (1927), 288–90
    3   G. P. Krapp, *MLN*, 40 (1925), 190–91
    4   F. Liebermann, *Archiv*, 149 (1925), 105–7

375   ——. "Old English Notes: 1. *Beowulf* 1408ff." *MLN*, 17 (1902), 209–10. (ana; 1408–10)

376   ——. "Old English *scúrheard*." *MLN*, 7 (1892), 253–54. (int, txt, wrd; 1033) Reply to Pearce [1622]; see also Hart [760].

377   ——. "The Possible Begetter of the Old English *Beowulf* and *Widsith*." *TCAAS*, 25 (1922), 281–346. (ana, com, hst, src)
Reviews:
    1   *Literary Review*, 3 (1922), 744
    2   *TLS*, 4 May 1922, p. 294
    3   E. Ekwall, *Beibl*, 34 (1923), 37–39
    4   H. M. Flasdieck, *ESt*, 58 (1924), 124–26
    5   F. Liebermann, *Archiv*, 143 (1922), 281–82
    6   J. Mansion, *Musée Belge*, 27 (1923), 55–56
    7   A. D. McKillop, *JEGP*, 23 (1924), 305–7
Separate repr., New Haven, 1922.

378   ——. "Theodebert of Austrasia." *JEGP*, 22 (1923), 424–27. (chr, hst; 1202)

379   ——. "Various Notes: . . . *Beowulf* 1408ff." *MLN*, 22 (1907), 146–47. (ana; 1408ff)

380   COOK, Albert S. *The Classic Line: A Study of Epic Poetry.* Bloomington, 1966. (epc)

381   COOK, S. Daniel. "The Structure of *Beowulf*." Unpub. Ph.D. diss., Univ. of California at Berkeley, 1955. *DDABAU*, 1954–55, no. 22, 249. (str)

382   COOLEY, Franklin Delany. "Contemporary Reaction to the Identification of Hygelac." In *Malone*, 269–74. (sch) On Grundtvig.
Review: R. M. Wilson, *YWES*, 30 (1949), 42

383   ——. "Criticism of *Beowulf* before 1855." Unpub. Ph.D.

diss., Johns Hopkins Univ., 1940. *DDABAU*, 1939–40, no. 7, 105. (sch)

384 ———. "Early Danish Criticism of *Beowulf*." *ELH*, 7 (1940), 45–67. (Fnb, hst, mth, sch) On Thorkelin, Rask, and Grundtvig.
Review: D. Whitelock, *YWES*, 23 (1942), 38–39

385 ———. "Grundtvig's First Translation from *Beowulf*." *SS*, 16 (1941), 234–38. (sch, on trl)

386 ———. "William Taylor of Norwich and *Beowulf*." *MLN*, 55 (1940), 210–11. (sch) Authorship of [2067].
Review: G. N. Garmonsway, *YWES*, 21 (1940), 37–38

387 CORNELIUS, Roberta D. "Palus inamabilis." *Speculum*, 2 (1927), 321–25. (ana, mth; 162a)

388 CORSON, Hiram. "A Passage of *Beowulf*." *MLN*, 3 (1888), 97. (epc, thm; 2724)

389 COSIJN, Peter Jacob. *Aanteekeningen op den "Beowulf."* Leiden, 1891–92. (ken)
Reviews:
    1 O. Erdman, *ZDP*, 25 (1893), 431
    2 F. Holthausen, *LGRP*, 16 (1895), 82 [884]
    3 H. Lübke, *AfdA*, 19 (1893), 341–42 [1269]
    4 A. Pogatscher, *Beitr*, 19 (1894), 544–45
    5 E. Sievers, *Beitr*, 18 (1894), 406–7 [1941]

390 ———. "*Beowulf* 1694b." *Taalkundige Bijdragen*, 1 (1877), 286. (lng, thm, txt; 1694)

391 ———. "Zum *Beowulf*." *Beitr*, 8 (1882), 568–74. (txt)

392 LA COUR, Vilhelm. "Lejrestudier." *DS*, 17 (1920), 49–67. (hst)

393 ———. "Lejrestudier: Mindesmaerkerne." *DS*, 18 (1921), 147–66. (hst)

394 ———. "Lejrestudier: Navnet." *DS*, 21 (1924), 13–22. (hst, nam) Cf. also A. F. Schmidt, "Lejrskov," *DS*, 23 (1926), 77–81.

395 ———. "Skjoldungefejden." *DS*, 23 (1926), 147–56. (hst, mth) Reply to Boer [144].

396 COURTHOPE, William J. *A History of English Poetry.* London and N.Y., 1895. Vol. I, chap. 3. (gen)

397 COX, Betty Smith. "Cruces of *Beowulf*." Unpub. Ph.D. diss., Univ. of Pittsburgh, 1964. *DA*, 26 (1965), 353. (for, int, lng, mth, rel, smb, tec)

398 COX, John Harrington. *Knighthood in Germ and Flower: The Anglo–Saxon Epic, "Beowulf," and the Arthurian Tale "Sir Gawain and the Green Knight."* Boston, 1910. (par) Popular paraphrase.

399   CRAIGIE, William Alexander. "Interpolations and Omissions in Anglo–Saxon Poetic Texts." *Philologica*, 2 (1925), 5–19. (mns; 31, 62, 139, 389, 403, 1931–62) Reply by Klaeber [1027].

400   ———. *Specimens of Anglo–Saxon Poetry.* Vol. III, *Germanic Legend and Anglo–Saxon History and Life.* Edinburgh, 1931. pp. 10–14. (edt, Fnb) Lines 1–85, 456–69, 871b–915, 1063–1159b, 1197–1214a, 1706b–22a, 1931b–62, 2020–60a, 2354b–96, 2425–2508a, 2602–25a, 2900–3007a

401   CRAIK, George L. *A Compendious History of English Literature, and of the English Language, from the Norman Conquest.* N.Y., 1877. Vol. I, p. 57. (gen, sch)

402   CRAMP, Rosemary. "*Beowulf* and Archaeology." *MArc*, 1 (1957), 55–77 and plates 9–11. (arc, img, int)

403   CRAWFORD, D. H. *"Beowulf" Translated into English Verse.* N.Y. and London, 1926. (bbl, Fnb, gen, nts, trl) Reviews:
        1   E. Blackman, *RES*, 3 (1927), 237–39
        2   S. J. Crawford, *MLR*, 22 (1927), 325–27
        3   M. Daunt, *YWES*, 7 (1926), 60
        4   M. S. MacLean, *Beibl*, 38 (1927), 312–14
        5   K. Malone, *MLN*, 42 (1927), 202–3

404   CRAWFORD, Samuel John. "*Beowulf*, ll. 168–9." *MLR*, 23 (1928), 336. (ana, int; 168–69)
        Review: M. Daunt, *YWES*, 9 (1928), 71

405   ———. "Beowulfiana." *RES*, 7 (1931), 448–50. (ana, mth, txt, wrd; 600a, 1724–68)
        Review: D. E. M. Clarke, *YWES*, 12 (1931), 69

406   ———. "Grendel's Descent from Cain." *MLR*, 23 (1928), 207–8. (ana, chr, nam, rel; 1691)
        Review: M. Daunt, *YWES*, 9 (1928), 71

406.1   ———. *Ibid.*, 24 (1929), 63. (ana, chr, nam, rel; 1691)
        Review: M. Daunt, *YWES*, 10 (1929), 92

407   ———. "Miscellaneous Notes: *Ealu-scerwen.*" *MLR*, 21 (1926), 302–3. (ana, int, wrd; 769a) Against Kock [1100].
        Review: M. Daunt, *YWES*, 7 (1926), 70

408   ———. (Untitled review of Sedgefield [1891]) *MLR*, 19 (1924), 104–8. (Fnb, lng, txt, wrd)

409   CREED, Robert Payson. "Afterword." Appendix to Raffel [1678], pp. 123–48. (com, for, hst, mtr, rel)

410   ———. "The *Andswarode*-system in Old English Poetry." *Speculum*, 32 (1957), 523–28. (dct, for, mtr; 258, 340)
        Review: R. M. Wilson, *YWES*, 38 (1957), 73

411   ——. *"Beowulf* 2231a: *sinc-fǣt (sōhte)." PQ*, 35 (1956),
       206–8. (mtr, txt; 2231a)
       Review: R. M. Wilson, *YWES*, 37 (1956), 72

412   ——. "The Making of an Anglo–Saxon Poem." *ELH*, 26
       (1959), 445–54. (dct, for, tec; 356–59) Replies by Fry
       [591], Greenfield [669], Lawrence [1186], and Stevick [2012].
       Review: R. M. Wilson, *YWES*, 40 (1959), 60

413   ——. "A New Approach to the Rhythm of *Beowulf."
       PMLA*, 81 (1966), 23–33. (mtr) Modifies Pope [1662].

414   ——. "On the Possibility of Criticizing Old English
       Poetry." *TSLL*, 3 (1961), 97–106. (for, img, stl; 1769–81)

415   ——. "The Singer Looks at His Sources." In *Brodeur*, pp.
       44–52. (ana, for, int, tec)
       Review: R. M. Wilson, *YWES*, 43 (1962), 57
       Also in *CL*, 14 (1962), 44–52.

416   ——. "Studies in the Techniques of Composition of the
       Béowulf Poetry in British Museum Ms. Cotton Vitellius
       A.XV." Unpub. Ph.D. diss., Harvard Univ., 1955. (dct,
       for, tec)

417   ——. "'. . . Wél-Hwelć Gecwæþ . . .': The Singer as
       Architect." *TSL*, 11 (1966), 131–43. (for)

418   CROSBY, H. Lamar, Jr. "Two Notes on *Beowulf." MLN*,
       55 (1940), 605–6. (hst, int, ken, wrd; 212, 216, 1910)
       Review: G. N. Garmonsway, *YWES*, 21 (1940), 36

419   CROSS, J. E. "On the *Wanderer*, Lines 80–84: A Study of
       a Figure and a Theme." *VSLA*, 1958–59, pp. 75–110. (dct,
       rht, thm; 1763ff)
       Review: R. M. Wilson, *YWES*, 40 (1959), 62

420   CROSSLEY-HOLLAND, Kevin. "The Finnesburh Frag-
       ment." In Bruce Mitchell, ed., *"The Battle of Maldon" and
       Other Old English Poems*. London, N.Y., 1965. pp. 45–48.
       (Fnb, gen, trl)
       Reviews:
          1   C. R. Barrett, *AUMLA*, 24 (1965), 296
          2   R. D. Stevick, *CE*, 27 (1966), 378

421   CROWNE, David K. "The Hero on the Beach: An
       Example of Composition by Theme in Anglo–Saxon Poetry."
       NM, 61 (1960), 362–72. (for, str, tec; 301–7, 518–21, 560–
       70, 1802–6, 1888–99, 1963–66) Expanded by Fry [588.1,
       589, 590].
       Review: R. M. Wilson, *YWES*, 41 (1960), 57

422   CULBERT, Taylor. "The Narrative Function of Beowulf's
       Swords." *JEGP*, 59 (1960), 13–20. (chr, str, tec)
       Review: R. M. Wilson, *YWES*, 41 (1960), 54

423   ——. "Narrative Technique in *Beowulf.*" *Neophilologus*, 47
        (1963), 50–61. (str, tec)
        Review: R. M. Wilson, *YWES*, 44 (1963), 71

424   ——. "The Single Combat in Medieval Heroic Narrative."
        Unpub. Ph.D. diss., Univ. of Michigan, 1957. *DA*, 18
        (1958), 1416–17. (str, thm)

425   CURME, George O. "A History of the English Relative
        Constructions." *JEGP*, 11 (1912), 10–29, 180–204, 355–80.
        (lng)

426   ——. "Is the Gothic Bible Gothic?" *JEGP*, 10 (1911),
        151–90, 335–59. (lng)

427   ——. "The Origin and Growth of the Adjective Declen-
        sion." *JEGP*, 9 (1910), 439–82. (lng)

?428   DAHLMANN, F. C. *Forschungen auf dem Gebiete der Geschichte.*
        Altona, 1822. Esp. Vol. I, pp. 440–41. (chr, hst)

429   ——. *Geschichte von Dännemark.* Hamburg, 1840. Esp. Vol.
        I, p. 17. (chr, hst)

429.1   DAHLSTEDT, August. *Rhythm and Wordorder in Anglo–Saxon
        and Semi–Saxon.* Lund, 1901. (lng, mtr)

430   DAHN, Therese. *Beowulf.* In Felix L. S. Dahn and Therese
        Dahn, eds., *Walhall: Germanische Götter- und Heldensagen.*
        Kreuznach, 1883. pp. 361–405. (Fnb, par) Selected and
        recast German prose paraphrase, based on Simrock [1952].
        2d ed., 1883; 3d ed., 1883; 4th ed., 1883; 5th ed., 1884; 6th
        ed., 1884; 7th ed., 1885; 8th ed., 1887; 9th ed., 1889; 10th
        ed., 1890; 11th ed., 1891; 12th ed., Leipzig, 1898; 13th ed.,
        1903.

431   DAICHES, David. *A Critical History of English Literature.*
        N.Y., 1960. (gen)
        Review: T. S. Dorsch, *YWES*, 42 (1963), 9–10

432   DALE, Edmund. *National Life and Character in the Mirror of
        Early English Literature.* Cambridge, 1907. (hst)

433   D'ARDENNE, S. T. R. O. "Shakespeare, a West Midland
        Man." *RLV*, 31 (1965–66), 547–54. (inf; 499–528) Source
        of *Julius Caesar*, I, ii, 99–110.

434   DAUNT, Marjorie. "Minor Realism and Contrast in *Beo-
        wulf.*" In *Mossé*, pp. 87–94. (img, str, tec)
        Review: R. M. Wilson, *YWES*, 40 (1959), 60

435   ——. "Old English." *YWES*, 25 (1944), 215–21. (sch)

436   ——. *Ibid.*, 26 (1945), 38–46. (sch)

437   ——. *Ibid.*, 27 (1946), 58–65. (sch)

438   ——. "Old English Studies." *YWES*, 7 (1926), 50–72.
        (sch)

438.1   ——. *Ibid.*, 8 (1927), 74–95. (sch)

438.2   ——. *Ibid.*, 9 (1928), 64–81. (sch)

438.3   ——. *Ibid.*, 10 (1929), 76–102. (sch)

438.4   ——. *Ibid.*, 11 (1930), 52–73. (sch)

439   ——. *Ibid.*, 13 (1932), 57–75. (sch)

440   ——. "Old English Verse and English Speech Rhythm."
        TPS, 1946, pp. 56–72. (mtr; 1255–1354)
        Review: R. M. Wilson, *YWES*, 27 (1946), 30–31

441   DAVIDSON, Charles. "Differences between the Scribes of
        Beowulf." *MLN*, 5 (1890), 43–45. (lng, mns) Answer by
        McClumpha [1527].

442   ——. "The Differences between the Scribes of *Beowulf.*"
        MLN, 5 (1890), 189–90. (lng, mns) Answer to McClum-
        pha [1527].

443   ——. "The Phonology of the Stressed Vowels of *Béowulf.*"
        PMLA, 6 (1891), 106–33. (lng)
        Review: G. E. Karsten, *ESt*, 17 (1892), 417–20

444   DAVIDSON, Hilda R. Ellis. "The Hill of the Dragon:
        Anglo–Saxon Burial Mounds in Literature and Archaeo-
        logy." *Folk-Lore*, 61 (1950), 169–85 and plate X. (arc, mth)

445   ——. *The Sword in Anglo–Saxon England: Its Archaeology and
        Literature.* Oxford, 1962. (arc, hst)
        Reviews:
            1   *TLS*, 20 April 1962, p. 263
            2   N. F. Blake, *N&Q*, 107 (1962), 351–53
            3   V. I. Evison, *MAE*, 32 (1963), 136–40
            4   D. H. Green, *MLR*, 57 (1962), 591–92
            5   F. E. Harmer, *RES*, 14 (1963), 276–77
            6   J. D. A. Ogilvy, *JEGP*, 61 (1962), 908–9
            7   R. M. Wilson, *YWES*, 43 (1962), 53

446   DAVIES, Constance. "Beowulf and Grendel." *TLS*, 28
        Dec. 1935, p. 899. (ana, img, src) Reply to Buck [264]
        about Davies [447].

447   ——. "Beowulf's Fight with Grendel." *TLS*, 9 Nov. 1935,
        p. 722. (ana, mth) Replies by Buck [264] and MacKenzie
        [1286].
        Review: D. E. M. Clarke, *YWES*, 16 (1935), 81

448   Item canceled.

 †   DAVIS, Norman, see [2278].

449   DEDERICH, Hermann. *Historische und geographische Studien*

zum angelsächsischen Beowulfliede. Cologne, 1877. (Fnb, hst, nam)

Reviews:

?1   *Revue Critique*, 52 (1876)

2   K. Körner, *ESt*, 1 (1877), 481–95 [1127]

3   K. Müllenhoff, *AfdA*, 3 (1877), 172–82

4   H. Suchier, *Jenaer Literatur-Zeitung*, 47 (1877), 732

5   R. Wülker, *LitCbl*, 1877, p. 1461

450   DEHMER, Heinz. "Die Grendelkämpfe Beowulfs im Lichte moderner Märchenforschung." *GRM*, 16 (1928), 202–18. (mth)

451   ——. *Primitives Erzählungsgut in den Íslendinga-Sögur.* Leipzig, 1927. (mth)

Reviews:

1   W. Krause, *AfdA*, 47 (1929), 157–60

2   H. Reuschel, *LGRP*, 51 (1938), 180–82

452   DELATTRE, Floris. *English Fairy Poetry.* Oxford, 1912. (mth)

453   DELBRÜCK, Berthold. "Der Germanische Optativ im Satzgefüge." *Beitr*, 29 (1904), 201–304. (lng)

454   ——. "Das schwache Adjektivum und der Artikel im Germanischen." *IF*, 26 (1909), 187–99. (lng)

455   ——. "Zu den Germanischen Relativsätzen." *Abhandl. der philol.-hist. Klasse der Königl. Sächsischen Gesellschaft der Wissenschaften*, 27, no. 19. Leipzig, 1909. (lng)

456   ——. (Untitled review of Ries [1710]) *AfdA*, 31 (1907–8), 65–76. (lng)

457   DENING, Wilhelm. *Zur Lehre von den Ruhe- und Richtungskonstruktionen.* Leipzig diss., 1912. (lng)

458   DENNER, Karl. "The Dative of Accompaniment in Old English Poetry." Unpub. Ph.D. diss., Johns Hopkins Univ., 1951. *DDABAU*, 1950–51, no. 18, 227. (lng)

459   DEROLEZ, R. L. M. "'And that difficult word, *garsecg*' (Gummere)." *MLQ*, 7 (1946), 445–52. (lng, wrd; 49, 515, 537)

460   ——. "Beowulfiana." *RBPH*, 40 (1962), 844–57. (sch)

461   ——. "Filologie en oudheidkunde: De *Beowulf* voor en na de ontdekking van Sutton Hoo." *HZM*, 15 (1961), 139–57. (arc, int)

462   DESKAU, H. *Zum Studium des "Beowulf": Berichte des freien deutschen Hochstiftes.* Frankfurt, 1890. (gen, hst, lng, txt)

463   DETTER, Ferdinand. "Der Baldrmythus." *Beitr*, 19 (1894), 495–516. (ana, chr, hst, mth)

464   ——. "Über die Heaðobarden im *Beowulf*." *Verhandlungen der Wiener Philologenversammlung*, May 1893, pp. 404–13. Leipzig, 1894. (hst, mth; 2021–70) Summarized in *ESt*, 19 (1894), 167–68.

465   ——. "Zur Ynglingasaga.   2. Der Baldrmythus; König Hygelac." *Beitr*, 18 (1894), 82–88. (ana, chr, hst, mth)

466   ——. *Ibid.* 4. Ingeld und die Svertinge." *Beitr*, 18 (1894), 90–96. (chr, hst)

467   DEUTSCHBEIN, Max. "Beowulf der Gautenkönig."   In *Morsbach*, 291–97. (hst)

468   ——. "Die sagenhistorischen und literarischen Grundlagen des Beowulfepos." *GRM*, 1 (1909), 103–19. (ana, hst, mth) Reply by Olson [1596].

469   ——. *Zur Entwicklung des englischen Alliterationsverses*. Leipzig Habilitationschrift. Halle a.S., 1902. (mtr)

†   DE VRIES, see VRIES, Jan de.

470   DICKHOFF, E. *Das zweigliedrige Wortasyndeton in der älteren deutschen Sprache*. Berlin, 1906. pp. 17–18. (dct, lng, stl)

471   DICKINS, Bruce. "Beowulf and the Monster."   *TLS*, 5 June 1943, p. 271   (ana)   On Bayeaux tapestry; refers to Paden [1612] and Ch.fneux [320].

472   ——. "English Names and Old English Heathenism." *E&S*, 19 (1934), 148–60. (nam, rel)

473   ——. "J. M. Kemble and Old English Scholarship."   Sir Israel Gollancz Memorial Lecture read 15 March 1939. *PBA*, 25 (1939), 51–84. (bbl, sch)
       Review: G. N. Garmonsway, *YWES*, 21 (1940), 43–44

474   ——. "Queen Cynethryth of Mercia." *PLPLS*, 4, part 1 (1936), 54. (ana)

475   ——. *Runic and Heroic Poems of the Old Teutonic Peoples*. Cambridge, 1915. (Fnb only: bbl, edt, hst, int, nts, trl)

476   DIETER, F. "Englische Litteratur, Altenglische Periode." In R. Bethge, ed., *Ergebnisse und Fortschritte der germanistischen Wissenschaft im letzten Vierteljahrhundert*. Leipzig, 1902. pp. 348–56. (sch)

477   DIETRICH, Franz. "Rettungen." *ZDA*, 11 (1859), 409–48. (int, lng, txt, wrd)

478   D'ISRAELI, Isaac. "Beowulf: The Hero-Life."   In his *Amenities of Literature*. London and N.Y., 1841. Vol. I, pp. 80–92. (mth)
       New ed., ed. by B. Disraeli, 1859. pp. 51–58

479   DIXON, W. MacNeile. *English Epic and Heroic Poetry.* London, 1912. (Fnb: gen, trl) Translates *Finnsburh* into English verse and prose.
       Reviews:
       1   *Dial*, 55 (1 April 1913), 83–86
       2   *Nation*, 97 (30 Oct. 1913), 412–13

480   DOBBIE, Elliott Van Kirk. *"Beowulf" and "Judith."* Anglo–Saxon Poetic Records, 4. N.Y., 1953. (bbl, com, edt, Fnb, hst, mns, nts, rel, txt)
       Reviews:
       1   *TLS*, 7 April 1954, p. 298
       2   F. L. Cassidy, *GR*, 30 (1955), 42–47
       3   N. D., *RES*, 6 (1955), 299–302
       4   F. P. Magoun, *MLN*, 71 (1956), 209–11
       5   A. McDonald, *ES*, 38 (1957), 212–13
       6   E. von Schaubert, *Speculum*, 33 (1958), 533–38
       7   R. M. Smith, *JEGP*, 53 (1954), 448–51
       8   R. M. Wilson, *YWES*, 34 (1953), 46–47

481   ——. "Finnsburg." In his *Anglo–Saxon Minor Poems.* Anglo–Saxon Poetic Records, 6. N.Y., 1942. (Fnb: bbl, com, edt, gen, mns, nts)
       Reviews:
       1   A. G. Kennedy, *MLQ*, 5 (1944), 492–94
       2   H. Larsen, *JEGP*, 42 (1943), 412–14
       3   F. P. Magoun, *MLN*, 59 (1944), 497–502
       4   H. Meroney, *MP*, 41 (1944), 198–200
       5   D. Whitelock, *YWES*, 23 (1942), 32–33

482   ——. "'Mwatide,' *Beowulf* 2226." *MLN*, 67 (1952), 242–45. (txt; 2226b)   Reply by Magoun [1303].
       Review: R. M. Wilson, *YWES*, 33 (1952), 41

483   DONAHUE, Charles. "*Beowulf*, Ireland and the Natural Good." *Traditio*, 7 (1949–51), 263–77. (com, hst, rel)

484   ——. "Grendel and the *Clanna Cain*." *Celtic Studies*, 1 (1950), 167–75. (int, mth, rel)

485   DONALDSON, E. Talbot. *Beowulf.* N.Y., 1966: Norton paperback. (gen, nts, trl)   Based on Klaeber [1026].

†   DRAAT, P. Vijn van, see VAN DRAAT.

486   DUBOIS, Arthur E. "*Beowulf*, 489–490." *MLN*, 50 (1935), 89–90. (int, txt; 489–90)
       Review: D. E. M. Clarke, *YWES*, 16 (1935), 83

487   ——. "*Beowulf* 1107 and 2577: Hoards, Swords, and Shields." *ESt*, 69 (1935), 321–28. (epc, mth, txt, wrd; 1107, 2577)
       Review: D. E. M. Clarke, *YWES*, 16 (1935), 81–82

488   ——. "The Dragon in *Beowulf.*" *PMLA*, 72 (1957), 819–
       22. (img, smb)
       Review: R. M. Wilson, *YWES*, 38 (1957), 75

489   ——. "Gifstol." *MLN*, 69 (1954), 546–49. (int, rel, wrd;
       168)
       Review: R. M. Wilson, *YWES*, 35 (1954), 40

490   ——. "'Hafelan Hydan,' *Beowulf*, ll. 446, 1372." *MLN*,
       70 (1955), 3–5. (int, ken; 446, 1372)
       Review: R. M. Wilson, *YWES*, 36 (1955), 61

491   ——. "Stod on Stapole." *MLQ*, 16 (1955), 291–98.
       (img, int; 926)   See also Griffith [685].
       Review: R. M. Wilson, *YWES*, 36 (1955), 61

492   ——. "The Unity of *Beowulf.*" *PMLA*, 49 (1934), 374–405.
       (hst, mth, rel, smb, stl, str, thm, unt)
       Review: M. Serjeantson, *YWES*, 15 (1934), 62

493   DUBOIS, Marguerite-Marie. *La littérature anglaise du moyen
       age.* Paris, 1962. (gen)
       Reviews:
            1   B. Cottle, *JEGP*, 62 (1963), 201–2
            2   P. Gradon, *EA*, 16 (1963), 273–74
            3   R. M. Wilson, *YWES*, 43 (1962), 54

494   DUFF, J. Wright. "Homer and *Beowulf:* A Literary
       Parallel." *Saga-Book*, 4, part 2 (1906), 382–406. (ana)
       Popular.

495   DUNSTAN, A. C. "*Beowulf*, ll. 223–4: Þa waes sund liden /
       eoletes aet ende." *MLR*, 20 (1925), 317–18. (int; 223–24)
       Review: E. V. Gordon, *YWES*, 6 (1925), 78

 †   ——, see [969].

496   DURANT, Jack. "The Function of Joy in *Beowulf.*" *TSL*,
       7 (1962), 61–69. (chr, str, tec, thm, unt)

497   EARLE, John. *Anglo–Saxon Literature (The Dawn of European
       Literature).* London, 1884. pp. 120–39. (com, gen, rel)
       Review: *Nation*, 11 Sept. 1884, no. 1002

498   [——]. "The Beowulf." *Times* (London), 25 Aug. 1884,
       p. 6. (ana, com, hst, mth)   Unsigned.

499   ——. "*Beowulf* I." *Ibid.*, 30 Sept. 1885, p. 3. (ana, com,
       hst, mth)

500   ——. "*Beowulf* II." *Ibid.*, 29 Oct. 1885, p. 3. (ana, com,
       hst, mth)

501   ——. *The Deeds of "Beowulf": An English Epic of the Eighth
       Century, Done into Modern Prose.* Oxford, 1892. (ana, com,

gen, hst, nts, trl, txt) Trans. into archaic English prose, based on Heyne [815], 4th and 5th eds.
Reviews:

    1 *Athenaeum*, 100, 1892, no. 3388, 445–46
    2 *SRL*, 73 (1893), 274
    3 J. M. Garnett, *Nation*, 57 (1893), 295 [618]
    4 E. Koeppel, *ESt*, 18 (1893), 93–95

Repr. 1892 and 1910, without introd. or notes. Partially repr. in J. W. Cunliffe, J. F. A. Pyre, and Karl Young, eds., *Century Readings for a Course in English Literature*. N.Y., 1915

502 [——]. "A Primitive Old Epic." *Household Words*, 17 (1857–58), 459–64. (par) English paraphrase, unsigned.

† ——, see [957].

503 EBELING, Friedrich W. *Angelsächsisches Lesebuch*. Leipzig, 1847. pp. 121–22. (edt) Lines 1063–1124 of Leo [1229] text.

504 EBERT, Karl Wilhelm Adolf. *Allgemeine Geschichte der Literatur des Mittelalters im Abendlande*. Leipzig, 1874–87. Vol. III, pp. 27–37. (gen)
New ed., 1880–89; no change in Vol. III

505 EBERT, Max. "Die Bootfahrt ins Jenseits." *Praehistorische Zeitschrift*, 12 (1919), 179–96. (hst)

506 ——. *Reallexikon der Vorgeschichte*. Berlin, 1924–32. (hst)

507 EDWARDES, Marian. *A Summary of the Literatures of Modern Europe (England, France, Germany, Italy, Spain) from the Origins to 1400*. London and N.Y., 1907. pp. 8–11. (bbl, Fnb, gen)

508 EDWARDS, Paul. "The Horse-Races in *Beowulf*." *Folklore*, 70 (1959), 336–37. (int, mth, str)

509 EHRISMANN, G. "Religionsgeschichtliche Beiträge zum germanischen Frühchristentum." *Beitr*, 35 (1909), 209–39. (rel)

510 EINARSSON, Stefán. "*Beowulf* 249: *Wlite* = Icelandic *Litr*." *MLN*, 64 (1949), 347. (dct, int, wrd; 250b)
Review: R. M. Wilson, *YWES*, 30 (1949), 42

511 ——. "Beowulfian Place Names in East Iceland." *MLN*, 76 (1961), 385–92. (hst, nam)
Review: R. M. Wilson, *YWES*, 42 (1963), 57–58

512 ——. "Bjolfur and Grendill in Iceland." *MLN*, 71 (1956), 79–80. (nam)

513 ——. "*Kyning-Wuldor* and *Mann-Skratti*." *MLN*, 75 (1960), 193–94. (dct, lng; 665)
Review: R. M. Wilson, *YWES*, 41 (1960), 55

514 EINENKEL, Eugen. "Die englische Verbalnegation." *Anglia*, 35 (1911), 187–248, 401–24. (lng)

515 ——. "Erklärung gegen Schipper." *Anglia*, 6 (1883), 64–66. (mtr) Answer to Schipper [1799].

516 EISEN, M. J. Über den Pekokultus bei den Setukesen." *Finnisch-Ugrische Forschungen*, 6 (1906), 104–11. (hst, mth) On Scyld.

517 EISMANN, A. *Der Konjunktiv in Nebensätzen in der ae. Poesie.* Kiel diss., 1921. (lng) Unpublished.

518 EKWALL, Eilert. (Untitled review of Chambers [307]) *Beibl*, 33 (1922), 177–85. (ana, hst, nam)

† ——, see also [119].

519 ELIASON, Norman E. "*Beowulf* Notes." *Anglia*, 71 (1953), 438–55. (int, txt, wrd; 73, 142a, 168–69, 175–88, 330, 478b–79, 759b–65a, 942a–46a, 1030–31, 1355b–57a, 1377b–78a, 2333–35a, 2645–46a)
Review: R. M. Wilson, *YWES*, 34 (1953), 48

520 ——. "The 'Improvised Lay' in *Beowulf.*" *PQ*, 31 (1952), 171–79. (epc, int, src, tec)
Review: R. M. Wilson, *YWES*, 33 (1952), 40

521 ——. "The 'Thryth-Offa Digression' in *Beowulf.*" In *Magoun*, pp. 124–38. (chr, hst; 1925–62)

522 ——. "The Þyle and Scop in *Beowulf.*" *Speculum*, 38 (1963), 267–84. (chr, int, tec, wrd; 78ff, 587, 1159ff, 1455–91, 1569, 1807–12)
Review: R. M. Wilson, *YWES*, 44 (1963), 74

523 ——. "Wulfhlið (*Beowulf*, l. 1358)." *JEGP*, 34 (1935), 20–23. (img, int; 1358)
Review: D. E. M. Clarke, *YWES*, 16 (1935), 84

524 ——. (Untitled review of Habicht [731]) *JEGP*, 60 (1961), 569–71. (int, stl)

525 ELLIOT, Ralph W. "Byrhtnoth and Hildebrand: A Study in Heroic Technique." In *Brodeur*, pp. 53–70. (epc, for, nam, thm, txt; 2633–38, 2708–09)
Repr. in *CL*, 14 (1962), 53–70

526 ELMORE, James Anna. "The Function of Vocabulary and Syntax in the Style of *Beowulf.*" Unpub. Ph.D. diss., Indiana Univ., 1945. (dct, lng)

527 EMERSON, Everett H. "On Translating *Beowulf.*" *SAQ*, 56 (1957), 369–79. (about trl)

528 EMERSON, Oliver Farrar. "Grendel's Motive in Attacking Heorot." *MLR*, 16 (1921), 113–19. (chr, rel)
Review: A. Brandl, *Archiv*, 145 (1923), 156

529 ——. "Legends of Cain, Especially in Old and Middle English." *PMLA*, 21 (1906), 831–929. (mth, rel)

530 ——. "The Punctuation of *Beowulf* and Literary Interpretation." *MP*, 23 (1926), 393–405. (int, lng, txt)
Review: M. Daunt, *YWES*, 7 (1926), 60–62

531 ——. "Transverse Alliteration in Teutonic Poetry." *JEGP*, 3 (1900), 127–37. (mtr) Attacked by Lewis [1239].

532 ENDTER, Wilhelm. *König Alfreds des Grossen Bearbeitung der Soliloquien des Augustinus*. Hamburg, 1922. (mns)
Review: E. E. Wardale, *YWES*, 3 (1922), 30–31

533 ENGEL, E. *Geschichte der englischen Litteratur*. Leipzig, 1883. (epc, lng)

534 ENGELHARDT, George J. "*Beowulf* 3150." *MLN*, 68 (1953), 535–38. (chr, int; 3150) Reply by Pope [1659].
Review: R. M. Wilson, *YWES*, 34 (1953), 48–49

535 ——. "*Beowulf*: A Study in Dilatation." *PMLA*, 70 (1955), 825–52. (com, rht, stl, str, tec, unt; 489–90)
Review: R. M. Wilson, *YWES*, 36 (1955), 59

536 ——. "On the Sequence of Beowulf's 'Geogoð.'" *MLN*, 68 (1953), 91–95. (epc, int, str, thm)
Review: R. M. Wilson, *YWES*, 34 (1953), 47

537 ENKVIST, Nils Erik. *The Seasons of the Year: Chapters on a Motif from "Beowulf" to "The Shepheardes Calendar."* Copenhagen, 1957. (ana, img, int)
Review: R. M. Wilson, *YWES*, 38 (1957), 73–74

538 ENTWHISTLE, William James, and GILLETT, Eric. *The Literature of England, A.D. 500–1942*. London, 1943. (gen)
Review: U. Ellis-Fermor, *YWES*, 24 (1943), 10

539 ENZENBERGER, C. "Das altenglische *Judith*-gedicht als Stilgebilde." *Anglia*, 82 (1964), 433–57. (stl; 1–121)
Review: R. M. Wilson, *YWES*, 45 (1964), 62

540 EPPELSHEIMER, Hanns W. *Handbuch der Weltliteratur*. Frankfurt, 1947. Vol. I, pp. 127–28. (bbl)

541 ERDMANN, Axel. *Über die Heimat und den Namen der Angeln*. Uppsala, 1890–91. pp. 40–54. (nam)

542 ERICSON, Eston Everett. "Old English *swa* in Worn-down Correlative Clauses." *ESt*, 65 (1931), 343–50. (lng; 93, 2608)
Review: D. E. M. Clarke, *YWES*, 12 (1931), 67–68

543 ——. "The Use of O.E. *swā* as a Pseudo-Pronoun." *JEGP*, 30 (1931), 6–20. (lng; 93, 1396, 2608)
Review: D. E. M. Clarke, *YWES*, 12 (1931), 67

544 ——. *The Use of Swa in Old English*. Göttingen and Baltimore, 1932. (lng)

Reviews:
   1   M. Daunt, *YWES*, 13 (1932), 72
   2   G. W. Small, *MLN*, 49 (1934), 537–39
545   ——. "The Uses of Old English *Swa* in Negative Clauses."
In *Collitz*, pp. 159–75. (lng)
†   ERICSSON, Mann, see [32].
546   ERLEMANN, Edmund. *Das landschaftliche Auge der angelsächsischen Dichter*. Berlin diss., 1902. (stl)
547   ESTRICH, Robert M. "The Throne of Hrothgar: *Beowulf*
ll. 168–169." *JEGP*, 43 (1944), 384–89. (hst, int, smb;
168–69)
Review: M. Daunt, *YWES*, 25 (1944), 217
548   ETTMÜLLER, Ludwig. *Beowulf: Heldengedicht des achten
Jahrhunderts: Zum ersten Male aus dem Angelsächsischen in das
Neuhochdeutsche stabreimend übersetzt und mit Einleitung und
Anmerkungen versehen*. Zurich, 1840. (com, Fnb, hst, nts, trl)
Literal German verse translation of *Finnsburh* and *Beowulf*,
based on Kemble [989] text.
549   ——. *Carmen de Beovvulfi Gautarum regis rebus praeclare gestis
atque interitu, quale fuerit antequam in manus interpolatoris, monachi
Vestsaxonici, inciderat*. Zurich, 1875. (Edt, nts, rel, str)   2896
lines with deletion of "interpolated" (i.e., Christian) por-
tions.
Reviews:
   1   A. Schönbach, *AfdA*, 3 (1877), 36–46 [1819]
   2   H. Suchier, *Jenaer Literatur-Zeitung*, 47 (1876), 732
550   ——. *Engla und Seaxna Scopas und Bōceras Anglosaxeum poetae
atque scriptores prosaici, quorum partim integra opera, partim loca
selecta collegit, correxit*. Quedlinburg and Leipzig, 1850. (edt,
Fnb, txt)   Text of 210–498, 607–61, 710–836, 991–1650,
2516–2820, 3110–82, and *Finnsburh*.
551   ——. *Handbuch der deutschen Literaturgeschichte*. Leipzig, 1847.
pp. 122–30. (Fnb, gen)
†   EVANS, Austin P., see [559].
†   EVANS, B. Ifor, see [1001].
552   EVANS, David. "The Sequence of Events in *Beowulf*, ll.
207–216." *MAE*, 32 (1963), 214–16. (int; 207–16)
Review: R. M. Wilson, *YWES*, 44 (1963), 73–74
553   EXNER, P. *Typische Adverbialbestimmungen in frühenglischer
Poesie*. Berlin diss., 1912. (lng)

554   FAHLBECK, Pontus. "Beovulfskvädet såsom källa för
nordisk fornhistoria." *ATS*, 8, no. 2 (1884), 1–88. (hst)
Review: *Academy*, 29 (1886), 12

?555   ——. "Beowulfskvädet som Källa för nordisk fornhistoria."
        N. F. Kungl. Vitterhets Historie och Antikvitets Akademiens Hand-
        lingar, 13, no. 3 (1913). (hst)
        Review: F. Klaeber, *ESt*, 48 (1914–15), 435–37
        ?Reissued as a monograph, 33, no 2 (1924).

556   FALK, Hjalmar.   "Altnordische Waffenkunde."   *Viden-*
        skapsselskapets Skriften II. Hist.- Filos. Klasse, no. 6.   Kristian,
        1914. (hst)

557   ——.   "Altnordisches Seewesen."   *Wörter und Sachen*, 4
        (1912), 1–122. (hst)

 †   ——, see [1916].

558   FANGER, Donald.   "Three Aspects of Beowulf and His
        God." *NM*, 59 (1958), 172–79. (mth, rel; 960–63)   Answer
        by Frankis [582].
        Review: R. M. Wilson, *YWES*, 39 (1958), 72

559   FARRAR, Clarissa P., and EVANS, Austin P.   *Bibliography
        of English Translations from Medieval Sources.*   Columbia
        Records of Civilization, 39.   N.Y. and London, 1946.   (bbl,
        about trl, Fnb)
        Review: F. L. Utley, *Speculum*, 21 (1946), 529–33

560   FAUST, Cosette, and THOMPSON, Stith.   *Old English
        Poems Translated into the Original Meter.*   Chicago and N.Y.,
        1918. (Fnb, trl)

561   FERGUSON, Robert.   "The Anglo–Saxon Name Beowulf."
        Athenaeum, no. 3372 (11 June 1892), 763a–b.   (chr, mth,
        nam)   < Beadowulf.

 †   FINGER, Charles J., see [1714].

562   FINKENSTAEDT, Thomas.   "Das Zeitgefühl im alten-
        glischen *Beowulf*-Epos." *Antaios*, 3 (1961), 215–32. (hst)

563   FISCHER, R.   (Untitled review of Graz [659])   *AfdA*, 23
        (1897), 40–54.   (mtr)

564   FISCHER, Walther.   "Von neuerer deutscher *Beowulf-*
        Forschung." In *Behaghel*, pp. 419–31.   (com, int, mth, mtr,
        sch, txt)
        Review: M. Serjeantson, *YWES*, 15 (1934), 61–62

565   FISHER, Peter F.   "The Trials of the Epic Hero in *Beowulf*."
        PMLA, 73 (1958), 171–83.   (ana, epc, hst, img, rel, smb,
        str, thm)
        Review: R. M. Wilson, *YWES*, 39 (1958), 71–72

566   FISKE, Christabel F.   "Old English Modifications of
        Teutonic Racial Conceptions." In *Hart*, pp. 255–94.   (hst,
        mth)

567   FLASDIECK, Herman M.   "Nochmals A.E. 'Nefne.'"
        Anglia, 70 (1951), 46.   (lng, wrd)   See next item.

568   ——. "O.E. 'Nefne': A Revaluation. I." *Anglia*, 69 (1950),
       135–71. (lng, wrd) See previous item.

569   ——. (Untitled review of Klaeber [1026]) *ESt*, 58 (1924),
       119–24. (com)

570   FLINT, E. L. and M. K. *Poetry in Perspective: A Critical
       Anthology.* London, 1963. (par) Paraphrase for children.
       Review: T. S. Dorsch, *YWES*, 44 (1963), 36

571   FLOM, George T. "Alliteration and Variation in Old
       Germanic Namegiving." *MLN*, 32 (1917), 7–17. (nam)

572   FOG, Reginald. "Bjarkemaals 'Hjalte.'" *DS*, 16 (1919),
       29–35. (int, txt) Includes letter by Axel Olrik.

573   ——. "Trolden 'Grendel' i Bjovulf: En Hypothese." *DS*,
       14 (1917), 134–40. (int, mth)

574   FOGELMAN, Roger Harry. "Dialect and Oral-formulaic
       Composition in Homer and the *Beowulf.*" Unpub. M.A.
       thesis, Univ. of Virginia, 1961. (for, lng)

575   FONTENROSE, Joseph. *Python: A Study of Delphic Myth and
       Its Origins.* Berkeley and Los Angeles, 1959. Appendix 5,
       pp. 524–34. (ana, mth, smb)

576   FORD, Ford Madox. *The March of Literature from Confucius
       to Modern Times.* London, 1939. (gen)
       Review: F. E. Budd, *YWES*, 20 (1939), 7–8

577   FÖRSTER, Max. "Die *Beowulf*-Handschrift." *Berichte über
       die Verhandlungen der Sächsischen Akademie der Wissenschaften zu
       Leipzig*, 61, no. 4 (1919). (mns) See Hoops [895] and Sisam
       [1956].
       Reviews:
            1 G. Binz, *LGRP*, 41 (1920), 97–98
            2 H. Hecht, *DLZ*, 42 (1921), 146–49
            3 W. Keller, *Beibl*, 34 (1923), 1–5
            4 J. H. Kern, *ES*, 3 (1921), 91–92
            5 G. C. van Langenhove, *LB*, 13 (1921), 230–32
            6 W. Preusler, *LitCbl*, 73 (1922), 95
            7 E. Schröder, *AfdA*, 40 (1921), 85–86
            8 E. E. Wardale, *YWES*, 1 (1919–20), 35

578   ——. *Bêowulf-Materialien, zum Gebrauch bei Vorlesungen.*
       Braunschweig, 1900. (ana, hst, mth)
       Reviews:
            1 O. Behagel, *LGRP*, 23 (1902), col. 67
            2 F. Holthausen, *Beibl*, 11 (1900), 289
       2d ed., 1908
       3d ed., 1912
       Review: F. Wild, *Beibl*, 24 (1913), 166–67
       4th ed., 1920

5th ed., Heidelberg, 1928
Review: M. Daunt, *YWES*, 9 (1928), 72

579 ———. "Keltisches Wortgut im Englischen." In *Liebermann*, unpaginated (lng, nam)
Review: E. E. Wardale, *YWES*, 2 (1920–21), 36–37

580 FOSTER, Thomas Gregory. *Judith: Studies in Metre, Language and Style with a View to Determining the Date of the Oldenglish Fragment and the Home of Its Author.* Strasbourg, 1892. (mtr)

581 FOURQUET, J. *L'ordre des éléments de la phrase en germanique ancien.* Paris, 1938. (lng) Comment by Klaeber [1076].
Review: K. Schneider, *Beibl*, 50 (1939), 225–33

582 FRANKIS, P. J. "*Beowulf* and the One That Got Away." *NM*, 60 (1959), 173–75. (epc, int; 960–63) Answer to Fanger [558].
Review: R. M. Wilson, 40 (1959), 61

583 FRANTZEN, J. J. A. A. "Het Alliteratievers." *Neophilologus*, 3 (1918), 30–35. (mtr)

?584 FREDBORG, Emil Äng. *Det första årtalet i Sveriges historia.* Umeå Progr., 1917. (hst)

585 FREEBURG, V. O. (Untitled review of Schück [1836]) *JEGP*, 11 (1912), 488–97. (int, mth, nam, src)

586 FREY, Leonard Hamilton. *Readings in Early English Language History.* N.Y., 1966: Odyssey paperback. pp. 28–30. (edt, trl) Edits 1–52 and translates into literal English prose.

587 FRIEND, Joseph H. "The Finn Episode Climax: Another Suggestion." *MLN*, 69 (1954), 385–87. (int; 1142–47)
Review: R. M. Wilson, *YWES*, 35 (1954), 40

588 ———. "A New Reading of a *Beowulf* Crux." *MLN*, 74 (1959), 292–93. (int, lng; 1030–31)
Review: R. M. Wilson, *YWES*, 40 (1959), 61

588.1 FRY, Donald K. "Aesthetic Applications of Oral-formulaic Theory: *Judith* 199–216a." Unpub. Ph.D. diss., Univ. of California at Berkeley, 1966. *DA*, 27 (1967), 3838A. (Fnb, for, tec, thm) Expands O'Neil [1599] and Ramsey [1684] and amplifies Crowne [421].

589 ———. "The Hero on the Beach in *Finnsburh*." *NM*, 67 (1966), 27–31. (ana, arc, for, hst—Fnb only) Expands Crowne [421].

590 ———. "The Heroine on the Beach in *Judith*." *NM*, 68 (1967), 168–84. (Fnb, for, str, tec; 301–7a, 562–71, 1494b–1517, 1801–6, 1888–99, 1963–66) Amplifies Crowne [421].

591 ———. "Old English Formulas and Systems." *ES*, 48 (1967), 193–204. (dct, for; 78a, 356, 710a, 1195b, 1896a,

1905a) Answer to Rogers [1728.1], Creed [412], and Magoun [1306].

592 FRYE, Prosser Hall. "The Translation of *Beowulf.*" *MLN*, 12 (1897), 79–82. (about trl) For blank verse.

593 FUHR, Karl. *Die Metrik des westgermanischen Alliterations-verses: Sein Verhaltnis zu Otfrid, den Nibelungen, der Gudrun, usw.* Marburg, 1892. (mtr)
Reviews:
    1 A. Heusler, *AfdA*, 19 (1893), 122–28
    2 H. Hirt, *LGRP*, 1894, no. 3
    3 F. Saran, *IF*, Anz. 5 (1895), 84–91
    4 E. Sievers, *LitCbl*, 1893, no. 19

594 FULTON, Edward. "On Translating Anglo–Saxon Poetry." *PMLA*, 13 (1898), 286–96. (about trl) For "irregular four-accent line."

595 FUNKE, Otto Viktor Conrad Wilhelm. "Zur Rhythmik des altenglischen Alliterationsverses—Eine kurze Betrachtung." *Anglia*, 76 (1958), 60–63. (mtr)
Review: R. M. Wilson, *YWES*, 39 (1958), 71

596 FÜRST, Clyde. "The Oldest English Poem: The *Beowulf.*" In *A Group of Old Authors.* Philadelphia, [1899]. pp. 157–99. (trl) Popular partial translation.
Review: C. G. Child, *MLN*, 15 (1900), 31–32

597 FURUHJELM, Åke. "Beowulfiana." *Anglia*, 57 (1933), 317–20. (int, txt; 224a, 303–6, 3074ff)
Review: D. E. M. Clarke, *YWES*, 14 (1933), 88–89

598 ——. "Note on a Passage in *Beowulf.*" *NM*, 32 (1931), 107–9. (int, lng; 3066–75)

599 GADDE, Fredrik. "Viktor Rydberg and Some *Beowulf* Questions." *SN*, 15 (1942–43), 71–90. (chr, mth, sch) About Rydberg [1747].
Review: D. Whitelock, *YWES*, 23 (1942), 39

600 GAIDOZ, Henri. "Cûchulainn, Beowulf et Hercule." *Bibliothèque de l'École des hautes études . . . Section des sciences historiques et philologiques*, Deux Cent Trentième Fascicule. Paris, 1921. pp. 131–56. (ana, mth)

601 GALINSKY, Hans. "Sprachlicher Ausdruck und künstlerischer Gehalt germanischer Schicksalsauffassung in der angelsächsischen Dichtung." *ESt*, 74 (1941), 273–323. (thm)

602 GALLÉE, J. H. "*haf, gamel, bano.*" *Beitr*, 12 (1887), 561–63. (int, txt, wrd) Reply to Sievers [1925] and [1933].

603   GANG, T. M. "Approaches to *Beowulf*." *RES*, n.s. 3
       (1952), 1–12. (com, epc, smb, str, thm, unt) Against Ker
       [1003] and Tolkien [2095]; replies by Bonjour [161] and
       Wright [2253].
       Review: R. M. Wilson, *YWES*, 33 (1952), 38–39

604   GARBÁTY, Thomas Jay. "Feudal Linkage in *Beowulf*."
       N&Q, 204 (1959), 11–12. (ana, epc, hst; 2633–38, 2864–72)
       Review: R. M. Wilson, *YWES*, 40 (1959), 61

605   GARDNER, Thomas. "Old English gārsecg." *Archiv*, 117
       (1966), 431–36. (lng, wrd; 19, 515, 537)

606   GARLANDA, Frederico. *Beowulf: Origini, bibliografia,
       metrica, contenuto, saggio di versione letterale, significato storico,
       etico, sociologico.* Rome, 1906. (bbl, com, hst, int, mtr)

607   GARMONSWAY, G. N. "Anglo–Saxon Heroic Attitudes."
       In *Magoun*, pp. 139–46. (chr, int; 2419–20)

608   ——. "A Note on a Passage in *Beowulf*." *Aberystwyth
       Studies*, 4 (1922), 67–68. (wrd; 1150) "Waefre."

609   ——. "Old English." *YWES*, 20 (1939), 23–40. (sch)

610   ——. *Ibid.*, 21 (1940), 32–45. (sch)

611   ——. *Ibid.*, 22 (1941), 43–50. (sch)

612   Item canceled.

613   Item canceled.

614   GARNETT, James Mercer. *Beowulf: An Anglo–Saxon Poem,
       and the "Fight at Finnsburg."* Boston, 1882. (bbl, Fnb, gen,
       nam, nts, trl) Translates into English four-stress verse.
       Reviews:
           1   *Nation*, 36 (8 Feb. 1883), 133–34
           2   J. W. Bright, *LGRP*, 10 (1883), 386–87
           3   J. A. Harrison, *AJPhil*, 4 (1883), 84–85 [757]. Reply
               by Garnett, *ibid.*, 243–46
           4   T. Krüger, *ESt*, 8 (1885), 133–38 [1166]
           5   J. Schipper, *Anglia*, 6 (1884), Anz., 120–24 [1800].
       2d ed., 1885. Collated with Grein/Wülker [677], Grein
       [676], and Heyne [815].
       Review: T. Krüger, *ESt*, 9 (1886), 151–52
       3d ed., 1893; repr. 1899
       4th ed., 1900; bibliography by Julian Huguenin
       Repr. 1902, 1904, 1906, 1910, 1912, each with new bib-
       liography

615   ——. "Recent Translations of O. E. Poetry." *PMLA*, 18
       (1903), 445–51, 455–58. (bbl, about trl)

616   ——. "The Translation of A.S. Poetry." *PMLA*, 6 (1891),
       95–105. (about trl) Concurs with Gummere [723].

617   ———. (Untitled review of Lumsden [1278])   *AJPhil*, 2
       (1881), 355–61. (about trl)

618   [———]. (Untitled review of Earle [501] and Hall [738])
       Nation, 57 (19 Oct. 1893), 295–96. (mtr, nam, smb, str)

619   GARNETT, Richard, and GOSSE, Edmund. *English Litera-
       ture: An Illustrated Record.* London and N.Y., 1903. Vol. I
       by Garnett. (com, Fnb, gen, hst) Popular.
       Review: E. Koeppel, *ESt*, 34 (1904), 373
       Vol. I repr. 1905, 1906, 1908, 1923, 1926

620   ———. (Untitled review of Gering [627])   *AJPhil*, 1 (1880),
       492. (ana, mth)

621   GASKIN, James R. "Structural Principle and Device in
       Beowulf." Unpub. Ph.D. diss., Univ. of N.C., 1952. Sum-
       mary in *U.N.C. Record*, no. 520, *Research in Progress* (1953),
       109–10. (str)

622   GATTIKER, Godfrey Leonard. "The Syntactic Basis of the
       Poetic Formula in *Beowulf.*" Unpub. Ph.D. diss., Univ. of
       Wisconsin, 1962–63. *DA*, 23 (1962), 2114–15. (for, lng)
       Uses O'Neil [1599]; summarized in Cassidy [294].

623   GELLING, Margaret. "The 'Gumstool.'"   *MLR*, 48
       (1953), 176–77. (nam, wrd; 1952)

624   GENZMER, Felix. *"Beowulf" und das "Finnsburg-Bruch-
       stück," aus dem Angelsächsischen übertragen.* Leipzig and Stutt-
       gart, 1951. (Fnb, par) German paraphrase.
       Review: E. A. Philippson, *JEGP*, 51 (1952), 91–92
       Repr. 1953

625   ———. "Die scandinavischen Quellen des *Beowulfs.*" *ANF*,
       65 (1950), 17–62. (src)

626   GERING, Hugo. *"Beowulf" nebst dem "Finnsburg-Bruchstück"
       übersetzt und erläutert.* Heidelberg, 1906. (Fnb, nts, trl)
       German verse.
       Reviews:
            1   G. Binz, *LGRP*, 31 (1910), 397–98
            2   R. C. Boer, *Museum*, 16 (1908), 139
            3   T. von Grienberger, *ZOG*, 59 (1908), 423–28
            4   H. Jantzen, *LitCbl*, 58 (1907), 64–65
            5   W. W. Lawrence, *JEGP*, 7 (1908), 129–33
            6   J. Ries, *AfdA*, 33 (1909), 143–47 [1711]
            7   A. Zehme, *Monatsschrift*, 14 (1909), 597–600
       2d ed., 1913
       Repr. 1930
       Review: M. Daunt, *YWES* 11 (1930), 73

627   ———. "Der *Béowulf* und die isländische *Grettissaga.*" *Anglia*,
       3 (1880), 74–87. (ana, mth, src)

Review: R. Garnett, *AJPhil*, 1 (1880), 492 [620]

628   ——. (Untitled review of Heyne [815]) *ZDP*, 12 (1881), 122–25. (gen, int, txt; 208ff, 303, 643)

629   GEROULD, Gordon Hall. *"Beowulf."* In his *Old English and Medieval Literature.* N.Y., 1929. (trl) Partial translation into English verse.
Rev. eds., 1933, 1935

630   ——. *"Beowulf" and "Sir Gawain and the Green Knight".* Poems *of Two Great Eras with Certain Contemporary Pieces.* N.Y., 1929. (gen, nts, trl) Trans. into English alliterative verse.
Repr. 1933, 1935

631   ——. "Offa and Labhraidh Maen." *MLN*, 17 (1902), 201–3. (ana, hst, mth)

632   GIBB, John. *"Gudrun" and Other Stories, from the Epics of the Middle Ages.* London and Edinburgh, 1881. (par) Selected English prose paraphrase.
2d ed., *"Gudrun," "Beowulf," and "Roland," with Other Medieval Tales.* London, 1884. pp. 135–68
Review: *RC*, no. 49 (1883)

633   GILLAM, Doreen M. E. "The Connotations of O. E. *fǣge:* With a Note on *Beowulf* and Byrhtnoth." *SGG*, 4 (1962), 165–202. (wrd)
Review: K. H. Göller, *Anglia*, 83 (1965), 90–91

634   ——. "The Connotations of the Old English Terms *sceacan, faege, æglæca:* A Study in the Method of Determining the Poetic Values of Old English Words." Unpub. M.A. thesis, London, Royal Holloway College, 1958–59. (dct, wrd)

635   ——. "The Use of the Term *aeglaeca* in *Beowulf* at Lines 813 and 2592." *SGG*, 3 (1961), 145–69. (wrd; 813, 2592)

†   GILLETT, Eric, see [538].

636   GIRVAN, Ritchie. *"Beowulf" and the Seventh Century.* London, 1935. (com, dct, hst, lng, mth, rel) Answer by Malone [1318].
Reviews:
     1 *TLS*, (4 Jan. 1936), 17
     2 D. E. M. Clarke, *YWES*, 16 (1935), 73–74
     3 E. V. K. Dobbie, *MLN*, 53 (1938), 455–57
     4 J. R. Hulbert, *MP*, 34 (1936), 76–77
     5 W. Jungandreas, *ZFDG*, 63 (1939), 339
     6 W. W. Lawrence, *Speculum*, 11 (1936), 297–98
     7 K. Malone, *ES*, 18 (1936), 223
     8 F. Mossé, *RG*, 27 (1936), 398–99
     9 J. Raith, *Beibl*, 48 (1937), 68–70

10   R. M. Wilson, *MLR*, 32 (1937), 330
11   C. L. Wrenn, *RES*, 13 (1937), 464–67

637   ——. "Finnsburuh." *PBA*, 26 (1940), 327–60. Sir Israel Gollancz Memorial Lecture for 1941, read 26 March 1941. (ana, chr, com, Fnb, int, tec)
Reviews:
1   K. Malone, *MAE*, 13 (1945), 88–91
2   D. Whitelock, *YWES*, 23 (1942), 36–37

638   ——. "The Medieval Poet and His Public." *EST*, (1951), 85–97. (com, rel)

639   ——. (Untitled review of Hoops [894]) *MLR*, 28 (1933), 244–46. (int, txt, wrd)

640   GLUNZ, Hans. *Die Verwendung des Konjunktivs im Altenglischen. Beitr*, 11 (1929). (lng)
Reviews:
1   M. Daunt, *YWES*, 11 (1930), 62–63
2   F. Klaeber, *Beibl*, 41 (1930), 261–63

641   GNEUSS, Helmut. *Lehnbildungen und Lehnbedeutungen im Altenglischen.* Berlin, 1955. (int, lng, smb, wrd)
Reviews:
1   G. Graband, *ZAA*, 3 (1957), 367–71
2   C. E. Reed, *MLQ*, 17 (1956), 371
3   K. Schneider, *Archiv*, 192 (1957), 201
4   E. G. Stanley, *MLR*, 50 (1955), 565

642   GOEBEL, Julius. "The Evolution of the *Nibelungensaga.*" *JEGP*, 17 (1918), 1–20. (ana, mth)

643   ——. "On the Original Form of the Legend of Sigfrid." *PMLA*, 12 (1897), 461–74. (ana, mth)

644   GOLDSMITH, Margaret E. "The Choice in *Beowulf.*" *Neophilologus*, 48 (1964), 60–72. (chr, epc, rel, smb, str)
Reply to Mitchell [1455].
Review: R. M. Wilson, *YWES*, 45 (1964), 59

645   ——. "The Christian Perspective in *Beowulf.*" *CL*, 14 (1962), 71–90. (com, int, rel, smb, src, thm)
Review: R. M. Wilson, *YWES*, 43 (1962), 56
Repr. in *Brodeur*, pp. 71–90; in Nicholson [1560], pp. 373–86

646   ——. "The Christian Theme of *Beowulf.*" *MAE*, 29 (1960), 81–101. (ana, int, rel, smb, src, thm)   Reply by Mitchell [1455].
Review: R. M. Wilson, *YWES*, 41 (1960), 54

647   GOLTHER, Wolfgang. *Handbuch der germanischen Mythologie.* Leipzig, 1895. (mth)

648   ——. (Untitled review of Panzer [1618]) *NJKA*, 25 (1910), 610–13. (ana, mth)

649 GORDON, Eric Valentine. *The Battle of Maldon.* London, 1937. pp. 23–30. (dct, Fnb, mtr, str, thm, unt)

650 ——. "Old English Studies." *YWES*, 5 (1924), 66–77. (sch)

651 ——. *Ibid.*, 6 (1925), 67–82. (sch)

652 ——. "Wealhþeow and Related Names." *MAE*, 4 (1935), 169–75. (chr, hst, lng, nam)
Review: D. E. M. Clarke, *YWES*, 16 (1935), 84

† ——, see [1916].

653 GORDON, R. K. *"The Song of Beowulf" Rendered into English Prose.* London, Toronto, and N.Y., [1923]. (Fnb, trl)
Translates *Beowulf* and *Finnsburh* into English prose.
Repr. in his *Anglo-Saxon Poetry.* London and N.Y., 1927: Everyman's Library no. 794; repr. 1930
Review: M. Daunt, *YWES*, 8 (1927), 85–86
Rev. ed. of repr., 1954; repr. 1964
Review: R. M. Wilson, *YWES*, 35 (1954), 39

654 GORRELL, Joseph Hendren. *Indirect Discourse in Anglo-Saxon.* Baltimore, 1895. (lng)

† GOSSE, Edmund, see [619].

655 GOUGH, A. B. *The Constance Saga.* Palaestra 23. Berlin, 1902. pp. 53–83. (hst, mth)
Reviews:
 1 E. Eckhardt, *ESt*, 32 (1903), 110–13
 2 M. Weyrauch, *Archiv*, 111 (1903), 453–54

656 GRAF, Nanette. *Beowulf Notes.* Lincoln, Neb., 1966. (bbl, dct, cpc, gen, ken, lng, mtr, nam, par, rel, str, thm) Popular student aid; paraphrases poem.

657 GRAMM, Willi. *Die Körperpflege der Angelsachsen: eine kultur-geschichtliche etymologische Untersuchung.* Heidelberg, 1938. (hst, lng, wrd)
Reviews:
 1 E. V. K. Dobbie, *GR*, 14 (1939), 225–26
 2 F. Holthausen, *Beibl*, 51 (1940), 27
 3 F. Klaeber, *Archiv*, 176 (1939), 82–84
 4 A. MacDonald, *MLR*, 35 (1940), 77
 5 H. Marquardt, *ESt*, 75 (1942), 216–17
 6 C. L. Wrenn, *YWES*, 19 (1938), 41–42

658 GRAU, Gustav. *Quellen und Verwandtschaften der älteren germanischen Darstellungen des jüngsten Gericht.* Halle a.S., 1908. pp. 145–56. (com, rel)
Reviews:
 1 K. Guntermann, *ZDP*, 41 (1909), 401–15
 2 H. Hecht, *Archiv*, 130 (1913), 424–30

659   GRAZ, Friedrich. *Die Metrik der sog. Caedmonschen Dichtungen
      mit Berücksichtigung der Verfasserfrage.* Weimar, 1894. (mtr)
      Reviews:
         1   O. Brenner, *ESt*, 22 (1896), 74–75
         2   P. Cosijn, *Museum*, 3 (1895), 203–4.
         3   R. Fischer, *AfdA*, 23 (1897), 40–54 [563]
         4   H. Hirt, *LitCbl*, 1895, no. 36, cols. 1288–90
         5   M. Trautmann, *Beibl*, 6 (1895–96), 1–4

660   GREEN, A. Wigfall. *Beowulf, Literally Translated.* Boston,
      1935. (trl)   Literal English prose.

661   GREEN, Alexander. *The Dative of Agency: A Chapter of
      Indo-European Case-Syntax.* Columbia Univ. Germanic
      Studies. N.Y., 1913. pp. 95–102. (lng)

662   ——. "An Episode in Ongenþeow's Fall (*Beowulf*, ll. 2957–
      2960)." *MLR*, 12 (1917), 340–43. (int; 2957–60)

663   ——. "The Opening of the Episode of Finn in *Beowulf*."
      PMLA, 31 (1916), 759–97 and one facsimile. (Fnb, str, tec;
      Fep)

664   GREEN, Charles. *Sutton Hoo: The Excavation of a Royal Ship-
      Burial.* London and N.Y., 1963. (arc, com, Fnb)
      Reviews:
         1   T. C. Lethbridge, *Spectator*, 17 Jan. 1964, pp. 81–82
         2   R. M. Wilson, *YWES*, 44 (1963), 67–68

665   GREEN, J. R. *The Making of England.* London, 1881.
      (gen)
      2d ed., London and N.Y., 1882.

666   ——. *A Short History of the English People.* Ed. Mrs. J. R.
      Green and Kate Norgate. London and N.Y., 1893. (hst)

667   GREENFIELD, Stanley B. "*Beowulf* 207B–228: Narrative
      and Descriptive Art." *N&Q*, 211 (1966), 86–90. (dct, int,
      lng, tec, wrd; 207b–28)

668   ——. "*Beowulf* and Epic Tragedy." *CL*, 14 (1962), 91–105.
      (epc, stl)
      Review: R. M. Wilson, *YWES*, 43 (1962), 56
      Repr. in *Brodeur*, pp. 91–105

669   ——. "The Canons of Old English Criticism." *ELH*, 34
      (1967), 141–55. (dct, for)   Answer to Creed [412], Lawrence
      [1186], and Whallon [2192] and [2193].

670   ——. *A Critical History of Old English Literature.* N.Y., 1965;
      London, 1966. (epc, Fnb, for, mns, mth, str, tec, thm)
      Reviews:
         1   *TLS*, 20 Oct. 1966, p. 957
         2   P. Bacquet, *EA*, 19 (1966), 279–81

3   M. W. Bloomfield, *Speculum*, 41 (1966), 330–32

4   R. Stevick, *CE*, 27 (1966), 578

671   ——. "The Exile-Wanderer in Anglo–Saxon Poetry." Unpub. Ph.D. diss., Univ. of California at Berkeley, 1950. *DDABAU*, (1949–50), no. 17, 196. (epc, int, mth, wrd; 1137, 3018–19)

672   ——. "The Formulaic Expression of the Theme of 'Exile' in Anglo–Saxon Poetry." *Speculum*, 30 (1955), 200–6. (chr, for, img, thm)
Review: R. M. Wilson, *YWES*, 36 (1955), 59

673   ——. "Geatish History: Poetic Art and Epic Quality in *Beowulf*." *Neophilologus*, 47 (1963), 211–17. (epc, hst, tec, thm; 2349b–99a, 2425–2515, 2910b–3000)
Review: R. M. Wilson, *YWES*, 44 (1963), 74–75

†   ——, see [2276].

674   GREG, W. W. "The 'Five Types' in Anglo–Saxon Verse." *MLR*, 20 (1925), 12–17. (mtr)
Review: E. V. Gordon, *YWES*, 6 (1925), 75–77

675   GREIN, Christian Wilhelm Michael. "Beóvulf" and "Ueberfall in Finnsburg." In his *Bibliothek der angelsächsischen Poesie*. Göttingen, 1857. Vol. I, pp. 255–343. (edt, Fnb) Collation of previous editions.

676   ——. *"Beovulf", nebst den "Fragmenten Finnsburg" und "Waldere."* Cassel and Göttingen, 1867. (edt, Fnb) Collation of previous editions.

677   ——. "*Beowulf*." In his *Dichtungen der Angelsachsen, stabreimend übersetzt*. Göttingen, 1857. Vol. I, pp. 222–308. (trl) Literal German alliterative verse.
Repr. Kassel and Göttingen, 1863; repr. 1930
Reviews:
1   W. Fischer, *LGRP*, 52 (1931), 428
2   J. Hoops, *ESt*, 67 (1932), 261–62
3   F. Klaeber, *Beibl*, 41 (1930), 257–58
4   E. Schwentner, *IF*, 52 (1934), 82–83
2d ed., Kassel, 1883, by R. Wülker. *Beowulf* separately, with new manuscript corrections by Grein.
Reviews:
1   E. Kölbing, *ESt*, 7 (1884), 482–89 [1124.1]
2   T. Krüger, *ESt*, 8 (1884), 139–42

678   ——. "Die historischen Verhältnisse des Beowulfliedes." *Jahrbuch für romanische und englische Literatur*, 4 (1862), 260–85. (Fnb, hst, int)

679   ——. "Zur Textkritik der angelsächsischen Dichter: *Finnsburg*." *Germania*, 10 (1865), 416–29. (Fnb, txt)

680   GRIENBERGER, T. von. "Bemerkungen zum *Beowulf.*"
       Beitr, 36 (1910), 77–101. (int) Opposed by Sievers [1931].

681   ——. "Zu *Beowulf.*" *Anglia*, 27 (1904), 331–32. (int, wrd;
       1107) Opposes Holthausen [865].

682   ——. (Untitled review of Heyne [815], 7th ed.) *ZOG*, 56
       (1905), 744–61. (lng, mtr, txt)

683   ——. (Untitled review of Holthausen [845]) *ZOG*, 59
       (1908), 333–46. (lng)

684   GRIERSON, Herbert J. C., and SMITH, J. C. *A Critical*
       History of English Poetry. London, 1944. (gen)
       Reviews:
            1   M. Daunt, *YWES*, 25 (1944), 216
            2   E. Seaton, *YWES*, 25 (1944), 7–8

685   GRIFFITH, D. D. "Stod on Stapole: Addendum." *MLQ*,
       16 (1955), 298–99. (img, int; 926) Agrees with DuBois
       [491].
       Review: R. M. Wilson, *YWES*, 36 (1955), 61

686   GRIMM, Jacob Ludwig Karl. *Andreas und Elene.* Cassel,
       1840. pp. xxiv–xliv. (gen, stl)

687   ——. *Deutsche Mythologie.* Göttingen, 1835. (hst, mth)
       2d ed., 1844; 3d ed., 1854.
       4th ed., Berlin, 1875–78. Ed. by Elard H. Meyer. Vol. III.
       Angelsächsische Stammtafeln. pp. 377–401.
       4th ed. trans. into English by James Steven Stallybrass as
       Teutonic Mythology. London, 1880–84. 4 vols.

688   ——. *Geschichte der deutsche Sprache.* Leipzig, 1848. (hst)
       2d ed., 1853; 3d ed., 1868; 4th ed., 1880

689   ——. "Sintarfizilo." *ZDA*, 1 (1841), 2–6. (ana, mth)

690   ——. "Über das Verbrennen der Leichen." *Adhandl. der*
       philol.-hist. Klasse der königl. Akademie der Wissenschaften zu
       Berlin, 1849, pp. 191–274. (hst)
       Repr. in his *Kleinere Schriften*, II (Berlin, 1865), 211–313

690.1 ——. "Über die Stammtafel der Westsachsen von John M.
       Kemble." In his *Kleinere Schriften*, V (Munich, 1856), 240–
       44. (lng, src)

691   ——. (Letter to J. M. Kemble dated 13 July 1833) *Briefe*
       der Brüder Grimm, ed. by Hans Gürtler. Jena, 1923. pp.
       76–78. (lng, sch; 71) Praising Kemble [989].

692   ——. (Letter to J. M. Kemble dated 26 April 1834) *Briefe*
       der Brüder Grimm, ed. by Hans Gürtler. Jena, 1923. pp.
       78–79. (lng, sch) Praising Kemble.

693   ——. (Letter to J. M. Kemble dated 23 Dec. 1839) *Briefe*
       der Brüder Grimm, ed. by Hans Gürtler. Jena, 1923. pp.
       92–94. (sch) About Leo [1229].

694   ——. (Untitled review of Grundtvig [707]) *Göttingische gelehrte Anzeiger*, 2 Jan. 1823, pp. 1–12. (hst)
Repr. in his *Kleinere Schriften*, IV (Berlin, 1869), 178–86

695   GRIMM, Paul. *Beiträge zum Pluralgebrauch in der altenglischen Poesie.* Halle diss., 1912. (lng)

696   GRIMM, Wilhelm. *Die Deutsche Heldensage.* Göttingen, 1829. pp. 13–17. (ana, hst, mth, trl) Partial translation into German.
2d ed., rev. by Karl Müllenhoff, Berlin, 1867
3d ed., Gütersloh, 1889

697   ——. "Einleitung über die Elfen." In *Irische Elfenmärchen: Übersetzt von den Brüdern Grimm.* Leipzig, 1826. pp. cxix–cxxiv. (mth)
Repr. in his *Kleinere Schriften*, I (Berlin, 1881), 405 and 467

698   ——. "Einleitung zur Vorlesung über *Gudrun.*" In his *Kleinere Schriften*, IV (1887), 557–60. (hst) Otherwise unpub. lecture given 6 times between 1843 and 1849.

699   GRINDA, Klaus R. "Einige Handwerke in der ae. Dichtung und in zeitgenössischen Inschriften: Gesichtspunkte der Darstellung und soziale Wertung." In *Hübener*, pp. 77–90. (hst, smb, thm, wrd)

700   GRION, Cav. Giusto. *Beowulf: Poema epico Anglosassone del VII secolo, tradotto e illustrato.* In *Atti della Real Accademia lucchese di scienze, lettere ed arti*, 22 (Lucca, 1883), 197–380. (bbl, Fnb, hst, mth, nts, trl, txt) First Italian translation; in literal Italian verse, based on all texts.
Review: T. Krüger, *ESt*, 9 (1886), 64–77

700.1   GROENE, Horst. *Die lehrhaften Elemente im "Beowulf": Züge eines Christlichen Fürstenspiegels.* Unpub. Kiel diss., 1966. (rel)

701   GRØNBECH, Vilhelm. *Vor Folkeæt i Oldtiden.* Copenhagen, 1909–12. (hst)
Reviews:
    1   E. Ekwall, *Beibl*, 31 (1920), 1–9
    2   L. M. Hollander, *JEGP*, 9 (1910), 269–78
    3   *Ibid.*, 14 (1915), 124–35
    4   G. Neckel, *ESt*, 47 (1913–14), 108–16
Trans. into English by William Worster as *The Culture of the Teutons.* Copenhagen and London, 1932. Rev. by Grønbech.
Trans. into German as *Kultur und Religion der Germanen.* Hamburg, 1937–39.

702   GROSSMANN, H. *Die Relativa im Beowulf.* Berlin, 1906. (lng)

?703 GROTH, E. *Composition und Alter der Exodus.* Göttingen, 1883. (com, lng)

704 GRUNDTVIG, Nik. Fred. Sev. *Beowulfes Beorh eller Bjovulfs-Drapen.* London and Copenhagen, 1861. (ana, edt, Fnb, mns) Uses Thorkelin [2081] and [2082].

705 ——— . *Bibliotheca Anglo–Saxonica: Prospectus and Proposals of a Subscription for the Publication of the Most Valuable Anglo–Saxon Manuscripts Illustrative of the Early Poetry and Literature of Our Language, Most of Which Have Never Yet Been Printed.* London, 1830. (gen) *Beowulf* would have been Vols. I and II.
Rev. ed., 1831

706 ——— . "Bjovulfs Drape–eller det Oldnordiske Heltedigt."
Brage og Idun, 4 (1841), 481–538. (ana, str)

707 ——— . **Bjowulfs Drape: Et Gothisk Helte-Digt fra forrige Aar-Tusinde af Angel-Saxisk paa Danske Rüm.* Copenhagen, 1820. (com, Fnb, gen, hst, nts, rel, smb, trl, txt, unt) Translates *Beowulf* into Danish ballad measure and *Finnsburh* into unrhymed verse.
Review: J. Grimm, *Göttingische gelehrte Anzeigen,* 2 Jan. 1823, pp. 1–12 [694]
2d ed., 1865

708 ——— . "Et Par Ord om det nys udkomne angelsaxiske Digt."
Nyeste Skilderie af Kjøbenhavn, no. 60 (1815), cols. 945, 998, 1009, 1025, 1030, 1045. (chr, hst, about trl, txt) Review of Thorkelin [2080]; reply by Thorkelin [2083]. Hygelac = Chochilaicus.

709 ——— . "Nok et Par Ord om Bjovulfs Drape." *Nyeste Skilderie af Kjøbenhavn,* no. 60 (1815), cols. 1106, 1121, 1139. (chr, hst, about trl, txt) Reply to Thorkelin [2083].

710 ——— . *Nordens Mythologi.* 2d ed., Copenhagen, 1832. pp. 571–94. (par) First ed., 1808, contains no *Beowulf.*
3d ed., 1869

711 ——— . "Om Bjovulfs Drape." *Dannevirke,* 2 (1817), 207–89. (chr, com, epc, hst) Hygelac = Chochilaicus.

712 ——— . "Stykker af Skjoldung-Kvadet eller Bjovulfs Minde."
Dannevirke, 4 (1819), 234–62. (trl)

713 ——— . (Untitled review of Thorkelin [2080]). *Göttingische gelehrte Anzeigen,* 1818, pp. 41–48. (epc, int) In German.

714 GRUNER, H. *Mathei Pariensis Vitae Duorum Offarum, in ihrer Manuskript- und Textgeschichte.* Munich diss., 1907. (ana, hst)

715 GUERBER, Hélène Adeline. "Anglo–Saxon Epic." In her *Book of the Epic: The World's Greatest Epics Told in Story.* Lon-

don and Philadelphia, 1913. (epc)
Repr. 1941

716 GUEST, Edwin. *A History of English Rhythms.* London, 1838. (mtr)
Rev. ed. by W. W. Skeat, London, 1882.
Review: J. M. Garnett, *AJPhil*, 4 (1883), 478

717 GUMMERE, Francis B. *The Anglo–Saxon Metaphor.* Freiburg diss., Halle a.S., 1881. (img, stl)

718 ——. *The Beginnings of Poetry.* N.Y. and London, 1901. (gen, hst)

719 ——. *Germanic Origins: A Study in Primitive Culture.* N.Y., 1892. (hst, nts, trl) Translates 402–661 into English verse.
Rev. ed. by F. P. Magoun, Jr., *Founders of England.* N.Y., 1930. Uses translations from Gummere [720].
Reviews:
1 M. Daunt, *YWES*, 11 (1930), 72–73
2 G. Hübener, *Beibl*, 42 (1931), 1–3
3 F. Klaeber, *ESt*, 66 (1931), 146–47
4 K. Malone, *MLN*, 46 (1931), 488–89

720 ——. *The Oldest English Epic: "Beowulf," "Finnsburg," "Waldere," "Deor," "Widsith," and the German "Hildebrand" Translated in the Original Metres.* N.Y., 1909. (Fnb, gen, nts, trl) English verse; see also Gummere [719].
Reviews:
1 *Athenaeum*, 1909, II, 151–52
2 G. C. Child, *MLN*, 24 (1909), 253–54 [323]; reply by Gummere [724] and reply to that by Child [324]
3 J. Derocquigny, *RG*, 6 (1910), 356–57
4 J. L. Hall, *SR*, 18 (1910), 373–76
5 W. J. Sedgefield, *ESt*, 41 (1910), 402–3 [1901]
6 M. Trautmann, *Beibl*, 21 (1910), 353–60 [2118]
Repr. 1910, 1914, 1920, 1922, 1923
Translation of *Beowulf* only included in C. W. Eliot, ed., Harvard Classics, XXXXIX. N.Y., 1910. pp. 5–94.

721 ——. *The Popular Ballad.* Boston and N.Y., 1907. (gen, hst)

722 ——. "The Sister's Son." In *Furnivall*, pp. 133–49. (hst)

723 ——. "The Translation of *Beowulf*, and the Relation of Ancient and Modern English Verse." *AJPhil*, 7 (1886), 46–78. (trl; 1–52) Translates 1–52 into alliterative English verse; argues for original metre; Garnett [616] concurs.

724 ——. "Translation of Old English Verse." *MLN*, 25 (1910), 61–63. (about trl) Reply to Child [323]; Child [325] replies.

725   ——. (Untitled review of Bode [135]). *MLN*, 2 (1887), 17–19. (ken)

726   GUTENBRUNNER, S. *Die germanischen Götternamen der antiken Inschriften.* Halle, 1936. (ana, chr, hst, mth, nam)

727   HAACK, Otto. *Zeugnisse zur altenglischen Heldensage.* Kiel diss., 1892. (hst, mth)

728   HAARDER, Andreas. "Et gammelt indlaeg i en ny debat: G.s vurdering af *Beowulf* som kunstværk." *Grundtvig Studier*, 1965, pp. 7–36. (str, unt) Answers Malone [1333].

729   HABER, Tom Burns. "*Beowulf* and the *Aeneid.*" *MLN*, 48 (1933), 207–8. (ana, epc, src) Reply to P. F. Jones, *MLN*, 47 (1932), 264–66, which is a review of Haber [730].

730   ——. "A Comparative Study of the *Beowulf* and the *Aeneid.*" Ph.D. diss., Ohio State Univ., 1929. (ana, bbl, epc)
         Pub. in book form, same title, Princeton and London, 1931
         Reviews:
         1 *TLS*, 24 Dec. 1931. pp. 1043
         2 M. Ashdown, *RES*, 8 (1932), 462–63
         3 D. E. M. Clarke, *YWES*, 12 (1931), 62–64
         4 H. Dehmer, *NS*, 41 (1933), 464–65
         5 R. Girvan, *MLR*, 27 (1932), 466–70
         6 P. F. Jones, *MLN*, 47 (1932), 264–66; reply by Haber [729]
         7 F. Klaeber, *Beibl*, 43 (1932), 229–32
         8 F. M., *RG*, 24 (1933), 52
         9 R. B. Onions, *Classical Review*, 47 (1933), 200–1

731   HABICHT, Werner. *Die Gebärde in englischen Dichtungen des Mittelalters.* Abhandlungen der bayerischen Akademie der Wissenschaften. Munich, 1959. (com, hst, img, tec)
         Reviews:
         1 D. S. Brewer, *MLR*, 56 (1961), 465
         2 K. Brunner, *Anglia*, 78 (1960), 228–30
         3 N. E. Eliason, *JEGP*, 55 (1961), 569–71 [524]
         4 N. E. Enkvist, *SN*, 33 (1961), 206–8
         5 H. Oppel, *NS*, 1960, pp. 505–7
         6 A. Renoir, *MLN*, 76 (1961), 165–66
         7 M. Schlauch, *KN*, 8 (1960), 235–36
         8 H. M. Smyser, *Speculum*, 35 (1960), 456–60
         9 E. Standop, *Archiv*, 197 (1961), 203–4

732   HACKENBERG, Erna. *Die Stammtafeln der angelsächsischen Königreiche.* Berlin diss., 1918. (hst)
         Reviews:
         1 E. Ekwall, *ESt*, 54 (1920), 307–10

      2 W. Fischer, *Beibl*, 31 (1920), 73–74

      3 F. Liebermann, *DLZ*, 1 March 1919, p. 181

733   HAEUSCHKEL, Bruno. *Die Technik der Erzählung im Beowulfliede*. Breslau diss., 1904. (stl, tec)

734   HAGEN, Silvert N. "Classical Names and Stories in the *Beowulf*." *MLN*, 19 (1904), 65–74, 156–65. (ana, mth, nam, src)

735   ——. "Yrsa og Rolv Krake." *DS*, 20 (1923), 180–82. (nam)

736   HAHN, E. Adelaide. "Waes Hrunting nama." *Language*, 37 (1961), 476–83. (lng, nam; 1457)

737   HAIGH, Daniel H. *The Anglo-Saxon Sagas: An Examination of Their Value as Aids to History; A Sequel to the History of the Conquest of Britain by the Saxons*. London, 1861. (com, Fnb, hst, mth, nam, trl) Prose translation of *Finnsburh* only.

738   HALL, John Lesslie. "*Beowulf*, an Anglo-Saxon Epic Poem, Translated from the Heyne-Socin Text." Ph.D. diss., Johns Hopkins Univ., 1892. (lng, nam, nts, sch, trl, txt) English verse, based on [815].

Pub. as book, same title, Boston, 1892.

Reviews:

      1 *Athenaeum*, 1892, II, 445

      2 *Critic*, 21 [n.s. 18] (13 Aug. 1892), 79

      3 *Dial*, 13 (Aug. 1892), 107

      4 *MLN*, 7 (1892), 128

      5 *SR*, 1 (1893), 504–6

      6 *SRL*, 73 (1892), 274

      7 J. M. Garnett, *Nation*, 57 (1893), 295–96 [618]

      8 O. Glöde, *ESt*, 19 (1894), 257–60

      9 F. Holthausen, *Beibl*, 4 (1894), 33–36

    10 T. Miller, *YBVS*, 1 (1909), 91–92

    11 P., *Poet Lore*, 6 (1894), 566 (Charlotte Porter)

Repr. 1893 (Student ed)

Repr. Boston, 1892, 1893, 1900, 1904, 1906, 1908, 1911 (includes corrections to glossary of [815])

  †   ——, see [66].

739   HALL, John R. Clark. *Beowulf: A Metrical Translation into Modern English*. Cambridge, 1914. (trl)

Reviews:

      1 F. Klaeber, *Beibl*, 26 (1915), 170–72

      2 W. J. Sedgefield, *MLR*, 10 (1915), 387–89 [1903]

740   ——. "*Beowulf*," and the "*Fight at Finnsburg*": A Translation into Modern English Prose, with an Introduction and Notes. London, 1901. (bbl, com, dct, Fnb, hst, lng, mtr, nts, str, trl) Based on Wyatt [2267] text. Comment by Klaeber [1029].

Reviews:

1 *Academy*, 60 (1901), 342
2 *Athenaeum*, 1901, II, 56
3 W. Dibelius, *Archiv*, 109 (1902), 403–4
4 F. Holthausen, *Beibl*, 13 (1902), 225–28 [879]
5 D. Stedman, *YBVS*, 3 (1912), 72–74
6 C. B. Tinker, *JEGP*, 4 (1902), 379–81
7 W. Viëtor, *NS*, 11 (1903–4), 439
8 R. Wülker, *LitCbl*, 53 (1902), 30–31

2d ed., 1911
Reviews:

1 *Academy*, 1911, I, 225–26
2 *Archiv*, 126 (1911), 492–93
3 G. Binz, *LGRP*, 32 (1911), 232
4 E. Björkmann, *ESt*, 44 (1912), 127–28
5 F. Klaeber, *Beibl*, 26 (1915), 170–72
6 A. Mawer, *MLR*, 6 (1911), 542

Rev. ed. by C. L. Wrenn, with preface by J. R. R. Tolkien [2096], London, 1940
Review: G. N. Garmonsway, *YWES*, 21 (1940), 33–35
New rev. ed., London, 1950; corrected translation, new intro. and additional notes
Review: R. M. Wilson, *YWES*, 31 (1950), 46
Repr. 1954, 1958, 1963

741 ——. "A Note on *Beowulf* 1142–1145." *MLN*, 25 (1910), 113–14. (Fnb, int; 1142–45)

† ——, see [2018].

742 HALVERSON, John. "*Beowulf* and the Pitfalls of Piety." *UTQ*, 35 (1966), 259–78. (rel, smb)

743 HALVORSON, Henry G. H. "A Study of Old English Dithematic Personal Names: deuterothemes." Unpub. Ph.D. diss., Harvard Univ., 1937. *DDABAU*, 1936–37, no. 4, 87. (chr, nam)

744 HAMEL, Anton Gerard van. "Hengest and His Name-sake." In *Klaeber*, pp. 159–71. (ana, chr, Fnb, hst, nam; Fep)

745 HAMILTON, Marie Padgett. "The Religious Principle in *Beowulf*." *PMLA*, 61 (1946), 309–30. (rel)
Review: M. Daunt, *YWES*, 27 (1946), 60
Repr. in Nicholson [1560], pp. 105–35

746 HANSCOM, Elizabeth Deering. "The Feeling for Nature in Old English Poetry." *JEGP*, 5 (1903–5), 439–63. (img, stl, thm)

747   HANSEN, Adolf. *Bjovulf, oversat.* Copenhagen and Cristiana, 1910. Posthumously ed. by Viggo J. von H. Rathlou; see his [1689]. (Fnb, trl) Translates into Danish. Review: A. Olrik, *DS*, 6 (1910), 112–13

748   ——. "Et Brudstykke af *Beowulf.*" *GDM*, 1904, pp. 468–78. (trl) Translates 491–924 into Danish verse.

749   HANSON, Howard. "The Lament for Beowulf." Musical work for mixed chorus and orchestra. Boston, 1925. Opus 25. First performed Ann Arbor Festival 1926. Recorded by the Eastman School Choir and Eastman Rochester Symphony Orchestra, Victor Masterworks VM 889 and later Victor 11–8114/6, set M889. (trl) Based on Morris and Wyatt [1482]. Cf. David Ewing, *The Complete Book of 20th Century Music.* Englewood Cliffs, N.J., 1959. pp. 162–63.

750   HARDY, J. P. "Tydre Treowlogan Tyne." *N&Q*, 205 (1960), 324. (epc, int, thm; 2847) Disagrees with Brodeur [229].
       Review: R. M. Wilson, *YWES*, 41 (1960), 55

751   HARGROVE, H. L. *King Alfred's Old English Version of St. Augustine's Soliloquies.* N.Y., 1902. (mns) Attacked by F. Holthausen, *Beibl*, 15 (1904), 321–28, and by Sisam [1956].

752   HARRISON, James Albert. "*Beówulf*": *Academy*, no. 653 (8 Nov. 1884), 308–9. (sch) See Powell [1667].

753   ——. *Beówulf. 1. Text: Edited from M. Heyne.* Boston, 1882. (edt) First American ed., based on Heyne [815].

754   ——, and SHARP, Robert. "*Beówulf*": *An Anglo–Saxon Poem; The "Fight at Finnsburh": A Fragment.* Boston, 1883. (edt, Fnb, nts) Based on Heyne [815].
       Reviews:
         1   J. W. Bright, *LGRP*, 1884, pp. 221–23
         2   E. Kölbing, *ESt*, 7 (1884), 482 [1124.1]
         3   F. Y. Powell, *Academy*, 26 (1884), 220–21 [1668]; reply by Harrison, *ibid.*, 308–9; reply by Powell, *ibid.*, 327
       2d ed., 1885; 3d ed., 1888
       4th ed., 1894
       Reviews:
         1   O. Glöde, *ESt*, 20 (1894), 417–18
         2   R. Wülker, *Beibl*, 5 (1894), 65–67
       Repr. 1895

755   ——. "List of Irregular (Strong) Verbs in *Béowulf.*" *AJPhil*, 4 (1883), 462–77. (lng)

756   ——. "Old Teutonic Life in *Beowulf.*" *Overland Monthly*, 2d ser., 4 (July 1884), 14–24, and (Aug. 1884), 152–61.

(ana, com, hst, img, mns, mth, rel, tec, wrd)   Attacks March [1410].
Partially repr. in *Critic*, 18 Oct. 1884, pp. 188–90

757   ——— . (Untitled review of Garnett [614]).   *AJPhil*, 4, no. 1 (1883), 84–85.   (sch, about trl)   Reply to Wülker [2261].

†   ——— , see [66].

758   HART, James Morgan.   "Allotria III."   *MLN*, 18 (1903), 117–18.   (chr, lng, nam, wrd; 524, 1931)

759   ——— .   "*Beowulf*, 168–9."   *MLN*, 27 (1912), 198.   (int, lng; 168–69)

760   ——— .   "Scurheard."   *MLN*, 8 (1893), 61.   (int, lng, wrd; 1033)   Reply to Pearce [1622].

761   ——— .   *Syllabus of Anglo–Saxon Literature*.   Cincinnati, 1881. (gen)   Adapted from ten Brink [222]

761.1   HART, Thom.   "*Beowulf*: A Study of the Tectonic Structures and Patterns."   Unpub. Ph.D. diss., Univ. of Wisconsin at Madison, 1966.   *DA*, 28 (1967), 631A.   (dct, mns, str, tec).

762   HART, Walter Morris.   *Ballad and Epic: A Study in the Development of Narrative Art*.   Harvard Studies and Notes in Philology and Literature, 11.   Boston, 1907.   (com, epc, gen, str, tec)
Review: *Archiv*, 119 (1907), 468

†   HARTMAN, J. W., see [1594].

763   HARVEY, H. Paul.   *The Oxford Companion to English Literature*.   Oxford, 1932.   (Fnb, gen)
Review: B. I. Evans, *YWES*, 14 (1933), 10–12
Repr. 1932; corrected repr. 1933; repr. 1934
2d ed., 1937.   Abridged as *The Concise Oxford Dictionary of English Literature*, by John Mulgan.   Oxford, 1937.   pp. 41, 178
Review: F. E. Budd, *YWES*, 20 (1939), 22
2d ed. repr. 1938 with corrections, 1940, 1942
3d ed., 1946, repr. 1948, 1950, 1953, 1955, 1958, 1960
4th ed., 1967

764   HASTE, G. T.   "On *Beowulf*."   *Academy*, 24 (1882), 109–11. (hst)

765   HATTO, Arthur T.   "Snake-Swords and Boar-Helms in *Beowulf*."   *ES*, 38 (1957), 145–60, 257–59.   (hst, img, smb; 1459)
Review: R. M. Wilson, *YWES*, 38 (1957), 75

766   HAUPT, M.   "Zum *Beowulf*."   *ZDA*, 5 (1845), 10.   (ana, chr, hst)

767 Item canceled.

768 HEATH, A. Frank. "The Old English Alliterative Line."
TPS, 2 (1893), 375–95. (mtr)
Reviews:
1 *Academy*, n.s. 43 (1893), 549
2 *Athenaeum*, 1893, I, 769

769 HECHT, Hans. "Zu Holthausens Bericht über v. Sydow,
Beowulf och Bjarke." *Beibl*, 35 (1924), 218–19. (int, nam)
On Holthausen, *Beibl*, 34 (1923), 357–58, a review of von
Sydow [2045].

770 HEIDEMANN, Gerhard. "Die Flexion des Verb. subst.
in Ags." *Archiv*, 147 (1924), 30–46. (lng)

771 HEIMS, Wilhelm. *Der germanische Alliterationsvers und seine
Vorgeschichte: Mit einem Exkurs über den Saturnier.* Münster
diss., 1914. (mtr)

772 HEINZEL, Richard. "Beschreibung der ìsländ. Saga."
*Sitzungsberichte der philos.-histor. Classe der K. Akademie der
Wissenschaften*, 97 (1881), 107–308. Vienna. (ana)

773 ——. *Über den Stil der altgermanischen Poesie.* Strasbourg,
1875. (stl)
Review: H. Zimmer, *AfdA*, 2 (1876), 294–300

774 ——. (Untitled review of Möller [1460] and Rönning
[1730]) *AfdA*, 10 (1884), 215–39. (com, Fnb, stl, str)

775 ——. (Untitled review of ten Brink [223]) *AfdA*, 15 (1889),
153–82. (stl)

776 ——. (Untitled review of Heyne/Socin [815]) *AfdA*, 15
(1889), 189–94. (lng, txt; 126–33, 246, 1059, 1081, 1143,
1334, 1808–15, 1877, 2551–52, 2922, 3136)

777 ——. (Untitled review of Müllenhoff [1504]). *AfdA*, 16
(1890), 264–75. (ana, hst, mth, nam, thm)

778 HELM, Karl. *Altgermanische Religionsgeschichte. II. Die nach-
römische Zeit.* Heidelberg, 1937. Vol. I. *Die Ostgermanen.*
(mth)

779 HELMER, William Floyd. "Critical Estimates of *Beowulf*
from the Early Nineteenth Century to the Present." Unpub.
Ph.D. diss., Univ. of Pennsylvania, 1963. *DA*, 24 (1964),
5385–86. (sch)

780 HENDERSON, Ebenezer. *Iceland; or, The Journal of a Resi-
dence between 1814 and 1815.* Edinburgh, 1818. Vol. II, pp.
329–30. (sch) On Thorkelin [2080].
2d ed., 1819; abridged ed., Boston, 1831

781 HENEL, Heinrich. "Stanboga im *Beowulf*." *Anglia*, 55
(1931), 273–81. (int; 2545a, 2561a, 2718a)
Review: D. E. M. Clarke, *YWES*, 12 (1931), 68–69

782   HENK, O. *Die Frage in der ae. Dichtung.* Heidelberg, 1904.
       (stl)

783   HENNING, R. "Sceaf und die westsächsische Stammtafel."
       ZDA, 41 (1897), 156–69. (chr, hst, mth, nam)

784   HENRY, P. L. "*Beowulf* Cruces." *ZVS*, 77 (1961), 140–59.
       (int, wrd; 130, 224, 769, 989, 1329, 2342, 2577, 2586, 2680)
       Review: R. M. Wilson, *YWES*, 42 (1963), 58

785   ——. "The Opening of the *Finnsburg Fragment.*" *Die
       Sprache*, 8 (1962), 66–71. (ana, Fnb, tec)
       Review: R. M. Wilson, *YWES*, 43 (1962), 58

786   HERAUCOURT, W. "Figurengestaltung im *Beowulf-
       Epos.*" *NS*, 49 (1941), 170–72. (img)

787   HERBEN, Stephen J., Jr. "Beowulf, Hrothgar and
       Grendel." *Archiv*, 173 (1938), 24–30. (hst, mth, nam, rel)
       Review: C. L. Wrenn, *YWES*, 19 (1938), 51

788   ——. "Heorot." *PMLA*, 50 (1935), 933–45. (hst, nam)

789   ——. "A Note on the Helm in *Beowulf.*" *MLN*, 52 (1937),
       34–36. (arc)

790   HERRMANN, Paul. *Erläuterungen zu den ersten neun Büchern
       der Dänischen Geschichte des Saxo Grammaticus.* Part II, *Die
       Heldensage des Saxo.* Leipzig, 1922. (chr, hst)

791   ——. *Die Geschichte von Hrólf Kraki.* Torgau, 1905. (ana,
       src)

792   ——. *Die Heldensagen des Saxo Grammaticus.* Leipzig, 1922.
       (hst, mth)

793   HERTZ, Wilhelm. "*Beowulf*, das älteste germanische
       Epos." *Nord und Süd*, 29 (1884), 229–53. (hst, mth)

794   HEUSINGKVELD, Arthur H., and BASHE, Edwin J. "A
       Bibliographical Guide to Old English." *Univ. of Iowa
       Humanistic Studies*, 4, no. 5 (1931), pp. 56–61, 78–80. (bbl,
       Fnb)
       Reviews:
           1 J. Hoops, *ESt*, 69 (1935), 432
           2 F. Klaeber, *Beibl*, 43 (1932), 200–2
           3 K. M., *MLN*, 49 (1934), 352
           4 F. P. Magoun, *Speculum*, 7 (1932), 286–89

795   HEUSLER, Andreas. *Die altgermanische Dichtung.* In Oskar
       Walzel, ed., *Handbuch der Literaturwissenschaft.* Berlin-
       Neubabelsberg, 1923. Vol. XI. (gen, mtr)
       Review: E. Mogk, *Beibl*, 37 (1926), 1–4
       2d ed., Babelsberg, 1943

796   ——. "Altgermanische Sittenlehre und Lebensweisheit."
       In Hermann Nollau, ed., *Germanische Wiedererstehung.* Heidel-
       berg, 1926. pp. 156–204. (hst)

797   ——. *"Beowulf."* RL, 1 (1912), 245–48. (bbl, hst, mth)

798   ——. *Deutsche Versgeschichte mit Einschluss des altenglischen und altnordischen Stabreimverses.* Berlin and Leipzig, 1925–27. Vol. I, 1, Einführendes, Grundbegriffe, 1925. Vol. I, 2, Die altgermanische Vers, 1927. *PGrdr*, 8.1. (mtr)

799   ——. "Der Dialog in der altgermanischen erzählenden Dichtung." *ZDA*, 46 (1902), 189–284. (stl, tec)

800   ——. "Dichtung." *RL*, 1 (1912–13), 439–62. (gen)

801   ——. "Geschichtliches und Mythisches in der germanischen Heldensage." *Sitzungsberichte der Königl. Preussischen Akademie der Wissenschaften.* 1909, no. 38, 920–45. (hst, mth)

802   ——. "Heldensage." *RL*, 2 (1913–15), 488–97. (epc, gen, nam, src)

803   ——. *"Heliand,* Liedstil und Epenstil." *ZDA*, 57 (1919–20), 1–48. (epc, Fnb, gen, mtr, stl)

804   ——. "Hengest." *RL*, 2 (1913–15), 505–6. (chr, epc, Fnb, gen)

805   ——. "Heremod." *RL*, 2 (1913–15), 509. (chr, gen, src)

806   ——. *Lied und Epos in germanischer Sagendichtung.* Dortmund, 1905. (com, epc, Fnb, gen, hst, str)
Reviews:
    1   K. Helm, *LGRP*, 28 (1907), 237–38
    2   E. Kauffmann, *ZDP*, 38 (1906), 546–48
    3   R. M. Meyer, *Archiv*, 115 (1905), 403–4
    4   J. Seemüller, *AfdA*, 34 (1910), 129–35

807   ——. "Stabreim." *RL*, 4 (1918–19), 231–40. (mtr)

808   ——. "Zeitrechnung im Beowulfepos." *Archiv*, 124 (1910), 9–14. (hst)

809   ——. "Zur Skiöldungendichtung." *ZDA*, 48 (1906), 57–87. (epc, hst) Also in *RL*, 4 (1918–19), 187–91.

810   ——. (Untitled review of Olrik [1588]) *AfdA*, 35 (1912), 169–83. (ana, hst, stl)

811   ——. (Untitled review of Imelmann [936]) *AfdA*, 41 (1922), 27–35. (mth, nam, thm)

812   ——. (Untitled review of Schneider [1813]) *AfdA*, 54 (1935), 102–8. (lng, mtr, thm, txt)

813   ——. (Untitled review of Panzer [1618]) *ESt*, 42 (1910), 289–98. (ana, mth)

814   HEYNE, Moritz. *Beowulf: Angelsächsisches Heldengedicht.* Paderborn, 1863. (Fnb, trl) Trans. into German blank verse, based on his text [815].
Review: A. Holtzmann, *Germania*, 8 (1863), 506–7
2d ed., 1898

Reviews:
> 1   F. Holthausen, *Archiv*, 103 (1899), 373–76 [876]
> 2   H. Jantzen, *ESt*, 25 (1898), 271–73
> 3   G. W. C. Löhner, *ZOG*, 49 (1898), 563
> 4   R. Wülker, *Beibl*, 9 (1898), 1–2

3d ed., 1915

815   ——. *"Beowulf," Mit ausführlichem Glossar*. Paderborn, 1863.
(edt, Fnb, nts)
Reviews:
> 1   C. W. M. Grein, *LitCbl*, 15 (1864), 137–38
> 2   A. Holtzmann, *Germania*, 8 (1863), 506–7

2d ed., 1868
Reviews:
> 1   *LitCbl*, 19 (1868), 283
> 2   M. Rieger, *ZDP*, 2 (1870), 371–74
> 3   W. Scherer, *ZOG*, 20 (1869), 89–112 [1793]

3d ed., 1873
Reviews:
> 1   *AZ*, 86 (1873), no. 42, 12
> 2   *Wissenschaft. Monatsblatt*, 1 (1873), 56–58
> 3   E. Sievers, *LitCbl*, 1873, pp. 662–63

4th ed., 1879; uses a collation by E. Kölbing
Reviews:
> 1   O. Brenner, *ESt*, 4 (1881), 135–39 [211]
> 2   H. Gering, *ZDP*, 12 (1881), 122–25 [628]
> 3   E. Henrici, *Zeitschrift für deutsche Gymnasialschulwesen*,
>   34 (1880), 331–32

5th ed., Paderborn and Münster, 1888; rev. by Adolf Socin
Reviews:
> 1   R. Heinzel, *AfdA*, 15 (1889), 189–94 [776]
> 2   E. Koeppel, *ESt*, 13 (1889), 466–72
> 3   E. Schöer, *LGRP*, 1889, pp. 170–71
> 4   E. Sievers, *ZDP*, 21 (1889), 354–65 [1949]

6th ed., 1898
Reviews:
> 1   O. Brenner, *Blatt für bayrische Gymnasien*, 38 (1902),
>   144
> 2   K. D. Bülbring, *Museum*, 11 (1903), 10
> 3   F. Holthausen, *Beibl*, 10 (1899–1900), 265–74 [878]
> 4   H. Jantzen, *Archiv*, 103 (1899), 175–76
> 5   G. Sarrazin, *ESt*, 28 (1900), 408–10 [1781]
> 6   M. Trautmann, *Beibl*, 10 (1899–1900), 257–62 [2117]

7th ed., 1903
Reviews:
> 1   T. von Grienberger, *ZOG*, 56 (1905), 744–61 [682]
> 2   F. Holthausen, *Beibl*, 18 (1907), 193–94

  3   F. Klaeber, *Beibl*, 18 (1907), 289–91
  4   E. A. Kock, *ANF*, 22 (1905–6), 215
  5   E. Kruisinga, *ESt*, 35 (1905), 401–2
8th ed., Paderborn, 1908; rev. by L. L. Schücking
Reviews:
  1   R. C. Boer, *Museum*, 16 (1908), 139
  2   T. von Grienberger, *ZOG*, 60 (1909), 1089–90
  3   R. Imelmann, *DLZ*, 30 (1909), 995–1000 [937]
  4   F. Klaeber, *ESt*, 39 (1908), 425–33 [1069]
  5   W. W. Lawrence, *MLN*, 25 (1910), 155–57 [1208]
9th ed., 1910
Reviews:
  1   W. J. Sedgefield, *ESt*, 43 (1911), 267–69
  2   F. Wild, *ZOG*, 64 (1915), 153–55
10th ed., 1913
Reviews:
  1   *ESt*, 49 (1915–16), 424
  ?2 Degenbart, *Blätter für Gymnasienschulwesen*, 51 (1914), 130
  3   F. Klaeber, *Beibl*, 24 (1913), 289–91 [1067]
  4   E. A. Kock, *ANF*, 32 (1915–16), 222–23
11th and 12th eds., 1918
Reviews:
  1   E. Björkman, *Beibl*, 30 (1919), 121–22, 180–81 [125]
  2   W. Fischer, *ESt*, 53 (1919–20), 338–39
  3   F. Holthausen, *ZDP*, 48 (1919–20), 127–31 [888]
  4   G. C. van Langenhove, *LB*, 13 (1921), 234–35
13th and 14th eds., 1929 and 1931, unchanged
Review: F. Klaeber, *Beibl*, 42 (1931), 370–71
15th ed., 1940; rev. by Else von Schaubert; 3 parts
Reviews:
  1   F. Klaeber, *ESt*, 74 (1941), 219–23
  2   K. Schneider, *Beibl*, 52 (1941), 1–6
16th ed., text 1946, commentary 1949, glossary 1949, all reprints
17th ed., 1958–59; text reprint of 15th ed.; new glossary and notes
Review: E. Standop, *Anglia*, 80 (1962), 443–46
18th ed., text 1963, commentary and glossary 1961
Reviews:
  1   E. A. Ebbinghaus, *JEGP*, 62 (1963), 676–78
  2   E. G. Stanley, *MLR*, 58 (1963), 454–55

816   ——— . *Fünf Bücher deutscher Hausaltertümer: Von den ältesten geschichtlichen Zeiten bis zum 16 Jahrhundert.* Leipzig, 1899–1903. 3 vols. (hst)
Repr. 1966

817   ———. *Ueber die Lage und Konstruction der Halle Heorot im angelsächsischen "Beowulfliede": Nebst einer Einleitung über angelsächsischen Burgenbau.* Paderborn, 1864. (hst)

818   HICKES, George. *Linguarum Veterum Septentrionalium
Thesaurus.* Oxford, 1705. Vol. I, pp. 192–93. (Fnb only:
edt) First edition of *Finnsburh.* See Wanley [2163].

819   HICKETIER, Franz. *Grendel.* Berlin, 1914. (ana, chr,
mth)

820   HIEATT, Constance B. *"Beowulf" and Other Old English
Poems.* N.Y., 1967: Odyssey paperback. Introd. by A. Kent
Hieatt. (Fnb, for, hst, ken, mtr, nam, nts, rel, str, thm, trl)
Translates *Beowulf* and *Finnsburh* into English prose.

821   HIGGINS, William. "Dramatic Functions of the Unferth
Incident." *IEY*, 9 (1964), 43–46. (chr, tec)

821.1   HIGHET, Gilbert. *The Classical Tradition.* N.Y. and London, 1949. (ana, epc, gen, rel, src)
3d printing corrected 1953; Galaxy paperback GB5, 1957.
Pages 22–28 repr. in F. H. Candelaria and W. C. Strange,
eds., *Perspectives on Epic.* Boston, 1965. pp. 41–50.

822   HILL, D. M. "Romance as Epic." *ES*, 44 (1963), 95–107.
(epc, str, tec)
Review: A. MacDonald and B. Hill, *YWES*, 44 (1963), 82

823   HILL, Thomas D. "Two Notes on Patristic Allusion in
Andreas." *Anglia*, 84 (1966), 156–62. (int, smb, src; 1841–
43, 2880–82)

824   HINTZ, Howard W. "The 'Hama' Reference in *Beowulf*
1197–1201." *JEGP*, 33 (1934), 98–102. (ana, chr, hst, mth,
txt; 1197–1201)
Review: M. Serjeantson, *YWES*, 15 (1934), 64

825   HIRT, Hermann. *Untersuchungen zur westgermanischen
Verskunst. I. Kritik der Neueren Theorien, Metrik des Ags.* Leip-
zig, 1889. (ken, lng, mtr, str)
Reviews:
         1   A. Heusler, *LGRP*, 1890, no. 6
         2   K. Luick, *Literaturzeitung*, 1890, no. 50
Also appeared in *Germania*, 36 (1891), 139–79, 279–307,
entitled "Zur Metrik des Altsächsischen und Hochdeutschen
Alliterations-verses."

826   HITTLE, Erla. *Zur Geschichte der ae. Präpositionen* mid *und*
wið *mit Berücksichtigung ihrer Beiderseitigen.* Heidelberg, 1900.
(lng)
Review: W. Franz, *ESt*, 29 (1901), 418–20
Repub. 1901 in Book II of J. Hoops's *Anglistischen Forschungen*

827   HODGKIN, R. H. *A History of the Anglo–Saxons*. Oxford, 1935. (arc, hst)
       Reviews:
    1   *TLS*, 10 Oct. 1935, p. 624
    2   A. Brandl, *Archiv*, 172 (1937), 81–84
    3   D. E. M. Clarke, *YWES*, 16 (1935), 68–69
    4   S. J. Herben, *NYTBR*, 25 Aug. 1935, pp. 10, 18
    5   R. Hoops, *ES*, 18 (1936), 173–74
    6   T. D. Kendrick, *Antiquaries Journal*, 15 (1935), 484–85
    7   F. P. Magoun, *MLN*, 52 (1937), 510–15
    8   K. Malone, *MAE*, 6 (1937), 57–60
    9   B. J. Whiting, *Speculum*, 12 (1937), 122–24
   10   R. M. Wilson, *Antiquity*, 10 (1936), 234–37
   11   D. Woodruff, *Spectator*, 155 (23 Aug. 1935), 296–97
       2d ed., 1940
       Review: *TLS*, 11 May 1939, p. 235
       3d ed., 1952; includes Bruce-Mitford [250]
       Review: F. P. Magoun, *Speculum*, 29 (1954), 125–26

828   HODLER, W. *Grundzüge einer germanischen Artikellehre*. Heidelberg, 1954. (lng)

829   HOFFMANN, A. *Der bildliche Ausdruck im "Beowulf" und in der Edda*. Breslau diss., 1882. (img, stl) Same title, *FSt*, 6 (1883), 163–216.

830   HOFFMANN, Otto. *Reimformeln im Westgermanischen*. Freiburg diss., Darmstadt, 1885. (dct, mtr, stl)
       Review: R. M. Meyer, *AfdA*, 13 (1897), 135–36

831   HOFFMANN, P. *Beówulf: Aeltestes deutsches Heldengedicht. Aus dem Angelsächsischen übertragen*. Zulliehau, [1893]. (com, Fnb, mth, trl, txt) Translates *Beowulf* and *Finnsburh* into Germanic *Nibelungenlied* stanzas, adding beginning and end to *Finnsburh*. Based on Grein [676].
       Reviews:
    1   F. Detter, *Österreiches Literaturblatt*, 5 (1896), 9
    2   O. Glöde, *ESt*, 19 (1894), 412–15
    3   C. Marold, *Deutsches Literaturblatt*, 23 (1891), 332
    4   G. Shipley, *MLN*, 4 (1894), 121–23
    5   R. Wülker, *Beibl*, 5 (1894–95), 67
    6   R. Wülker, *LitCbl*, 44 (1894), 1930
       2d ed., Hanover, 1900
       Review: J. M. Garnett, *PMLA*, 18 (1903), 445–51, 455–58

832   HOFFMANN, Richard L. "Guðrinc astah: *Beowulf* 1118b." *JEGP*, 64 (1965), 660–67. (int; 1118b)

833   HOLDER, Alfred. *Beowulf. I. Abdruck der Handschrift im Britischen Museum*. Freiburg i.B. and Tübingen, [1881]. (edt, mns) Diplomatic ed. from his 1875 collation.

Reviews:

  1 F. Kluge, *LGRP*, 4 (1883), 178

  2 R. Wülker, *LitCbl*, 33 (1882), 1035–36

  3 J. Zupitza, *Literaturzeitung*, 1882, pp. 805–6

2d ed., 1882

Review: E. Kölbing, *ESt*, 7 (1884), 482–89 [1124.1]

3d ed., 1895

Reviews:

  1 F. Dieter, *Beibl*, 6 (1895–96), 260–61

  2 E. Martin, *AfdA*, 22 (1895), 90

834   ——. *Beowulf.* IIa. *Berichtigter Text mit knappem Apparat und Wörterbuch.* Freiburg i.B. and Tübingen, 1884. (Edt, nts, txt)

Reviews:

  1 A. Brandl, *AfdA*, 23 (1897), 107

  2 T. Krüger, *LGRP*, 1884, pp. 468–70

  3 F. Y. Powell, *Academy*, 26 (1884), 220–21 [1668]

  4 R. Wülker, *LitCbl*, 1885, cols. 1008–9

  5 J. Zupitza, *Literaturzeitung*, 1885, pp. 489–90

2d ed., 1899.

Reviews:

  1 K. D. Bülbring, *Museum*, 11 (1903), 10

  2 J. Ellinger, *NRs*, 21 (1901), 67–68

  3 F. Holthausen, *LGRP*, 21 (1900), 60–62 [885]

  4 M. Trautmann, *Beibl*, 10 (1899–1900), 257–62 [2117]

  5 E. Wülfing, *ESt*, 29 (1901), 278–79

835   ——. *Beowulf.* IIb. *Wortschatz mit sämtlichen Stellennachweisen.* Freiburg, 1896. (ref) Concordance.

Reviews:

  1 P. J. Cosijn, *Museum*, 4 (1896), 16–17

  2 F. Dieter, *Beibl*, 6 (1895–96), 260–61

  3 F. Holthausen, *LGRP*, 17 (1896), 266–67

  4 R. Wülker, *LitCbl*, 49 (1897), 336

836   HOLLANDER, Lee M. "Beowulf 33." *MLN*, 32 (1917), 246–47. (txt; 33)

837   ——. "The Gautland Cycle of Sagas I." *JEGP*, 11 (1912), 61–81. (hst, int, nam)

838   ——. "The Gautland Cycle of Sagas II." *JEGP*, 11 (1912), 209–17. (hst, int, nam)

839   ——. "Litotes in Old Norse." *PMLA*, 53 (1938), 1–33. (rht, stl)

840   ——. *The Poetic Edda.* Austin, Tex., 1928. (ana)

2d ed., 1962

Repr. 1964

  †   ——, see [1587].

841 HOLTHAUSEN, Ferdinand. "Angelsächsisches Allerlei."
Beibl, 44 (1933), 349–50. (txt; 1728ff, 1755ff)
Review: D. E. M. Clarke, *YWES*, 14 (1933), 89

842 ——. "Beiträge zur Erklärung des altenglischen Epos.
I, Zum *Beowulf*; II, Zum *Finnsburg-fragment.*" *ZDP*, 37
(1905), 113–25. (Fnb, txt)

843 ——. "Beiträge zur Erklärung und Textkritik altenglischer
Dichter." *IF*, 4 (1894), 379–88. (txt; 2706)

844 ——. "Beiträge zur Textkritik altenglischer Dichtungen.
I. Zum *Beowulf.*" In *Viëtor*, p. 127. (txt; 224, 2251)

845 ——. *"Beowulf" nebst dem Finnsburg–Bruchstück. I. Texte und
Namenverzeichnis. II. Einleitung, Glossar und Anmerkungen.*
Heidelberg, 1905 and 1906. (bbl, edt, Fnb, gen, nts) See
Trautmann [2111].
Reviews:
    1 A. J. Barnouw, *Museum*, 14 (1906), 169–70
    2 M. Deutschbein, *Archiv*, 121 (1908), 162–64
    3 T. von Grienberger, *ZOG*, 59 (1908), 333–46 [683]
    4 H. Jantzen, *NRs*, 27 (1907), 18
    5 F. Klaeber, *MLN*, 24 (1909), 94–95 [1075]
    6 W. W. Lawrence, *JEGP*, 7 (1908), 125–29
    7 L. L. Schücking, *ESt*, 39 (1908), 94–111 [1860]
    8 R. Wülker, *DLZ*, 27 (1906), 285–86
2d ed., retitled *"Beowulf" nebst den kleineren Denkmälern der Heldensage*, *"Finnsburg," "Waldere," "Deor," "Widsith," "Hildebrand,"* 1908 and 1909.
Reviews:
    1 G. Binz, *LGRP*, 32 (1911), 53–55
    2 A. Brandl, *Archiv*, 121 (1908), 473; 124 (1910), 210
    3 A. Eichler, *Beibl*, 21 (1910), 129–33; 22 (1911),
      161–65
    4 E. Koeppel, *Beibl*, 23 (1912), 297
    5 L. L. Schücking, *ESt*, 42 (1910), 108–11 [1861]
3d ed., 1912 and 1913
4th ed., 1914 and 1919
Reviews:
    1 G. Binz, *LGRP*, 41 (1920), 316–17
    2 W. Fischer, *ESt*, 54 (1920), 404–6
5th ed., 1921 and 1929
6th ed., 1929
Reviews:
    1 M. Daunt, *YWES*, 10 (1929), 87
    2 F. Klaeber, *Beibl*, 41 (1930), 8–12
    3 K. Malone, *JEGP*, 29 (1930), 611–13
    4 K. Malone, *Speculum*, 5 (1930), 327–28

7th ed., 1938
Review: F. Klaeber, *Beibl*, 50 (1939), 161–62
8th ed., 1948; revises part I only with new emendations;
incorporates material from Sievers [1948]; additions and
corrections in Holthausen [877]
Review: F. Klaeber, *DLZ*, 70 (1949), 210–13

846   Item canceled.

847   ——. "Etymologien." *IF*, 14 (1903), 339–42.   (int, lng;
1363)   Reply to Wright [2252].

848   ——. "Ein lappisches Bärensohn-Märchen." *Beibl*, 31
(1920), 66–67.   (ana, mth)

849   ——. "Onsæl meoto." *Beibl*, 42 (1931), 249–50.   (lng,
wrd; 489)   Answer by Imelmann [934].

850   ——. "Wǣgbora." *Beibl*, 14 (1903), 49.   (lng, wrd; 1440a)

851   ——. "Zu ae. $\bar{\imath}$ für $\bar{e}$." *Beibl*, 44 (1933), 26–27.   (int, lng,
wrd)   Reply to Malone [1377]; reply by Malone [1372].

852   ——. "Zu alt- und mittelenglischen Dichtungen IX." 51.
Zum *Beowulf*." *Anglia*, 21 (1899), 366.   (int, wrd; 2298–99,
2488)

853   ——. "Zu altenglischen Denkmälern.   1. Zum *Beowulf*."
ESt, 51 (1917), 180.   (int; 1141)

854   ——. "Zu altenglischen Dichtungen." *Beibl*, 34 (1923),
89–91.   (int, tec; 769)

855   ——. "Zu altenglischen Dichtungen." *ESt*, 74 (1940–41),
324–28.   (int; 1107ff)

856   ——. "Zu *Beowulf* 457." *Beibl*, 45 (1934), 19.   (lng, nam,
txt; 457)
Review: M. Serjeantson, *YWES*, 15 (1934), 66–67

857   ——. "Zu *Beowulf* v. 489f. und v. 3114f." *Beibl*, 40 (1929),
90–91.   (int, lng, txt; 489–90, 3114–15)
Review: M. Daunt, *YWES*, 10 (1929), 92

858   ——. "Zu *Beowulf* v. 665." *Beibl*, 13 (1902), 204–05.   (int,
lng; 665)

859   ——. "Zu *Beowulf* v. 2577." *Beibl*, 13 (1902), 78–79.   (int,
lng; 2577)

860   ——. "Zu *Beowulf* v. 3074f." *Beibl*, 43 (1932), 157.   (int,
lng, 3074–75)

861   ——. "Zu *Beowulf* v. 3157." *Beibl*, 12 (1901), 146.   (int,
lng; 3157)

862   ——. "Zu *Finsburg* v. 36." *Beibl*, 43 (1932), 256.   (Fnb,
txt; Fnb 34)

863   ——. "Zum *Beowulf*." *Anglia*, 24 (1901), 267–68.   (int,
lng; 719–20)

864   ——. *Ibid. Archiv*, 105 (1900), 366–67. (int, txt; 497–98, 565ff)

865   ——. *Ibid. Beibl*, 13 (1902), 363–64. (int, txt; 1107, 1745ff)   Reply by von Grienberger [681].

866   ——. *Ibid.*, 34 (1923), 89–90. (int, lng; 769)

867   ——. *Ibid.*, 54–55 (1943), 27–30. (int, lng, txt; 406, 461, 769, 1174, 3075, 3168)

868   ——. *Ibid. ESt*, 69 (1935), 433–34. (int, lng; 224)   Reply by Krogmann [1160].

869   ——. "Zum *Beowulf* (v. 33)." *Beibl*, 14 (1903), 82–83. (int, lng; 33)

870   ——. "Zum Obigen." *Beibl*, 44 (1933), 191–92. (int, lng, wrd)   Reply to Malone [1372]; reply by Malone [1351].

871   ——. "Zur altenglischen Literatur. III. Zur Datierung des *Beowulf*; zu *Beowulf* v. 719." *Beibl*, 18 (1907), 77–78. (com, lng; 718–19)   On Morsbach [1484].

872   ——. "Zur altenglischen Literatur. XII." *Beibl*, 21 (1910), 300–1. (com, int, txt; 1440)

873   ——. "Zur altenglischen Wortkunde." *Beibl*, 53 (1942), 272–74. (int, lng, wrd; 1537)

874   ——. "Zur Textkritik altenglischer Dichtungen." *Beitr*, 16 (1892), 549–52. (int, txt; 1117)

875   ——. "Zur Textkritik des *Beowulf*." *SN*, 14 (1941–42), 160. (int, lng, txt; 460ff, 3168b)   Comment by Klaeber [1076]. Review: D. Whitelock, *YWES*, 23 (1942), 36

876   ——. (Untitled review of Heyne [814]) *Archiv*, 103 (1899), 373–76. (int, mtr, txt; 6, 7, 35, 58, 63, 75ff, 82–85, 104, 121, 126, 307, 315, 383, 444, 461, 466, 487, 501–3, 532, 553, 559, 600, 638, 641, 646, 671, 694, 721–24, 773, 777, 793, 804, 809, 815, 828, 837, 859, 871, 887, 914, 916, 923, 954, 992, 1009–12, 1022, 1027–28, 1036–37, 1047, 1073, 1083)

877   ——. (Untitled article) *Archiv*, 187 (1950), 125–26. (edt, txt)   Additions and errata to his [845], 8th ed.

878   ——. (Untitled review of Heyne/Socin [815], 6th ed.) *Beibl*, 10 (1899–1900), 265–74. (Fnb, txt)

879   ——. (Untitled review of Hall [740]) *Beibl*, 13 (1902), 225–28. (txt)

880   ——. (Untitled review of Schücking [1851]) *Beibl*, 32 (1921), 80–83. (Fnb, txt)

880.1 ——. (Untitled review of *Jespersen*) *Beibl*, 42 (1931), 133–37. (lng)   On Malone [1374].

881   ——. (Untitled review of *Klaeber*) *Beibl*, 42 (1931), 199–205. (txt)

882   ——. (Untitled review of Hoops [894]) *Beibl*, 43 (1932), 357–58. (txt)

883   ——. (Untitled review of Hoops [896]) *Beibl*, 44 (1933), 225–27. (txt)

884   ——. (Untitled review of Cosijn [389]) *LGRP*, 16 (1895), 82. (int, lng; 600)

885   ——. (Untitled review of Holder [834], 2d ed.) *LGRP*, 21 (1900), 60–62. (int, lng)

886   ——. (Untitled review of Trautmann [2107]) *LGRP*, 21 (1900), 62–64. (int, lng)

887   ——. (Untitled review of Sedgefield [1892], 3d ed.) *LGRP*, 59 (1938), 163–67. (int, lng)   Discusses Sievers [1948].

888   ——. (Untitled review of Heyne/Schücking [815], 11th and 12th eds.) *ZDP*, 48 (1919–20), 127–31. (int, lng, txt)

889   HOLTZMANN, Adolf. "Zu *Beowulf*." *Germania*, 8 (1863), 489–97. (edt, Fnb, int, trl, txt; 3157–73)   Translates 3157–73 into German.

890   HOOPS, Johannes, and KLAEBER, Frederick.   "Ae 'Ealuscerwen' und kein Ende." *ESt*, 66 (1931), 1–5.   (int, wrd; 769a)   Klaeber pp. 1–3; Hoops pp. 3–5.   Answer to Hoops [891]; answered by Krogmann [1151].
        Review: D. E. M. Clarke, *YWES*, 12 (1931), 70

891   ——. "Altenglisch *ealuscerwen, meoduscerwen*." *ESt*, 65 (1931), 177–80.   (ana, int, wrd; 769a)   Reply by Hoops and Klaeber [890].
        Review: D. E. M. Clarke, *YWES*, 12 (1931), 70

892   ——. "Altenglisch *gēap, horngēap, sǣgēap*." *ESt*, 64 (1929), 201–11.   (int, wrd; 82, 836, 1800, 1896)

893   ——. "*Beowulf* 457f.: *For werefyhtum* and *for arstafum*." *ESt*, 70 (1935–36), 77–80.   (int, txt, wrd; 382, 457–58)
        Review: D. E. M. Clarke, *YWES*, 16 (1935), 83

894   ——. *Beowulfstudien*. Heidelberg, 1932.   (int)   See Malone [1317]; answers Krogmann [1150] and his reply [1159].
        Reviews:
            1   M. Daunt, *YWES*, 13 (1932), 57–58
            2   R. Girvan, *MLR*, 28 (1933), 244–46 [639]
            3   W. v. d. Graaf, *Museum*, 43 (1935), 12–15
            4   F. Holthausen, *Beibl*, 43 (1932), 357–58 [882]
            5   G. Hübener, *LGRP*, 56 (1935), 241–43 [921]
            6   F. Klaeber, *ESt*, 67 (1932–33), 399–402 [1071]
            7   K. Malone, *ES*, 15 (1933), 94–96 [1398]
            8   K. Malone, *MLN*, 48 (1933), 206
            9   E. von Schaubert, *LGRP*, 57 (1936), 26–31 [1789]
           10   C. L. W., *RES*, 10 (1934), 94–95

895 ——. "Die Foliierung der *Beowulf*-Handschrift." *ESt*, 63 (1928), 1–11. (mns) Attacks Förster [577].
Review: M. Daunt, *YWES*, 9 (1928), 74–75

896 ——. *Kommentar zum "Beowulf."* Heidelberg, 1932. (Fnb, int, nts)
Reviews:
  1 M. Daunt, *YWES*, 13 (1932), 57–58
  2 W. v. d. Graaf, *Museum*, 43 (1935), 12–15
  3 J. R. H., *MP*, 31 (1934), 322 (J. R. Hulbert?)
  4 F. Holthausen, *Beibl*, 44 (1932), 225–27 [883]
  5 G. Hübener, *LGRP*, 56 (1935), 241–43 [921]
  6 P. F. Jones, *MLN*, 49 (1934), 115–16
  7 F. Klaeber, *ESt*, 68 (1933), 112–15 [1072]
  8 K. Malone, *ES*, 15 (1933), 149–51 [1399]
  9 W. J. Sedgefield, *MLR*, 28 (1933), 373–75 [1904]
  10 C. L. W., *RES*, 10 (1934), 94–95

897 ——. "Das Meer als Schwanenstrasse." *Wörter und Sachen*, 12 (1929), 251–52. (dct, img, ken)

898 ——. "'Orcneas.'" *Anglia*, 57 (1933), 110–11. (int, lng, txt, wrd; 112)
Review: D. E. M. Clarke, *YWES*, 14 (1933), 83–84

899 ——. "Das Preislied auf *Beowulf* und die Sigemund-Heremod-Episode." *Beiträge zur neueren Literaturgeschichte*, 16 (*Deutsch-kundliches, Fr. Panzer überreicht*). Heidelberg, 1930. pp. 34–36. (ana, lng, stl; 867–915)
Review: M. Daunt, *YWES*, 11 (1930), 60
Repr. in his [894], pp. 52–54

900 ——. "Das Verhüllen des Haupts bei Toten, ein angelsächsisch-nordischer Brauch." *ESt*, 54 (1920), 19–23. (hst, int; 446)

901 ——. "War Beowulf König von Dänemark?" In *Förster* pp. 26–30. (hst, int, txt; 3005b)
Review: M. Daunt, *YWES*, 10 (1929), 85
Repr. in his [894], pp. 78ff

† HOPPER, Vincent F., see [2084].

902 HORGAN, A. G. "*Beowulf*, Lines 224–25." *EPS*, 8 (1963), 24–29. (txt, wrd; 224–25)
Review: R. M. Wilson, *YWES*, 44 (1963), 74

903 HORN, Wilhelm. "Textkritische Bemerkungen. I and II." *Anglia*, 29 (1906), 129–31. (txt; 69ff)

904 HORNBURG, J. *Die Komposition des "Beowulf."* Programm des Kaiserlichen Lyceums zu Metz, 1877. (com, hst, int, mtr, src, str)

Review: F. Hummel, *Archiv*, 62 (1879), 231–33 (includes summary)
Repr. *Archiv*, 72 (1884) 333–404 with same title

905   HORNING, E. L. *Zur Grammatik des "Beowulf."* Göttingen diss., 1891. (lng)

906   —— . "The English Homer." *Canadian Magazine*, 2 (Nov. 1893), 62. (gen)

907   HOSFORD, Dorothy G. *By His Own Might: The Battles of Beowulf.* N.Y., 1947. (par) English paraphrase; illustrated by Laszlo Matulay.
Review: H. Armstrong, *Horn Book*, 23 (Sept. 1947), 366–69
Repr. 1955, 1957

908   —— . "Our Northern Heritage." *Horn Book*, 23 (Sept. 1947), 370–77. (gen)

909   HOTZ, G. *On the Use of the Subjunctive Mood in Anglo–Saxon, and Its Further History in Old English.* Zurich, 1882. (lng)
Review: T. Wissmann, *LGRP*, 4 (1883), 61–62

910   HOWREN, Robert. "A Note on *Beowulf* 168–9." *MLN*, 71 (1956), 317–318. (img, int, thm; 168–69)
Review: R. M. Wilson, *YWES*, 37 (1956), 72

911   HUBBARD, Frank Gaylord. "*Beowulf* 1598, 1996, 2026; Uses of the Impersonal Verb *geweorþan*." *JEGP*, 17 (1918), 119–24. (lng, wrd; 1598, 1996, 2026)

912   —— . "The Plundering of the Hoard in *Beowulf*." *UWSLL*, no. 11 (1920), 5–20. (int, mth) Opposes Lawrence [1201].
Review: T. S. Graves, *SAQ*, 20 (1921), 371

913   HÜBENER, Gustav. "*Beowulf* and Germanic Exorcism." *RES*, 11 (1935), 163–81. (ana, mth) See Magoun [1315] and Clarke [336].
Review: D. E. M. Clarke, *YWES*, 16 (1935), 79–80

914   —— . "*Beowulf* und die Psychologie der Standesentwicklung." *GRM*, 14 (1926), 352–71. (hst, int, mth)
Review: M. Daunt, *YWES*, 7 (1926), 57–60

915   —— . "*Beowulf* und nordische Dämonenaustreibung. (Grettir, Herakles, Theseus u.s.w.)." *ESt*, 62 (1927–28), 293–327. (mth)
Review: M. Daunt, *YWES*, 9 (1928), 68–70

916   —— . "Beowulf's 'Seax,' the Saxons and an Indian Exorcism." *RES*, 12 (1936), 429–39. (mth, nam) Refuted by Magoun [1315]. Also appeared as "*Beowulf*, ein indisches Messerexorzismus und die Sachsen," in *Deutschbein*, pp. 60–71 with two illustrations.
Review: M. Serjeantson, *YWES*, 17 (1936), 59–60 (both)

917   ——— . *England und die Gesittungsgrundlage der europäischen Frühgeschichte.* Frankfurt a.M., 1930. pp. 67–104. (mth)
        Reviews:
          1   M. Daunt, *YWES*, 11 (1930), 65–66
          2   P. F. Jones, *MLN*, 46 (1931), 347–48
          3   K. Malone, *Speculum*, 6 (1931), 148–50

918   ——— . "Das Problem des Flexionsschwundes im Angelsächsischen." *Beitr*, 45 (1921), 85–102. (com, lng) Answer by Cohn [347].
        Review: E. E. Wardale, *YWES*, 2 (1921–22), 39–40

919   ——— . "Richtigstellung." *ESt*, 69 (1934–35), 154–58. (int)
        Reply to Keller [985]; reply by Keller [987].
        Review: M. Serjeantson, *YWES*, 15 (1934), 65

920   ——— . "Zur Erklärung der Wortstellungsentwicklung im Angelsächsischen." *Anglia*, 39 (1916), 277–302. (lng)

921   ——— . (Untitled review of Hoops [894] and [896]) *LGRP*, 56 (1935), 241–43. (dct, hst, mtr, thm)

922   HUGUENIN, Julian. "Secondary Stress in Anglo–Saxon (Determined by Metrical Criteria)." Unpub. Ph.D. diss., Johns Hopkins Univ., 1901. (lng, mtr)

†   ——— , see [614].

923   HULBERT, James Root. "The Accuracy of the B-Scribe of *Beowulf*." *PMLA*, 43 (1928), 1196–99. (mns) Opposes Rypins [1749].
        Review: M. Daunt, *YWES*, 9 (1928), 71

924   ——— . "*Beowulf* and the Classical Epic." *MP*, 44 (1946), 65–75. (chr, epc, str, tec)
        Review: M. Daunt, *YWES*, 27 (1946), 60–61

925   ——— . "The Genesis of *Beowulf:* A Caveat." *PMLA*, 66 (1951), 1168–76. (com, mth, rel, sch)

926   ——— . "A Note on Compounds in *Beowulf*." *JEGP*, 31 (1932), 504–8. (dct, lng, nam) Opposes Magoun [1309]; uses Krackow [1131].
        Review: M. Daunt, *YWES*, 13 (1932), 60

927   ——— . "A Note on the Psychology of the *Beowulf* Poet." In *Klaeber*, pp. 189–95. (com, img, tec) Opposes Lawrence [1203].
        Review: M. Daunt, *YWES*, 10 (1929), 79

928   ——— . "A Sketch of Anglo–Saxon Literature." In Bright [216], pp. lxxxvii–cxxxii. (gen)

929   ——— . "Surmises Concerning the *Beowulf*-Poet's Source." *JEGP*, 50 (1951), 11–18. (Src)

†   ——— , see [216] and [1468].

930   HUPPÉ, Bernard F. "A Reconsideration of the Ingeld
        Passage in *Beowulf.*" *JEGP*, 38 (1939), 217–25. (hst, int;
        2032ff)   Answer by Malone [1389]; continues Steadman
        [1999].
        Review: G. N. Garmonsway, *YWES*, 20 (1939), 25–26

 †   HUTCHINGS, H., see [1919].

931   HUYSHE, Wentworth. *Beowulf: An Old English Epic (The
        Earliest Epic of the Germanic Race).*   London and N.Y., 1907.
        (bbl, com, Fnb, hst, mns, nts, trl)   Translates *Beowulf* and
        Finnsburh into English prose, based (?) on Wyatt text [2267].
        Reviews:
            1   *Athenaeum*, 1907, II, 96
            2   *N&Q*, 115 (1907), 58
            3   J. M. Garnett, *AJPhil*, 29 (1908), 344–46
            4   F. Klaeber, *Beibl*, 19 (1908), 257–59

932   IMELMANN, Rudolph. "*Beowulf* 303ff und 3074ff." *ESt*,
        67 (1932–33), 325–29. (ana, int, txt; 303ff, 3074ff)
        Review: D. E. M. Clarke, *YWES*, 14 (1933), 85–86

933   ———. "*Beowulf*, 489f." *ESt*, 65 (1930–31), 190–96. (txt;
        489–90)
        Review: D. E. M. Clarke, *YWES*, 12 (1931), 69–70

934   ———. "*Beowulf* 489f., 600, 769." *ESt*, 66 (1932), 321–45.
        (int, wrd; 489–90, 599–600, 769a)   Answer to Holthausen
        [849].
        Review: M. Daunt, *YWES*, 13 (1932), 61–62

935   ———. "*Beowulf* 3074ff: Nachprüfung." *ESt*, 68 (1933),
        1–5. (txt; 2748, 3074ff)
        Review: D. E. M. Clarke, *YWES*, 14 (1933), 85–86

936   ———. *Forschungen zur altenglischen Poesie.*   Berlin, 1920. (chr,
        edt, Fnb, hst, int, src, txt; Fep, 1409, 1931b)   Edits Finns-
        burh episode and fragment.
        Reviews:
            1   A. Heusler, *AfdA*, 41 (1922), 27–35 [811]
            2   F. Holthausen, *Anglia*, 46 (1922), 55–60
            3   H. Jantzen, *Zeitschrift für franz. und engl. Unterricht*, 22
                (1923), 223

937   ———. (Untitled review of Heyne/Schücking [815], 8th ed.)
        DLZ, 30 (1909), 995–1000. (int, lng, txt; Fep)

938   ———. (Untitled review of Boer [138]) *DLZ*, 34 (1913), cols.
        1062–66. (lng, txt)

 †   IRVINE, Helen Douglas, see [1215].

939 IRVING, Edward B. "Ealuscerwen: Wild Party at Heorot." *TSL*, 11 (1966), 161–68. (lng, wrd; 769)

940 ISAACS, Neil David. "A Note on *Beowulf* 2570b–2575a." *N&Q*, 202 (1957), 140. (int, lng, tec; 2570b–75a)
Review: R. M. Wilson, *YWES*, 38 (1957), 75

941 ——. "Personification in *Beowulf*." Unpub. Ph.D. diss., Brown Univ., 1959. DA, 20 (1959), 2276. (for, stl, tec, thm)

942 ——. "Six *Beowulf* Cruxes." *JEGP*, 62 (1963), 119–28. (epc, for, int, tec, thm; 168–69, 303b–6a, 1020b, 1290b–91, 2255–66, 2570b–75a) Personification.
Review: R. M. Wilson, *YWES*, 44 (1963), 73

943 ISSHIKI, Masaho. "The Kennings in *Beowulf*." In *Otsuka*, pp. 257–73. (img, ken, lng, mtr, stl, var)
Review: R. M. Wilson, *YWES*, 39 (1959), 72

944 JACKSON, William T. H. *The Literature of the Middle Ages.* N.Y., 1960. (gen)
Review: R. M. Wilson, *YWES*, 41 (1960), 51–52

945 ——. *Medieval Literature: A History and a Guide.* London and N.Y., 1966: Collier paperback 05229. (Fnb, gcn)

946 JANOTTA, Georg. *Wörterbuch zum "Beowulf," sachlich geordnet.* Rostock diss., 1923. (dct, lng) Summary pub. Rostock, 1923.

947 JELINEK, Vladimir. "Three Notes on *Beowulf*." *MLN*, 71 (1956), 239–42. (int, txt; 31–32, 208–9, 736–38)
Review: R. M. Wilson, *YWES*, 37 (1956), 72

948 JELLINEK, Max Hermann, and KRAUS, Carl. "Die Widersprüche in *Beowulf*." *ZDA*, 35 (1891), 265–81. (com, int, txt)

949 ——. "Zum "*Finnsburgfragment*." *Beitr*, 15 (1891), 428–31. (Fnb, int, txt)

950 JENTE, Richard. *Die mythologischen Ausdrücke im altenglischen Wortschatz: Eine kulturgeschichtlich-etymol. Untersuch.* Heidelberg, 1921. (dct, hst, lng, mth, nam, rel, wrd)
Reviews:
    1 E. Ekwall, *Beibl*, 34 (1923), 133–36
    2 F. R. Schröder, *GRM*, 10 (1922), 189
    3 E. E. Wardale, *YWES*, 2 (1920–21), 37–38

† JESPERSEN, Otto, see [97].

951 JIRICZEK, Otto Luitpold. *Die Deutsche Heldensage.* Strasbourg, 1898. (ana, hst)

Partially trans. by M. G. Bentinck-Smith. *Northern Hero Legends.* London, 1902.
2d ed., Leipzig, 1900; 3d ed., 1902; 4th ed., Berlin and Leipzig, 1913

952   JOBES, Gertrude. "Beowulf." *Dictionary of Mythology Folklore and Symbols.* N.Y., 1961. Vol. I, p. 203. (mth)

953   JOHANSSON, Gust. *Beowulfsagans Historiska fragment.* Göteborg, 1964. (bbl)

954   ——. *Beowulfsagans Hronesnaesse, Lekmannafunderingar angående det Gamla Götland.* Göteborg, 1947. (hst, int, mth)
       Review: F. P. Magoun, *Speculum,* 27 (1952), 225–26

955   JOHNSON, Samuel Frederich. "*Beowulf.*" *Explicator,* 9 (1950–51), item 52. (mth, str)

956   JONES, Eustace Hinton. *Beowulf.* In George W. Cox and E. H. Jones. *Popular Romances of the Middle Ages.* London, 1871. pp. 382–98. (par)   Selected English prose paraphrase. See his [957].
       2d ed., 1880 (actually 1879)

957   ——. "*Beowulf.*" *Canadian Monthly and National Review,* 2 (1872), 83–91. (par)   Selected from his [956]. English prose paraphrase, falsely attributed to John Earle.

958   JONES, George Fenwick. "Lov'd I Not Honour More: The The Durability of a Literary Motif." *CL,* 11 (1959), 131–43. (hst, int; 2884–91)

959   JONES, Putnam Fennell. "*Beowulf* 2596–99." *MLN,* 45 (1930), 300–301. (str, thm; 2596–99)
       Review: M. Daunt, *YWES,* 11 (1930), 55

960   JORDAN, Richard. *Eigentümlichkeit des anglischen Wortschatzes.* Heidelberg, 1906. (lng)

961   JORDANS, Wilhelm. *Der germanische Volksglaube von den Toten und Dämonen im Berg und ihrer Beschwichtigung/die Spuren in England.* Bonn, 1933. (mth)

962   JOSEPH, Eugen. "Zwei Versversetzungen im *Beowulf.*" *ZDP,* 22 (1890), 385–97. (mtr, txt; 901–15, 1404–7)

963   JOYNES, Mary Lou. "Structural Analysis of Old English Metrics." Unpub. Ph.D. diss., Univ. of Texas, 1958. *DA,* 19 (1959), 1076. (mtr)

964   JUSSERAND, Jean Andrien Antoine Jules. *A Literary History of the English People from the Origins to the Civil War.* London, 1895. (gen)
       2d ed., N.Y., 1906–9; 3d ed., 1926–31

965 KAHLE, B. (Untitled review of Panzer [1618]) *ZDP*, 43 (1911), 383–94. (ana, mth)

966 KAIL, J. "Über die Parallelstellen in der angelsächsischen Poesie." *Anglia*, 12 (1889), 21–40. (ana)

967 KALMA, D. *Kening Finn. Frisia-Rige*, no. 3, 1937. (Fnb, gen, trl; Fep) Translates Finnsburh episode and fragment into alliterative Frisian verse.

968 KALUZA, Max. *Der altenglische Vers: eine metrische Untersuchung.* Part I. *Kritik der bisherigen Theorien.* Part II. *Die Metrik des Beowulfliedes.* Berlin, 1894. (mtr) Scans lines 1–1000.
Reviews:
1 P. J. Cosijn, *Museum*, 2 (1895), 353–54
2 A. Heusler, *AfdA*, 21 (1895), 313–17
3 H. Hirt, *LitCbl*, 1895, no. 36, and 1896, no. 1, 5
4 K. Luick, *Beibl*, 5 (1894–95), 198
5 E. Martin, *ESt*, 20 (1895), 293–96 [1419]
6 F. Saran, *ZDP*, 27 (1895), 539–43
7 M. Trautmann, *Beibl*, 5 (1894–95), 131–36

969 ——. *Englische Metrik in historischer Entwicklung dargestellt.* Berlin, 1909. (mtr)
Trans. by A. C. Dunstan. *A Short History of English Versification.* London and N.Y., 1911.

970 ——. *Prolegomena zu einer Beowulfausgabe. Teutonia*, 1 (1902). (gen)

971 ——. "Die Schwellverse in der altenglischen Dichtung." *ESt*, 21 (1895), 337–84. (mtr)

972 ——. "Zur Betonungs- und Verslehre des Altenglischen." In *Schade*, pp. 101–33. (mtr)

973 ——. (Untitled review of Kistenmacher [1010]). *ESt*, 27 (1900), 121–22. (lng, txt)

974 KASKE, Robert E. "'Hygelac' and 'Hygd.'" In *Brodeur*, pp. 200–206. (chr, nam, smb)
Review: R. M. Wilson, *YWES*, 44 (1963), 74

975 ——. "*Sapientia et Fortitudo* as the Controlling Theme of *Beowulf.*" *SP*, 55 (1958), 423–57. (hst, rel, str, thm)
Review: R. M. Wilson, *YWES*, 39 (1958), 71
Repr. in Nicholson [1560], pp. 269–310

976 ——. "The Sigemund-Heremod and Hama-Hygelac Passages in *Beowulf.*" *PMLA*, 74 (1959), 489–94. (epc, int, str, thm; 874–915, 1179–1214, 1709–52)
Review: R. M. Wilson, *YWES*, 40 (1959), 61

977   ——. "Weohstan's Sword." *MLN*, 75 (1960), 465–68.
       (chr, epc, int)
       Review: R. M. Wilson, *YWES*, 41 (1960), 55

978   KAUFFMANN, Friedrich. *Deutsche Altertumskunde*.
       Munich, 1913. (hst)

979   ——. "Die sogenannten Schwellverse der alt- und angel-
       sächsischen Dichtung." *Beitr*, 15 (1891), 360–76. (mtr)
       Simplifies Sievers [1926] and Karl Luick, *Beitr*, 13 (1888),
       388–94.

980   KEE, Kenneth. "*Beowulf* 1408ff: A Discussion and a Sug-
       gestion." *MLN*, 75 (1960), 385–89. (int, txt; 1408–12)
       Review: R. M. Wilson, *YWES*, 41 (1960), 55

981   KEILLER, Alexander, and PIGGOTT, Stuart. "Cham-
       bered Tomb in *Beowulf*." *Antiquity*, 13 (1939), 360–61. (arc)

982   KEISER, Albert. "The Influence of Christianity on the
       Vocabulary of Old English Poetry." Ph.D. diss., Univ. of
       Illinois, 1918. (dct, rel)
       Published, same title, Univ. of Illinois Studies in Language
       and Literature, V, 1 and 2. Urbana, Ill., 1919.
       Reviews:
            1 A. Brandl, *Archiv*, 147 (1924), 144
            2 J. W. Bright, *MLN*, 36 (1921), 315–18
            3 L. Faucett, *SR*, 28 (1920), 607–8
            4 O. Funke, *LGRP*, 43 (1922), 94–102
            5 F. Karpf, *NS*, 31 (1923), 230–31
            6 F. Klaeber, *ESt*, 56 (1922), 88–90
            7 W. Preusler, *LitCbl*, 72 (1921), 785–86
            8 H. Schöffler, *Beibl*, 32 (1921), 55
            9 L. L. Schücking, *MLR*, 16 (1921), 176–77

983   KELLER, May Lansfield. *The Anglo–Saxon Weapon Names
       Treated Archaeologically and Etymologically*. Heidelberg, 1906.
       (arc, dct, lng, nam, wrd)

984   KELLER, Wolfgang. *Angelsächsische Paleographie*. Berlin,
       1906. Vol. I. (mns)

985   ——. "Beowulf der riesige Vorkämpfer." *ESt*, 68 (1933–
       34), 321–38. (ana, chr, wrd) Reply by Hübener [919].
       Review: M. Serjeantson, *YWES*, 15 (1934), 64–65

986   ——. "Zur Worttrennung in den angelsächsischen Hand-
       schriften." In *Förster*, pp. 89–105. (mns)
       Review: M. Daunt, *YWES*, 10 (1929), 85

987   ——. (Untitled note) *ESt*, 69 (1934–35), 158. Response
       to Hübener [919]. (txt)

988   KELLOGG, Robert L. "The South Germanic Oral Tradition." In *Magoun*, pp. 66–74. (ana, dct, for)

989   KEMBLE, John Mitchell. *The Anglo–Saxon Poems of "Beowulf," "The Travelers Song," and the "Battle of Finnesburh."* London, 1833. (com, dct, edt, Fnb, gen, hst, ken, mns, mth, nts, trl, wrd) Translates into literal English prose.
2d ed., Vol. I (same title, contains edited text), 1835; Vol. II, *A Translation of the Anglo–Saxon Poem of "Beowulf,"* 1837 (dated 1835).

990   ——. *History of the English Language: First, or Anglo–Saxon Period.* Cambridge, 1834. (lng)

991   ——. *The Saxons in England: A History of the English Commonwealth till the Period of the Norman Conquest.* London, 1849. (hst, mth) Trans. into German by H. B. C. Brandes. *Die Sachsen in England.* Leipzig, 1853–54.
2d ed., rev. by Walter de Gray Birch, 1876
Trans. into French as introd. of Pierquin [1650].

992   ——. *Über die Stammtafeln der Westsachsen.* Munich, 1836. (hst, mth, nam)
Review: J. Grimm, *GGA*, 28 April 1836, pp. 649–57; repr. in his *Kleinere Schriften*, V (Berlin, 1871), 240–45.

993   ——. (Untitled letter dated 1837) In Francisque Michel, ed., *Bibliothèque Anglo–Saxonne*, which is Vol. II of F. Michel and Phillipe de Larenaudière, eds., *Anglo–Saxonica.* Paris and London, 1836–37. pp. 1–63. (mns, txt) Corrections to Conybeare [356] and Thorkelin [2080].

994   KENNEDY, Arthur Garfield, and KRAPP, George Philip. *An Anglo–Saxon Reader.* N.Y., 1929. (edt) Edits lines 64–158, 710–836, 2550–2835.

995   ——. *A Bibliography of Writings on the English Language from the Beginnings of Printing to the End of 1922.* Cambridge and New Haven, 1927. (bbl, lng)
Repr., N.Y., 1961

996   KENNEDY, Charles W. *An Anthology of Old English Poetry.* N.Y., 1960. (Fnb, trl) Translates *Finnsburh* and *Beowulf* 1066–1159, 2200–2354, 2510–2614, 2631–2891, 3110–82.

997   ——. *Beowulf. The Oldest English Epic.* N.Y., London, and Toronto, 1940. (ana, bbl, epc, Fnb, hst, mns, mth, rel, trl) Translates *Beowulf* into English alliterative verse, based on Klaeber [1026].
Reviews:
1   *N&Q*, 180 (1941), 234
2   *TLS*, 15 Feb. 1941, p. 83
3   G. N. Garmonsway, *YWES*, 21 (1940), 33–35

> 4   H. S. V. Jones, *JEGP*, 40 (1941), 456
> 5   T. M., *Catholic World*, 152 (1940), 372–73
> 6   M. B. Ruud, *MLQ*, 2 (1941), 138–39
> 7   P. W. Souers, *Speculum*, 16 (1941), 351–52

Repr. 1942, 1948

998   ——. *The Earliest English Poetry.* London, Toronto, and N.Y., 1943. (ana, epc, Fnb, gen, hst, int, mth, rel, src, str, trl) Translates part of *Beowulf* and *Finnsburh* into English alliterative verse.
Reviews:

> 1   C. Baker, *NYTB*, 23 July 1944, p. 22
> 2   P. F. Baum, *SAQ*, 43 (1944), 104–5
> 3   M. D. Coogan, *Catholic World*, 158 (1944), 505–6
> 4   K. Jost, *ES*, 28 (1947), 116–17
> 5   H. Larsen, *JEGP*, 43 (1944), 453–55
> 6   K. Malone, *MLN*, 59 (1944), 194–95
> 7   H. Meroney, *Speculum*, 19 (1944), 508–9
> 8   D. Whitelock, *YWES*, 24 (1943), 28–29
> 9   Mother Williams, *Thought*, 19 (1944), 348–49

Repr. 1948

999   ——. *Old English Elegies.* Princeton, 1936. (trl) Translates lines 2231–70 into English verse, based on Klaeber [1026].
Review: M. Serjeantson, *YWES*, 17 (1936), 64

†   KENNEDY, Horace M., see [225].

1000 KER, Neil Ripley. *Catalogue of Manuscripts Containing Anglo–Saxon.* Oxford, 1957. (bbl, Fnb, mns; 869) *Beowulf* no. 216, *Finnsburh* no. 282, *Beowulf* 869 in no. 229.
Reviews:

> 1   *TLS*, 19 Dec. 1958, p. 740
> 2   R. Derolez, *ES*, 39 (1958), 126–28
> 3   D. J. V. Fisher, *EHR*, 74 (1959), 480–82
> 4   H. Gneuss, *Anglia*, 76 (1958), 539–44
> 5   K. Sisam, *RES*, 10 (1959), 68–71
> 6   D. Whitelock, *Antiquity*, 32 (1958), 129–32
> 7   R. Willard, *JEGP*, 59 (1960), 129–37
> 8   R. M. Wilson, *YWES*, 38 (1957), 72–73
> 9   C. E. Wright, *MAE*, 28 (1959), 53–57

1001 KER, William Paton. *The Dark Ages.* Edinburgh and London, 1904. (gen)
Repr. 1955 with preface by B. I. Evans
Reviews:

> 1   F. Mossé, *EA*, 9 (1956), 344
> 2   R. M. Wilson, *YWES*, 36 (1955), 58

Repr. 1961

1002 ——. *English Literature: Medieval.* N.Y. and London, [1912]. (Fnb, gen)

1003 ——. *Epic and Romance: Essays on Medieval Literature.* N.Y. and London, 1897. (com, Fnb, gen, hst, tec)
Reviews:
    1 A. Brandl, *Archiv*, 100 (1898), 198–200
    2 R. Fischer, *Beibl*, 10 (1899–1900), 133–35
2d ed., 1908
Repr. 1922

1004 KERN, H. "Angelsaksische Kleinigheden." *Taalkundige Bijdragen*, 1 (1877), 193–203. (lng, wrd; 2766)

1005 KERN, J. H. "Zum Vokalismus einiger Lehnwörter im Altenglischen." *Anglia*, 37 (1913), 54–61. (lng)

† KERRIGAN, Anthony, see [172].

† KERSHAW, Nora, see CHADWICK, Nora Kershaw.

1006 KIER, Chr. *Beowulf: Et Bidrag til Nordens Oldhistorie.* Copenhagen, 1915. (hst, nam)
Review: E. Björkman, *Beibl*, 27 (1916), 244–46

† KILDE, Jacob Elle, see [1594].

1007 KINLOCK, A. Murray. "A Note on *Beowulf* L. 1828B." *MLR*, 51 (1956), 71. (txt; 1828b)
Review: R. M. Wilson, *YWES*, 37 (1956), 72

† KIRBY, John P., see [33].

1008 KIRTLAN, Ernest J. B. *The Story of Beowulf: Tr. from Anglo-Saxon into Modern English Prose.* London, 1913. (gen, nts, trl) Illustrations by Frederic Lawrence.
Reviews:
    1 *Athenaeum*, 1914, II, 71
    2 F. Klaeber, *Beibl*, 27 (1916), 129–31
Repr. 1914

1009 KISSACK, Robert Ashton, Jr. "The Sea in Anglo–Saxon and Middle English Poetry." *Washington Univ. Studies, Humanistic Series*, 13, no. 2 (1926), 371–89. (img, thm)

1010 KISTENMACHER, Richard. *Die Wörtlichen Wiederholungen im "Beowulf."* Greifswald diss., 1898. (dct, stl, var)
Reviews:
    1 M. Kaluza, *ESt*, 27 (1900), 121–22 [973]
    2 W. E. Mead, *JEGP*, 2 (1898–99), 546–47

1011 KITTREDGE, George Lyman. "Zu *Beowulf*, 107ff." *Beitr*, 13 (1888), 210. (rel; 107ff) On Cain.

1012 Item canceled.

1013 KLAEBER, Frederick. "Aeneis und Beowulf." *Archiv*, 126 (1911), 40–48, 339–59. (ana, src; 2358)

1014 ———. "Altenglische wortkundliche Randglossen." *Beibl*, 40 (1929), 21–32. (lng; 107–8, 600, 769)
Review: M. Daunt, *YWES*, 10 (1929), 101

1015 ———. "Die ältere *Genesis* und der *Beowulf*." *ESt*, 42 (1910), 321–38. (com, src)

1016 ———. "Anmerkungen zum *Beowulf*-Text." *Archiv*, 188 (1951), 108–9. (int, txt; 473, 867ff, 982ff, 1382, 2356, 2372, 2706, 3027, 3117)

1017 ———. "Attila's and Beowulf's Funerals." *PMLA*, 42 (1927), 255–67. (ana, hst, src)
Review: M. Daunt, *YWES*, 8 (1927), 80–81

1018 ———. "Aus Anlass von *Beowulf* 2724f." *Archiv*, 104 (1900), 287–92. (int; 2724–25)

1019 ———. "Eine Bemerkung zum altenglischen Passivum." *ESt*, 57 (1923), 187–95. (lng)

1020 ———. "Bemerkungen zum *Beowulf*." *Archiv*, 115 (1905), 178–82. (Fnb, txt; Fnb 8b)

1021 Item canceled.

1022 ———. "*Beowulf*, 62." *MLN*, 21 (1906), 255–56; 22 (1907), 160. (int, lng; 62) Continues his [1042].

1023 ———. "*Beowulf* 769." *ESt*, 67 (1932), 24–26. (int; 769a)

1024 ———. "*Beowulf* 769 und *Andreas* 1526ff." *ESt*, 73 (1939), 185–89. (ana, int, lng, str, wrd; 769) On "ealuscerwen."
Review: G. N. Garmonsway, *YWES*, 20 (1939), 31–32

1025 ———. "*Beowulf* 2041: *beah*." *Beibl*, 51 (1940), 206–7. (int, lng, wrd; 2041b)

1026 ———. "*Beowulf*" and "*The Fight at Finnsburg*" Edited, with *Introduction, Bibliography, Notes, Glossary, and Appendices*. Boston, N.Y., Chicago, 1922. London, 1923. (ana, bbl, com, edt, Fnb, hst, lng, mns, mth, mtr, nts, rel, stl, str, txt)
Reviews:
    1 *TLS*, 8 Feb. 1923, p. 95
    2 H. M. Flasdieck, *ESt*, 58 (1924), 119–24 [569]
    3 H. Hecht, *AfdA*, 43 (1924), 46–51
    4 F. Holthausen, *Beibl*, 34 (1923), 353–57
    5 E. A. Kock, *ANF*, 39 (1923), 185–89 [1108]
    6 H. Larsen, *PQ*, 2 (1923), 156–58
    7 W. W. Lawrence, *JEGP*, 23 (1924), 294–300 [1207]
    8 R. J. Menner, *N.Y. Evening Post Literary Review*, 20 Jan. 1923, p. 394
    9 E. E. Wardale, *YWES*, 4 (1923), 39–43
2d ed., 1928, with supplement

Reviews:

   1 A. Brandl, *Archiv*, 156 (1929), 304–5

   2 K. Malone, *JEGP*, 28 (1929), 416–17

3d ed., Boston, 1936

Reviews:

   1 A. Brandl, *Archiv*, 171 (1937), 220–22

   2 F. Holthausen, *Beibl*, 48 (1937), 65–66

   3 H. S. V. Jones, *JEGP*, 37 (1937), 92–93

3d ed., with supplement, 1941; 3d ed., with second supplement, 1950

1027 ——. "Beowulfiana." *Anglia*, 50 (1926), 107–22, 195–244. (Fnb, hst, mns, txt; 14ff, 20ff, 22–24, 26, 76–77, 78, 82–83, 106–7, 162, 168–69, 175ff, 189–90, 208–9, 223–24, 232, 272, 287–89, 299–300, 305–6, 374–75, 389–90, 414, 427–28, 445–46, 455, 489–90, 748, 769, 785, 804, 810, 865ff, 870–71, 902ff, 948–49, 968, 1013ff, 1022, 1174, 1210–11, 1214, 1223–24, 1231, 1240, 1321ff, 1342, 1374–75, 1376, 1408, 1409, 1459, 1461, 1543, 1604, 1637–38, 1657–58, 1688ff, 1696–97, 1725ff, 1728–29, 1737–38, 1756–57, 1769ff, 1807–8, 1814–16, 1825, 1833, 1836–37, 1865, 1907, 1992–93, 2018, 2029–31, 2034, 2044, 2047, 2085, 2106, 2179, 2215, 2223, 2243, 2260–62, 2295, 2353, 2423–24, 2457, 2481, 2484–85, 2570ff, 2628, 2649–50, 2717–19, 2766) Opposes Craigie [399].
Review: M. Daunt, *YWES*, 7 (1926), 50–51.

1028 ——. "Beowulfiana Minora." *Anglia*, 63 (1939), 400–425. (ana, dct, Fnb, img, int, ken, lng, mtr, nam, sch, stl, str, trl, txt, var, wrd; 83ff, 115ff, 129–30, 133, 156, 161, 172–74, 218, 232, 262ff, 305–6, 356–59, 403, 450–51, 455, 457, 506, 636–38, 640, 681, 708–9, 730, 749, 1011–12, 1020, 1024, 1033, 1056–57, 1071–72, 1082, 1099, 1106, 1107–8, 1131–32, 1142ff, 1199ff, 1247, 1302, 1351, 1357, 1372, 1379, 1425ff, 1440, 1458, 1720, 1850, 1865, 2018, 2047ff, 2059, 2106, 2163ff, 2179, 2251ff, 2468, 2697, 2951, 3019, 3027, 3061, 3071–72, 3084, 3098, 3163)
Review: G. N. Garmonsway, *YWES*, 20 (1939), 25–26 [609]

1029 ——. "Beowulf's Character." *MLN*, 17 (1902), 162. (chr, int; 2738–40) Concerns Hall [740].

1030 ——. "Die christlichen Elemente im *Beowulf*." *Anglia*, 35 (1912), 111–36, 249–70, 453–82; 36 (1912), 169–99. (ken, rel, var)

1031 ——. "Concerning the Functions of Old English *geweorðan* and the Origins of German *gewähren lassen*." *JEGP*, 18 (1919), 250–71. (lng, wrd; 1598, 1996, 2026)

1032 ——. "Concerning the Relation between *Exodus* and *Beowulf*." *MLN*, 33 (1918), 218–24. (ana, com, src)

1033 ——. "Cynewulf's *Elene* 1262f." *JEGP*, 6 (1907), 197. (ana, lng; 2261)

1034 ——. "Drei Anmerkungen zur Texterklärung." *ESt*, 70 (1936), 333-36. (chr, Fnb, int, nam) On Garulf and Guthere.
Review: M. Serjeantson, *YWES*, 17 (1936), 63-64

1035 ——. "A Few *Beowulf* Jottings." *Beibl*, 50 (1939), 330-32. (Fnb, int, lng; 62ff, 168ff, 194, 600, 670, 1151ff, 1210, 1212-14a, 1440, 2178, 2362, 3146, Fnb 6, 16)
Review: G. N. Garmonsway, *YWES*, 20 (1939), 26

1036 ——. "A Few *Beowulf* Notes." *MLN*, 16 (1901), 14-18. (txt; 70, 423, 459, 847b, 1206, 3024ff, 3170)

1037 ——. "A Few Recent Additions to *Beowulf* Bibliography and Notes." *Beibl*, 52 (1941), 135-37. (bbl, nts)

1038 ——. "Garulf, Guthlafs Sohn, im *Finnsburg–Fragment*." *Archiv*, 162 (1932), 116-17. (chr, nam, Fnb only) Opposes Scott-Thomas [1886].
Review: M. Daunt, *YWES*, 13 (1932), 61

1039 ——. "Eine germanisch-englische Formel: Ein stilisch-syntaktischer Streifzug." In *Förster*, pp. 1-22. (dct, lng, stl; 286, 356)
Review: M. Daunt, *YWES*, 10 (1929), 84

1040 ——. "Das Grändelsmôr–eine Frage." *Archiv*, 131 (1913), 427. (mth, nam)

1041 ——. "Der Held Bēowulf in deutscher Sagenüberlieferung." *Anglia*, 46 (1922), 193-201. (ana)

1042 ——. "Hrothulf." *MLN*, 20 (1905), 9-11. (chr, hst, int, txt) Answer to Abbott [2]; continued by his [1022].

1043 ——. "Eine kleine Nachlese zum *Beowulf*." *Anglia*, 56 (1932), 421-31. (Fnb, hst, int, str, txt; 61, 850, 1142, 1724ff, 1741)
Review: M. Daunt, *YWES*, 13 (1932), 59

1044 ——. "Minor Notes on the *Beowulf*." *JEGP*, 6 (1907), 190-96. (int, lng)

1045 ——. "Miscellen zum *Beowulf*." *ESt*, 39 (1908), 463-67. (int, lng, txt; 1120, 1440, 1655-56, 1728-29, 1769ff, 2034ff, 2252, 2297, 2337, 2564, 2586ff, 2764-65, 2784ff, 2957)

1046 ——. "Noch einmal *Exodus* 56-58 und *Beowulf* 1408-1410." *Archiv*, 187 (1950), 71-72. (ana, lng; 1408-10)
Review: R. M. Wilson, *YWES*, 31 (1950), 46

1047 ——. "A Notelet on the Ingeld Episode in *Beowulf*." *Beibl*, 50 (1939), 223-24. (ana, epc, thm)
Review: G. N. Garmonsway, *YWES*, 20 (1939), 25

1048 ——. "Notizen zum *Beowulf:* Über den Gebrauch einiger Adjectiva und Verwandtes." *Anglia,* 29 (1906), 378–82. (lng)

1049 ——. "Notizen zur Cynewulfs *Elene.*" *Anglia,* 29 (1906), 271–72. (ana, lng)

1050 ——. "Notizen zur Texterklärung des *Beowulf.*" *Anglia,* 28 (1905), 439–47. (Fnb, txt; Fnb 5)

1051 ——. "Observations on the Finn Episode." *JEGP,* 14 (1915), 544–49. (Fnb, int; Fep)

1052 ——. "Old English *beagas.*" *Beibl,* 52 (1941), 179–80. (int, wrd)

1053 ——. "Eine Randbemerkung zur Nebenordnung und Unterordnung im Altenglischen." *Beibl,* 52 (1941), 216–19. (lng)

1054 ——. "Randglossen zur Texterklärung des *Beowulf.*" *Beitr,* 72 (1950), 120–26. (txt)

1055 ——. "Some Further Additions to *Beowulf* Bibliography and Notes." *Beibl,* 54–55 (1944), 274–80. (bbl, nts)

1056 ——. "Studies in the Textual Interpretation of Beowulf. Part I." *MP,* 3 (1905–6), 235–65. (lng, rht, txt, var, wrd)

1056.1 ——. "Studies in the Textual Interpretation of *Beowulf.* Part II." *MP,* 3 (1905–6), 445–65. (lng, txt, wrd)

1057 ——. "Textual Notes on *Beowulf.*" *MLN,* 34 (1919), 129–34. (txt) Answer to Koch [1096].

1058 ——. "Textual Notes on the *Beowulf.*" *JEGP,* 8 (1909), 254–59. (txt)

1059 ——. "Unferð's Verhalten im *Beowulf.*" *Beibl,* 53 (1942), 270–72. (int)

1060 ——. "Zum Bedeutungsinhalt gewisser altenglischer Wörter und ihrer Verwendung." *Anglia,* 46 (1922), 232–38. (wrd)

1061 ——. "Zum *Beowulf.*" *Anglia,* 28 (1905), 448–56. (Fnb, hst, txt)

1062 ——. *Ibid. Archiv,* 108 (1902), 368–70. (lng, txt; 497–98, 1745–47)

1063 ——. "Zum *Finnsburg-Kampfe.*" *ESt,* 39 (1908), 307–8. (txt, Fnb only)

1064 ——. "Zum Rhythmus der *Beowulf*-verse." *Archiv,* 185 (1948), 121–24. (mtr)

1065 ——. "Zur Texterklärung altenglischer Dichtungen." *Beibl,* 54–55 (1944), 170–76. (txt; 404)

1066   ——. "Zur Texterklärung des *Beowulf.*" *Beibl*, 22 (1911),
         372–74. (txt; 769, 1129–30)

1067   ——. (Untitled review of Heyne/Schücking [815], 10th ed.)
         Beibl, 24 (1913), 289–91. (txt, wrd; 94, 138, 455, 457, 918,
         1004, 1106, 1174, 1223, 1252, 1539, 2044, 2149, 2394, 2526,
         2591, 2814, 2845)

1068   ——. (Untitled review of Leonard [1231]) *Beibl*, 32 (1921),
         145–48. (about trl)

1069   ——. (Untitled review of Heyne/Schücking [815], 8th ed.)
         ESt, 39 (1908), 425–33. (int, lng, mtr)

1070   ——. (Untitled review of Sedgefield [1892]) *ESt*, 44 (1911–
         12), 119–26. (int, lng, txt)

1071   ——. (Untitled review of Hoops [894]) *ESt*, 67 (1932–33),
         399–402. (int, lng, txt, wrd; 769)

1072   ——. (Untitled review of Hoops [896]) *ESt*, 68 (1933),
         112–15. (int, lng, wrd; 480, 531, 2041)

1073   ——. (Untitled review of Stjerna [2018]) *JEGP*, 13 (1914),
         167–73 (arc)

1074   ——. (Untitled review of Trautmann [2106]) *MLN*, 20
         (1905), cols. 83–87. (dct, int, txt, var, wrd)

1075   ——. (Untitled review of Holthausen [845]) *MLN*, 24
         (1909), 94–95. (int, lng, txt)

1076   ——. (Untitled review of *Ekwall Miscellany, Studia Neophil.*
         14 (1942) and 15 (1942–43).) *SN*, 15 (1942–43), 337–56.
         (Fnb, int, mns, txt, wrd; 1166, 2599, 2994) Comments on
         Fourquet [581], Holthausen [875], Kökeritz [1119], and
         Malone [1387].

†   ——, see also [890].

1077   KLEMAN, (Sister) M. Maurice. "Three Old English Verbs
         for 'Cleanse,' 'Purge.'" *IALR*, 1 (1953), 179–84. (dct, lng,
         wrd)

1078   KLIPSTEIN, Louis F. *Analecta Anglo–Saxonica.* N.Y., 1849.
         (edt, Fnb, nts, trl) Edits *Finnsburh* and *Beowulf* lines 1–114,
         320–70, 499–661, 710–90, 1321–82, 2694–2751, 3137–82;
         translates 1–17, 31–52, 85–106, 317–31.

?1079   KLÖPPER, C. "Heorot-Hall in the Anglo–Saxon poem of
         Beowulf." In *Krause.* (hst)

1080   KLUGE, Friedrich. *Angelsächsisches Lesebuch.* 3d ed., Halle,
         1902. pp. 127–28. (edt, Fnb only) Not in first two eds.

1081   ——. "Der *Beowulf* und die Hrolfs Saga Kraka." *ESt*, 22
         (1896), 144–45. (ana, hst, mth; 61–62, 753, 925, 1678)

1082   ——. "Sprachhistorische Miscellen." *Beitr*, 8 (1882), 506–
         39. (lng, txt; 63, 1026, 1234, 1266)

1083   ——. "Zeugnisse zur germanischen Sage in England."
        ESt, 21 (1895), 446–48. (hst, mth)

1084   ——. "Zum *Beowulf.*" *Beitr*, 9 (1884), 187–92. (txt; 31,
        112, 275, 360, 444, 490, 586, 650, 695, 856, 992, 1032, 1075,
        1151, 1232, 1254, 1402, 1546, 1557, 1862, 1876, 2031ff, 2196,
        2594, 2607, 2706, 2767, 2995)

1085   ——. "Zur Geschichte des Reimes im Altgermanischen."
        Beitr, 9 (1884), 422–50. (lng, mtr)

1086   KNÖRK, M. *Die Negation in der altenglischen Dichtung.* Kiel
        diss., 1907. (lng)

1087   Item canceled.

†   KNOTT, Thomas A., see [1468].

1088   KNUDSEN, G. "Udlejre." *DS*, 19 (1922), 176–77. (hst,
        nam)

1089   KOBAN, Charles. "Substantive Compounds in Beowulf."
        Unpub. Ph.D. diss., Univ. of Illinois, 1964. *DA*, 24 (1964),
        4175–76. (dct, lng, nam)

1090   KOCK, A. "Är Skåne de gamles Scandinavia?" *ANF*, 34
        (1917–18), 71–88. (hst, nam) Opposes Lindroth [1257];
        answer by Lindroth [1258] and [1259].

1091   ——. "Vidare om *Skåne* och *Scadinavia.*" *ANF*, 36 (1919–
        20), 74–85. (hst, nam) Answer to Lindroth [1258] and
        [1259].

1092   KOCK, Ernest A. "Altgermanischer Parallelismus." In
        Ehrismann, pp. 21–26. (ana, lng)

1093   ——. *The English Relative Pronouns.* Lund, 1897. (lng)

1094   ——. "Fornjermansk Forskning." *LUA*, n.s. I, 18, no. 1
        (1922). (txt)

1095   ——. "Interpretations and Emendations of Early English
        Texts: III." *Anglia*, 27 (1904), 218–37. (int, txt; 6)
        Answer by Sievers [1944].

1096   ——. "Interpretations and Emendations of Early English
        Texts: IV." *Anglia*, 42 (1918), 99–124. (int, txt) Reply by
        Klaeber [1057].

1097   ——. "Interpretations and Emendations of Early English
        Texts: V." *Anglia*, 43 (1919), 298–312. (int, txt; 16ff, 22,
        32–33, 44, 54, 63–64, 67, 99, 297–98, 1489, 1926, 2030, 2328,
        2419–24, 3066–67)

1098   ——. "Interpretations and Emendations of Early English
        Texts: VI." *Anglia*, 44 (1920), 97–114. (Fnb, int, txt; 23,
        154–56, 189–90, 489–90, 581–83, 1745–47, 1820–21, 1931–32,
        1992–93, 2164)

1099   ——. "Interpretations and Emendations of Early English
Texts: VII." *Anglia*, 44 (1920), 245–60. (int, txt; 1230–31,
1404, 1553–56)

1100   ——. "Interpretations and Emendations of Early English
Texts: VIII." *Anglia*, 45 (1921), 105–31. (Fnb, txt; 769)
Reply by Crawford [407].

1101   ——. "Interpretations and Emendations of Early English
Texts: IX." *Anglia*, 46 (1922), 63–96. (int, txt; 241–43,
245–47, 305–6, 988–90, 1013–17, 1030–34, 1071–74, 1170–74,
1214, 1233–38, 1292–93, 1338–43, 1508–9, 1687–89, 1688–90,
1689–92, 1703–6, 1725–27, 1728–31, 1737–38, 1807–12,
1814–16, 1822–25, 1834–35, 1836–37, 1840, 1863–65, 1942–
43, 1944, 2016–18, 2095–96, 2200–22, 2283–84, 2350–53,
2354–58, 2484–88, 2638–41, 2909–10, 2954–55)

1102   ——. "Interpretations and Emendations of Early English
Texts: X." *Anglia*, 46 (1922), 173–90. (int, txt; 2032–37,
2044–45, 2069–70, 2105–6, 2187–88, 2209–10, 2212, 2255,
2256ff, 2353–54, 2455–57, 2457–59, 2482–85, 2570–75, 2709–
11, 2764–66, 2857, 3084)

1103   ——. "Jubilee Jaunts and Jottings: 250 Contributions to
the Interpretations and Prosody of Old West Teutonic Alliterative Poetry." *LUA*, n.s. I, 14, no. 26 (1918), 1–82. (int,
mtr)
Reviews:
    1 F. Holthausen, *Beibl*, 30 (1919), 1–5
    2 F. Klaeber, *JEGP*, 19 (1920), 409–13

1104   ——. "Notationes Norrœnæ." *LUA*, n.s. I, 19 (1923).
(int, lng, txt)

1105   ——. "Old West Germanic and Old Norse." In *Klaeber*,
pp. 14–20. (dct, lng)

1106   ——. "Plain Points and Puzzles, 60 Notes on Old English
Poetry." *LUA*, n.s. I, 17, no. 7 (1922). (int, lng, txt)
Reviews:
    1 H. M. Flasdieck, *Beibl*, 33 (1922), 223
    2 F. Klaeber, *JEGP*, 22 (1923), 313–15

1107   ——. "Zu *Anglia* XXVII 219f., Beitr. Z. Gesch. D. D. Spr.
U. Lit. XXIX, 560ff." *Anglia*, 28 (1905), 140–42. (int, txt;
5, 6)   Reply to Sievers [1944].

1108   ——. (Untitled review of Klaeber [1026]) *ANF*, 39 (1923),
185–89. (arc, hst, int, lng, txt; 14–15, 81ff, 189–90, 459,
489–90, 1140–41)

1109   KÖGEL, Rudolf. "Beowulf." *ZDA*, 37 (1893), 268–76.
(chr, mth, nam, smb)   Attacked by Sievers [1932].

1110 ——. *Geschichte der deutschen Litteratur bis zum Ausgange des Mittelalters.* Strasbourg, 1894. (Fnb, gen, mth, stl, var)

1111 Item canceled.

1112 ——. (Untitled review of Ferdinand Wrede. *Über die Sprache der Ostgoten in Italien.* Strasbourg, 1891) *AfdA*, 18 (1892), 43–60. (lng, mth, nam) Etymology of "Beowulf."

1113 KÖHLER, Artur. "Die beiden Episoden von Heremod im Beovulfliede." *ZDP*, 2 (1870), 314–20. (com, str) Multiple authorship.

1114 ——. "Die Einleitung des Beovulfliedes: Ein Beitrag zur Frage über die Liedertheorie." *ZDP*, 2 (1870), 305–14. (com, str) Multiple authorship.

1115 ——. "Germanische Alterthümer im *Beóvulf.*" *Germania*, 13 (1868), 129–58. (Fnb, hst, rel)

1116 ——. "Über den Stand berufsmässiger Sänger im nationalen Epos germanischer Völker." *Germania*, 15 (1870), 27–50. (hst)

1117 KÖHLER, Karl. *Der syntaktische Gebrauch des Infinitivs und Particips im "Beowulf."* Münster diss., 1886. (lng)

1118 KÖKERITZ, Helge. "*Finnsburg Fragment*, 5a." *MLN*, 58 (1943), 191–94. (int, Fnb only; 5a) From his [1119].
Review: D. Whitelock, *YWES*, 24 (1943), 33

1119 ——. "Two Interpretations, *Finnsburg Fragment*, l. 5a." *SN*, 14 (1941–42), 277–79. (Fnb, int; 2069b, Fnb 4–5) Repeated in his [1118].
Reviews:
1 F. Klaeber, *SN*, 15 (1942–43), 337–56 [1076]
2 D. Whitelock, *YWES*, 23 (1942), 36

1120 KOLB, Eduard. "*Beowulf* 568: An Emendation." *ES*, 46 (1965), 322–23. (hst, int, txt; 568)

1121 KÖLBING, Eugen. "Kleine Beiträge zur Erklärung und Textkritik englischer Dichter. I." *ESt*, 3 (1880), 92–105. (int, txt; 168–69)

1122 ——. "Zum *Beowulf.*" *ESt*, 22 (1896), 325. (int, txt; 1027ff)

1123 ——. "Zur *Beovulf*-Handschrift." *Archiv*, 56 (1876), 91–118. (edt, mns) Collation.

1124 ——. (Untitled review of Wülker [2259]) *ESt*, 5 (1882), 239–41. (mns)

1124.1 ——. (Untitled review of Grein/Wülker [677], Harrison [754], Holder 2d ed. [833], Wülker [2259], and Zupitza [2278]) *ESt*, 7 (1884), 482–89. (mns)

1125   ——. (Untitled review of Wülker [2262]) *ESt*, 23 (1897), 306. (int, txt, wrd; 748)

†   ——, see also [815], 4th ed.

1126   KONRATH, W. "Zu *Beowulf* 445b–446a." *Archiv*, 99 (1897), 417–18. (int, lng; 445–46)

1127   KÖRNER, Karl. (Untitled review of Dederich [449]) *ESt*, 1 (1877), 481–95. (ana, hst, int, mth)

1128   ——. (Untitled review of Sweet [2038]) *ESt*, 1 (1877), 500. (int, lng, txt)

1129   ——. (Untitled review of Botkine [174]) *ESt*, 2 (1879), 248–51. (txt; 168ff, 287, 489–90)

1130   KÖRTING, Gustav Carl Otto. *Grundriss der Geschichte der englischen Litteratur.* Münster, 1887. pp. 28–33. (gen)
        2d ed., 1893; 3d ed., 1899; 4th ed., 1905; 5th ed., 1910

1131   KRACKOW, Otto. *Die Nominalcomposita als Kunstmittel im altenglischen Epos.* Weimar and Berlin, 1903. (stl) Used by Hulbert [926].
        Review: E. Björkman, *Archiv*, 117 (1906), 189–90

1132   ——. "Zu *Beowulf* v. 1225 und 2222." *Archiv*, 111 (1903), 171–72. (int, txt; 1225, 2222)

1133   KRALIK, Richard von. *Das deutsche Götter- und Heldenbuch.* Stuttgart, Munich, and Vienna, 1903. Vol. II, pp. 246–80. (trl) Trans. into German alexandrines.

1134   KRAPP, George Philip. *Andreas and the Fates of the Apostles.* Boston, 1906. (ana, src) Introd. only.

1135   ——. "Miscellaneous Notes: II. *Scurheard, Beowulf* 1033, *Andreas* 1133." *MLN*, 19 (1904), 234. (int, lng, wrd: 1033)

1136   ——. "Notes on the *Andreas.*" *MP*, 2 (1905), 405–7. (int, lng; 28, 234, 580, 1916, 1965)

1137   ——. "The Parenthetic Exclamation in Old English Poetry." *MLN*, 20 (1905), 33–37. (rht, stl)

†   ——, see [994].

1138   KRAPPE, Alexander Haggerty. "Der blinde König." *ZDA*, 72 (1935), 161–71. (hst)

1139   ——. "La Légende des Harlungen." In *Études de mythologie et de folklore germaniques.* Paris, 1928. pp. 137–74. (ana, hst, mth)

1140   ——. "Eine mittelalterlich-indische Parallele zum *Beowulf.*" *GRM*, 15 (1927), 54–58. (ana, mth) On Somadeva's *Katha Sarit Sāgara* ; answered by Chambers [314].
        Review: M. Daunt, *YWES*, 8 (1927), 83

1141   ——. "The Offa-Constance Legend." *Anglia*, 61 (1937), 361–69. (hst, mth)

1142   ——— . (Untitled review of F. R. Schröder. *Germanentum und Hellenismus.* Heidelberg, 1924) *Litteris*, 2 (1925), 170–73. (ana, hst, mth, smb)

1143   KRAUEL, Hans. *Der Haken- und Langzeilenstil im "Beowulf."* Göttingen diss., 1908, and *SEP*, 32 (1908). (mtr, var)

†   KRAUS, Carl, see [948].

?1144   KRAUS, Karl. "Hrodulf." In *Moneta*, pp. 4ff.

1145   KRAUSE, Wolfgang. *Die Kenning als typische Stilfigur der altgermanischen und keltischen Dichtersprache.* Halle, 1930. (ken) Review: S. Singer, *IF*, 51 (1933), 164–67

1146   KRETSCHMER, P. "Scandinavia." *Glotta*, 17 (1928), 148–51. (hst) On "Scedenig" and "Scedeland."

1147   KROGMANN, Willy. "Ae. ēolet." *Anglia*, 58 (1934), 351–57. (lng, wrd; 224a) Review: M. Serjeantson, *YWES*, 15 (1934), 81–82

1148   ——— . "Ae *gang.*" *Anglia*, 57 (1933), 216–17. (lng, wrd; 1009, 1295, 1316) Review: D. E. M. Clarke, *YWES*, 14 (1933), 89

1149   ——— . "*Æ̅ orc.*" *Anglia*, 57 (1933), 110. (lng, wrd; 112) Review: M. Daunt, *YWES*, 14 (1933), 83–84

1150   ——— . "*Æ̅ orcneas.*" *Anglia*, 56 (1932), 40–42. (lng, wrd; 112) Answer in Hoops [894]; reply by Krogmann [1159]. Review: M. Daunt, *YWES*, 13 (1932), 61; 14 (1933), 83–84

1151   ——— . "Ae *scerwan.*" *ESt*, 66 (1932), 346. (dct, int, wrd; 769a) Answer to Klaeber [890]. Review: M. Daunt, *YWES*, 13 (1932), 61

1152   ——— . "Altengl. *Ā̆NTĪD* und seine Sippe." *ESt*, 70 (1935–36), 40–45. (int, lng, wrd; 219) Review: D. E. M. Clarke, *YWES*, 16 (1935), 82

1153   ——— . "Altengl. *isig.*" *Anglia*, 56 (1932), 438–39. (int, wrd; 33a)

1154   ——— . "Altenglisches." *Anglia*, 61 (1937), 351–60. (int, lng, wrd; 677)

1155   ——— . *Ibid.*, 63 (1939), 398–99. (int; 3114–15, 3155)

1156   ——— . "Bemerkungen zum *Beowulf.*" *ESt*, 68 (1933), 317–19. (int, lng; 84, 460, 850, 1737, 2079) Review: D. E. M. Clarke, *YWES*, 14 (1933), 87–88

1157   ——— . "*Bēowulf.*" *ESt*, 67 (1932), 161–64. (mth, nam) Review: M. Daunt, *YWES*, 13 (1932), 60

1158   ——— . "*Ealuscerwen* und *Meodoscerwen.*" *ESt*, 67 (1932), 15–23. (int, lng, wrd; 769a)

1159   ——— . "*Orc* und *orcneas.*" *Anglia*, 57 (1933), 396. Reply to Hoops [894]. (wrd; 112)

1160   ———. "Richtigstellung." *ESt*, 70 (1935–36), 323–24. (int, wrd; 224) Reply to Holthausen [868].

1161   KROHMER, W. *Altengl. in und on.* Berlin, 1904. (lng)

1162   KROHN, Kaarle. "Sampsa Pellervoinen < Njordr Freyr?" *Finnisch-Ugrische Forschungen*, 4 (1904), 231–48. (hst, mth) On Scyld.

1163   KRÜGER, Thomas. "Über Ursprung und Entwicklung des Beowulfliedes." *Archiv*, 71 (1884), 129–52. (com, sch)

1164   ———. "Zum *Beowulf*." *Beitr*, 9 (1884), 571–78. (int, lng; 424–26, 524, 744–45, 766, 1546–47, 2359–60, 2362, 2587ff, 2729, 2771, 3151–52)

1165   ———. *Zum Beowulfliede.* Program des städtischen Realgymnasiums Bromberg, 1884. (mtr, sch) Superseded by Wülker [2263].
        Reviews:
          1 F. Kluge, *LGRP*, 5 (1884), 428–29
          2 E. Kölbing, *ESt*, 9 (1886), 150

1166   ———. (Untitled review of Garnett [614]). *ESt*, 8 (1885), 133–38. (int, lng, txt)

1167   KUHN, Hans. "Zur Wortstellung und -betonung im Altgermanischen." *Beitr*, 57 (1933), 1–109. (lng)
        Reviews:
          1 K. Jost, *Beibl*, 47 (1936), 225–31
          2 G. Neckel, *AfdA*, 52 (1933), 161–63

1168   KUHN, Sherman M. "The Sword of Healfdene." *JEGP*, 42 (1943), 82–95. (epc, txt; 1020)
        Review: D. Whitelock, *YWES*, 24 (1943), 33

1169   LABORDE, Edward Dalrymple. "Grendel's Glove and His Immunity from Weapons." *MLR*, 18 (1923), 202–4. (chr, int)

1170   ———. "The Style of *The Battle of Maldon*." *MLR*, 19 (1924), 401–17. (stl)
        Review: E. V. Gordon, *YWES*, 5 (1924), 75–76

†   LA COUR, Vilhelm, see COUR.

1171   LAISTNER, Ludwig. *Nebelsagen.* Stuttgart, 1879. pp. 88ff and 264ff. (chr, mth, smb)

1172   ———. *Das Rätsel der Sphinx: Grundzüge einer Mythengeschichte.* Berlin, 1889. Vol. II, pp. 15–34. (chr, mth)

1173   LAMB, Evelyn M. Hemming. "*Beowulf*: Hemming of Worchester." *N&Q*, 121 (1910), 26. (com, mns)

1174   ——. "*Beowulf* Queries–1." *N&Q*, 149 (1925), 243–44.
(com, mns, nam, txt; 953, 1916, 1665, 2347, 2499, 2562,
2612, 2659, 2680, 2681, 2687)

1175   LANGEBEK, J. "Langfeðgatal fra Noa til varra Konunga."
Scriptores Rerum Danicum Medii Ævi. Copenhagen, 1772. Vol.
I, p. 9, n. R; p. 44, n. E; and p. 2, table I. (Fnb, nam, sch)
About Wanley [2163].

1176   LANGENFELT, Gösta. "*Beowulf* och Fornsverige: Ett
försök till datering av den fornengelska hjältedikten."
Ortnamnssällskapets i Uppsala Årsskrift 1961–1962. pp. 35–55
(1961); 23–38 (1962). (com, hst)

1177   ——. "Notes on the Anglo–Saxon Pioneers: VII. *Beowulf*
Problems." *ESt*, 66 (1931–32), 236–44. (ana, hst, nam)
Review: D. E. M. Clarke, *YWES*, 12 (1931), 77–78

1178   LANIER, Sidney. "Nature in Early English and in Shakespere: *Beowulf* and *Midsummer Night's Dream.*" In his
Shakespere and His Forerunners. N.Y., 1902. Vol. I, pp. 43–74.
(img, thm)

1179   LAPPENBERG, J. M. *Geschichte von England.* Hamburg,
1834. Vol. I. (gen)
Transl. by Benjamin Thorpe as *History of England under the
Anglo–Saxon Kings.* London, 1845. Rev. ed. by E. C. Otté,
London, 1884

1180   ——. (Untitled review of *The Heimskringla; or, Chronicle of
the Kings of Norway* Transl. by Samuel Laing. London,
1845) *Edinburgh Review*, 82 (1845), 267–318. (gen)

†   LARSEN, H. A., see [1594].

1181   LARSEN, Henning. "Wudga: A Study in the Theodoric
Legends." *PQ*, 1 (1922), 128–36. (ana, hst)

1182   LARSON, Laurence Marcellus. *The King's Household in England before the Norman Conquest.* Ph.D. diss., Univ. of Wisconsin, 1904 (hst) Pub. in *Bulletin of the Univ. of Wisconsin*, 100
(1904).

1183   LATTIMORE, Richmond. "Finnsburg." *Hudson Review*,
16 (1963), 50–51. (trl, Fnb only) Translates into alliterat-
ing English verse.
Repr. in his *Stride of Time: New Poems and Translations 1966.*
Ann Arbor, Mich., 1966

†   LAUN, H. van, see [2057].

1184   LAUR, Wolfgang. "Die Heldensage vom Finnsburgkampf."
ZDA, 85 (1954), 107–36. (com, Fnb, hst, int, nam, txt, Fep)

1185   LAWRENCE, John. *Chapters on Alliterative Verse.* London
diss., 1893. (mtr)

Reviews:
  1   K. Luick, *Beibl*, 4 (1893–94), 193–201
  2   E. Sievers, *LitCbl*, 1894, no. 4, col. 124

1186   LAWRENCE, R. F. "The Formulaic Theory and Its Appli-
       cation to English Alliterative Poetry." In Roger Fowler, ed.,
       Essays on Style and Language. London, 1966. pp. 166–83.
       (dct, for)   Refers to Creed [412]; developed by Greenfield
       [669].

1187   LAWRENCE, William Witherle. "Battle of Ravenswood."
       ASR, 22 (1934), 112–17. (hst, mth)

1188   ———. *"Beowulf" and Epic Tradition*. Cambridge, Mass.,
       1928. (ana, bbl, epc, Fnb, gen, hst, mth, sch, str)
       Reviews:
           1   E. Blackman, *RES*, 5 (1929), 333–35
           2   A. G. Brodeur, *Univ. of Calif. Chronicle*, 31 (Jan. 1929),
               97–104
           3   R. W. Chambers, *MLR*, 24 (1929), 334–37
           4   M. Daunt, *YWES*, 9 (1929), 66–67
           5   F. Delatte, *RBPH*, 8 (1929), 1252–54
           6   O. L. Jiriczek, *Beibl*, 40 (1929), 193–202
           7   H. Larsen, *MLN*, 44 (1929), 189–90
           8   K. Malone, *Speculum*, 3 (1928), 612–15 [1405]
       Repr., 1930 with minor alterations
       Repr., London and N.Y., 1961 and 1963
       Review: E. G. Stanley, *MLR*, 57 (1962), 589–91

1189   ———. *"Beowulf* and the *Saga of Samson the Fair."* In *Klaeber*,
       pp. 172–81. (ana, epc, mth, rel, src)
       Review: M. Daunt, *YWES*, 10 (1929), 79

1190   ———. *"Beowulf* and the Tragedy of Finnsburg." *PMLA*, 30
       (1915), 372–431. (Fnb, int; Fep)

1191–1199   Items canceled.

1200   ———. "The Breca Episode in *Beowulf."* In *Kittredge*, pp.
       359–66. (hst, mth)

1201   ———. "The Dragon and His Lair in *Beowulf." PMLA*, 33
       (1918), 547–83. (int, mth)   Reply by Hubbard [912].

1202   ———. "Grendel's Lair." *JEGP*, 38 (1939), 477–80. (ana,
       dct, img, int, mth)   Refutes Mackie [1288].
       Review: G. N. Garmonsway, *YWES*, 20 (1939), 28–29

1203   ———. "The Haunted Mere in *Beowulf." PMLA*, 27 (1912),
       208–45. (ana, mth)   Replies by Hulbert [927] and Mackie
       [1288].

1204   ———. *Medieval Story and the Beginnings of the Social Ideals of the
       English-speaking People*. N.Y., 1911. pp. 27–53. (gen) 2d
       ed., 1926.
       Review: K. Malone, *MLN*, 48 (1933), 482

1205   ——. "Some Disputed Questions in *Beowulf*-Criticism."
         PMLA, 24 (1909), 220–73. (ana, chr, mth)   Answer by
         Brandl [204].

1206   ——. (Untitled review of Sedgefield [1892])   *JEGP*, 10
         (1911), 633–40. (com, int, mth, txt)

1207   ——. (Untitled review of Klaeber [1026])   *JEGP*, 23 (1924),
         294–300. (int, mth)

1208   ——. (Untitled review of Heyne [815], 8th ed.)   *MLN*, 25
         (1910), 155–57. (Fnb, txt, wrd; 601, 817, 902, 1033, 1069ff,
         1107, 1169, 1195, 1799, Fnb 18)

1209   ——. (Untitled review of Panzer [1618])   *MLN*, 27 (1912),
         57–60. (ana, mth)

1210   LEACH, MacEdward. "Beowulf." In *Funk and Wagnalls
         Standard Dictionary of Folklore, Mythology, and Legend*, ed. by
         Maria Leach and Jerome Fried. N.Y., 1949. Vol. I, pp.
         136–37. (ana, mth)

1211   LEAKE, Jane Carol Acomb. "The Geats of *Beowulf*: A
         Study in the Geographical Mythology of the Middle Ages."
         Ph.D. diss., Univ. of Wisconsin, 1963. *DA*, 24 (1963), 1149–
         50. (hst, mth, nam, src)
         Pub. same title, Madison, 1966.

1212   Item canceled.

1213   ——. "Middle English Glosses in the *Beowulf*-Codex."
         MLQ, 23 (1962), 229–32. (mns)
         Review: R. M. Wilson, *YWES*, 43 (1962), 57–58

1214   LEE, Alvin A. "From Grendel to the *Phoenix*: A Critical
         Study of Old English Poetry." Unpub. Ph.D. diss., Univ. of
         Toronto, 1961. (epc, hst, int, mth, rel)

1215   LEGOUIS, Émile, and CAZAMIAN, Louis. *Histoire de la
         littérature anglaise*. Paris, 1924. (gen)
         Review: L. Abercrombie, *YWES*, 5 (1924), 7
         Trans. by H. D. Irvine as *A History of English Literature: The
         Middle Ages and Renascence (650–1660)*. London and Toronto,
         1926.
         Repr. in various forms, 1930, 1933, 1947, 1954

1216   LEHMANN, Edvard. "Fandens Oldemor." *Dania*, 8
         (1901), 179–94. (chr, mth)   On Grendel and his mother.
         In German: "Teufels Grossmutter." *Archiv für Religion-
         swissenschaft*, 8 (1905), 411–30.

1217   LEHMANN, Hans. *Brünne und Helm im angelsächsischen
         Beowulfliede*. Göttingen diss., Leipzig, 1885. (arc, hst)
         Reviews:
             1   F. Schulz, *ESt*, 9 (1886), 471
             2   R. Wülker, *Anglia*, 8 Anz., (1885), 167–70

1218   ——. "Über die Waffen im angelsächsischen Beowulfliede."
        Germania, 31 (1886), 486–97. (arc, hst)

1219   LEHMANN, Winfred Philipp, and TABUSA, Takemitsu.
        The Alliterations of the "Beowulf." Austin, Tex., 1958. (dct,
        for, mtr, ref, stl)

1220   ——. "*Beowulf* 33, *isig.*" *MLN*, 74 (1959), 577–78. (dct,
        mth, wrd; 33a)
        Review: R. M. Wilson, *YWES*, 40 (1959), 61

1221   ——. "*Beowulf* 2298." In *Wolff*, pp. 107–10. (int, lng, txt;
        2298)

1222   ——. *The Development of Germanic Verse Form.* Austin, Tex.,
        1956. (ken, mtr)
        Review: R. M. Wilson, *YWES*, 37 (1956), 71

1223   ——. "The *Finnsburg Fragment* 34a: 'Hwearflacra hraer.'"
        Univ. of Texas Studies in English, 34 (1955), 1–5 (Fnb, int, lng,
        txt; Fnb 34a)

1224   LEHNERT, Martin. *Beowulf: Eine Auswahl mit Einführung,
        teilweiser Übersetzung, Anmerkungen, und etymologischem Wörter-
        buch.* Berlin, 1939. (edt, nts, trl) 1044 lines.
        Reviews:
            1   K. Brunner, *Beibl*, 52 (1941), 51–54
            2   W. Horn, *Archiv*, 178 (1943), 47
        2d ed., 1949; 3d ed., 1959; 4th ed., 1966

1225   LEICHER, Richard. *Die Totenklage in der deutschen Epik von
        der ältesten Zeit bis zur Nibelungen-Klage.* Germanistische
        Abhandlungen 58. Breslau, 1927. (ana, epc)

1226   LEISI, Ernst. "Gold und Manneswert im *Beowulf.*" *Anglia*,
        71 (1952–53), 259–73. (hst, mth)
        Review: R. M. Wilson, *YWES*, 34 (1953), 48

1227   Item canceled.

1228   LEO, Heinrich. *Altsächsische und Angelsächsische Sprachproben.*
        Halle, 1838. pp. 88–92. (edt; 1063–1162a)

1229   ——. Bëówulf: Das älteste deutsche, in angelsächsischer
        *Mundart erhaltene Heldengedicht nach seinem Inhalte, und nach seinen
        historischen und mythologischen Beziehungen betrachtet: Ein Beitrag
        zur Geschichte alter deutscher Geisteszustände.* Halle, 1839. (com,
        hst, mth, par) Chap. V is a selected German prose para-
        phrase from Kemble text [989].

1230   LEONARD, William Ellery. *Beowulf: A New Verse Transla-
        tion for Fireside and Classroom.* London and N.Y., 1923. (gen,
        Fnb, trl)
        Reviews:
            1   *Archiv*, 147 (1924), 300
            2   M. W. Croll, *Literary Review*, 7 July 1923, p. 811

3   F. Klaeber, *Beibl*, 34 (1923), 321–23

4   L. Lewisohn, *Nation* (N.Y.), 6 June 1923, p. 660
Reissued as *The Random House "Beowulf,"* illustrated by Rockwell Kent. N.Y., 1932
Review: *SR*, 9 May 1932, p. 659
Re-issued as *Beowulf*, illustrated by Lynd Ward. N.Y., 1939

1231   ———. *"Beowulf* and the *Nibelungen* Couplet." *UWSLL*, 2 (1918), 99–152.   (mtr, trl)   Translates 559–661 into *Nibelungen* couplets.
Review: F. Klaeber, *Beibl*, 32 (1921), 145–48 [1068]

1232   ———. "Four Footnotes to Papers on Germanic Metrics." In *Klaeber*, pp. 1–13.   (mtr)

1233   ———. "The Recovery of the Metre of the *Cid.*" *PMLA*, 46 (1931), 289–306.   (mtr)
Another version in Spanish: *Revista de Archivos*, 32 (1928), 334–52; 34 (1930), 16–40; 35 (1931), 195–210, 302–28, 401–21

1234   ———. "The Scansion of Middle English Alliterative Verse." *UWSLL*, 11 (1920), 57–103.   (mtr, trl)

1235   LEPAGE, R. B. "Alliterative Patterns as a Test of Style in Old English Poetry." *JEGP*, 58 (1959), 434–41.   (mtr, stl)

1236   ———. "A Rhythmical Framework for the Five Types." *EGS*, 6 (1957), 92–103.   (mtr)   Modification of Pope [1662].
Review: R. M. Wilson, *YWES*, 38 (1957), 73

1237   LEVANDER, Lars. "Sagotraditioner om Sveakonungen Adils." *ATS*, 18 (1908).   (ana, chr, hst, mth, nam)   On Eadgils.

1238   LEVINE, Robert. "Direct Discourse in *Beowulf:* Its Meaning and Function." Unpub. Ph.D. diss., Univ. of California at Berkeley, 1962–63. *DA*, 24 (1964), 4191–92.   (rht, str, tec)

1239   LEWIS, C. M. "Notes on Transverse Alliteration." *MLN*, 16 (1901), 43–44, or cols. 85–88.   (mtr)   Opposes Emerson [531].

1240   LEWIS, Clives Staples. *A Preface to "Paradise Lost."* London, 1942. pp. 12–18, 19, 24–25.   (dct, epc, tec)

1241   LEYEN, Friedrich von der. *Deutsche Philologie: Eine Einführung in ihr Studium.* Stuttgart, 1952. pp. 98–99.   (epc, gen)

1242   ———. *Die Deutschen Heldensage.* Munich, 1912. pp. 107–23, 345–47.   (gen)

1243   LEYERLE, John. "Beowulf the Hero and King." *MAE*, 34 (1965), 89–102.   (chr, int, str, tec, thm)

1244   LICHTENHELD, A. "Das schwache Adjectiv im Angel-
       sächsischen." *ZDA*, 16 (1873), 325–93. (com, lng)

1245   LIEBERMANN, F. "Grendel als Personenname." *Archiv*,
       126 (1911), 180. (nam)

1246   ——. "Ort und Zeit der Beowulfdichtung." *Nachrichten von
       der Königl. Gesellschaft der Wissenschaften zu Göttingen, Philologie-
       historische Klasse*, 1920, 253–76. (com, hst, nam)
       Reviews:
           1   A. Brandl, *Archiv*, 141 (1921), 307–8
           2   E. Ekwall, *Beibl*, 33 (1922), 67–69

1247   ——. "Zu *Beowulf*, v. 770." *Archiv*, 143 (1922), 247–48.
       (hst, int; 769)

1248   LIESTØL, Knut. "*Beowulf* and Epic Tradition." *ASR*, 18
       (1930), 370–73. (ana, epc)   On waterfall trolls.

1249   LINDENSCHMIT, L. *Handbuch der deutschen Alterthumskunde*.
       Part I. *Die Alterthümer der merovingischen Zeit*. Brunswick,
       1880–89. (hst)

1250   LINDERHOLM, E. "Vendelshögens konunganamn i sock-
       nens 1600–tals tradition." *NB*, 7 (1919), 36–40. (hst, nam)

1251   LINDQVIST, Sune. "*Beowulf*" *Dissectus: Snitt ur fornkvädet
       jämte svensk tydning av Sune Lindqvist*. Uppsala, 1958. (bbl,
       com, hst, nts, trl, txt)   With English summary, pp. 137–42.
       Partial translation into Swedish.

1252   ——. *Hednatemplet i Uppsala*. *Fornvännen*, 18 (1923). (hst)
       Heorot and wooden churches.

1253   ——. "Sutton Hoo och *Béowulf*." *Fornvännen*, 43 (1948),
       94–110 (arc, com, hst, img)   With English summary.
       Trans. by Rupert L. S. Bruce–Mitford as "Sutton Hoo and
       Beowulf." *Antiquity*, 22 (1948), 131–40. Abridged and foot-
       noted by the translator.
       Review: R. M. Wilson, *YWES*, 29 (1948), 59–60

1254   ——. "Uppsala Högar och Ottarshögen." *Kungl. Vitterhets
       Hist. och Ant. Akademien*. Stockholm, 1936. (arc)
       Review: T. D. Kendrick, *Antiquity*, 11 (1937), 247–48

1255   ——. "Vendelhjälmarnas ursprung: De Koniska hjälmarna
       hos de utomnordiska folken under folkvandringstiden."
       Fornvännen, 20 (1925), 181–207, 227–40. (arc, hst)

1256   ——. "Ynglingaättens Gravskick." *Fornvännen*, 16 (1921),
       83–194. (arc, hst)

†   ——, see [32].

1257   LINDROTH, Hjalmar. "Är Skåne de gamles Scadinavia?"
       NB, 3 (1915), 10–28. (hst, nam)   Replies by Kock [1090],
       Noreen [1575], and Björkman [118].

1258   ——. "Äro Scadinavia och Skåne samma Ord." *ANF*, 35
        (1918), 29–47. (hst, nam) Reply to Kock [1090], Noreen
        [1575], and Björkman [118]; reply by Kock [1091].

1259   ——. "Skandinavien och Skåne." *NB*, 6 (1918), 104–12.
        (hst, nam) Reply to Kock [1090], Noreen [1575], and
        Björkman [118]; reply by Kock [1091].

  †   LOCKE, Louis G., see [33].

1260   LOHR, Evelyn. "Patristic Demonology in Old English
        Literature." Ph.D. diss., New York Univ., 1947. *DDABAU*,
        1946–47, no. 14, 82. (img, smb, src)
        Issued in separate, abridged ed., N.Y., 1949
        Review: A. H. C. Meertens, *ES*, 31 (1950), 124–25

1261   [LONGFELLOW, Henry Wadsworth.] "Anglo–Saxon
        Literature." *North American Review*, 47 (1838), 90–134.
        (Fnb, gen, trl) Translates into English verse lines 18–40,
        53–83, 189–257, 1789–1803, 2455–62, based on Conybeare
        [356].
        Repr. in his *Poets and Poetry of Europe*. Cambridge and
        Philadelphia, 1845; N.Y., 1857. pp. 1–10. 2d ed., 1871;
        repr. 1896
        Repr. in his *Collected Prose*. Boston, 1857. Vol. I, pp. 384–
        411. Rev. ed., 1866; repr., Boston and N.Y., 1886; repr.,
        Boston, 1894.

1262   LOOMIS, Roger S. *Introduction to Medieval Literature, Chiefly
        in England.* N.Y. and Oxford, 1948. (ref)
        Review: R. M. Wilson, *YWES*, 29 (1948), 57

1263   LORD, Albert Bates. "Beowulf and Odysseus." In
        Magoun, pp. 86–91. (ana, for, src)

1264   ——. "Homer and Other Epic Poetry." In Alan J. B.
        Wace and F. H. Stubbings, eds., *A Companion to Homer.* Lon-
        don and N.Y., 1963. pp. 179–214. (epc, for, mth, mtr)

1265   ——. *The Singer of Tales.* Cambridge, Mass., 1960. (ana,
        epc, for)
        Review: A. Campbell, *MLR*, 57 (1962), 75–76
        Repr. 1964, in paperback 1965

1266   LORZ, Anton. *Aktionsarten des Verbums im "Beowulf."*
        Würzberg diss., 1908. (lng)

1267   LOTSPEICH, C. M. "Old English Etymologies." *JEGP*,
        40 (1941), 1–4. (lng, wrd; 224)

1268   LOTSPEICH, Henry G. "*Beowulf* 1363, *hrinde bearwas*."
        JEGP, 29 (1930), 367–69. (Mth; 1363b)
        Review: M. Daunt, *YWES*, 11 (1930), 55

1269   LÜBKE, H. (Untitled review of Cosijn [389]) *AfdA*, 19 (1893), 341–42. (dct, lng, txt, wrd; 305, 1064)

1270   LUECKE, (Sister) Jane Marie. "Meter and the Free Rhythm of *Beowulf*." Unpub. Ph.D. diss., Notre Dame Univ., 1964. *DA*, 25 (1964), 2495–96. (mns, mtr)

1271   LUEHRS, Phoebe M. "Summary of Sarrazin's Studies in *Beowulf*." *Bulletin of Western Reserve Univ.*, 7 (1904), 146–65. (com, Fnb, gen, lng, mth, sch, src, stl) Summarizes Sarrazin [1770].

1272   LUICK, Karl. *Englische Metrik: Geschichte der heimischen Versarten*. PGrdr, II, 994. (mtr)
        2d ed., II, 2 (1905), 141–60

1272.1 ——. "Über den Versbau des angelsächsischen Gedichtes *Judith*." *Beitr*, 11 (1886), 470–92. (mtr)

1273   ——. "Zur ae. und alts. Metrik (Schwellvers und Normalvers, Alliteration und Versrhythmus)." *Beitr*, 15 (1891), 441–54. (mtr; 375, 1023, 1969, 2388, 2432, 2476, 2673, 2775) Opposes Kauffmann [979].

1274   LUKMAN, N. C. *Skjoldunge und Skilfinge, Hunnen- und Herulerkönig in ostnordischer Überlieferung*. Copenhagen, 1943. (hst)

1275   LUMIANSKY, Robert M. "The Contexts of O.E. 'ealuscerwen' and 'meoduscerwen.'" *JEGP*, 48 (1949), 116–26. (int; 769a)

1276   ——. "The Dramatic Audience in *Beowulf*." *JEGP*, 51 (1952), 545–50. (tec)
        Review: R. M. Wilson, *YWES*, 33 (1952), 40

1277   ——. "Wiglaf." *CE*, 14 (1953), 202–6. (chr, thm)

1278   LUMSDEN, Henry William. *Beowulf: An Old English Poem, Translated into Modern Rhymes*. London, 1881. (Fnb, nts, trl) Partial trans. of *Beowulf* and *Finnsburh* into English ballad measure. Based on Grein [675] and Arnold [36].
        Reviews:
            1   *Athenaeum*, April 1881, p. 587
            2   *WR*, 119 (1883), 298–99
            3   J. M. Garnett, *AJPhil*, 2 (1881), 355–61 [617]
            4   F. Y. Powell, *Academy*, 19 (1881), 273
            5   R. Wülker, *Anglia*, 4 Anz. (1881), 69–78 [2261]
        2d ed., 1883, rev. and corrected, complete trans.
        Reviews:
            1   *SRL*, 57 (1884), 583
            2   F. Y. Powell, *Academy*, 26 (1884), 220–21 [1668]

 †   LUNDBERG, Oskar, see [32].

1279   LUNING, Otto. *Die Natur ihre Auffassung und poetische Verwendung in der altgermanischen und mittelhochdeutschen Epik bis zum Abschluss der Blütezeit.* Zurich, 1889. (thm)
Reviews:
  1   E. Ballerstedt; *AfdA*, 16 (1890), 71–74
  2   O. Frankel, *LGRP*, 11 (1890), 439–44
  3   W. Golther, *DLZ*, 10 (1889), 710–12
  4   K. Weinhold, *ZDP*, 22 (1890), 246–47

1280   LUSSKY, George F. "The Verb Forms Circumscribed with the Perfect Participle in the *Beowulf.*" *JEGP*, 21 (1922), 32–69. (lng)

1281   LYONS, Clifford P. "A Note on *Beowulf* 760." *MLN*, 46 (1931), 443–44. (int; 760)
Review: D. E. M. Clarke, *YWES*, 12 (1931), 71–72

[For names beginning with *Mc*, see after *My.*]

1282   MacCULLOCH, John Arnott. *The Mythology of All Races.* Boston, 1930. Vol. II, *Eddic.* (mth)

1283   MacDONALD, A. "An Anglo-Saxon Survival?" *N&Q*, 206 (1961), 47–48. (ana; 612–14, 620–22, 2020–21)
Review: A. MacDonald and B. Hill, *YWES*, 42 (1963), 63

1284   Item canceled.

 †   MacDOWALL, M. W., see [2159].

1285   MACKAYE, Percy. *Beowulf: An Epical Drama of Anglo-Saxon Times.* Leipzig, 1899. Play based on the poem.

1286   MacKENZIE, Donald A. (Untitled note) *TLS*, 23 Nov. 1935, p. 770. (ana) Reply to Davies [447].
Review: D. E. M. Clarke, *YWES*, 16 (1935), 81

1287   Item canceled.

1288   MACKIE, W. S. "The Demons' Home in *Beowulf.*" *JEGP*, 37 (1938), 455–61. (ana, int, tec; 1359, 1516) Attacks Lawrence [1203]; reply by Lawrence [1202].
Review: C. L. Wrenn, *YWES*, 19 (1938), 50

1289   ——. "The Fight at Finnsburg." *JEGP*, 16 (1917), 250–73. (com, edt, nts, txt, Fnb only)

1290   ——. *Ibid. MLR*, 17 (1922), 288. (txt, Fnb only; Fnb 35, 40) Opposes Sedgefield [1897].

1291   ——. "Notes on O.E. Poetry: III. *Beowulf*, ll. 223–4." *MLR*, 21 (1926), 301. (int, txt; 223b)
Review: M. Daunt, *YWES*, 7 (1926), 70

1292   ——. "Notes upon the Text and the Interpretation of
          Beowulf." *MLR*, 34 (1939), 515–24. (Fnb, int, txt; 1142)
          Review: G. N. Garmonsway, *YWES*, 20 (1939), 27–28

1293   ——. "Notes upon the Text and Interpretation of *Beowulf:*
          II." *MLR*, 36 (1941), 95–98. (int, txt; 2266, 2588, 2863)
          Review: G. N. Garmonsway, *YWES*, 22 (1941), 47 [611]

1294   MAGOUN, Francis Peabody, Jr. "Abbreviated Titles for
          the Poems of the Anglo–Saxon Poetic Corpus." *EA*, 8
          (1955), 138–46. (Fnb, ref)
          Review: R. M. Wilson, *YWES*, 36 (1955), 59

1295   ——. "*Béowulf Á:* A Folk-Variant." *Arv*, 14 (1958), 95–
          101. (ana, com, str; 2009b–2176) Answer by Witke [2227].

1296   ——. "*Beowulf*" *and* "*Judith*": *Done in a Normalized Ortho-
          graphy.* Cambridge, Mass., 1959. (edt, Fnb, txt) Expan-
          sion of his [1307], based on Wrenn [2244].
          2d ed., rev. by J. B. Bessinger, Jr.   Harvard Old English
          Series, I.   1966

1297   ——. "Beowulf and King Hygelac in the Netherlands."
          ES, 35 (1954), 193–204. (ana, hst, src)
          Review: R. M. Wilson, *YWES*, 35 (1954), 40

1298   ——. "*Béowulf B:* A Folk-Poem on Béowulf's Death." In
          Smith, pp. 127–40. (chr, com, for, int, mtr, str; 1845–53,
          2183–89, 2430–34)
          Review: R. M. Wilson, *YWES*, 44 (1963), 73

1299   ——. "Beowulf in Denmark: An Italo-Brazilian Variant."
          In *Mossé*, pp. 247–55. (ana) Concerns [25].
          Review: R. M. Wilson, *YWES*, 40 (1959), 61

1300   ——. "The Burning of Heorot: An Illustrative Note."
          MLN, 42 (1927), 173–74. (ana; 82–83)
          Review: M. Daunt, *YWES*, 8 (1927), 84

1301   ——. "Danes, North, South, East, and West, in *Beowulf.*"
          In *Malone*, pp. 20–24. (dct, hst, nam; 383, 392, 463, 616,
          783, 828, 1578, 1996)
          Review: R. M. Wilson, *YWES*, 30 (1949), 42

1302   ——. "The Geography of Hygelac's Raid on the Lands of
          the West Frisians and Hætt-ware, ca. 530 A.D." *ES*, 34
          (1953), 160–63. (hst)
          Review: R. M. Wilson, *YWES*, 34 (1953), 48

1303   ——. "*Inwlatide < Onfunde?*" *MLN*, 68 (1953), 540–41.
          (ana, int, txt; 2226b) Concurs with Dobbie [482].
          Review: R. M. Wilson, *YWES*, 34 (1953), 48

1304   ——. "A Note on Old West-Germanic Poetic Unity." *MP*,
          43 (1945), 77–82. (ana, hst)
          Review: M. Daunt, *YWES*, 26 (1945), 44

1305   ——. "The Old-Germanic Altar- or Oath-Ring (*Stalla-hringr*)." *APS*, 20 (1949), 277–93. (hst; 1204–13)

1306   ——. "The Oral-formulaic Character of Anglo–Saxon Narrative Poetry." *Speculum*, 28 (1953), 446–67. (dct, for)
Replies by Rogers [1728.1] and Fry [591].
Review: R. M. Wilson, *YWES*, 34 (1953), 45
Repr. in Nicholson [1560], pp. 189–221

1307   ——. *The Poems of British Museum MS. Cotton Vitellius A. XV: "Beowulf" (fol. 132a–201b) and "Judith" (fol. 202b–209b).* Cambridge, Mass., 1955. (edt, Fnb) Based on Wrenn [2244], and see [1296].

1308   ——. "Readings from the *Beowulf*." Harvard Vocarium LP Record no. L6000–01, 1950. (Recording)

1309   ——. "Recurring First Elements in Different Nominal Compounds in *Beowulf* and in the *Elder Edda*." In *Klaeber*, pp. 73–78. (dct, img, nam) Answer by Hulbert [926].
Review: M. Daunt, *YWES*, 10 (1929), 76

1310   ——. "Some Notes on Anglo–Saxon Poetry." In *Baugh*, pp. 273–83. (Fnb, for; 235–36, 1024–26, 1046–49, 1880–85, 1900–1903, Fnb 1–7)

1311   ——. "The Sutton Hoo Ship-Burial: A Chronological Bibliography." *Speculum*, 29 (1954), 116–24. (arc, bbl, hst)
Continued by Bessinger [103].

1312   ——. "The Theme of the Beasts of Battle in Anglo–Saxon Poetry." *NM*, 56 (1955), 81–90. (Fnb, for, img, thm; 3024–27)
Review: R. M. Wilson, *YWES*, 36 (1955), 59

1313   ——. "Two Verses in the Old English "Waldere" Characteristic of Oral Poetry." *Beitr*, 80 (1958), 214–18. (for)

1314   ——. "Zu *Etzeln Burc*, *Finns Buruh* und *Brunan-Burh*." *ZDA*, 77 (1940), 65–66. (nam)

1315   ——. "Zum heroischen Exorzismus des Beowulfepos." *ANF*, 54 (1938–39), 215–28. (mth) Refutes Hübener [913] and [916].
Review: G. N. Garmonsway, *YWES*, 20 (1939), 29

  †   ——, see [719].

1316   MALONE, Kemp. "*Beowulf*." *ES*, 29 (1948), 161–72. (gen, rel, smb, str, tec)
Review: R. M. Wilson, *YWES*, 29 (1948), 57–58
Repr. in F. H. Horn, ed., *Literary Masterpieces of the Western World*. Baltimore, 1953
Review: T. S. Dorsch, *YWES*, 34 (1953), 17
Repr. in Nicholson [1560], pp. 137–54

1317   ——. "Beowulfiana." *MAE*, 2 (1933), 58–64. (lng, txt; 304, 645–51, 3005, 3074) On Hoops [894].
Review: D. E. M. Clarke, *YWES*, 14 (1933), 86–87

1318   ——. "The Burning of Heorot." *RES*, 13 (1937), 462–63. (ana, hst, int) Opposes Girvan [636].
Review: D. E. M. Clarke, *YWES*, 18 (1937), 54–55

1319   ——. "Coming Back from the Mere." *PMLA*, 69 (1954), 1292–99. (str, tec)
Review: R. M. Wilson, *YWES*, 35 (1954), 40

1320   ——. "Danes and Half-Danes." *ANF*, 42 (1926), 234–40. (hst, nam; 1069, 1076)
Review: M. Daunt, *YWES*, 7 (1926), 51–52

1321   ——. "The Daughter of Healfdene." In *Klaeber*, pp. 135–58. (chr, hst, nam, txt; 62)
Review: M. Daunt, *YWES*, 10 (1929), 78–79
Repr. in *SHL & CS*, pp. 124–41

1322   ——. "Ealhhild." *Anglia*, 55 (1931), 266–72. (chr, nam)

1323   ——. "Ecgtheow." *MLQ*, 1 (1940), 37–44. (chr, nam, txt; 262–66, 372–76, 459–72, 2428–33)
Review: D. Whitelock, *YWES*, 23 (1942), 37–38

1324   ——. "Eleven *Beowulf* Notes." In *Flasdieck*, pp. 192–99. (int, txt; 4–5, 9–10, 15, 62, 101, 194–95, 247, 445, 461, 1015, 2032–66, 2041, 2042)
Review: R. M. Wilson, *YWES*, 41 (1960), 55

1325   ——. "Epithets and Eponym." *Names*, 2 (1954), 109–12. (nam) Reply to Ramsay [1683].
Repr. in *SHL & CS*, pp. 189–92

1326   ——. "The Finn Episode in *Beowulf*." *JEGP*, 25 (1926), 157–72. (chr, Fnb, int, trl, txt; Fep)
Review: M. Daunt, *YWES*, 7 (1926), 52–54

1327   ——. "The Finn Episode Once Again." In *Fischer*, pp. 1–3. (int; Fep, 1125–29)
Reviews:
    1 T. S. Dorsch, *YWES*, 40 (1959), 17
    2 R. M. Wilson, *YWES*, 40 (1959), 61

1328   ——. "Finn's Stronghold." *MP*, 43 (1945), 83–85. (Fnb, img, int, lng; 1125–27a, 2252)
Review: M. Daunt, *YWES*, 26 (1945), 39–40

1329   ——. "Finnsburg." In his *Ten Old English Poems Put into Modern English Alliterative Verse*. Baltimore, 1941. pp. 25–26. (Fnb, nts, trl) Based on Klaeber [1026].
Reviews:
    1 R. Humphries, *Nation*, 153 (1941), 97
    2 G. Scarborough, *SR*, 100 (1942), 264–65

1330 ——. "Freawaru." *ELH*, 7 (1940), 39–44. (chr, hst, nam)
Review: D. Whitelock, *YWES*, 23 (1942), 37
Repr. in *SHL & CS*, pp. 197–201

1331 ——. "Grendel and Grep." *PMLA*, 57 (1942), 1–14.
(ana, chr, hst, mth, src)
Review: D. Whitelock, *YWES*, 23 (1942), 38

1332 ——. "Grendel and His Abode." In *Spitzer*, pp. 297–308.
(ana, img, rel)
Review: R. M. Wilson, *YWES*, 40 (1959), 60–61

1333 ——. "Grundtvig as *Beowulf* Critic." *RES*, 17 (1941), 129–
38. (sch) Answer by Haarder [728].
Review: G. N. Garmonsway, *YWES*, 22 (1941), 46

1334 ——. "Grundtvigs oversættelse af Beowulf." *Grundtvig
Studier*, (1960), 7–25. (sch, about trl)
Review: R. M. Wilson, *YWES*, 41 (1960), 55

1335 ——. "Grundtvig's Philosophy of History." *JHI*, 1 (1940),
281–98. (hst, sch)

1336 ——. "Hagbard and Ingeld." In *Brown*, pp. 1–22. (ana,
chr, nam; 82–84, 2047–52)
Repr. in *SHL & CS*, pp. 63–81

1337 ——. "Healfdene." *ESt*, 70 (1935–36), 74–76. (chr, hst,
nam; 1069)
Review: D. E. M. Clarke, *YWES*, 16 (1935), 82–83

1338 ——. "Hildeburg and Hengest." *ELH*, 10 (1943), 257–84.
(chr, Fnb, int; Fep)
Review: D. Whitelock, *YWES*, 24 (1943), 31

1339 ——. "Hrethric." *PMLA*, 42 (1927), 268–313. (chr, hst)
Review: M. Daunt, *YWES*, 8 (1927), 81–82

1340 ——. "Humblus and Lotherus." *SHL & CS*, pp. 168–80.
(chr, hst, nam)
Review: G. N. Garmonsway, *YWES*, 20 (1939), 29–30

1341 ——. "Hunlafing." *MLN*, 43 (1928), 300–304. (int, nam;
1143)
Review: M. Daunt, *YWES*, 9 (1928), 70

1342 ——. "Hygd." *MLN*, 56 (1941), 356–58. (chr, int, nam;
1926, 1932)
Review: G. N. Garmonsway, *YWES*, 22 (1941), 46

1343 ——. "Hygelac." *ES*, 21 (1939), 108–19. (ana, chr, hst,
nam)

1344 ——. "The Identity of the *Geatas*." *APS*, 4 (1929–30),
84–90. (hst, nam) Reply to Wadstein [2156].
Review: M. Daunt, *YWES*, 10 (1929), 89–90

1345 ——. "*Ifarr* and *Inwaer*." *PMLA*, 45 (1930), 626–28. (chr,
hst) Opposes Cawley [297]; reply by Cawley [298].

1346 ——. "Ingeld." *MP*, 27 (1929–30), 257–76. (ana, hst, int)
See his [1360] and [1384], and Woolf [2235]
Review: M. Daunt, *YWES*, 11 (1930), 53.

1347 ——. "The Kenning in *Beowulf* 2220." *JEGP*, 27 (1928),
318–24. (ken, mtr, txt; 2220a)
Review: M. Daunt, *YWES*, 9 (1928), 70

1348 ——. "King Alfred's 'Geats.'" *MLR*, 20 (1925), 1–11.
(hst)
Review: E. V. Gordon, *YWES*, 6 (1925), 77–78

1349 ——. "King Alfred's Götland." *MLR*, 23 (1928), 336–39.
(hst)

1350 ——. "King Aun in the Rök Inscription." *MLN*, 39
(1924), 223–26. (ana, chr, hst, nam)

1351 ——. "Last Word." *Beibl*, 44 (1933), 192. (int, lng, wrd)
Reply to Holthausen [870].

1352 ——. "Lift-Patterns in Old English Verse." *ELH*, 8
(1941), 74–80. (mtr)
Review: D. Whitelock, *YWES*, 23 (1942), 34–35

1353 ——. *The Literary History of "Hamlet."* I. *The Early Tradition.*
Heidelberg, 1923. (chr, Fnb, hst, mth)   See Woolf [2235].
Reviews:
    1 *LitCbl*, 74 (1923), 485
    2 A. L. R. Andrews, *PQ*, 3 (1924), 318–20; reply by
    Malone, *PQ*, 4 (1925), 158–60
    3 W. D. Briggs, *JEGP*, 24 (1925), 413–24 [215]

1354 ——. "A Note on *Beowulf* 377ff." *MLN*, 68 (1953), 354–56.
(int, lng; 377ff)
Review: R. M. Wilson, *YWES*, 34 (1953), 48

1355 ——. "A Note on *Beowulf* 489–90." *MLR*, 56 (1961), 212.
(int, txt; 489–90)
Review: R. M. Wilson, *YWES*, 42 (1963), 58

1356 ——. "A Note on *Beowulf* 1231." *MLN*, 41 (1926), 466–67.
(int, tec, txt; 1231)
Review: M. Daunt, *YWES*, 7 (1926), 62

1357 ——. "A Note on *Beowulf* 2466." *JEGP*, 50 (1951), 19–21.
(txt; 2466)

1358 ——. "A Note on *Beowulf* 2928 and 2932." *PQ*, 8 (1929),
406–7. (chr, hst, int, nam, txt; 2928, 2932)
Review: M. Daunt, *YWES*, 10 (1929), 91

1359 ——. "A Note on *Beowulf* l. 1379." *MLR*, 25 (1930), 191.
(mtr, txt; 1379a)
Review: M. Daunt, *YWES*, 11 (1930), 55

1360   ——. "A Note on *Beowulf*, l. 2034." *MLR*, 24 (1929), 322–
        23. (lng, txt; 2034a) See his [1346].
        Review: M. Daunt, *YWES*, 10 (1929), 90

1361   ——. "Note on *Grottasǫngr*." *APS*, 4 (1929), 270. (ana,
        chr, hst) On Halfdane.

1362   ——. "Notes on *Beowulf*." *Anglia*, 69 (1950), 295–300.
        (chr, int; 2183–89) Reply to Bonjour [159], pp. 24–27; reply
        by Bonjour [169].
        Review: R. M. Wilson, *YWES*, 31 (1950), 46

1363   ——. "Notes on *Beowulf:* I." *Anglia*, 53 (1929), 335–36,
        439. (lng, mtr, txt, wrd; 51b, 106, 1026, 1142)
        Review: M. Daunt, *YWES*, 10 (1929), 92

1364   ——. "Notes on *Beowulf:* II, III, IV." *Anglia*, 54 (1930),
        1–7. (int, txt; 2003, 2542–44, 3005, 3058–60, 3066–75)
        Review: M. Daunt, *YWES*, 11 (1930), 54–55

1365   ——. "Notes on *Beowulf:* V." *Anglia*, 54 (1930), 97–98.
        (int, lng, wrd; 2003, 2542)

1366   ——. "Notes on *Beowulf:* VI." *Anglia*, 56 (1932), 436–37.
        (int, ken, nam; 1710)
        Review: M Daunt, *YWES*, 13 (1932), 61

1367   ——. "Notes on *Beowulf:* VII." *Anglia*, 57 (1933), 218–20.
        (int; 2061)
        Review: D. E. M. Clarke, *YWES*, 14 (1933), 88

1368   ——. "Notes on *Beowulf:* VIII." *Anglia*, 57 (1933), 313–16.
        (int, lng; 982, 1011, 1068, 2076, 2817, 2957, 3134)
        Review: D. E. M. Clarke, *YWES*, 14 (1933), 88

1369   ——. "Notes on *Beowulf:* IX–XI." *Anglia*, 63 (1939), 103–
        12. (int, nam, txt; 1176, 1944, 1961, 2034–35, 2466)
        Review: G. N. Garmonsway, *YWES*, 20 (1939), 25–26

1370   ——. "Notes on *Beowulf:* XII–XIII." *Anglia*, 65 (1941),
        227–29 (int, lng, txt)

1371   —— *The Nowell Codex: British Museum Cotton Vitellius A.
        XV, Second MS.* Early English Manuscripts in Facsimile, 12.
        Copenhagen, 1963. (edt, mns, txt) Facsimile of [226], same
        negatives as [2278], 2d ed.
        Reviews:
            1 L. D. Benson, *Speculum*, 39 (1964), 722–23
            2 N. F. Blake, *Anglia*, 83 (1965), 230–33
            3 M. D. Clubb, *PQ*, 43 (1964), 558–67
            4 N. Davis, *RES*, 16 (1965), 409–11
            5 J. D. A. Ogilvy, *ELN*, 1 (1964), 295–96
            6 R. M. Wilson, *YWES*, 44 (1963), 70

1372   ——. "The OE Sound-Shift ē > ī Once More." *Beibl*, 44 (1933), 190–91. (int, lng, wrd; 3173)   Reply to Holthausen [851] and his reply [870].

1373   ——. "Old English *beagas*." *Beibl*, 52 (1941), 179–80. (int, lng, wrd; 1528, 2041, 2055, 2635)

1374   ——. "Old English *(Ge)hȳdan* 'Heed.'" In *Jespersen*, pp. 45–54. (lng, wrd; 2235, 3059)   Reply by Holthausen [880.1]
        Review: M. Daunt, *YWES*, 11 (1930), 61–62

1375   ——. *The Old English Period*. In A. C. Baugh, ed., *A Literary History of England*. London and N.Y., 1948.   Book I, part 1, pp. 1–105.   (Fnb, gen, mtr, stl)
        Reviews:
            1   C. Duffy, *NYTBR*, 23 May 1948, p. 25
            2   D. Ferguson, *NYHTB*, 2 May 1948, p. 11
            3   R. M. Wilson, *YWES*, 29 (1948), 56–57
        2d ed., 1967; adds 7 pages of bibliography

1376   ——. "On *Finnsburg* 39." *RES*, 21 (1945), 126–27.   (Fnb, txt; Fnb 39)
        Review: M. Daunt, *YWES*, 26 (1945), 40

1377   ——. "On the OE Sound-shift *ē* > *ī*." *Beibl*, 43 (1932), 284–87. (int, lng, wrd; 3173)   Restatement of his [1374]; reply by Holthausen [851].

1378   ——. "Readings from the Thorkelin Transcripts of *Beowulf*." *PMLA*, 64 (1949), 1190–1218. (mns, txt)   Collation of Thorkelin [2081–82] and Zupitza [2278].
        Review: R. M. Wilson, 30 (1949), 42

1379   ——. "Royal Names in Old English Poetry." *Names*, 1 (1953), 153–62. (nam)   Answer to R. L. Ramsay, *Names*, 1 (1953), 20–29; answer by Ramsay [1683].
        Repr. in *SHL & CS*, pp. 181–88

1380   ——. "Some *Beowulf* Readings." In *Magoun*, pp. 120–23. (mns, txt; 1228–29, 2223–27, 2339ff, 3150ff, 3174ff)

1381   ——. "The Suffix of Appurtenance in *Widsith*." *MLR*, 28 (1933), 315–25. (hst, lng, nam; 2494)

1382   ——. "Swerting." *GR*, 14 (1939), 235–57. (ana, txt; 1960)

1383   ——. "Symbolism in *Beowulf*: Some Suggestions." *English Studies Today*, 2d series. (1959), 81–91. (chr, smb)
        Review: T. S. Dorsch, *YWES*, 42 (1963), 14–15

1384   ——. "The Tale of Ingeld." *SHL & CS*, pp. 1–62. (ana, hst, int)   Rev. version of his [1346].
        Review: R. M. Wilson, *YWES*, 40 (1959), 58

1385 ———. "The Text of *Beowulf.*" *Proceedings of the American Philosophical Society*, 93 (1949), 239–43. (mns, sch, txt) On Thorkelin [2081–82].

1386 ———. *The Thorkelin Transcripts of "Beowulf" in Facsimile.* Early English Manuscripts in Facsimile, 1. Copenhagen, London, and Baltimore, 1951. (mns) Facsimile of Thorkelin [2081–82].
Reviews:
    1 *DUJ*, 44 (1951), 108
    2 "Romance of Scholarship," *TLS*, 18 April 1952, p. 265
    3 R. Girvan, *MLR*, 48 (1953), 198–99
    4 F. P. Magoun, *Speculum*, 28 (1953), 194–95
    5 F. Mossé, *EA*, 6 (1953), 47
    6 J. L. N. O'Loughlin, *MAE*, 23 (1954), 63–65
    7 J. C. Pope, *MLN*, 68 (1953), 506–8
    8 G. G. Smith, *Emory Univ. Quarterly*, 8 (1952), 123–24
    9 H. B. Woolf, *ES*, 35 (1954), 81–83
    10 C. L. Wrenn, *RES*, 4 (1953), 274–76

1387 ———. "Thorkelin's Transcripts of *Beowulf.*" *SN*, 14 (1941–42), 25–30. (mns, txt) Comment by Klaeber [1076].
Review: D. Whitelock, *YWES*, 23 (1942), 39

1388 ———. "Three Notes on *Beowulf.*" *JEGP*, 29 (1930), 233–36. (int, lng, txt, wrd; 303–6, 646–51, 708–9, 1053–57)
Review: M. Daunt, *YWES*, 11 (1930), 52–53

1389 ———. "Time and Place in the Ingeld Episode of *Beowulf.*" *JEGP*, 39 (1940), 76–92. (chr, int, txt; 2041, 2058ff)
Answer to Huppé [930]; reply by Brodeur [229], pp. 157–81.
Review: G. N. Garmonsway, *YWES*, 21 (1940), 35–36

1390 ———. "Two Notes on *Widsith.*" *MLN*, 47 (1932), 367–71. (hst, nam; 464, 1710)
Review: M. Daunt, *YWES*, 13 (1932), 74–75

1391 ———. "Ubbo Fresicus at Brávellir." *C&M*, 8 (1946), 116–20. (ana, hst) Answer to A. Olrik, "Brávellir," *NB*, 2 (1914), 297–312.
Repr. in *SHL & CS*, pp. 82–86

1392 ———. "When did Middle English begin?" *Curme Volume of Linguistic Studies.* Baltimore, 1930. pp. 110–17. (lng)

1393 ———. *Widsith.* London, 1936. (hst, nam)
Reviews:
    1 L. Abercrombie, *SR*, 46 (1938), 124–28
    2 H. M. Ayres, *MLN*, 52 (1937), 296–98
    3 A. Brandl, *Archiv*, 160 (1937), 243–45

    4 A. Campbell, *Viking Soc. Saga Book*, 11 (1936), 297–98

    5 [B. Dickins], *TLS*, 22 Feb. 1936, p. 165

    6 W. Fischer, *ES*, 19 (1937), 211–14

    7 F. Holthausen, *Beibl*, 48 (1937), 33–34

    8 K. Jost, *LGRP*, 58 (1937), 252–54

    9 J. M. Menner, *SSN*, 14 (1937), 205–7

  10 F. Mezger, *AJPhil*, 58 (1937), 378–79

  11 F. Mossé, *LM*, 34 (1937), 486

  12 ——, *RAA*, 13 (1937), 510

  13 ——, *RG*, 28 (1937), 176–77

  14 S. Potter, *MLR*, 33 (1938), 58–60

  15 F. R. Schröder, *GRM*, 24 (1936), 233

  16 M. S. Serjeantson, *YWES*, 17 (1938), 62–63

  17 P. W. Souers, *Speculum*, 11 (1936), 532–36; reply by Malone, *Notes on a Review*. Baltimore, 1936

  18 J. M. Steadman, *EA*, 1 (1936), 21

  19 A. E. H. Swaen, *Neophilologus*, 22 (1936), 70–71

  20 C. L. W[renn], *RES*, 14 (1938), 235–37

2d ed., Copenhagen, 1962; Anglistica 13

Reviews:

    1 K. Brunner, *ES*, 46 (1965), 494–96

    2 J. E. Cross, *JEGP*, 63 (1964), 136–37

    3 U. Dronke, *Anglia*, 82 (1964), 368–71

    4 R. M. Wilson, *YWES*, 43 (1962), 58

1394   ——. "*Widsith* and the *Hervararsaga*." *PMLA*, 40 (1925), 769–813. (ana, chr, hst, nam)

1395   ——. "*Widsith*, *Beowulf*, and Bravellir." In *Hammerich*, pp. 161–67. (ana, hst, nam)

1396   ——. "Words of Wisdom in *Beowulf*." In *Taylor*, pp. 180–94. (thm, wrd)

1397   ——. "Young Beowulf." *JEGP*, 36 (1937), 21–23. (int, mth, tec; 2177–89)

Review: D. E. M. Clarke, *YWES*, 18 (1937), 54

1398   ——. (Untitled review of Hoops [894]) *ES*, 15 (1933), 94–96. (int, lng, nam)

1399   ——. (Untitled review of Hoops [896]) *ES*, 15 (1933), 149–51. (int; 2359b–62)

1400   ——. (Untitled review of Sedgefield [1892], 3d ed.) *ES*, 18 (1936), 257–58. (int, lng, txt)

1401   ——. (Untitled review of Storms [2025]) *ES*, 41 (1960), 200–205. (dct, for, hst, int, nam)

1402   ——. (Untitled review of Williams [2221]) *JEGP*, 25 (1926), 114–17. (hst, int, txt)

1403   ——. (Untitled review of Marquardt [1413]) *MLN*, 55 (1940), 73–74. (ken; 304, 1359, 2035, 2128, 2220, 2847)

1404   ——. (Untitled review of Brodeur [229]) *MLN*, 75 (1960), 347–53. (for, hst, int; 2032–62)

1405   ——. (Untitled review of Lawrence [1188]) *Speculum*, 3 (1928), 612–15. (Fnb, hst, int)

1406   ——. (Untitled review of Wessén [2187]) *Speculum*, 5 (1930), 134–35. (hst)

1407   ——. (Untitled review of Bonjour [159]) *Speculum*, 26 (1951), 148–50. (int, str, txt; 120, 1960)

1408   MANLY, John M. "Narrative Writing in Anglo–Saxon Times." *Reader*, 7 (1902), 102–9. (tec)

1409   MARCH, Francis A. *Introduction to Anglo–Saxon: An Anglo–Saxon Reader.* N.Y., 1872. (edt, gen, nts, trl) Edits lines 1–11, 26–52, 64–82a, 89b–98, 99–129a, 144–52a, 194–228, 229–69, 286–92, 301–19, 612–46a, 651b–53, 867b–74a, 1455–64, 1512b–36, 1557–64, 1687–98a, 1789b–1803a; translates 867b–74a.
Repr. 1896.

1410   ——. "The World of *Beowulf*." *Proceedings of the American Philological Association*, 13 (1882), xxi–xxiii. (hst, stl) Answer by Harrison [756].

1411   MARKLAND, Murray F. "The Craven Comitatus." *CE*, 22 (1961), 341–43. (int, str, thm, unt)

1412   MARKMAN, Alan. "Apology for *Beowulf*." *CEA*, 22 (1960), ii, 4–5, 11. (gen, sch)

1413   MARQUARDT, Hertha. *Die altenglischen Kenningar: Ein Beitrag zur Stilkunde altgermanischer Dichtung.* Schriften der Königsberger Gelehrten Gesellschaft, Geisteswissenschaftliche Klasse, 14 Jahr, Heft 3. Halle, 1938. (dct, int, ken, txt) Modeled on Meissner [1429].
Reviews:
    1   A. G. v. Hamel, *ES*, 21 (1939), 12–15
    2   F. Klaeber, *Beibl*, 49 (1938), 321–26
    3   H. Koziol, *ESt*, 74 (1940), 107–10
    4   K. Malone, *MLN*, 55 (1940), 73–74 [1403]
    5   S. Potter, *MLR*, 34 (1939), 128
    6   J. W. Rankin, *JEGP*, 38 (1939), 282–85
    7   F. R. Schröder, *GRM*, 26 (1938), 45
    8   C. L. Wrenn, *YWES*, 19 (1938), 58–59

1414   ——. "Fürsten- und Kriegerkenning im *Beowulf*." *Anglia*, 60 (1936), 390–95. (dct, ken; 1020, 1507, 2261, 2345)
Review: M. Serjeantson, *YWES*, 17 (1936), 61

1415   ———. "Zur Entstehung des *Beowulf*." *Anglia*, 64 (1940), 152–58. (com, src)

1416   MARSH, George Perkins. *The Origin and History of the English Language and of the Early Literature It Embodies*. N.Y., 1862. (gen, lng)
2d ed., 1865; 3d ed., 1869
Rev. eds., 1885, 1892, 1898

1417   MARSHALL, H. E. *Stories of "Beowulf" Told to the Children*. London and N.Y., 1908. (par) English paraphrase.

1418   MARTIN, Ernst. *Der Versbau des Heliand und der altsächsischen Genesis*. *Q&F*, 100. Strasbourg, 1907. (mtr)

1419   ———. (Unitled review of Kaluza [968]) *ESt*, 20 (1895), 293–96. (mtr; 1514, 3027)

†   ———, see [223].

1420   MASSEY, B. W. A. "Compound Adjectives in Shelley and Keats [and *Beowulf*]." *N&Q*, 144 (1923), 464–68. (dct, lng; 251, 295, 305, 528, 572, 1111, 1256, 1278, 1406, 1490, 1533, 1546, 1584, 1649, 1802, 2517, 2820, 2929)

1421   MATTER, Hans. *Englische Gründungssagen von Geoffrey of Monmouth bis zur Renaissance*. *AF*, 58. Heidelberg, 1922. (chr, Fnb, hst; Fep) On Hengist.
Review: F. Holthausen, *Beibl*, 35 (1924), 41–42

1422   MATTHES, Heinrich Christoph. "Beowulfstudien." *Anglia*, 71 (1953), 148–90. (chr, hst, lng, txt; 59–63)
Review: R. M. Wilson, *YWES*, 34 (1953), 49

1423   ———. "Hygd." In *Spira*, pp. 14–31. (chr; 1925–62)
Review: T. S. Dorsch, *YWES*, 42 (1963), 16

1424   MAYNARD, W. A. "The Fight at Finnsburg." *MLR*, 44 (1949), 228. (Fnb, txt; Fnb 34)
Review: R. M. Wilson, *YWES*, 30 (1949), 42–43

1425   MEAD, Douglas S. "*Beowulf* 11b: 'þæt wæs god cyning.'" *Explicator*, 2 (1943), 2. (hst, thm; 11b)

1426   MEAD, G. W. "Wiðergyld of *Beowulf*, 2051." *MLN*, 32 (1917), 435–36. (chr, int; 2051)

1427   MEAD, William E. "Color in Old English Poetry." *PMLA*, 14 (1899), 169–206. (img, stl)

1428   MEIGS, Carl. "*Beowulf*, Mythology and Ritual: A Common-Reader Exploration." *Xavier Univ. Studies*, 3 (1964), 89–102. (mth, rel)

1429   MEISSNER, Rudolf. *Die Kenningar der Skalden: Ein Beitrag zur skaldischen Poetik*. Bonn and Leipzig, 1921. (ken) See Marquardt [1413].

1430   MENNER, Robert. "The Date and Dialect of *Genesis A*, 852–2936." *Anglia*, 70 (1952), 285–94. (dct)

1431   MERBACH, Hans. *Das Meer in der Dichtung der Angelsachsen.* Breslau diss., 1884. (img, thm)

1432   MERBOT, Reinhold. *Ästhetische Studien zur angelsächsischen (altenglischen) Poesie.* Breslau diss., 1883. (stl)
Pub. Breslau, 1883.
Reviews:
    1 F. Kluge, *ESt*, 8 (1885), 480–82
    2 E. A. Kock, *Anglia*, 6 (1883), 100–103

1433   MERITT, Herbert. "Three Studies in Old English." *AJPhil*, 62 (1941), 331–39. (txt; 1031)

1434   MERONEY, Howard. "Full Name and Address in Early Irish." In *Malone*, pp. 124–31. (ana; 237ff)

1435   ——. "Old English *dær* 'if.'" *JEGP*, 41 (1942), 201–9. (lng; 2570ff)

1436   METCALF, Allan. "Ten Natural Animals in *Beowulf*." *NM*, 64 (1963), 378–89. (img, smb, tec)
Review: R. M. Wilson, *YWES*, 44 (1963), 73

1437   METCALFE, Frederick. *The Englishman and the Scandinavian; or, A Comparison of Anglo–Saxon and Old Norse Literature.* London, 1880. (gen)
Review: H. Sweet, *Academy*, 29 May 1880

†   MEURS, J. C. van, see VAN MEURS.

1438   MEYER, Elard Hugo. *Germanische Mythologie.* Berlin, 1891. pp. 299–300. (mth, smb) Grendel = storm.

1439   ——. *Indogermanische Mythen.* Berlin, 1887. Vol. II, pp. 557, 565, 634. (ana, mth, smb, thm; 710, 714)

1440   ——. *Mythologie der Germanen.* Strasbourg, 1903. (mth)

†   ——, see [687].

1441   MEYER, Kuno. *Fianaigecht.* Royal Irish Academy Proceedings, Todd Lecture Series, 16 (Dublin, 1910). (ana)

1442   MEYER, Richard M. *Die altgermanische Poesie nach ihren formelhaften Elementen beschrieben.* Berlin, 1889. (stl)

1443   MEYER, Willy. *Beiträge zur Geschichte der Eroberung Englands durch die Angelsachsen.* Halle diss., 1912. (chr, edt, Fnb, hst; Fep) Edits Finnsburh episode.

1444   ——. "Wĕalhþēo(w)." *Beibl*, 33 (1922), 94–101. (chr, hst)

1445   ——. "Zum Finnsburg Fragment, Vers 6–8a." *Beibl*, 54–55 (1943–44), 125–26. (Fnb, int, nam, wrd; 1110–12, Fnb 6–8a)

1446   MEZGER, Fritz. "O.E. 'Hāmweorðung': *Beowulf* 2998."
        JEGP, 50 (1951), 243–45. (dct, lng; 2998a)

1447   ——. "*On faeder feorme, Beowulf*, Line 21." *MLN*, 59 (1944),
        113–14. (txt; 21b)
        Review: M. Daunt, *YWES*, 25 (1944), 219

1448   ——. "Self-Judgment in O.E. Documents." *MLN*, 67
        (1952), 106–09. (dct, hst, img, wrd)
        Review: R. M. Wilson, *YWES*, 33 (1952), 41

1449   ——. "Two Notes on *Beowulf*." *MLN*, 66 (1951), 36–38.
        (hst, int, txt; 253, 446)

  †   MICHEL, Francisque, see [993].

1450   MILLER, Thomas. "The Position of Grendel's Arm in
        Heorot." *Anglia*, 12 (1889), 396–400. (int; 834ff, 925ff,
        982ff)

1451   MILOSH, Joseph. "Sisam's *Structure of "Beowulf"* and
        Realism in Criticism: A Review Essay." *Cithara*, 5 (1966),
        52–58. (sch)
        Review of Sisam [1962].

1452   MINCOFF, M. "Zur angelsächsischen Dichtersprache."
        Sofiskiya Universitet (Sofia); *Istoriko-filologicheski fakultet; Godish-
        nik*, 39 (1942–43). (dct)

1453   MITCHELL, Bruce. *A Guide to Old English.* Oxford, 1965.
        (hst, lng, ref)
        Review: R. I. Page, *MAE*, 35 (1966), 175–76

1454   ——. "Pronouns in Old English Poetry: Some Syntactical
        Notes." *RES*, n.s. 15 (1964), 129–41. (lng; 2056)
        Review: R. M. Wilson, *YWES*, 45 (1964), 59

1455   ——. "'Until the Dragon Comes . . .': Some Thoughts on
        Beowulf." *Neophilologus*, 47 (1963), 126–38. (rel, smb)
        Reply to Goldsmith [646]; reply by Goldsmith [644].
        Review: R. M. Wilson, *YWES*, 44 (1963), 72–73

  †   ——, see [420].

1456   MOGK, Eugen. "Altgermanische Spukgeschichten: Zug-
        leich ein Beitrag zur Erklärung der Grendel-episode im
        Beowulf." *NJKA*, 43 (1919), 103–17. (mth, src)

1457   ——. "Die dämonischen Gestalten der Einzelnen Ele-
        mente." *PGrdr*, 2d ed., III, 301–2. (mth)

1458   ——. "Die germanische Heldendichtung mit besonderer
        Rücksicht auf die Sage von Siegfrid und Brunhild." *NJKA*,
        1 (1898), 68–80. (ana, mth)

1459   MOHR, Wolfgang. *Kenningstudien.* Stuttgart, 1933. (ken,
        rel)
        Review: A. Brandl, *Archiv*, 165 (1934), 290 [207]

1460 MÖLLER, Hermann. *Das altenglische Volksepos in der ursprünglichen strophischen Form.* Kiel, 1883. (com, edt, Fnb, int, str; Fep) Reconstructs "original" in 344 4-line stanzas; *Finnsburh* as 14 quatrains. Reply to Schönbach [1819]. Reviews:
    1 R. Heinzel, *AfdA*, 10 (1884), 215–33 [774]
    2 A. Schönbach, *ZOG*, 35 (1884), 37–46

1461 ——. (Untitled review of ten Brink [223]) *ESt*, 13 (1889), 247–315. (com, hst, lng)

1462 MONCRIEFF, Charles K. Scott. *"Beowulf" Translated.* London, 1921. (Fnb, trl) Literal, alliterative English verse.
Review: F. Klaeber, *Beibl*, 34 (1923), 321–23
Repr. in his *"Widsith," "Beowulf," "Finnsburgh," "Waldere," "Deor," Done into Common English after the Old Manner.* London and N.Y., 1921. Introd. by Viscount Northcliffe.
Lines 1–52 repr. in Richard Aldington, ed., *Viking Book of Poetry of the English-speaking World.* N.Y., 1941. pp. 1–2.

1463 MONE, Franz Joseph. *Untersuchungen zur Geschichte der teutschen Heldensage.* Quedlinburg and Leipzig, 1836. (Fnb, hst, mth)

1464 Item canceled.

† MONNET, Camille, see [1582].

1465 MONTELIUS, Oscar. "Ynglingaäten." *NTVKI*, 1918, 213–38. (ana, chr, hst) Swedish kings.

1466 MOORE, Arthur K. "Beowulf's Dereliction in the Grendel Episode." *MLN*, 68 (1953), 165–69. (hst, int, mth)
Review: R. M. Wilson, *YWES*, 34 (1953), 47–48

1467 MOORE, Samuel. *"Beowulf* Notes." *JEGP*, 18 (1919), 205–16. (txt; 489–90, 599, 1082ff, 3005–6, 3074–75, 3123–24)

1468 ——, and KNOTT, Thomas A. *The Elements of Old English.* 8th ed., Ann Arbor, 1940. (edt) Includes lines 102–5, 115–34, 194–201, 671–90, 702–90, 809–24. No *Beowulf* in first 7 eds.
9th ed., 1942; 10th ed., 1955, rev. by James R. Hulbert

1469 ——. "Notes on *Beowulf.*" In *Klaeber*, pp. 208–12. (txt; 1104–6, 2032–40, 3117–19)

1470 MOORMAN, Charles. "The Essential Paganism of *Beowulf.*" *MLQ*, 28 (1967), 3–18. (int, mth, rel, str, thm)

1471 ——. "Suspense and Foreknowledge in *Beowulf.*" *CE*, 15 (1954), 379–83. (tec)

1472 MOORMAN, Frederic William. "English Place-Names and Teutonic Sagas." *E&S*, 5 (1914), 75–103. (ana, com, hst, mth, nam)

1473   ——. *The Interpretation of Nature in English Poetry from "Beo-wulf" to Shakespeare.* Strasbourg, 1905. *Q&F*, 95. (img, thm)
Review: R. Wülker, *DLZ*, 18 Nov. 1905, col. 2867

1474   MORGAN, Bayard Q. "Zur Lehre von der Alliteration in der westgermanischen Dichtung: I. Die Tonverhältnisse der Hebungen im *Beowulf.* II. Die gekreuzte Alliteration." Leipzig diss., 1907. (mtr, txt)
Pub. in *Beitr*, 33 (1908), 95–181.

1475   MORGAN, Edwin. *Beowulf: A Verse Translation into Modern English.* Aldington, Kent, 1952; N.Y., 1953. (gen, nam, trl)   Based on Klaeber [1026].
Reviews:
    1   *TLS*, 7 May 1954, p. 298
    2   B. Kimpel, *Poetry*, 83 (Oct. 1953), 44–48
    3   F. Mossé, *EA*, 7 (1954), 413
    4   R. M. Wilson, *YWES*, 33 (1952), 38
Repr. in paperback (Cal–67), Berkeley and Los Angeles, 1962
Review: R. M. Wilson, *YWES*, 44 (1963), 71

1476   MORLEY, Henry. "*Beowulf.*" In his *Manual of English Literature*, rev. by Moses Coit Tyler. N.Y., 1879. pp. 17–18. (gen)

1477   ——. *English Writers.* London, 1864–67. Vol. I. (bbl, chr, com, Fnb, hst, mth, trl)   Translates part of *Beowulf* into English verse with summaries of remainder, and *Finnsburh* into English prose.
2d ed., London, Paris, Melbourne, and N.Y., 1887
Review: J. M. Garnett, *MLN*, 3 (1888), 190–94
3d ed., 1889; 4th ed., 1891

1478   ——. *A First Sketch of English Literature.* London, 1873. (gen)
2d ed., 1892

1479   ——. *Longer Works in English Verse and Prose.* London, 1881. (gen)

1479.1 MORRELL, Minnie Cate. *A Manual of Old English Biblical Materials.* Knoxville, Tenn., 1965. pp. 31–36. (mns)

1480   MORRIS, John. "Ring-Mail." *JEGP*, 33 (1934), 194–204. (hst)
Review: M. Serjeantson, *YWES*, 15 (1934), 76

1481   ——. "Sidney Lanier and Anglo–Saxon Verse-Technique." *AJPhil*, 20 (1899), 435–38. (mtr)

1482   MORRIS, William, and WYATT, Alfred J. *The Tale of Beowulf, Sometime King of the Folk of the Weder Geats.* (1st ed. untitled; this is title of 2d ed.) Hammersmith, 1895. (trl) English verse, based on Wyatt [2267] and Wyatt's prose paraphrase.
Review: *Athenaeum*, 106 (10 Aug. 1895), 181–82
2d ed., London and N.Y., 1898
Review: W. H. Hulme, *MLN*, 15 (1900), 25–26
Repr. 1904; repr. in May Morris, ed., *The Collected Works of William Morris.* London and N.Y., 1911. Vol. X.

1483   ——. (Summaries in Wyatt [2266]). (par)

1484   MORSBACH, Lorenz. "Zur Datierung des *Beowulf* Epos." *Nachrichten der K. Gesellschaft der Wissenschaften zu Göttingen, Philologisch-historische Klasse*, (1906), 251–77. (com, lng, mtr) Reply by Holthausen [871].

1485   MORTON, Lena. "The Influence of the Sea upon the English Poetry from the Anglo–Saxon Period to the Victorian Period." Unpub. Ph.D. diss., Western Reserve Univ., 1947. *DDABAU*, 14 (1946–47), 84. (dct, img, smb, thm; 515, 518–19, 579–80, 1691–93, 1904–5)

1486   MOSSÉ, Fernand. *Manuel de l'anglais du moyen âge des origines au XIVe siècle.* I. *Vieil-anglais.* Paris, 1945. pp. 273–85. (edt) Edits *Beowulf* 499–603a, 710–836, 1345–76a, 2711b–2820.

1487   MOULTON, Charles Wells. "Beowulf." In his *Library of Literary Criticism of English and American Authors.* N.Y., 1902. Vol. I, pp. 17–21. (sch)
Repr., 1929, 1935

1488   MOUREK, V. E. *Zur Negation im Altgermanischen.* Prague, 1903. (lng)

1489   ——. "Zur Syntax des Konjunktivs im *Béowulf.*" *Prager Deutsche Studien*, 8 (1908), 121–37. (lng)

1490   MUCH, Rudolf. *Die Germania des Tacitus erläutert.* Heidelberg, 1937. (hst)
Review: H. Rosenfeld, *Archiv*, 173 (1938), 74–78
2d ed., 1959

1491   ——. "Orendel." *Wörter und Sachen*, 4 (1912), 170–73. (hst, nam)

1492–99   Items canceled.

1500   ——. "*Widsith:* Beiträge zu einem Commentar." *ZDA*, 62 (1925), 113–50. (chr, hst) On Breca and Hoc.

1501   ——. (Untitled review of Friedrich Panzer. *Hilde-Gudrun.* Halle, 1901) *Archiv*, 108 (1902), 406–10. (ana, Fnb, mth)

† MULGAN, John, see [763].

1502 MÜLLENHOFF, Karl. "Die alte Dichtung von den Nibelungen. I. Von Sigfrids Ahnen." *ZDA*, 23 (1879), 113–173. (ana, mth; 886–900).

1503 ———. "Die austrasische Dietrichssage." *ZDA*, 6 (1847), 435–59. (hst, mth) On Hygelac's expedition.

1504 ———. *Beovulf: Untersuchungen über das angelsächsische Epos und die älteste Geschichte der germanischen Seevölker.* Berlin, 1889. (com, Fnb, gen, hst, mth) pp. 110–65 reprint his [1507].
Reviews:
    1 L. Ehrhardt, *Hist Zs*, 69 (1892), 481–82
    2 R. Heinzel, *AfdA*, 16 (1890), 264–75 [777]
    3 F. Holthausen, *LGRP*, 1890, pp. 370–73
    4 E. Koeppel, *ZDP*, 23 (1891), 110–13
    5 E. Koeppel, *Münchner Neueste Nachrichten*, 1889, p. 428
    6 A. Kraus, *DLZ*, 12 (1891), 1820–22
    7 F. Liebermann, *Deutsche Zeitschrift für Geschichtswissenschaft*, 6 (1891), 135–37
    8 H. Logemann, *MA*, 3 (1890), 226–67
    9 E. Otto, *AZ*, 1890, no. 8
    10 G. Sarrazin, *ESt*, 16 (1892), 71–85 [1780]
    11 G. Schirmer, *Anglia*, 12 (1889), 465–67
    12 R. Wülker, *LitCbl*, 1890, no. 2, 58–59

1505 ———. *Deutsche Altertumskunde.* Berlin, 1900. Vol. IV. (hst) 2d ed., 1920

1506 ———. "Die deutschen Völker an Nord- und Ostsee in ältester Zeit: Eine Kritik der neueren Forschungen mit besonderer Rücksicht auf Tacitus, *Beovulf* und Scopesvidsith." *Nordalbingische Studien*, 1 (1844), 111–74. (chr, Fnb, hst)

1507 ———. "Die innere Geschichte des *Beovulfs.*" *ZDA*, 14 (1869), 193–244. (com, str)
Repr. in his [1504], pp. 110–65

1508 ———. "Der Mythus von *Beowulf.*" *ZDA*, 7 (1849), 419–41. (mth)

1509 ———. "Sceáf und seine Nachkommen." *ZDA*, 7 (1849), 410–19. (chr, hst, mth)

1510 ———. "Verderbte Namen bei Tacitus." *ZDA*, 9 (1853), 248. (nam; 438)

1511 ———. "Zeugnisse und Excurse zur deutschen Heldensage." *ZDA*, 12 (1865), 253–386. (Fnb, hst, nam)

1512 ———. "Zur Kritik des angelsächsischen Volkepos, 2, *Widsith.*" *ZDA*, 11 (1859), 272–94. (Fnb, mth)

† ——, see [696].

1513   MÜLLER, Hugo. *Über die ags. Versus gnomici.*" Jena, 1893. (mtr)

1514   MÜLLER, Johannes. *Das Kulturbild des Beowulfepos.* Halle a.S., 1914. *SEP* 53. Inaugural diss., Göttingen, 1914. (hst). Reviews:
    1   K. Brunner, *Archiv*, 138 (1919), 242–43
    2   F. Klaeber, *Beibl*, 27 (1916), 241–44

1515   MÜLLER, Nathanael. *Die Mythen im "Beowulf" in ihrem Verhältnis zur germanischen Mythologie betrachtet.* Heidelberg diss., Leipzig, 1878. Deutsche Studienblätter von Rottsch, III, 13 and 14. (mth)

1516   MÜLLER, Thomas. "*Angelsächsisches Lesebuch.*" 1855. pp. 103–27. (edt) Lines 1–836. Never published.

1517   MUNN, James B. "Beowulf." In H. A. Watt and James B. Munn, eds., *Ideas and Forms in English and American Literature.* Chicago, 1925. (trl) English prose.

1518   MURPHY, James Michael. "Beowulf's Forearm: A New Look At." *Moderator*, 5 (Feb. 1966), 46. (sch) Parody.

1519   MUSGROVE, S. "Beowulf on Perelandra." *N&Q*, 188 (1945), 140–42. (ana, img, inf, src)
    Review: M. Daunt, *YWES*, 26 (1945), 41

1520   MUSSOFF, L. "Lighting up the Dark Ages: Contrasting *Beowulf* with the *Canterbury Tales.*" *English Journal*, 52 (1963), 525–27. (gen)

1521   MUST, Hildegard Reisman. *Beow und Pekko: Ein Beitrag zur Beowulfforschung.* Hamburg diss., 1948. (ana)

1522   MUSTANOJA, Tauno F. "The Unnamed Woman's Song of Mourning over Beowulf and the Tradition of Ritual Lamentation." *NM*, 68 (1967), 1–27. (ana, hst, txt; 3150–55)

1523   MYERS, Irene T. *A Study in Epic Development.* YSE 11. N.Y., 1901. (epc, gen, hst)

1524   MYRES, J. N. L. "The English Settlements." In R. G. Collingwood and J. N. L. Myres, eds., *Roman Britain and the English Settlements.* Oxford, 1936. (chr, hst) On Hengist. 2d ed., 1937.
    Repr. 1941, 1945, 1949
    Reviews:
    1   H. A. Crowne, *History*, 22 (1938), 350–51
    2   K. Malone, *MLN*, 53 (1938), 220–22

1525   McCAIN, R. "*Beowulf*, the Epic of the Saxons." *Education*, 27 (Nov. 1906), 136–42. (epc, gcn)

1526   McCLELLAND, Charles B. "Horses in *Beowulf:* A Horse of a Different Color." *TSL*, 11 (1966), 177–87. (dct, hst, img, smb)

1527   McCLUMPHA, Charles Flint. "Differences between the Scribes of *Beowulf.*" *MLN*, 5 (1890), 123. (lng, mns)
Reply to Davidson [441]; see his reply [442].

1528   ——. "On Stopford Brooke's *Beowulf* in His *History of Early English Literature.*" *MLN*, 8 (1893), 27–29. (com, src) On Brooke [239].

1529   McELROY, Davis D. "England's First Poet-Critic?" *N&Q*, 204 (1959), 305–6. (for, tec; 867ff)
Review: R. M. Wilson, *YWES*, 40 (1959), 61

1530   McGALLIARD, John C. "*Beowulf* and Bede." In Robert S. Hoyt, ed., *Life and Thought in the Early Middle Ages.* Minneapolis, 1967. pp. 101–21. (com, hst)

1531   ——. "The Complex Art of *Beowulf.*" *MP*, 59 (1962), 276–82. (for, hst, ken, lng, thm, unt, var)
Review of Brodeur [229].

1532   McNAMEE, Maurice B. "*Beowulf*–An Allegory of Salvation?" *JEGP*, 59 (1960), 190–207. (ana, chr, mth, rel, smb, src) Answer by Bonjour [156].
Review: R. M. Wilson, *YWES*, 41 (1960), 54
Repr. in Nicholson [1560], pp. 331–52

1533   ——. *Honor and the Epic Hero.* N.Y., 1960. (com, epc, rel, thm)

1534   McNARY, Sarah J. "Beowulf and Arthur as English Ideals." *Poet-Lore*, 6 (1894), 529–36. (gen, hst)

1535   NADER, Engelbert. *Dativ und Instrumental im Béowulf.* Vienna, 1883. (lng)
Review: E. Klinghardt, *ESt*, 7 (1884), 368–70

1536   ——. *Der Genitiv im "Béowulf."* Brünn, 1882. (lng)
Review: E. Klinghardt, *ESt*, 6 (1883), 288

1537   ——. "Tempus und Modus im *Beowulf.*" *Anglia*, 10 (1888), 542–63; 11 (1889), 444–99. (lng)

1538   ——. "Zur Syntax des *Beowulf* (Accusativ)." *Programm der Staats-Oberrealschule, in Brünn am Schluss des Schuljahrs 1879.* 1879–80. (lng)
Review: E. Bernhardt, *LGRP*, 1 (1880), 439–40. Reply by Nader and Bernhardt's reply, *LGRP*, 2 (1881), 119–20

1539   NAGANO, Moriji. *The Beowulf.* Tokyo, 1966. (trl) Prose.

1540 NAUMANN, Hans. *Altnordische Namenstudien*. Berlin, 1912. pp. 179-82. (hst, mth, nam)

1541 ———. *Frühgermanentum, Heldenlieder und Sprüche übersetzt und eingeleitet*. Munich, 1926. (Fnb, trl) Alliterative verse.

1542 ———. *Frühgermanisches Dichterbuch: Zeugnisse und Texte für Übungen und Vorlesungen über ältere germanische Poesie*. Berlin, 1931. (edt, Fnb) Edits *Beowulf* 867b-97, 1063-1159a, 3137-82.
Review: F. Klaeber, *Beibl*, 43 (1932), 325-27

1543 NECKEL, Gustav. "Adel und Gefolgschaft: Ein Beitrag zur germanischen Altertumskunde." *Beitr*, 41 (1916), 385-436. (hst)

1544 ———. *Altgermanische Kultur*. Leipzig, 1925. (hst)

1545 ———. *Beiträge zur Eddaforschung, Anhang: Die altgermanische Heldenklage*. Dortmund, 1908. (epc, int, hst)

1546 ———. "Etwas von germanischer Sagenforschung." *GRM*, 2 (1910), 1-14. (epc)

1547 ———. "Ragnacharius von Cambrai." *Mitt. d. Schlesischen Gesellschaft für Volkskunde*, 13-14 (1911), 121-54. (ana, hst)

1548 ———. "Sigmunds Drachenkampf." *Edda*, 13 (1920), 122-40, 204-29. (ana, mth)

1549 ———. "Studien über Fróði." *ZDA*, 48 (1906), 163-86. (hst)

1550 ———. *Die Überlieferungen vom Gotte Balder dargestellt und vergleichend untersucht*. Dortmund, 1920. (ana, chr, hst, mth)

1551 NEELOV, A. A. ["Some Data on the Frequency of Compound Words in *Beowulf*."] *Problems of English Philology*. [Rostov-on-Don, 1966]. (lng) In Russian.

† NEHRING, A., see [1821].

1552 NERMAN, Birger. *Det svenska Rikets Uppkonst*. Stockholm, 1925. (hst)

1553 ———. "Ottar Vendelkråka och Ottarshögen i Vendel." *Upplands Fornminnesförenings Tidskrift*, 7 (1917), 309-34. (arc, hst)

1554 ———. *Studier över Svärges hedna litteratur*. Uppsala, 1913. (arc, hst) On Swedish mounds.

1555 ———. *Vilka konungar ligga i Uppsala högar?* Uppsala, 1913. (arc, hst) On Aun, Egill, Aðils.

1556 ———. "Ynglingasagan i arkeologisk Belysning." *Fornvännen*, 12 (1917), 226-61. (ana, arc, hst)

1557 NEUHAUS, J. "Om Skjold." *ANF*, 35 (1918), 166-72. (nam) Corrections to Olrik [1588].

1558   NEUNER, Erich. *Über ein- und dreihebige Halbverse in der altenglischen alliterienden Poesie."* Berlin diss., 1920. (mtr)
Review: J. W. Bright, *MLN*, 36 (1921), 59–63

1559   NEWCOMER, A. G., and ANDREWS, A. E. *Twelve Centuries of English Poetry and Prose.* Chicago, 1910. (trl)
English prose selected and "improved" from Thorpe [2084].

1560   NICHOLSON, Lewis E. *An Anthology of "Beowulf" Criticism.* Notre Dame, 1963; NDP 27 paperback. Contains Baum [73], Blackburn [126], Bloomfield [131] and [132], Cabaniss [281], Chadwick [302], Goldsmith [645], Hamilton [745], Kaske [975], Magoun [1306], Malone [1316], McNamee [1532], Robertson [1716], Rogers [1728], Schücking [1852], Tolkien [2095], Wrenn [2248], and Wright [2253].
Reviews:
    1   B. Mitchell, *RES*, 15 (1964), 414–15
    2   E. G. Stanley, *N&Q*, 209 (1964), 122–23
    3   R. M. Wilson, *YWES*, 44 (1963), 71

1561   ——. "The Literal Meaning and Symbolic Structure of *Beowulf.*" *C&M*, 25 (1964), 151–201. (smb, str)

1562   ——. "Oral Techniques in the Composition of Expanded Anglo–Saxon Verses." Unpub. Ph.D. diss., Harvard Univ., 1957–58. (for, mtr) See his [1563].

1563   ——. "Oral Techniques in the Composition of Expanded Anglo–Saxon Verses." *PMLA*, 78 (1963), 287–92. (for, mtr; 1165–67, 2995–96a) See his [1562].

1564   NIEDERSTENBRUCH, A. "Germanisch-heidnische und christlich-kirchliche Elemente im *Beowulf.*" *Weltanschauung und Schule*, 3 (1940), 159–65. (mth, rel)

1565   NIEDNER, Felix. "Die Dioskuren im *Beowulf.*" *ZDA*, 42 (1898), 229–58. (mth)

1566   NIST, John Albert. "Alliterative Patterns in *Beowulf:* A Key to Authorship." *PMASAL*, 44 (1959), 347–53. (com, mtr, stl, txt)

1567   ——. "*Beowulf* and the Classical Epics." *CE*, 24 (1963), 257–62. (epc)

1568   ——. "Phonemics and Distinctive Features of *Beowulf.*" *SIL*, 13 (1958), 25–33. (lng)

1569   ——. *A Structural History of English.* N.Y., 1966. (gen)

1570   ——. "The Structure and Texture of Beowulf." Ph.D. diss., Indiana Univ., 1953. (lng, mns, mtr, stl, str)
Pub. with same title, São Paulo, 1959. Univ. de São Paulo Faculdade de filosofia, ciências e letras, Boletin no. 229: Lingua e literatura inglêsa, no. 1.

1571 ———. "The Structure of *Beowulf*." *PMASAL*, 43 (1958), 307–14. (str)

1572 ———. "Textual Elements in the *Beowulf* Manuscript." *PMASAL*, 42 (1957), 331–38. (mns, txt)

1573 Item canceled.

1574 NOLAN, Edward Francis. "Organic Repetition in the Structure of *Beowulf*." Unpub. Ph.D. diss., Princeton Univ., 1941. *DA*, 13 (1952), 70. *DDABAU*, 1940–41, no. 8, 120. (str, tec)

1575 NOREEN, Adolf. "Skandinavien och Skåne." In *Tegnér*, pp. 43–48. (hst, nam) Answer to Lindroth [1257]; answer by Lindroth [1258].

1576 ———. *Ynglingatal: Text, översättning och kommentar.* Kungl. Vitterhets Historie och Antikvitets Akademiens Handlingar, 28, no. 2. Stockholm, 1925. (ana, hst)
Review: G. Neckel, *Litteris*, 3 (1926), 181–82

1577 ———. "Yngve, Inge, Inglinge m. m." *NB*, 8 (1920), 1–8. (nam)

† NORTHCLIFFE, Viscount, see [1462].

1578 OCHS, E. "Healfdenes Tochter." *NM*, 52 (1951), 29–30. (chr)

1579 OERTEL, Hans. "Hildebrands Theory of Alliteration." *MLN*, 7 (1892), 144–46. (mtr)

1580 OGILVY, Jack David Angus. "Unferth: Foil to Beowulf?" *PMLA*, 79 (1964), 370–75. (ana, chr, epc, hst, int, tec) Opposes Rosier [1733].
Review: R. M. Wilson, *YWES*, 45 (1964), 59–60

1581 OLIVERO, Federico. "Beowulf." In *Traduzioni dalla poesia anglo-sassone.* Bari, 1915. pp. 73–119, 127–32. (Fnb, nts, trl) Translates 1100 lines into Italian.
Review: S. S. Smart, *MLR*, 11 (1916), 509

1582 ———. *Beowulf.* Turin, 1934. (bbl, com, gen, hst, mth, mtr, rel, stl, trl, txt) Trans. into literal Italian prose, based on Chamber's text [2267].
Reviews:
    1 A. B., *Archiv*, 164 (1933), 293–94
    2 J. R. H., *MP*, 31 (1934), 322
    3 H. Hecht, *AfdA*, 53 (1934), 141–43
    4 F. P. Magoun, *Speculum*, 11 (1936), 304–5
    5 K. Malone, *MLN*, 51 (1936), 416

Trans. into French by Camille Monnet. Turin, 1937
Reviews:
1 F. Klaeber, *Archiv*, 173 (1938), 80–82
2 K. Malone, *MLN*, 55 (1940), 241
3 F. Mossé, *EA*, 2 (1938), 42
4 H. Oppel, *Dichtung und Volkstum*, 38 (1937), 507–8

1583 Item canceled.

1584 O'LOUGHLIN, J. L. N. "*Beowulf*–Its Unity and Purpose."
MAE, 21 (1952), 1–13. (hst, rel, str, unt)
Review: R. M. Wilson, *YWES*, 33 (1952), 39–40

1585 ——. "The Location of *Beowulf*." *Scientific American*, 186
(April 1952), 42, 44. (arc, com, hst) On Sutton Hoo.

1586 ——. "Sutton Hoo–The Evidence of the Documents."
MArc, 8 (1964), 1–19. (arc, chr, hst, nam; 3134ff) Trans-
lates 3134ff.
Review: R. M. Wilson, *YWES*, 45 (1964), 56–57

1587 OLRIK, Axel. *Danmarks Heltedigtning: I. Rolf Krake og den
ældre Skjoldungrække*. Copenhagen, 1903. (epc, hst, mth)
Reviews:
1 W. Golther, *LGRP*, 28 (1907), 8–9
2 A. Heusler, *AfdA*, 30 (1906), 26–36
Trans. and rev. in collaboration with the author by L. M.
Hollander. *The Heroic Legends of Denmark*. Illustrated
Scandinavian Monographs, 4. N.Y., 1919.
Reviews:
1 G. T. Flom, *JEGP*, 19 (1920), 284–90
2 W. E. Mead, *Nation*, 110 (17 Apr. 1920), 520–21

1588 ——. *Danmarks Heltedigtning:* II, *Starkad den gamle og den
yngre Skjoldungrække*. Copenhagen, 1910. (epc, hst, mth)
Opposed by Neuhaus [1557].
Reviews:
1 R. C. Boer, *Museum*, 19 (1912), 171–74
2 A. Heusler, *AfdA*, 35 (1912), 169–83 [810]
3 H. Ussing, *DS*, 7 (1910), 193–203

1589 ——. "Epische Gesetze der Volksdichtung." *ZDA*, 51
(1909–10), 1–12. (epc)

1590 ——. "Epische love i folkedigtningen." *DS*, 5 (1908),
69–89. (epc)

1591 ——. "Er Uffesagnet indvandret fra England? Bemaer-
kningar til Müllenhoffs *Beovulf*." *ANF*, 8 (1892), 368–75.
(ana, hst, src)

1592 ——. *Kilderne til Sakses Oldhistorie:* II *Norröne sagaer og danske
sagn*. Copenhagen, 1894. pp. 177–83. (ana, src)

1593   ——. *Nogle Grundsaetninger for sagnforskning; efter forfatterens dφd udg. af dansk folkemindesamling ved Hans Ellekilde.* Copenhagen, 1921. (mth)
Review: W. Golther, *LGRP*, 43 (1922), 237–39

1594   ——. *Nordisk Aandsliv i Vikingetid og tidlig Middelalder.* Copenhagen and Cristiana, 1907. (hst)
Trans. into German by W. Ranisch. *Nordisches Geistesleben in heidnischer und frühchristlicher Zeit.* Heidelberg, 1908.
2d ed., rev. by Hans Elle Kilde, 1927
2d ed. trans. into English by J. W. Hartmann and H. A. Larsen. *Viking Civilization.* N.Y., 1930

†   ——, see [271] and [572].

1595   Item canceled.

1596   OLSON, Oscar Ludvig. *"Beowulf* and *The Feast of Bricriu."* *MP*, 11 (1914), 407–27. (ana, mth)   Opposes Deutschbein [468].

1597   ——. "The Relation of the *Hrólfs Saga Kraka* and the *Bjarkarímur* to *Beowulf:* A Contribution to the History of Saga Development in England and the Scandinavian Countries." Ph.D. diss., Univ. of Chicago, 1914. (ana, mth)
Pub. same title in *Publications of the Society for the Advancement of Scandinavian Study*, 3, no. 1, Urbana, Ill., 1916.
Review: L. M. Hollander, *JEGP*, 16 (1917), 147–49
Private ed., Univ. of Chicago Library, 1916

1598   OMAN, Charles William Chadwick. *England before the Norman Conquest.* London and N.Y., 1910. (hst)
2d ed., 1910; 3d ed., London only, 1913; 4th ed., 1919; 5th ed., 1921; 6th ed., 1921; 7th ed., 1929; 8th ed., 1938; 9th ed., 1949; 10th ed., 1958

1599   O'NEIL, Wayne Albert. "Oral-formulaic Structure in Old English Elegaic Poetry." Unpub. Ph.D. diss., Univ. of Wisconsin, 1960. *DA*, 21 (1960), 625. (dct, for)   Summary by Cassidy [294]; used by Fry [588.1] and Gattiker [622].

1600   O'NEILL, Mary Angelica. "Elegaic Elements in *Beowulf.*" Unpub. Ph.D. diss., Catholic Univ., 1932. (str, thm)

†   ONIONS, C. T., see [2038].

1601.   OROZ, Rudolph. *Lautische Unterschiede im Vokalismus der Starktonsilben bei den beiden Schreibern der Beowulf-Handschrift.* Leipzig diss., 1922. (lng, mns)   Summary in *Jahrb. d. phil. Fak. zu Leipzig*, 2 (1922), 28–29.

1602.   ORRICK, Allan H. "Beowulf's Fight with Grendel." In *French*, pp. 13–23. (dct, img, int, lng, txt; 745b–49)

1603   ——. "Reðes ond Hattres, *Beowulf* 2523." *MLN*, 71 (1956), 551–56. (int, mtr, txt; 2318–19, 2523) Answers by Pope [1660] and Stevick [2011].
         Review: R. M. Wilson, *YWES*, 37 (1956), 72

†   ORTON, Harold, see [1696.1].

1604   OSHITARI, Kinshiro. ["Trends of *Beowulf* Criticism."]. *F. Nakajima Festschrift*. Tokyo, 1965. pp. 503–512. (sch) In Japanese.

1605   OSTHEEREN, Klaus. *Studien zum Begriff der "Freude" und seinen Ausdrucksmitteln in altenglischen Texten (Poesie, Alfred, Aelfric)*. Heidelberg, 1964. (tec, thm)
         Review: A. Campbell, *RES*, n.s. 18 (1967), 177–79

1606   OSTHOFF, Hermann. *Zur Geschichte des schwachen deutschen Adjectivums*. Jena, 1876. (lng)

†   OTTÉ, E. C., see [1179].

1607   OTTO, Ernst. *Typische Motive in dem weltlichen Epos der Angelsachsen*. Berlin, 1901. (stl, str, tec, thm)
         Reviews:
             1   G. Binz, *ESt*, 32 (1903), 401–5
             2   H. Spies, *Archiv*, 115 (1905), 222

1608   ——. *Typische Schilderungen von Lebewesen, Gegenständlichem, und Vorgängen im weltlichen Epos der Angelsachsen*. Berlin, 1901. (epc)

1609   OUTZEN, Nicolaus. "Das angelsächsische Gedicht *Beowulf*, als die Schätzbarste Urkunde des höchsten Alterthums von unserm Vaterlande." *Kieler Blätter*, 3 (1816), 307–27. (ana, com, hst)
         Review of Thorkelin [2080]

1610   OVERTON, G. H. "*Beowulf* Can Be Fun: Account of an Unorthodox Approach." *English Journal*, 42 (1953), 392–93. (sch)

1611   PADELFORD, Frederick Morgan. *Old English Musical Terms*. Bonner Beitrage, 4. Bonn, 1899. (hst)

1612   PADEN, W. D. "Beowulf and the Monster." *TLS*, 22 May 1943, p. 247. (ana) Refers to Chefneux [320]; see also Dickins [471].
         Review: D. Whitelock, *YWES*, 24 (1943), 33

1613   PAETZEL, Walther. *Die Variationen in der altgermanischen Alliterationspoesie*. Berlin, 1913. Palaestra, 48. pp. 73–84. (Fnb, var) Develops from Berlin diss., 1905.
         Review: J. Franck, *AfdA*, 37 (1914), 6–14

1614 PALMER, Arthur H. (Untitled letter to editor) *MLN*, 8 (1893), 61. (int, wrd; 1033)

1615 PALMER, Bertha. "Beowulf and Grendel." In her *Stories from the Classic Literature of Many Nations*. London and N.Y., 1898. pp. 262–64. (par) English prose paraphrase from Hall [738].

1616 PANZER, Friedrich. *Das altdeutsche Volksepos*. Halle a.S., 1903. (epc, gen, hst)

1617 ——. *Deutsche Heldensage im Breisgau*. Heidelberg, 1904. (ana, hst; 1199–1201)

1618 ——. *Studien zur germanischen Sagengeschichte*. I. *Beowulf*. Munich, 1910. (ana, mth)
   Reviews:
   1 G. Binz, *Beibl*, 24 (1913), 321–37 [109]
   2 A. Brandl, *Archiv*, 126 (1911), 231–35 [205]
   3 W. Golther, *NJKA*, 25 (1910), 610–13 [648]
   4 A. Heusler, *ESt*, 42 (1910), 289–98 [813]
   5 B. Kahle, *ZDP*, 43 (1911), 383–94 [965]
   6 W. W. Lawrence, *MLN*, 27 (1912), 57–60 [1209]
   7 W. J. Sedgefield, *MLR*, 6 (1911), 128–31 [1902]
   8 C. W. von Sydow, *AfdA*, 35 (1911), 123–31 [2052]

1619 PAST, Raymond E. "A Note on *The Rhythm of 'Beowulf'*" *MLN*, 64 (1949), 310–11. (mtr) Opposes Pope [1662].
   Review: R. M. Wilson, *YWES*, 30 (1949), 42

1620 PATZIG, H. "Zum *Beowulf*-Text." *Anglia*, 47 (1923), 97–104. (txt; 29, 303, 489, 523, 574, 586, 645, 714, 935, 988, 1002, 1015, 1016, 1097, 1129, 1174, 1214, 1378, 1440, 1508, 1557, 1634, 1807, 1926, 2152, 2222, 2239, 2297, 2442, 2642, 2858, 2886, 2941, 2990, 3006, 3038, 3056, 3074, 3126)

1621 ——. "Zur Episode von Þryð im *Beowulf*." *Anglia*, 46 (1922), 282–85. (hst, int; 1931–62)

1622 PEARCE, J. W. "Anglo–Saxon *scūrheard*." *MLN*, 7 (1892), 193–94. (int, lng, wrd; 305, 1033) Replies by Cook [376] and Hart [760].

1623 PEARCE, Thomas M. "*Beowulf* and the Southern Sun." *AN&Q*, 4 (1966), 67–68, 151; 5 (1967), 25. (img, int, mth, rel, smb; 603–6)

1624 ——. "Beowulf's Moment of Decision in Heorot." *TSL*, 11 (1966), 169–76. (epc)

1625 PEARSON, Lucien Dean. *Beowulf*. Bloomington, 1965: Midland paperback MB-73. Introd. and notes by R. L. Collins. (bbl, dct, for, gen, int, mth, mtr, nts, rel, smb,

thm, trl, wrd)   Translates into English prose, based on
Klaeber [1026] and Wrenn [2244].
Review: N. Graf, *CE*, 27 (1966), 338

1626   PENTTILÄ, Erkki. "The Old English Verbs of Vision: A
Semantic Study." *Mémoires de la Société néophilologique de
Helsinki*, 18 (1956), 1–211. (dct, lng, wrd)

1627   PEPPERDENE, Margaret W. "Beowulf and the Coast-
guard." *ES*, 47 (1966), 409–19. (for, hst, int, lng, thm)

1628   ———. "Grendel's *Geis*." *JRSAI*, 85 (1955), 188–92. (mth)

1629   ———. "Irish Christianity and *Beowulf:* Basis for a New Interpretation of the Christian Elements." Unpub. Ph.D.
diss., Vanderbilt Univ., 1953. *DA*, 13 (1953), 798–99. (int,
mth, rel, src)

1630   PEREZ, Orestes Vera. *Beowulf*. Madrid, 1959. (edt, trl)
Review: U. T. Holmes, *BA*, 35 (1961), 271

1631   PETER, I. S. *"Beowulf" and the "Rāmāyana": A Study in Epic
Poetry*. London, 1934. (epc, gen)

1632   PETERS, Leonard J. "The Relationship of the Old English
Andreas to *Beowulf*." *PMLA*, 66 (1951), 844–63. (ana, dct,
rel, src)

1633   PETERSEN, C. "Germanische Heldendichtung in
Schleswig-Holstein." *Literar. Jahrbuch für Schleswig-Holstein*,
1925. (ana, chr, Fnb)

1634   PETHERAM, J. *Historical Sketch of Anglo–Saxon Literature in
England*. London, 1840. (gen)

1635   PFÄNDLER, Wilhelm. "Die Vergnügungen der Angelsachsen." *Anglia*, 29 (1906), 417–526. (hst)

1636   PFANNKUCHE, Karl. *Der Schild bei den Angelsachsen*. Halle
diss., 1908. (arc, hst)

1637   PFEIFER, H. *Über die Art der Redeführung in der ae. erzählenden
Dichtung, im Heliand und in Layamons Brut*. Halle diss., 1924.
(dct)

1638   PFEILSTÜCKER, Suse. *Spätantikes und germanisches Kunstgut
in der frühangelsächsischen Kunst, nach lateinischen und altenglischen
Schriftquellen*. Berlin, 1936. pp. 42–54. (arc, hst)   On
Heorot.
Reviews:
1   S. Beyschlag, *AfdA*, 56 (1937), 186–88
2   G. F., *JEGP*, 39 (1940), 165
3   A. MacDonald, *MLR*, 33 (1938), 573
4   B. S., *Geistige Arbeit*, 4 (1937), 4
5   F. R. Schröder, *GRM*, 25 (1937), 237
6   M. Serjeantson, *YWES*, 17 (1936), 57
7   J. Werner, *Beibl*, 48 (1937), 289–90

1639   PFOHL, Erica. *Zur "Beowulf"-Chronologie*. Rostock diss.,
        1921. (com)

1640   PHEIFER, J. D. *"Waldere* I. 29–31." *RES*, n.s. 11 (1960),
        183–85. (int, txt; 1417–20)

1641   PHELPS, Gilbert. *A Short History of English Literature*. Lon-
        don, 1962. (gen)
        Review: T. S. Dorsch, *YWES*, 43 (1962), 11

1642   PHILIPPSON, Ernst Alfred. *Germanisches Heidentum bei den
        Angelsachsen*. Kölner Anglistische Arbeiten, 4. Leipzig,
        1929. (chr, hst, mth)
        Reviews:
            1   S. J. Crawford, *RES*, 7 (1931), 224–26
            2   M. Daunt, *YWES*, 10 (1929), 92–94
            3   H. Dehmer, *NS*, 39 (1931), 296–97
            4   A. G. van Hamel, *ES*, 12 (1930), 114–16
            5   F. Holthausen, *Beibl*, 41 (1930), 4–5
            6   G. Hübener, *LGRP*, 52 (1931), 37–41
            7   F. Klaeber, *ESt*, 65 (1931), 443–46
            8   K. Malone, *MLN*, 45 (1930), 259–60
            9   O. Ritter, *Zeitschrift für Ortsnamenforschung*, 8 (1932),
                78–91
           10   E. Voigt, *ZDP*, 56 (1931), 327–40

1643   ——. "Neuere Forschung auf dem Gebiet der germanischen
        Mythologie." *GR*, 11 (1936), 4–19. (mth)

1644   PHILLIPS, C. W. "The Excavation of the Sutton-Hoo Ship
        Burial." In R. L. S. Bruce-Mitford, ed., *Recent Archaeological
        Excavations in Britain*. London, 1956. pp. 145–66. (arc)
        Repr. 1957.
        Abridged in M. W. Wheeler, ed., *History Was Buried*. N.Y.,
        1967. pp. 351–63

1645   PHILLPOTTS, Bertha S. *"The Battle of Maldon:* Some
        Danish Affinities." *MLR*, 24 (1929), 172–90. (ana, com,
        src)
        Review: M. Daunt, *YWES*, 10 (1929), 94–95

1646   ——. "Wyrd and Providence in Anglo–Saxon Thought."
        E&S, 13 (1928), 7–27. (rel, thm)
        Reviews:
            1   M. Daunt, *YWES*, 9 (1928), 64–66
            2   S. B. Liljegren, *Beibl*, 40 (1929), 12–14

1647   PHOENIX, Walter. *Die Substantivierung des Adjectivs, Parti-
        zips und Zahlwortes im Angelsächsischen*. Berlin diss., 1918.
        (lng)
        Review: W. Fischer, *Beibl*, 31 (1920), 10–12

?1648 "PIA." (Untitled review of Thorkelin [2080]). *Jenaische Litteratur-Zeitung*, 1816, Ergänzungsblätter, nos. 45, 46, pp. 353–65.

1649 PICKERING, James D. "The Conversion of the Haugbui." *Timarit Þjóðræknisfelags Islendinga i Vesturheimi*, 47 (1966), 55–69. (ana, img, rel, src)

1650 PIERQUIN, Hubert. *Le poème anglo–saxon de "Beowulf."* Paris, 1912. (edt, Fnb, hst, lng, mtr, trl) French prose trans. of *Beowulf* and *Finnsburh*, based on Kemble text [989]; Kemble [991] printed as introd.
   Reviews:
   1 *Academy* 2, (1912), 509–10
   2 J. Barat, *MA*, 26 (1913), 298–302
   3 R. Imelmann, *DLZ*, 34 (1913), 1062–63
   4 F. Klaeber, *Beibl*, 24 (1913), 138–39
   ?5 K. Luick, *Mitt. d. inst. für österr. gesch.-forsch.*, 36 (1913), 401.
   6 W. J. Sedgefield, *MLR*, 8 (1913), 550–52

† PIGGOTT, Stuart, see [981].

1651 PILCH, L. *Umwandlung des ae. Alliterationsverses in den me. Reimvers.* Königsberg, 1904. (mtr)

1652 PIPER, William Bowman. "The Case for 'weard Scildinga' (*Beowulf*, 305b–306a)." *PQ*, 35 (1956), 202–6. (dct, int, tec, txt; 305b–306a)
   Review: R. M. Wilson, *YWES*, 37 (1956), 72

1653 PIRKHOFER, Anton. *Figurengestaltung im Beowulf-Epos.* Heidelberg, 1940. AF 87. (chr, smb)
   Reviews:
   1 F. Klaeber, *ESt*, 75 (1943), 224–26
   2 B. J. Timmer, *ES*, 25 (1943), 109–11

1654 PIZZO, Enrico. "Zur Frage der ästhetischen Einheit des *Beowulf*." *Anglia*, 39 (1915), 1–15. (chr, rel, unt)

1655 PLANTA, J. *A Catalogue of the Manuscripts in the Cottonian Library Deposited in the British Museum.* London, 1802. (mns)

1656 POGATSCHER, Alois. "Altenglisch *Grendel*." In *Luick*, p. 151. (chr, lng, mth, nam)

1657 ——. "Zu *Beowulf* 168." *Beitr*, 19 (1894), 544–45. (int, mth, rel; 168–69, 1088, 1235–36)

† POLÍVKA, Georg, see [150].

1658 PONS, Émile. "Le thème et le sentiment de la nature dans la poésie anglo–saxonne." *Publications de la Faculté des lettres de l'Université de Strasbourg et Paris*, 25 (1925). Strasbourg and Oxford, 1925. (stl, thm) Summary by Pons in *Rev. de l'Ens. des Lang. Viv.*, Dec. 1925, 439–450.

Reviews:

1   E. C. B[atho], *RES*, 2 (1926), 496–97
2   A. Brandl, *Archiv*, 151 (1927), 297
3   C. Brown, *MLR*, 21 (1926), 343–44
4   F. Delatte, *Humanitas*, 3 (1928), 57–59
5   E. V. Gordon, *YWES*, 6 (1925), 70–72
6   F. Klaeber, *Beibl*, 38 (1927), 129–32
7   E. Legouis, *RAA*, 3 (Dec. 1925), 138–40
8   K. Malone, *MLN*, 43 (1928), 406–8
9   F. Mossé, *LM*, 23 (1925), 568–71
10 J. Vendryès, *Revue Celtique*, 42 (1925), 205–7

1659   POPE, John Collins. "*Beowulf* 3150–3151: Queen Hygd and the Word 'Geomeowle.'" *MLN*, 70 (1955), 77–87. (int, txt; 2931a, 3150–51) Reply to Engelhardt [534]. Review: R. M. Wilson, *YWES*, 36 (1955), 61

1660   ——. "The Emendation 'Oreðes ond Attres,' *Beowulf* 2523." *MLN*, 72 (1957), 321–28. (mtr, txt; 2523) Opposes Orrick [1603]; defended by Stevick [2011]. Review: R. M. Wilson, *YWES*, 38 (1957), 75

1661   ——. *Old English Versification with Particular Reference to the Normal Verses of "Béowulf."* New Haven, 1957. Mimeographed. (mtr)

1662   ——. *The Rhythm of "Beowulf": An Interpretation of the Normal and Hypermetric Verse Forms in Old English Poetry.* New Haven and Oxford, 1942. (mus, mtr, txt) See Creed [413], LePage [1236], and Past [1619]. Reviews:

1   G. O. Curme, *JEGP*, 42 (1943), 115–16
2   R. Girvan, *RES*, 19 (1943), 73–77
3   J. P. Oakden, *MLR*, 38 (1943), 136–37
4   D. Whitelock, *YWES*, 23 (1942), 34

Rev. ed., 1966

1663   ——. "Three Notes on the Text of *Beowulf*." *MLN*, 67 (1952), 505–12. (int, txt; 1376b–79a, 2528b, 3151) Review: R. M. Wilson, *YWES*, 33 (1952), 41

1664   ——. (Untitled review of Brodeur [229]). *Speculum*, 37 (1962), 411–17. (for, int, ken, tec, var; 168–69)

1665   PORTENGEN, Alberta J. *De Oudgermaansche dichtertaal in haar ethnologisch verband.* Leiden diss., 1915. (ken)

1666   POWELL, Frederick York. "*Beowulf* and Watanabe-No-Tsuna." In *Furnivall*, pp. 395–96. (ana, mth)

1667   ——. "Harrison's *Beowulf*." *Academy*, 26 (1884) 327. (int, wrd)

1668   ——. "Recent *Beowulf* Literature." *Academy*, 26 (1884), 220–21. (sch)

†   ——, see [2140].

1669   PRICE, Richard. (Untitled preface) In his ed. of Thomas Warton. *History of English Poetry*. London, 1824. Vol. I, pp. 43, 94–96. (ana)
          Abbrev. repr., London, 1840. Vol. I, pp. 33, 83–85
          New ed., 1871. Vol. I, pp. 30, 68–73

1670   PROKOSCH, Eduard. "Two Types of Scribal Errors in the *Beowulf*." In *Klaeber*, pp. 196–207. (mns)
          Review: M. Daunt, 10 (1929), 80–81

1671   PUHVEL, Martin. "*Beowulf* and Celtic Under-Water adventure." *Folklore*, 76 (1965), 254–61. (ana, mth)

1672   ——. "*Lices Feorm*, l. 451, *Beowulf*." *ELN*, 1 (1964), 159–63. (int, wrd; 451)
          Review: R. M. Wilson, *YWES*, 45 (1964), 60

1673   QUASHA, George. *Beowulf*. N.Y., 1965: Monarch Notes and Study Guides, 550–54. (bbl, epc, Fnb, hst, nam, rel, rht, stl, thm, unt)

1674   QUENNELL, Marjorie, and QUENNELL, Charles Henry Bourne. "Beowulf." In their *Everyday Life in Anglo–Saxon, Viking, and Norman Times*. London and N.Y., 1927. pp. 37–41. (gen, hst)

1675   QUIRK, Randolph. "Poetic Language and Old English Metre." In *Smith*, pp. 150–71. (dct, for, mtr, tec)
          Review: R. M. Wilson, *YWES*, 44 (1963), 69

1676   RADEMACHER, Margarete. *Die Worttrennung in ags. Handschriften*. Münster diss., 1921. (lng, mns)

1677   RADKE, George. *Die Epische Formel im Nibelungenliede*. Kiel diss., 1890. (ana, dct, epc)

1678   RAFFEL, Burton. *Beowulf*. N.Y., 1963. Paperback version Mentor MP 531 has "Afterword" by Robert Creed [409]. (gen, nam, trl)
          Translates into alliterative English verse, based on Klaeber [1026] and Wrenn [2244].
          Review: E. G. Stanley, *MLR*, 59 (1964), 252–53
          Repr. in Angel Flores, ed., *Medieval Age*. N.Y., 1963. pp. 19–31. Lines 64–239, 301–30, 506–606, 662–836

1679   ——. "On Translating *Beowulf*." *YR*, 54 (1965), 532–46. (about trl)

1680   RAGLAN, FitzRoy Richard Somerset. *The Hero: A Study in Tradition, Myth, and Drama.* London, 1936. (ana, mth) Repr. N.Y., 1956: Vintage paperback K 32

1681   RAGOZIN, Zenaïde Alexeivna. "Beowulf, the Hero of the Anglo–Saxons." In her *Tales of the Heroic Age: Siegfried, the Hero of the North, and Beowulf, the Hero of the Anglo–Saxons.* London and N.Y., 1898. pp. 211–322. (par) English prose paraphrase, based on Earle [501].
Review: W. H. Hulme, *MLN,* 15 (1900), 26
2d ed., N.Y., 1900

1682   RAITH, Josef. *Geschichte der englischen Literatur.* Munich, 1961. (gen)
Review: T. S. Dorsch, *YWES,* 42 (1963), 10

1683   RAMSAY, Robert Lee. "Scyldings and Shields." *Names,* 1 (1953), 274–76. (nam) Reply to Malone [1379]; reply by Malone [1325].

1684   RAMSEY, Lee Carter. "The Theme of Battle in Old English Poetry." Unpub. Ph.D. diss., Indiana Univ., 1965. *DA,* 26 (1965), 2758. (Fnb, for, img, str, tec, thm) See Fry [588.1].

1685   RANDALL, Dale B. J. "Was the Green Knight a Fiend?" *SP,* 57 (1960), 479–91. (img, mth, smb)
Review: A. MacDonald, *YWES,* 41 (1960), 63

 †   RANISCH, W., see [1594].

1686   RANKIN, James Walter. "Rhythm and Rime before the Norman Conquest." *PMLA,* 36 (1921), 401–28. (com, mtr)

1687   ——— . "A Study of the Kennings in Anglo–Saxon Poetry." *JEGP,* 8 (1909), 357–422; 9 (1910), 49–84. (dct, img, ken, src)

1688   RASK, Rasmus Kristian. *Angelsaksisk Sproglære tilligemed en kort læsbog.* Stockholm, 1817. pp. 163–66. (edt) Lines 53–114. Uses Thorkelin [2080].
Review: *Foreign Review,* 3 (1823), 234–40; repr. *Select Journal* 2, no. 3 (1833), 104–6
Trans. into English by Benjamin Thorpe. *A Grammar of the Anglo–Saxon Tongue, from the Danish of Erasmus Rask.* Copenhagen, 1830. 2d ed., rev., London, 1865.

1689   RATHLOU, Viggo Julius von Holstein. (Untitled review of Hansen [747]). *Tilskueren,* June 1910, pp. 557–62. (about trl)

1690   RATTRAY, R. F. "Beowulf." *TLS,* 6 Jan. 1927, p. 12. (mth, smb) On boar symbolism.

1691   REDBOND, W. J. "Notes on the word 'Garsecg.'" *MLR*,
       27 (1932), 204–6. (wrd; 49, 515, 537)

1692   REHRMANN, Heinrich. *Essay concerning Anglo–Saxon Poetry.*
       Program of Höhere Bürgerschule zu Lübben, 1877. (epc,
       gen, thm)

1693   REIMAN, Donald H. "Folklore and Beowulf's Defense of
       Heorot." *ES*, 42 (1961), 231–32. (mth, src)
       Review: R. M. Wilson, *YWES*, 42 (1961), 58

1694   REINO, Joseph C. "Significant Repetition and Echo in the
       Beowulf." Unpub. Ph.D. diss., Univ. of Pennsylvania, 1951.
       DDABAU, (1950–51), no. 18, 229. (str, tec)

1695   RENOIR, Alain. "The Heroic Oath in *Beowulf,* the *Chanson
       de Roland,* and the *Nibelungenlied.*" In *Brodeur,* pp. 237–66.
       (epc, int, thm)
       Review: R. M. Wilson, *YWES*, 44 (1963), 71–72

1696   ——. "Point of View and Design for Terror in *Beowulf.*"
       NM, 63 (1962), 154–67. (ana, for, img, str, tec; 702–21)
       Review: R. M. Wilson, *YWES*, 43 (1962), 56–57

1696.1 RENWICK, W. L., and ORTON, Harold. *The Beginnings
       of English Literature to Skelton 1509.* London, 1939. (bbl,
       Fnb, mns)
       Reviews:
           1   *TLS*, 13 May 1939, p. 277
           2   G. N. Garmonsway, *YWES*, 20 (1939), 23–25
       2d ed., 1952
       Review: R. M. Wilson, *YWES*, 33 (1952), 38
       3d ed., London and N.Y., 1966; rev. by Martyn F. Wakelin

1697   REXROTH, Kenneth. "Classics Revisited–IV, *Beowulf.*"
       Saturday Review, 10 April 1965, p. 27. (gen)

1698   REYNOLDS, Robert L. "An Echo of *Beowulf* in Athelstan's
       Charters of 931–933 A.D.?" *MAE*, 24 (1955), 101–3. (ana,
       nam, src, thm)
       Review: R. M. Wilson, *YWES*, 36 (1955), 60

1699   ——. "Note on *Beowulf* 's Date and Economic-social
       History." In *Sapori,* pp. 175–78. (com, hst, src)

1700   RHYS, John. *Lectures on the Origin and Growth of Religion as
       Illustrated by Celtic Heathendom.* The Hibbert Lectures for
       1886. London and Edinburgh, 1886. pp. 592, 603, 610.
       (mth)
       2d ed., 1888; 3d ed., 1898

1701   RICCI, A. "The Chronology of Anglo–Saxon Poetry."
       RES, 5 (1929), 257–66. (com, lng)
       Review: M. Daunt, *YWES*, 10 (1929), 96

1702   RICHTER, Carl. *Chronologische Studien zur angelsächsischen Literatur auf Grund sprachlich-metrischer Kriterien.* Halle, 1910. *SEP*, 33. pp. 8–15. (com, lng, mtr)
Reviews:
    1   G. Binz, *Beibl*, 22 (1911), 78–80
    2   R. W. Chambers, *Widsith* (Cambridge, 1912), 171–74
    3   H. Hecht, *Archiv*, 130 (1913), 430–32
    4   R. Imelmann, *DLZ*, 31 (1910), 2986–87

1703   RICKERT, Edith. "The Old English Offa Saga." *MP*, 2 (1904–5), 29–76, 321–76. (ana, hst; 2358)

1704   RIEGER, Max. "Die alt- und angelsächsische Verskunst." *ZDP*, 7 (1876), 1–64; separately, Halle, 1876. (mtr)
Review: T. Schmitz, *Anglia*, 33 (1910), 176

1705   ——. *Alt- und angelsächsisches Lesebuch nebst Altfriesischen Stücken.* Giessen, 1861. pp. 63–82. (edt, Fnb) Lines 867–915, 1008–1250, 2417–2541, 2724–2820, 2845–91.

1706   ——. "Bemerkungen zum *Hildebrandsliede*." *Germania*, 9 (1864), 295–320. (mtr; 100, 175, 345, 353, 525, 558, 575)

1707   ——. "Ingväonen, Istväonen, Herminonen." *ZDA*, 11 (1859), 177–205. (hst, nam)

1708   ——. "Zum *Beowulf*." *ZDP*, 3 (1871), 381–416. (Fnb, int, mth, txt; Fep)

1709   ——. "Zum Kampf in Finnsburg." *ZDA*, 48 (1905–6), 9–12. (Fnb, txt)

1710   RIES, John. *Die Wortstellung im "Beowulf."* Halle a.S., 1907. (lng)
Reviews:
    1   *LitCbl*, 58 (1907), 1474
    2   G. Binz, *Beibl*, 22 (1911), 65–78 [108]
    3   E. Borst, *ESt*, 42 (1910), 93–101
    4   B. Delbrück, *AfdA*, 31 (1907–8), 65–76 [456]
    5   P. Doin, *RC*, 64 (1908), 488
    6   R. Huchon, *RG*, 3 (1907), 634–38
    7   H. Reis, *LGRP*, 28 (1907), 328–30

1711   ——. (Untitled review of Gering [626]). *AfdA*, 33 (1909–10), 143–47. (about trl)

1712   RIGBY, Marjory. "*The Seafarer, Beowulf* l. 769, and a Germanic Conceit." *N&Q*, 207 (1962), 246. (ana, img, wrd; 769)

1713   RIGGERT, G. *Der syntaktische Gebrauch des Infinitivs in der altenglischen Poesie.* Kiel diss., 1909. (lng)

1714   RIGGS, Strafford. *The Story of Beowulf: Retold from the Ancient Epic.* London and N.Y., 1933. Illustrated by

Henry A. Pitz, foreword by Charles J. Finger. (par) Paraphrase.

1715 RINGLER, Richard N. "*Him Sēo Wēn Gelēah:* The Design for Irony in Grendel's Last Visit to Heorot." *Speculum*, 41 (1966), 49–67. (tec, thm)

1716 ROBERTSON, D. W., Jr. "The Doctrine of Charity in Medieval Literary Gardens: A Topical Approach through Symbolism and Allegory." *Speculum*, 26 (1951), 24–49. (alg, ana, rel, smb)
Repr. in Nicholson [1560], pp. 165–88

1717 ROBINSON, B. "*Beowulf* 's English." *English Journal*, 55 (1966), 180–81, 188. (ken, lng, thm) Teaching *Beowulf* to 8th graders.

1718 ROBINSON, Fred Colson. "*Beowulf* 1917–19." *N&Q*, 211 (1966), 407–8. (int; 1917–19)

1719 ——. "Beowulf's Retreat from Frisia: Some Textual Problems in Ll. 2361–2362." *SP*, 62 (1965), 1–16. (int, txt; 2361–62)

1720 ——. "Is Wealhþeow a Prince's Daughter?" *ES*, 45 (1964), 36–39. (chr, hst; 2174)
Review: R. M. Wilson, *YWES*, 45 (1964), 60

1721 ——. "Old English Research in Progress 1964–65." *NM*, 66 (1965), 235–50. (sch)

1722 ——. "Old English Research in Progress 1965–66." *NM*, 67 (1966), 191–205. (sch)

1723 ——. "Old English Research in Progress 1966–67." *NM*, 68 (1967), 193–208. (sch)

1724 ——. "Two Non-Cruces in *Beowulf*." *TSL*, 11 (1966), 151–60. (txt; 67–70, 247–51)

1725 ——. "Variation: A Study in the Diction of *Beowulf*." Unpub. Ph.D. diss., Univ. of North Carolina, 1961. *DA*, 22 (1962), 1962. (bbl, dct, for, img, ken, tec, var, wrd)

1726 ROBINSON, W. Clark. "*Beowulf*." In his *Introduction to Our Early English Literature*. London, Durham, and Heidelberg, 1885. (trl) Translates 1–52 into English prose, 89–98 into verse.

1727 ROEDER, Fritz. *Die Familie bei den Angelsachsen:* I. *Mann und Frau.* Halle a.S., 1899. *SEP*, 4. (hst)

1728 ROGERS, H. L. "Beowulf's Three Great Fights." *RES*, n.s. 6 (1955), 339–55. (chr, hst, stl, str, unt, wrd)
Review: R. M. Wilson, *YWES*, 36 (1955), 59–60
Repr. in Nicholson [1560], pp. 233–56

1728.1 ———. "The Crypto-Psychological Character of the Oral Formula." *ES*, 47 (1966), 89–102. (dct, for)   Attacks Magoun [1306]; answer by Fry [591].

1729   RONA, Eva. *English Literature from the Beginnings to the Renaissance.* Budapest, 1965. (gen)

1730   RÖNNING, F. *Beovulfs-Kvadet: en literær-historisk under-søgelse.* Copenhagen diss., 1883. (com, gen, str)
Review: R. Heinzel, *AfdA*, 10 (1884), 233–39. [774]

1731   ROOTH, Erik G. T. "Der Name Grendel in der Beowulf-sage." *Beibl*, 28 (1917), 335–40. (chr, mth, nam)

1732   ROPER, Alan H. "Boethius and the Three Fates of *Beowulf.*" *PQ*, 41 (1962), 386–400. (rel, src, thm)
Review: R. M. Wilson, *YWES*, 43 (1962), 56

1733   ROSIER, James L. "Design for Treachery: The Unferth Intrigue." *PMLA*, 77 (1962), 1–7. (chr, hst, mth, wrd)
Answer by Ogilvy [1580].
Review: R. M. Wilson, *YWES*, 43 (1962), 57

1734   ———. "*Icge Gold* and *Incge Lafe* in *Beowulf.*" *PMLA*, 81 (1966), 342–46. (int, txt, wrd; 1107, 2577).

1735   ———. "A Textual Ambiguity in *Beowulf:* stod on stapole." *MAE*, 34 (1965), 223–25. (int, txt; 926)

1736   ———. "The *Unhlitm* of Finn and Hengest." *RES*, n.s. 17 (1966), 171–74. (int, lng, txt, wrd; 1003, 1096–99, 1127–31)

1737   ———. "The Uses of Association: Hands and Feasts in *Beowulf.*" *PMLA*, 78 (1963), 8–14. (ana, chr, dct, img, str, tec, wrd)   Reply by Byers [279].
Review: R. M. Wilson, *YWES*, 44 (1963), 73

1738   ROSS, Alan S. C. "Philological Probability Problems." *Journal of the Royal Statistical Society*, Series B (Methodological), 12 (1950), 19–41. (mtr, stl)   On alliteration.

1739   ROSTEUTSCHER, J. "Germanischer Schicksalsglaube und angelsächsische Elegiendichtung." *ESt*, 73 (1938), 1–31. (hst, mth, rel; 572–73)
Review: C. L. Wrenn, *YWES*, 19 (1938), 60

1740   ROUTH, H. V. *God, Man, and Epic Poetry: A Study in Comparative Literature.* Cambridge, 1927. Vol. II, *Medieval.* (com, epc, rel)
Reviews:
   1   M. Daunt, *YWES*, 8 (1927), 84–85
   2   C. H. Herford, *MLR*, 23 (1928), 255–59
   3   F. P. Magoun, *Speculum*, 3 (1928), 124–27

1741   ROUTH, J. "Anglo–Saxon Meter." *MP*, 21 (1923–24), 429–34. (mtr)

1742   ———. "Our Earliest English Masterpiece." *SR*, 19 (1911), 29–42. (epc, mth, stl, str)

1743   ROUTH, James Edward, Jr. "Two Studies on the Ballad Theory of the *Beowulf*, Together with an Introductory Sketch of Opinion." Ph.D. diss., Johns Hopkins Univ., 1905. (com, mth, str, tec)
Published, same title, Baltimore, 1905.
Reviews:
    1   E. Eckhardt, *ESt*, 37 (1907), 404–5
    2   A. Heusler, *AfdA*, 31 (1908), 115–16
    3   L. L. Schücking, *DLZ*, 26 (1905), 1908–10

1744   RUMBLE, Thomas C. "The *Hyran-Gefrignan* Formula in *Beowulf*." *AM*, 5 (1964), 13–20. (dct, for)

1745   RUMMONS, Constance. *Ethnic Ideals of the British Isles.* Univ. of Nebraska Studies in Language, Literature, and Criticism, 3. Lincoln, 1920. (hst, thm)

1746   RYAN, J. S. "Othin in England." *Folklore*, 74 (1963), 460–80. (img, mth, rel) Noted in *Abstracts of Folklore Studies*, 2 (1964), 4.

1747   RYDBERG, Viktor. *Undersökningar i germanisk mytologi.* Stockholm, 1886–89. (ana, chr, mth) See Gadde [599].
Trans. by R. B. Anderson. *Teutonic Mythology: Gods and Goddesses of the Northland.* London and N.Y., 1907.

1748   RYPINS, Stanley I. "The *Beowulf* Codex." *MP*, 17 (1919–20), 541–47. (com, mns)
Review: E. E. Wardale, *YWES*, 1 (1919–20), 37
Rev. version, *Colophon*, 10 (1932), [9–12]
Review: M. Daunt, *YWES*, 13 (1932), 62–63
Repr. in his [1751], pp. vii–xiv

1749   ———. "A Contribution to the Study of the *Beowulf* Codex." *PMLA*, 36 (1921), 167–85. (lng, mns) Reply by Hulbert [923].
Reviews:
    1   E. Ekwall, *Beibl*, 38 (1927), 48–52
    2   J. Hoops, *ESt*, 61 (1926–27), 435–40
Repr. in his [1751], pp. xiv–xxix

1750   ———. "The OE. *Epistola Alexandri ad Aristotelem*." *MLN*, 38 (1923), 216–20. (lng, mns)
Repr. in his [1751], pp. xxxviii–xlii

1751   ———. *Three Old English Prose Texts in MS. Codex Vitellius A. XV Edited with an Introduction and Glossarial Index.* EETS, 161. London, 1924.. (com, lng, mns) Includes [1748–50].
Reviews:
    1   E. Ekwall, *Beibl*, 38 (1927), 48–52

2   E. V. Gordon, *YWES*, 5 (1924), 66–72

3   J. Hoops, *ESt*, 61 (1927), 435–40

4   F. P. Magoun, *MLN*, 42 (1927), 67–70

1752   RYTTER, Henrik. *"Beowulf" og "Striden um Finnsborg" frå Angelsaksisk.* Oslo, 1921. (Fnb, trl) Trans. into Norwegian "Landsmaal" alliterative verse.

1753   SAINTSBURY, George Edward Bateman. *A Short History of English Literature.* London and N.Y., 1898. (gen)
2d ed., London, 1929; 3d ed., 1937

1754   SALMON, Paul. "Anomalous Alliteration in Germanic Verse." *Neophilologus*, 42 (1958), 223–42. (lng, mtr)
Review: R. M. Wilson, *YWES*, 39 (1958), 71

1755   SALUS, Peter II. "OE *eoletes.*" *Lingua*, 12 (1963), 429–30. (int, lng, wrd; 224a) Answer by Taylor [2065].
Review: R. M. Wilson, *YWES*, 44 (1963), 74

1756   ——. "OE *eoletes* Once More." *Lingua*, 13 (1965), 451. (int, lng, wrd; 224a) Answer to Taylor [2065].

1757   SAMPSON, George. *The Concise Cambridge History of English Literature.* Cambridge and·N.Y., 1941. (gen)
Review: U. Ellis-Fermor, *YWES*, 22 (1941), 7–8
2d ed., 1961
Review: T. S. Dorsch, *YWES*, 42 (1963), 9

1758   SANDBACH, Francis E. *The Nibelungenlied and Gudrun in England and America.* London, 1904. pp. 22–23, 113, 118–21. (ana, trl; 875–900) Translates 875–900, from Holder text [834].

1759   SANDER, Greif. *Gliederung und Komposition des "Beowulfs."* Mainz diss., 1955. (com, str) Pub. same title, Mainz, Berlin, Frankfurt, Leipzig, 1955.
Review: T. Riese, *Archiv*, 193 (1958), 208

1760   SANDERLIN, George. "A Note on *Beowulf* 1142." *MLN*, 53 (1938), 501–03. (int, nam, txt; 1142–43)
Review: C. L. Wrenn, *YWES*, 19 (1938), 52

1761   SANDRAS, S. G. *De Carminibus Anglo-Saxonicis Cædmoni Adjudicatis Disquisitio.* Paris, 1859. pp. 8–19. (edt, trl) Selected trans. into Latin prose.

1762   SANDYS, E. V. *Beowulf.* N.Y., London, and Toronto, 1941. (par)

1763   SARAN, Franz. "Metrik." In Richard Bethge, ed., *Ergebnisse und Fortschritte der germanistischen Wissenschaft im letzten Vierteljahrnundert.* Leipzig, 1902. pp. 158–70. (mtr)

1764   SARRAZIN, Gregor. "Die Abfassungszeit des Beowulfliedes I." *Anglia*, 14 (1892), 399–415. (com, gen)

1765   ——. "Altnordisches im Beowulfliede." *Beitr*, 11 (1886),
528–41. (com, lng, src) See Sievers [1925].

1766   ——. "Der Balder-Kultus in Lethra." *Anglia*, 19 (1897),
392–97. (hst, mth) Addendum to his [1771].

1767   ——. "Beowa und Böthvar." *Anglia*, 9 (1886), 200–204.
(nam)

1768   ——. "*Beowulf* und Kynewulf." *Anglia*, 9 (1886), 515–50.
(ana, com) On *Elene* and *Andreas*.

1769   ——. "Die Beowulfsage in Dänemark." *Anglia*, 9 (1886),
195–99. (ana)

1770   ——. *Beowulf-Studien: ein Beitrag zur Geschichte altgermanischer
Sage und Dichtung.* Berlin, 1888. (com, Fnb, lng, mth, src,
stl) English summary in Luehrs [1271].
Reviews:
1   F. Dieter, *Archiv*, 83 (1889), 352–53
2   R. Heinzel, *AfdA*, 15 (1889), 182–89
3   F. Holthausen, *LGRP*, 11 (1890), 14–16
4   E. Koeppel, *ESt*, 13 (1889), 472–80; reply by Sarrazin, *ESt*, 14 (1890), 421–27; reply by Koeppel, *ESt*,
14 (1890), 427–32
5   A. Kraus, *DLZ*, 12 (1891), 1822–23
6   F. Liebermann, *Deut. Zeitschrift für Geschichtswissenschaft*, 6 (1891), 138–39
7   E. Otto, *AZ*, 1890, no. 8, 4
8   E. Sievers, *ZDP*, 21 (1889), 366
9   R. Wülker, *Anglia*, 11 (1889), 536–41
10   ——, *LitCbl*, 40 (1889), 315–16

1771   ——. "Die Hirsch-Halle." *Anglia*, 19 (1897), 368–92.
(hst, mth) His [1766] is addendum.

1772   ——. "Hrolf Krake und sein Vetter im Beowulfliede."
ESt, 24 (1898), 144–45. (ana, hst, mth)

1773   ——. "Neue *Beowulf*-Studien: I. König Hrodgeirr und seine
Familie. II. Das Skjöldungen-Epos. III. Das Drachenlied.
IV. Das Beowulflied und Kynewulfs *Andreas*." *ESt*, 23
(1897), 221–67. (ana, hst, mth, nam)

1774   ——. "Neue *Beowulf*-Studien: V. Beowulfs Kampfgenos-
sen." *ESt*, 35 (1905), 19–27. (hst, mth)

1775   ——. "Neue *Beowulf*-Studien: VI. Æt hærgtrafum.   VII.
Fyrgenstrēam. VIII. Der Grendelsee. IX. Personennamen;
Herkunft der Sage. X. Beowulfs Ende und Bödhvar Bjarkis
Fall." *ESt*, 42 (1910), 1–37. (ana, hst, img, mth, nam,
src; 175, 1359, 2128)

1776   ——. "Parallelstellen in altenglischer Dichtung." *Anglia*,
        14 (1892), 186–92. (dct)

1777   ——. "Der Schauplatz des ersten Beowulfliedes und die
        Heimat des Dichters." *Beitr*, 11 (1886), 159–83. (com, hst,
        lng)   Reply by Sievers [1933].

1778   ——. *Von Kädmon bis Kynewulf: Eine litterar-historische
        Studie*. Berlin, 1913. (com, gen)
        Reviews:
            1   W. A. Berendsohn, *LGRP*, 35 (1914), 386–88
            2   L. Dudley, *JEGP*, 15 (1916), 313–17
            3   O. Funke, *Beibl*, 31 (1920), 121–34

1779   ——. "Zur Chronologie und Verfasserfrage angelsäch-
        sischer Dichtungen." *ESt*, 38 (1907), 145–95. (ana, com,
        lng)

1780   ——. (Untitled review of Müllenhoff [1504]) *ESt*, 16
        (1892), 71–85. (com, epc, hst, int, lng, mth)

1781   ——. (Untitled review of Heyne-Socin [815], 6th ed.) *ESt*,
        28 (1900), 408–10. (int, lng, wrd; 927, 2021ff, 2567, 3050ff,
        3084)

1782   SAVAGE, David J. "Old English Scholarship in England,
        1800–1840." Unpub. Ph.D. Diss., Johns Hopkins Univ.,
        1935. *DDABAU*, 1934–35, no. 2, 86. (sch)

1783   SCARGILL, M. H. "Gold beyond Measure: A Plea for
        Old English Poetry." *JEGP*, 52 (1953), 289–93. (gen)
        Review: R. M. Wilson, *YWES*, 34 (1953), 45

1784   SCHAAR, Claes. "On a New Theory of O.E. Poetic Dic-
        tion." *Neophilologus*, 40 (1956), 301–5. (dct, for)
        Review: R. M. Wilson, *YWES*, 37 (1956), 71

1784.1 SCHABRAM, Hans. "*Andreas* und *Beowulf*." *Nachrichten
        der Giessener Hochschulgesellschaft*, 34 (1965), 201–18. (ana,
        com)

1785   ——. *Superbia: Studien zum altenglischen Wortschatz*. Part I:
        Die dialektale und zeitliche Verbreitung des Wortguts. Munich,
        1965. (rel, thm, wrd)
        Review: A. Campbell, *RES*, n.s. 18 (1967), 177–79

1786   SCHÄFER, Hermann. *Götter und Helden: Ueber religiöse Ele-
        mente in der germanischen Heldendichtung*. Tübingen, 1937.
        (mth)

1787   SCHALDEMOSE, Frederik. "*Beo-Wulf*" og "*Scopes Widsiŏ*"
        to Angelsaxiske Digte, med Oversættelse og oplysende Anmerkingar.
        Copenhagen, 1847. (edt, Fnb, nts, trl)   Trans. into literal,
        alliterative Danish prose, with verbatim Kemble text [989].
        2d ed., actually a repr., 1851

1788   SCHAUBERT, Else von. "Zur Gestaltung und Erklärung des *Beowulf*-Textes." *Anglia*, 62 (1938), 173–89. (chr, int, lng, txt; 28–31, 932–39, 1169–85, 1174, 1931b, 2032–38, 2105–6)
Review: C. L. Wrenn, *YWES*, 19 (1938), 52

1789   ———. (Untitled review of Hoops [894]) *LGRP*, 57 (1936), 26–31. (int, lng)

†   ———, see [815.4].

1790   SCHAUFFLER, Theodor. *Zeugnisse zur Germania der Tacitus aus der altnord. und ags. Dichtung.* Ulm Programm, 1898–1900. (hst)

1791   SCHEINERT, Moritz. "Die Adjectiva im Beowulfepos als Darstellungsmittel." *Beitr*, 30 (1905), 345–430. (img, lng)

1792   SCHEMANN, Karl. *Die Synonyma im Béowulfsliede mit Rücksicht auf Composition und Poetik des Gedichtes.* Münster diss., 1882. (dct, lng, stl, str, tec, var)
Review: F. Kluge, *LGRP*, 4 (1883), 62–63

1793   SCHERER, Wilhelm. (Untitled review of Heyne [815], 2d ed.) *ZOG*, 20 (1869), 89–112. (hst)
Repr. in his *Kleine Schriften*, 1 (1893), 471–96

1794   SCHICK, J. "Die Urquelle der Offa-Konstanze-Sage." In *Förster*, pp. 31–56. (ana, hst, mth, src)

1795   SCHILLING, Hugo. "The *Finnsburg-Fragment* and Finn-Episode." *MLN*, 2 (1887), 146–50. (Fnb, hst, int, lng, nam, txt; Fep)

1796   ———. "Notes on the Finnsaga. I and II." *MLN*, 1 (1886), 89–92, 116–17. (com, Fnb, int, txt)

1797   SCHIPPER, Jakob M. *Englische Metrik.* Part 1, *Altenglische Metrik.* Bonn, 1881–82. (Mtr) Basis for his [1798].
Reviews:
        1   E. Einenkel, *Anglia*, 5 (1882), Anz., 31–53
        2   J. M. Garnett, *AJPhil*, 3 (1882), 355–60
        3   T. Wissmann, *LGRP*, 1882, no. 4 and 7, cols. 133, 271; answer by Schipper, *ESt*, 5 (1882), 487–88 and *Litbl*, 1882, no. 9, cols. 369–70
        4   R. Wülker, *LitCbl*, 1883, no. 10, cols. 332–33

1798   ———. *Grundriss der englischen Metrik.* Vienna and Leipzig, 1895. (mtr) Rev. and abridged from his [1797].
Reviews:
        1   J. Ellinger, *Beibl*, 7 (1897), 36–37
        2   M. Kaluza, *LGRP*, 1896, no. 7
        3   L. Kellner, *ZOG*, 47 (1896), 601
        4   E. A. Kock, *Archiv*, 97 (1896), 406–9

     5 A. Schröer, *LitCbl*, 46 (1895), no. 51

     6 W. Wilke, *ESt*, 23 (1897), 295–99

Trans. into English as *A History of English Versification.* Oxford, 1910.

1799 ——. "Zur altenglischen Wortbetonung." *Anglia*, 5 (1882), Anz., 88–111. (mtr) Opposed by Einenkel [515].

1800 ——. (Untitled review of Garnett [614]) *Anglia*, 6 (1883), Anz., 120–24. (about trl)

1801 SCHIRMER, Walter F. *Geschichte der englischen Literatur.* Halle, 1937. (gen, str)
Review: K. Malone, *MLN*, 54 (1939), 626–27

1802 SCHLAUGH, Margaret. "Another Analogue of *Beowulf.*" *MLN*, 45 (1930), 20–21. (ana, mth) On *Flores Saga Konungs.*
Review: M. Daunt, *YWES*, 11 (1930), 55

1803 ——. "Chaucer's Constance and Accused Queens." Ph.D. diss., Columbia Univ., 1927. (ana, chr, hst) On *Vita Offarum.* Pub. same title, N.Y., 1927.

1804 ——. *English Medieval Literature and Its Social Foundations.* Warsaw and N.Y., 1956. (epc, gen, int, thm)
Reviews:
    1 *ZAA*, 5 (1957), 329–32
    2 W. Chwalewik, *Kwartalnik Neofilologiczny*, 4 (1957), 164–67
    3 A. B. Friedman, *Speculum*, 32 (1957), 861–63
    4 R. E. Morseberger, *BA*, 32 (1958), 324
    5 R. M. Wilson, *MLR*, 52 (1957), 580–81

1805 SCHLUTTER, Otto B. "Weitere Beiträge zur altengl. Wortforschung." *Anglia*, 48 (1924), 101–4, 375–92. (dct, lng, txt, wrd; 2649–51)
Review: E. V. Gordon, *YWES*, 5 (1924), 76–77; 6 (1925), 80

1806 ——. "Zur Altenglischen Wortkunde." *ESt*, 46 (1912–13), 156–63. (lng)

1807 SCHMELLER, J. A. "Ueber den Versbau in der allitericrenden Poesie besonders der Altsachsen." *Abhandlungen der Philos.-Philologischen Klasse der Königlich Bayerischen Akademie der Wissenschaften zu München*, 4 (1844), 207–27. (mtr)

  † SCHMIDT, E., see [223].

1808 SCHMIDT, Wolfgang. "*Beowulf* als Schullektüre in neuenglischer Übertragung?" *NMs*, 6 (1935), 456–58. (com, thm)

1809 SCHMITZ, Theodor. "Die Sechstakter in der altenglischen Dichtung." *Anglia*, 33 (1910), 1–76, 172–218. (mtr)

1810   SCHNEIDER, Friedrich. *Der Kampf mit Grendels Mutter: Ein Beitrag zur Kenntnis der Komposition des "Beowulf."* Programm des Friedrichs Real-Gymnasiums. Berlin, 1887. (com, str)

1811   SCHNEIDER, Hermann. *Englische und nordgermanische Heldensage.* Berlin, 1933. Sammlung Göschen, 1064. (epc, Fnb, gen)
Review: W. A. Berendsohn, *Beibl*, 44 (1933), 257–59

1812   ——. *Germanische Altertumskunde.* Munich, 1938. (hst)
Review: L. Wolff, *AfdA*, 58 (1939), 101–10

1813   ——. *Germanische Heldensage.* Issued in parts:
I. "Deutsche Heldensage." *PGrdr* 10 (1928), no. 1
Review: A. Dunstan, *MLR*, 24 (1929), 370
Expanded by Brandl [201]
II.1. "Nordgermanische Heldensage." *PGrdr* 10 (1933), no. 2
II.2. "Englische Heldensage." *PGrdr* 10 (1934), no. 3. (Fnb, mth, src)
Review: A. Heusler, *AfdA*, 54 (1935), 102–8 [812]

1814   ——. "Zur Sigmundsage." *ZDA*, 54 (1913), 339–43. (ana, mth)

1815   SCHNEIDER, Karl. *Die Stellungstypen des finiten Verbs im urgermanischen Haupt- und Nebensatz.* Heidelberg, 1938. (lng)

1816   SCHNEPPER, Heinrich. *Die Namen der Schiffe und Schiffsteile im Altenglischen.* Kiel diss., 1908. (hst, nam, wrd)

1817   SCHOFIELD, William Henry. "Signy's Lament." *PMLA*, 17 (1902), 262–95. (ana, mth)   On Sigemund.

  †   ——, see [269].

1818   SCHOLTZ, Hendrik van der Merwe. *The Kenning in Anglo–Saxon and Old Norse Poetry.* Utrecht diss., 1927. (dct, img, ken, wrd)   Pub., same title, Utrecht and Nijmegen, 1927; Oxford, 1929.
Reviews:
    1 M. Daunt, *YWES*, 10 (1929), 96–97
    2 H. A. C. Green, *MLR*, 25 (1930), 196–97

1819   SCHÖNBACH, Anton. (Untitled review of Ettmüller [549]) *AfdA*, 3 (1877), 36–46. (com, lng, stl, wrd)   Reply by Möller [1460].

1820   SCHÖNFELD, M. *Wörterbuch der altgermanischen Personen- und Völkernamen: Nach der Überlieferung des klassischen Altertums.* Heidelberg, 1911. (hst, nam)   See Schütte [1876].

1821   SCHRADER, O. *Reallexikon der indogermanischen Altertums-kunde.* Strasbourg, 1901. (arc, hst)
Rev. ed. by A. Nehring, 1917–29

1822   SCHREINER, Katharina. *Die Sage von Hengest und Horsa: Entwicklung und Nachleben bei den Dichtern und Geschichtsschreibern Englands.* Eberings Germanische Studien, 12. Berlin, 1921. (Fnb, hst)
        Reviews:
           1   F. Klaeber, *Archiv*, 144 (1922), 276–78
           2   F. Werner, *LitCbl*, 74 (1923), 484

1823   SCHRÖBLER, Ingeborg. "*Beowulf* und Homer." *Beitr*, 63 (1939), 305–46. (ana, epc, src)

1824   SCHRÖDER, Edward. "Beowulf." *Anglia*, 56 (1932), 316–17.. (chr, mth, nam, smb) Continued by his [1827].
        Review: M. Daunt, *YWES*, 13 (1932), 60

1825   ——. "Die Leichenfeier für Attila." *ZDA*, 59 (1922), 240–44. (ana, hst) See H. Naumann, "Zeugnisse der antiken und frühmittelalterlichen Autoren." *GRM*, 15 (1923), 270.

1826   ——. "Der Name Healfdene." *Anglia*, 58 (1934), 345–50. (chr, hst, nam)
        Review: M. Serjeantson, *YWES*, 15 (1934), 63

1827   ——. "Nochmals Beowulf = 'Bienenwolf.'" *Anglia*, 57 (1933), 400. (ana, mth, nam) Continues his [1824].
        Review: D. E. M. Clarke, *YWES*, 14 (1933), 89

1828   ——. "Steigerung und Häufung der Alliteration in der west-germanischen Dichtung. I. Die Anwendung alliterierenden Nominalcomposita." *ZDA*, 43 (1899), 361–85. (lng, mtr)

1829   SCHRØDER, Ludwig. *Om Bjovulfs-drapen: Efter en række foredrag på folske-höjskolen i Askov.* Copenhagen, 1875. (chr, hst)

1830   SCHRÖER, A. "Zur Texterklärung des *Beowulf*." *Anglia*, 13 (1891), 333–48. (int, txt; 1117, 1363, 1392, 1440, 1671–76, 1681–1765, 1802–5, 1807–12, 1830–35, 1873–76, 2127–28, 2156–62, 2212, 2240, 2347, 2410, 2518–21, 2957–60) See Sievers [1947].

1831   SCHRÖER, M. M. A. *Grundzüge und Haupttypen der englischen Literaturgeschichte.* Berlin, 3d ed., 1927. Sammlung Göschen, 286. Part I, pp. 40–54. (gen)

1832   SCHUBEL, F. *Englische Literaturgeschichte. I. Die alt- und mittelenglische Periode.* Berlin, 1954. Sammlung Göschen, B. 1114. (gen)
        Reviews:
           1   H. Marcus, *Archiv*, 191 (1956), 95
           2   R. M. Wilson, *YWES*, 35 (1954), 39

1833   SCHUBERT, Hermann. *De Anglo-Saxonum Arte Metrica.* Berlin diss., 1870. (mtr) Reply by Vetter [2138].

1834   SCHUCHARDT, Richard. *Die Negation im "Beowulf."*
        Berliner Beiträge zur germ. und roman. Philol., 38. Berlin,
        1910. (lng)

1835   SCHÜCK, Henrik. *Folknamnet Geatas i den fornengelska dikten
        "Beowulf."* Upsala Universitets Årsskrift, 1907, Program 2.
        Uppsala, 1907. (hst, nam)
        Reviews:
            1   V. O. Freeburg, *JEGP*, 11 (1912), 279–83
            2   A. Mawer, *MLR*, 4 (1908–9), 273

1836   ——. *Studier i Beowulfsagan.* Upsala Universitets Årsskrift,
        1909, Program 1. Uppsala, 1909. (com, hst, mth, str)
        Review: V. O. Freeburg, *JEGP*, 11 (1912), 488–97. [585]

1837   ——. *Studier i Ynglingatal.* Uppsala, 1905. (ana, hst)

1838   ——. *Sveriges förkristna konungalängd.* Uppsala, 1910. (hst)

†   ——, see [112].

1839   Item canceled.

1840   SCHÜCKING, Levin Ludwig. "Altengl. *scepen* und die
        sogen. idg. Vokativreste im Altengl." *ESt*, 44 (1911–12),
        155–57. (int, lng, wrd; 106) See Sievers [1923].

1841   ——. "Das angelsächsische Totenklagelied." *ESt*, 39
        (1908), 1–13. (dct, img, thm)

1842   ——. "Die angelsächsische und frühmittelenglische Dich-
        tung." Part I of his and Hans Hecht's *Die Englische Literatur
        im Mittelalter.* Potsdam, 1927. pp. 1–35. (gen) Sometimes
        listed as part of Oskar Walzel, ed., *Handbuch der Literaturwis-
        senschaft.*

1843   ——. "*Beowulf* 1174." *ESt*, 44 (1911–12), 157. (txt; 1174)
        Reply by Sievers [1928].

1844   Item canceled.

1845   ——. "Die Beowulfdatierung. Eine Replik." *Beitr*, 47
        (1923), 293–311. (com, hst)

1846   ——. *Beowulfs Rückkehr.* Halle a.S., 1905. *SEP*, 21. (com,
        lng, mtr, stl)
        Review: A. Brandl, *Archiv*, 115 (1905), 421–23

1847   ——. *Die Grundzüge der Satzverknüpfung im "Beowulf."* Part I.
        Halle a.S., 1904. *SEP*, 15. (Fnb, lng)
        Reviews:
            1   O. Behagel, *LGRP*, 28 (1907), 100–102
            2   E. Eckhardt, *ESt*, 37 (1907), 396–97
            3   H. Grossmann, *Archiv*, 118 (1907), 176–79
            4   A. Pogatscher, *DLZ*, 26 (1905), 922–23

1848   ——. *Heldenstolz und Würde im Angelsächsischen. Mit einem
        Anhang: Zur Charakterisierungstechnik im Beowulfepos.* Abhand-
        lungen der Sächsischen Akademie der Wissenschaften,

Philol.-Histor. Klasse, Vol. 42, no. 5, 1933.   (chr, stl, thm)
See his [1849].
Reviews:

1   W. F. Bryan, *JEGP*, 34 (1935), 104–5
2   S. Einarsson, *MLN*, 50 (1935), 108–11
3   F. Fiedler, *Zeitschrift für Neusprachlichen Unterricht*, 34 (1935), 120–21
4   H. Glunz, *Beibl*, 45 (1934), 257–65
5   H. Heuer, *LGRP*, 56 (1935), 19–21
6   A. Heusler, *AfdA*, 53 (1934), 219–20
7   A. MacDonald, *MLR*, 30 (1935), 221–22
8   K. Malone, *ES*, 16 (1935), 141
9   W. Mann, *Neue Jahrbücher für Wissenschaft und Jugendbildung*, 10 (1934), 562
10 F. Ranke, *ZDP*, 61 (1936), 215–16
?11 H. Schneider, *DL*, 6 (1935), 547–48
12 F. Schröder, *GRM*, 22 (1934), 327

1849   ——. "Heldenstolz und Würde im Angelsächsischen." *FuF*, 10 (1935), 4–5.   (chr, stl, thm)   See his [1848].

1850   ——. "Heroische Ironie im ags. "Seefahrer.'"   In *Deutschbein*, pp. 72–74.   (stl, tec, thm)
Review: M. Serjeantson, *YWES*, 17 (1936), 64

1851   ——. *Kleines angelsächsisches Dichterbuch: Lyric und Heldensagen: Text und Textproben, mit kurzer Einleitung und ausführlichem Wörterbuch.*   Cöthen, 1919.   (edt, Fnb)   Edits *Beowulf* 1063–1160a, 1888–2199; and *Finnsburh*.
Reviews:

1   G. Binz, *LGRP*, 41 (1920), 315–16
2   W. Fischer, *ESt*, 54 (1920), 302–3
3   F. Holthausen, *Beibl*, 32 (1921), 80–83 [880]
4   R. Imelmann, *DLZ*, 40 (1919), 423–25
Repr. Leipzig, 1933

1852   ——. "Das Königsideal im *Beowulf*."   *MHRA Bulletin*, 3 (1929), 143–54.   (hst, mth, rel, src, thm)
Also in *ESt*, 67 (1932), 1–14.
Review: M. Daunt, *YWES*, 13 (1932), 58–59
Repr. in Nicholson [1560], pp. 35–49, trans. into English

1853   ——. "Noch einmal: *Enge ānpaðas, uncūð gelād*."   In *Klaeber*, pp. 213–16.   (com, int, src; 1409–11)
Review: M. Daunt, *YWES*, 10 (1929), 81

1854   ——. "*Sōna* im *Beowulf*."   In *Förster*, pp. 85–88.   (lng, wrd)
Review: M. Daunt, *YWES*, 10 (1929), 87

1855   ——. *Untersuchungen zur Bedeutungslehre der angelsächsischen Dichtersprache.*   Heidelberg, 1915.   (dct, lng, wrd)

1856   ——. "Wann entstand der *Beowulf?* Glossen, Zweifel und Fragen."   *Beitr*, 42 (1917), 347–410.   (com, hst)

1857   ——. "Wiðergyld (*Beowulf* 2051)." *ESt*, 53 (1919–20), 468–70. (chr, int; 2051)

1858   Item canceled.

1859   ——. (Untitled review of Trautmann [2106]) *Archiv*, 115 (1905), 417–21. (int, lng, txt)

1860   ——. (Untitled review of Holthausen [845], 1st ed.) *ESt*, 39 (1908), 94–111. (int, lng; 14–15, 31, 44, 143, 149, 442ff, 489–90, 572–73, 599, 710, 720, 749, 913ff, 915, 976, 1032, 1129ff, 1231, 1260, 1271, 1334, 1382, 1459, 1783, 1885, 1923, 1931ff, 2048, 2051, 2109, 2245, 2353, 2468, 2766, 2829, 3074ff)

1861   ——. (Untitled review of Holthausen [845], 2d ed.) *ESt*, 42 (1910), 108–111. (int, lng, mns; 1121–22, 2505)

1862   ——. (Untitled review of Wyatt/Chambers [2267]) *ESt*, 55 (1921), 88–100. (int, txt)

1863   ——. (Untitled review of Barnouw [62]) *GGA*, 167 (1905), II, 730–40. (lng, txt)

†   ——, see [815], 8th ed.

1864   SCHUHMANN, G. "Beovulf, antichissimo poema epico de' popoli germanici." *Giornale napoletano di filosofia e lettere, scienze morali e politiche*, Anno 4 (1882), Vol. 7, 25–36, 175–90. (trl) First Italian translation.

1865   SCHULTZE, Martin. *Alt-Heidnisches in der angelsächsischen Poesie, speciell im Beowulfsliede.* Berlin, 1877. (hst, mth, rel) Review: A. Chuquet, *RC*, n.s. 4 (1877), no. 32, 72.

1866   ——. "Ueber das Beowulfslied." *Programm der städtischen Realschule zu Elbing*, 1864. (mth) Summary in *Archiv*, 37 (1865), 232.

1867   SCHULZ, F. *Die Sprachformen des Hildebrands-Liedes im "Beowulf."* Programm der Realschule auf der Burg zu Königsberg in Preussen, no. 17, 1882. pp. 1–21. (ana, dct)

1868   SCHÜTT, J. H. "A Guide to English Studies: The Study of Old and Middle English Literature." *ES*, 9 (1927), 140–48. (bbl)

1869   SCHÜTTE, Gudmund. "Anglian Legends in Danish Traditions." *APS*, 16 (1943), 233–38. (ana, mth, src)

1870   ——. "Daner og Eruler." *DS*, 24 (1927), 65–74. (hst, nam) Opposes Wessén [2187].

1871   ——. "Episoderne med Hygelac og Ongentheow." *DS*, 37 (1940), 49–58. (epc, int, thm)

1872   ——. "Ethnische Prunknamen." *ZDA*, 67 (1930), 129–39. (dct, int, nam)

1873 ——. "Geaterspørgsmaalet." *DS*, 27 (1930), 70–81. (hst)

1874 ——. "The Geats of *Beowulf*." *JEGP*, 11 (1912), 574–602. (hst)

1875 ——. *Gotthiod und Utgard: Altgermanischen Sagengeographie in neuer Auffassung*. Copenhagen and Jena, 1935–36. (hst, mth)

1876 ——. "Notes til Schönfelds Navnesamling." *ANF*, 33 (1911), 22–49. (hst, nam) On Schönfeld [1820].

1877 ——. "Offa I Reduced ad Absurdum." *APS*, 19 (1947–49), 179–96. (chr, epc, hst, nam) On Ingeld.

1878 ——. "Skjoldungsagnene i ny Læsemaade." *DS*, 39 (1942), 81–100. (ana, epc, hst, thm)

1879 ——. "Vidsid og Slægtssagnene om Hengest og Angantyr." *ANF*, 36 (1919–20), 1–32. (ana, Fnb, nam)

1880 ——. *Vor Folkegruppe: Gottjod*. Copenhagen, 1926. (hst, nam)
Review: M. Schönfeld, *APS*, 3 (1928), 86–89.
Trans. into English by Jean Young as *Our Forefathers the Gothonic Nations*. Cambridge, 1929, 1933. 2 vols. rev. of 1926 ed.
Reviews:
  1 *TLS*, 22 Aug. 1929, p. 647
  2 W. E. Collinson, *MLR*, 25 (1930), 231–34
  3 E. Ekwall, *Antiquity*, 4 (1930), 527–28
  4 K. Malone, *MLN*, 50 (1935), 106–8
  5 A. Mawer, *EHR*, 45 (1930), 641–42

1881 SCHÜZ, Monika. "Beowulf." In *Kindlers Literatur Lexicon*. Zurich, 1964. Vol. I, cols. 1500–1502. (bbl, gen)

1882 SCHWARTZKOPFF, Werner. *Rede und Redeszene in der deutschen Erzählung bis Wolfram von Eschenbach*. Palaestra, 74. Berlin, 1909. (stl)

1883 SCHWEITZER, Henry P. "The Idea of the King in Old English Literature." Unpub. Ph.D. diss., Fordham Univ., 1941. *DDABAU*, 1940–41, no. 8, 118. (epc, hst, int, thm)

1884 SCOTT, N. F. "Vowel Alliteration in Mn. E." *MLN*, 30 (1915), 233–37. (mtr)

1885 SCOTT, (Sir) Walter. "Essay on Romance." In his *Essays on Chivalry, Romance and the Drama*. London and Edinburgh, 1824. (gen)

1886 SCOTT-THOMAS, H. F. "The *Fight at Finnsburg*: Guthlaf and the Son of Guthlaf." *JEGP*, 30 (1931), 498–505. (Fnb, int, lng, nam) Answer by Klaeber [1038].
Review: D. E. M. Clarke, *YWES*, 12 (1931), 71

1887   SCRIPTURE, E. W. "Experimentelle Untersuchungen über die Metrik im *Beowulf.*" *Archiv für die gesamte Psychologie*, 66 (1928), 203–15. (mtr)
Review: M. Daunt, *YWES*, 9 (1928), 72–74

1888   ——. "Die Grundgesetze des altenglischen Stabreimverses." *Anglia*, 52 (1928), 69–75. (mtr)
Review: M. Daunt, *YWES*, 9 (1928), 72–74

1889   ——. *Grundzüge der englischen Verswissenschaft.*   Marburg, 1929. (mtr)
Reviews:
   ?1   A. Brandl, *DL*, 51 (1930), 23–26
   2   B. E. C. Davis, *MLR*, 25 (1930), 358–59
   3   G. Panconcelli-Calzia, *LGRP*, 51 (1930), 195–97
   4   R. A. Williams, *Beibl*, 41 (1930), 357–62

1890   SEAL, Gabriel. "Heorot in *Beowulf.*"   *N&Q*, 174 (1938), 245. (hst, nam)   On location of Heorot.

1891   SEDGEFIELD, Walter John.   *An Anglo–Saxon Verse-Book.* Manchester and London, 1922.   (edt, Fnb, hst, mth)   Edits 1160 rearranged lines.
Reviews:
   1   S. J. Crawford, *MLR*, 19 (1924), 104–8 [408]
   2   H. M. Flasdieck, *Beibl*, 35 (1924), 165–66
   3   F. Klaeber, *JEGP*, 23 (1924), 121–24
   4   E. E. Wardale, *YWES*, 3 (1922), 27–29
Repr. in his *An Anglo–Saxon Book of Verse and Prose.*   London and Manchester, 1928
Reviews:
   1   *TLS*, 10 Oct. 1929, p. 792
   2   L. Cooper, *JEGP*, 28 (1929), 541–42
   3   M. Daunt, *YWES*, 9 (1928), 76
   4   E. von Erhardt-Siebold, *ESt*, 67 (1932), 108–12
   5   K. Malone, *MLN*, 44 (1929), 204
   6   A. H. Smith, *SN*, 1 (1928), 151–52

1892   ——. *Beowulf edited with Introduction, Bibliography, Notes, Glossary, and Appendices.*   Publications of the Univ. of Manchester, no. 238, English Series 2.   Manchester, 1910.   (ana, bbl, com, edt, Fnb, hst, lng, mns, mth, mtr, nam, nts, str, txt, unt)
Reviews:
   1   *Nation*, 92 (1911), 505b–c
   2   A. Brandl, *Archiv*, 126 (1911), 279
   3   F. Klaeber, *ESt*, 44 (1911–12), 119–26 [1070]
   4   W. W. Lawrence, *JEGP*, 10 (1911), 633–40 [1206]
   5   P. G. Thomas, *MLR*, 6 (1911), 266–68 [2075]

6 F. Wild, *Beibl*, 23 (1912), 253–60

2d ed., 1913

Reviews:

    1   *MLR*, 9 (1914), 429

    2   F. Klaeber, *Beibl*, 25 (1914), 166–68

    3   W. W. Lawrence, *JEGP*, 14 (1915), 609–11

3d ed., 1935

Reviews:

    1   D. E. M. Clarke, *YWES*, 16 (1935), 74–76

    2   E. V. K. Dobbie, *MLN*, 53 (1938), 456–57

    3   J. R. H., *MP*, 33 (1936), 439

    4   F. Holthausen, *LGRP*, 59 (1938), 163–67 [887]

    5   K. Malone, *ES*, 18 (1936), 257–58 [1400]

    6   H. Marcus, *Beibl*, 47 (1936), 129–31

1893   ——. "Emendations of the *Beowulf* Text." *MLR*, 27 (1932), 448–51. (txt; 32, 33, 387, 489–90, 617–618, 936, 1107–8, 1375, 2575–77, 2764–66, 2989, 3074–75)
Review: M. Daunt, *YWES*, 13 (1932), 59–60

1894   ——. "The Finn Episode in *Beowulf*." *MLR*, 28 (1933), 480–82. (hst, int, nam; Fep)
Review: D. E. M. Clarke, *YWES*, 14 (1933), 84–85

1895   —— "Further Emendations of the *Beowulf* Text." *MLR*, 28 (1933), 226–30. (txt; 357, 667 68, 1833, 2241–43, 2288, 2333–35, 2455–57, 3014–15)
Review: D. E. M. Clarke, *YWES*, 14 (1933), 85

1896   Item canceled.

1897   ——. "Miscellaneous Notes: Suggested Emendations in Old English Texts." *MLR*, 16 (1921), 59. (Fnb, txt; Fnb 35, 40) Opposed by Mackie [1290].

1898   ——. "Notes on *Beowulf*." *MLR*, 5 (1910), 286–88. (int, lng, txt; 31, 204, 223–24, 413–14, 567, 985, 991, 1134–35, 1161, 2029, 2333–35, 2475, 2525, 2558–59, 2659, 2766, 2854)

1899   ——. "Old English Notes." *MLR*, 18 (1923), 471–72. (int, lng, mtr, wrd; 223–24)

1900   ——. "The Scenery in *Beowulf*." *JEGP*, 35 (1936), 161–69. (com, hst, img)
Review: M. Serjeantson, *YWES*, 17 (1936), 62

1901   ——. (Untitled review of Gummere [720]) *ESt*, 41 (1910), 402–3. (about trl)

1902   ——. (Untitled review of Panzer [1618]) *MLR*, 6 (1911), 128–31. (ana, mth)

1903   ——. (Untitled review of Hall [739]) *MLR*, 10 (1915), 387–89. (mtr, about trl)

1904   ——. (Untitled review of Hoops [896]) *MLR*, 28 (1933), 373–75. (int, lng, mtr, txt; 150, 305, 399, 410, 758, 1086, 1106, 1169, 1379, 1382, 1892, 1931, 2488, 2629, 2673)

1905   SEEBOHM, Frederic. *Tribal Custom in Anglo–Saxon Law.* London and N.Y., 1902. (hst)

1906   SEIFFERT, Friedrich. *Die Behandlung der Wörter mit aus-lautenden ursprünglich silbischen Liquiden oder Nasalen und mit Kontraktionsvokalen in der Genesis A und im Beowulf.* Halle diss., 1913. (com, lng)

1907   SERJEANTSON, Mary S. "Old English." *YWES*, 15 (1934), 60–82. (sch)

1907.1 ——. "Old English." *YWES*, 17 (1936), 57–69. (sch)

1908   SERRAILLIER, Ian. *Beowulf, the Warrior.* London, 1954. (trl)

1909   SETZLER, Edwin B. *On Anglo–Saxon Versification from the Standpoint of Modern-English Versification.* Univ. of Virginia Studies in Teutonic Languages, 5. (Baltimore, 1904. (mtr)

1910   SEVERINSEN, P. "Kong Hugleiks Dødsaar." *DS*, 16 (1919), 96. (hst)

1911   SEWELL, William A. P. "A Reading in *Beowulf*." *TLS*, 11 Sept. 1924, p. 556. (hst, int, nam; 6a)

1912   SHAHAN, Thomas J. "Beowulf." In his *A Book of Famous Myths and Legends.* Boston, 1901. (par) English summary. Repr. in Hamilton W. Mabie; ed., *Legends That Every Child Should Know.* N.Y., 1906.

†   SHARP, Robert, see [754].

1913   SHAW, Thomas B. *Shaw's New History of English Literature.* Ed. by Truman J. Backus. N.Y., 1874. pp. 14–16. (gen)

1914   SHEARIN, H. G. "The Expression of Purpose in Old English Poetry." *Anglia*, 32 (1909), 235–52. (epc, lng)

1915   SHEPHERD, R. A. "Resuscitating the Epic." *English Journal* (High School Ed.), 21 (1932), 64–65. (epc, ref; 380–645, 916–1001, 1410–1585)

1916   SHETELIG, Haakon, and FALK, Hjalmar. *Scandinavian Archaeology.* Trans. with additional notes by E. V. Gordon. Oxford, 1937. (arc, hst)
        Reviews:
            1 J. Blomfield, *RES*, 14 (1938), 333–37
            2 C. L. Wrenn, *YWES*, 19 (1938), 40–41

1917   SHIMIZU, Tokio. "Pleonasm in *Beowulf*." In *Nakayama*, pp. 243–57. (dct, lng, var)

1918   SHIPLEY, George. "The Genitive Case in Anglo–Saxon Poetry." Ph.D. diss., John Hopkins Univ., 1903. (lng) Published, same title, Baltimore, 1903.

Reviews:

   1   E. A. Kock, *ESt*, 35 (1905), 92–95

   2   V. Mourek, *AfdA*, 30 (1906), 172–74

1919   SHUMAN, R. Baird, and HUTCHINGS, H. Charles, III. "The *un*-Prefix: A Means of Germanic Irony in *Beowulf*." *MP*, 57 (1960), 217–22. (int, lng, rht, stl, about trl)
Review: R. M. Wilson, *YWES*, 41 (1960), 54

1920   SIDDHANTA, N. K. *Heroic Age of India*. London and N.Y., 1929. (ana, epc)

1921   SIEBS, Theodor. "Altfriesische Literatur." *PGrdr*, IIa (1893), 494–95. (Fnb, gen, mth, nam)
2d ed., 1902, pp. 523–24

1922   SIEPER, Ernst. *Die altenglische Elegie*. Strasbourg, 1915. (gen)
Review: L. L. Schücking, *ESt*, 51 (1917), 97–115

1923   SIEVERS, Eduard. "Ags. *scepen*." *ESt*, 44 (1912), 295–96. (int, lng, wrd; 106, 1174) Reply to Schücking [1840].

1924   ——. *Altgermanische Metrik*. Halle, 1893. (mtr)
Reviews:

   1   J. Franck, *AfdA*, 20 (1894), 337–43

   2   H. Hirt, *LGRP*, 1893, no. 9, cols. 455–57

   3   K. Luick, *AIS*, 3 (1894), 144–55

 ?4   O. Lyon, *Zeitschrift für deutschen Unterricht*, 7 (1893), 281–82

   5   W. Streitberg, *LitCbl*, (1893), no. 24, cols. 1865–66

 ?6   J. E. Wackernell, *Das Österreichische Literaturblatt*, 2 (1893), 4

Abridged in *PGrdr*, IIa (1893), 861–97; 2d ed., IIb (1905), 1–38

1925   ——. "Altnordisches im Beowulf?" *Beitr*, 12 (1887), 168–200. (com, lng) Opposes Sarrazin [1765]; reply by Gallée [602].

1926   ——. "Der angelsächsische Schwellvers." *Beitr*, 12 (1887), 454–82. (mtr) Continued by Kauffmann [979].

1927   ——. "*Beowulf* 240f." *Beitr*, 21 (1896), 436. (mtr; 240–41)

1928   ——. "*Beowulf* 1174." *ESt*, 44 (1912), 296–97. (txt; 1174) Answer to Schücking [1843].

1929   ——. "*Beowulf* 3066ff." *Beitr*, 55 (1931), 376. (com, lng, txt; 3066–73)

1930   ——. "*Beowulf* und Saxo." *Berichte über die Verhandlungen der Königl. Sächsischen Gesellschaft der Wissenschaften zu Leipzig, Philol.-Hist. Classe*, 47 (1895), 175–92. (ana, chr, hst, mth)

1931   ——. "Gegenbemerkungen zum *Beowulf*." *Beitr*, 36 (1910), 397–434. (int) Opposes von Grienberger [680].

1932   ——. "Grammatische Miscellen." *Beitr*, 18 (1894), 407–16. (chr, mth, nam) On the name "Beowulf"; opposes Kögel [1109].

1933   ——. "Die Heimat des Beowulfdichters." *Beitr*, 11 (1886), 354–62. (com, lng) Opposes Sarrazin [1777]; reply by Gallée [602].

1934   ——. *Heliand*. Halle, 1878. pp. 389–495. (ana, dct) Review: M. Roediger, *AfdA*, 5 (1879), 267–68

1935   ——. "Lückenbüsser." *Beitr*, 27 (1902), 572. (int, txt; 33) Review of Trautmann [2107].

1936   ——. "Metrische Studien IV: Die altschwedischen Upplandslagh nebst Proben formverwandter germanischen Sagendichtung." *Abhandlungen der Königl. sächsischen Gesellschaft der Wissenschaften, Philol.-hist. Klasse*, 35. Leipzig, 1918–19. (mtr)

1937   ——. "Sceaf in den nordischen Genealogien." *Beitr*, 16 (1892), 361–63. (chr, hst, mth)

1938   ——. *Ziele und Wege der Schallanalyse*. Heidelberg, 1924. (mtr)

1939   ——. "Zu Cynewulf." In *Luick*, pp. 60–81. Mtr)

1940   ——. "Zum *Beowulf*." *Beitr*, 9 (1884), 135–44, 370. (txt)

1941   ——. *Ibid.*, 18 (1894), 406–7. (txt; 283) Review of Cosijn [389].

1942   ——. *Ibid.*, 28 (1903), 271–72. (txt; 48ff, 515) Review of Trautmann [2107].

1943   ——. *Ibid.*, 29 (1904), 305–31. (txt) Opposes Trautmann [2107]; reply by Trautmann [2104].

1944   ——. *Ibid.*, pp. 560–76. (txt; 6) Reply to Kock [1095]; reply by Kock [1107].

1945   ——. "Zur Rhythmik des germanischen Alliterationsverses: I. Vorbemerkungen: Die Metrik des *Beowulf*." *Beitr*, 10 (1885), 209–314. (mtr) Separate repr., N.Y., 1909

1946   ——. "Zur Rhythmik des germanischen Alliterationsverses. III." *Beitr*, 12 (1887), 454–82. (mtr; 1164–69, 1706–8, 2996–97)

1947   ——. "Zur Texterklärung des *Beowulf*." *Anglia*, 14 (1892), 133–46. (int, txt) Opposes Schröer [1830].

1948   ——. (Unpub. ed. of *Beowulf*) Univ. of Leipzig Library. (edt) An ed. based on "Schallanalyse"; see Holthausen [845] and [887].

1949   ——. (Untitled review of Heyne/Socin [815], 5th ed.) *ZDP*, 21 (1889), 354–65. (txt)

1950   SILVER, Thomas. "A Lecture on the Study of Anglo–Saxon." Valedictory lecture 1822 Rawlinson Chair. Oxford, 1822. (gen, hst, lng)

1951   SIMONS, L. *Beowulf: Angelsaksich Volkepos vertaald in stafrijm en mit inleiding en aanteekeningen.* Koninklijke Vlaamsche Academie voor Taal- & Letterkunde. Ghent, 1896. (com, epc, Fnb, hst, mns, mth, mtr, nts, rel, trl, txt) Literal Dutch verse based on Heyne-Socin [815], 5th ed.
Reviews:
    1 O. Glöde, *ESt*, 25 (1898), 270–71
    2 C. C. Uhlenbeck, *Museum*, 5 (1898), 217–18

1952   SIMROCK, Karl. *Beowulf: Das älteste deutsche Epos.* Stuttgart and Augsburg, 1859. (chr, com, Fnb, trl) Translated *Beowulf* and *Finnsburh* into German alliterative verse, based on Grein [675].

1953   SINGER, S. "Miscellen." *Beitr*, 12 (1887), 211–15. (txt; 1107)

1954   SISAM, Kenneth. "Addendum: The Verses Prefixed to *Gregory's Dialogues.*" *SHOEL*, pp. 225–31. (mns) Answer to Dobbie [481].

1955   ——. "Anglo–Saxon Royal Genealogies." *PBA*, 39 (1953), 288–348. (chr, hst, mth, nam, src)
Review: R. M. Wilson, *YWES*, 34 (1953), 42–43

1956   ——. "The *Beowulf* Manuscript." *MLR*, 11 (1916), 335–37. (lng, mns; 70, 475, 2141, 2197) Opposes Hargrove [751]; continued by Förster [577].
Review: E. F. Wardale, *YWES*, 1 (1919–20), 37
Repr. in *SHOEL*, pp. 61–64

1957   ——. "Beowulf's Fight with the Dragon." *RES*, n.s. 9 (1958), 129–40. (com, img, int, stl, tec, txt; 3069–73)
Reviews:
    1 *AES*, 1 (1958), no. 1057
    2 R. M. Wilson, *YWES*, 39 (1958), 72

1958   ——. "The Compilation of the *Beowulf* Manuscript." *SHOEL*, pp. 65–96. (lng, mns, txt; 1799)

1959   ——. "Cynewulf and His Poetry." The Sir Israel Gollancz Memorial Lecture, read 8 March 1933. *PBA*, 18 (1932), 303–31. (com, dct, var; 344–53)
Repr. in *SHOEL*, pp. 1–28

1960   ——. "Dialect Origins of the Earlier Old English Verse." *SHOEL*, pp. 119–39. (com, dct, Fnb, lng)

1961   ——. "Notes on Old English Poetry: The Authority of Old English Poetical Manuscripts." *RES*, 22 (1946), 257–68.

(Fnb, mns, nam, txt; 61, 152, 461, 467, 875, 901, 1127–48,
1261, 1709, 1931, 1960–61, 1981, 2158, 2453, 2780, 3150)
Review: M. Daunt, *YWES*, 29 (1946), 62
Repr. in *SHOEL*, pp. 29–44

1962   ——— . *The Structure of "Beowulf."* Oxford, 1965.   (chr, for,
hst, int, rel, str; 837–927, 1164, 1888–2199)
Reviews:
   1   C. R. Barrett, *AUMLA*, 24 (1965), 294–95
   2   M. W. Bloomfield, *Speculum*, 41 (1966), 368–71
   3   A. G. Brodeur, *ELN*, 4 (1966), 133–35 [234]
   4   T. Finkenstaedt, *Anglia*, 83 (1965), 490–91
   5   M. E. Goldsmith, *N&Q*, 210 (1965), 469–70
   6   J. Milosh, *Cithara*, 5 (1966), 52–58 [1451]
   7   B. Mitchell, *RES*, 17 (1966), 190–91
   8   W. Riehle, *Archiv*, 118 (1967), 300–302
   9   K. Shinobu, *SELJ*, 42 (1966), 265–68 (in Japanese)
  10   J. B. Trahern, *JEGP*, 65 (1966), 701–2
  11   J. C. van Meurs, *ES*, 47 (1966), 140–43
  12   W. Whallon, *MP*, 64 (1966), 68–69

1963   ——— . *Studies in the History of Old English Literature.*   Oxford,
1953. Collection of essays, including his [1954, 1956, 1958–
1961].
Reviews:
   1   *DUJ*, 45 (1953), 123
   2   *TLS*, 27 Mar. 1953, p. 203
   3   D. Bethurum, *Speculum*, 29 (1954), 162–64
   4   K. Brunner, *Anglia*, 72 (1954–55), 469–73
   5   J. R. Hulbert, *MP*, 52 (1954), 273–74
   6   K. Jost, *MAE*, 24 (1955), 129–35
   7   F. Mossé, *EA*, 7 (1954), 227
   8   T. F. Mustanoja, *NM*, 56 (1955), 232–39
   9   G. Storms, *ES*, 36 (1955), 314–18
  10   B. J. Timmer, *RES*, 5 (1954), 275–77
  11   R. M. Wilson, *MLR*, 49 (1954), 62–63
  12   R. M. Wilson, *YWES*, 34 (1953), 43–44
Corrected repr., 1962

1964   SKEAT, Walter William.   *English Dialects from the Eighth
Century to the Present Day.* Cambridge, 1911. pp. 7–9. (ana,
txt, wrd; 1357b–76)
Repr. 1912

1965   ——— . "Essay on Alliterative Poetry."   In F. J. Furnivall
and J. W. Hales, eds., *Bishop Percy's Folio Manuscript.* London, 1868. Vol. III, pp. xi–xxxix. (mtr)

1966   ——— . "The Name Beowulf."   *Academy*, 11 (1877), 163c.
(chr, mth, nam)

1967   ———. "On the Signification of the Monster Grendel in the Poem of *Beowulf;* with a Discussion of Lines 2076-2100." *Journal of Philology*, 15 (1886), 120-31. (chr, mth; 2076-2100)

†   ———, see [716].

1968   SKEMP, Arthur R. "The Transformation of Scriptural Story, Motive, and Conception in Anglo-Saxon Poetry." *MP*, 4 (1906-7), 423-70. (rel, src, tec)

1969   SLAY, D. "Some Aspects of the Technique of Composition of Old English Verse." *TPS* (London), 1952, pp. 1-14. (mtr)

1970   SMITH, Arthur H. "The Photography of Manuscripts." *London Medieval Studies*, 1 (1938), 179-207. (mns, txt)

1971   SMITH, Charles Alphonso. *An Old English Grammar and Exercise Book.* Boston, 1896. (edt) Edits 611-61, 739-836, 2711b-51, 2792b-2820.
        2d ed., 1898; 3d ed., 1903; 4th ed., 1903; 5th ed., [1910]; 6th ed., 1913

1972   SMITH, Charles Sprague. "*Beowulf* Gretti." *New Englander*, 40 (1881), 49-67. (ana, trl) Translates into English verse 711-838, 1493-1652.

†   SMITH, J. C., see [684].

1973   SMITH, L. W. "Race Permanence and the War: The *Nibelungenlied* and *Beowulf* Compared." *SR*, 25 (1917), 187-92. (ana, thm)

1974   SMITHERS, G. V. "Five Notes on Old English Texts." *EGS*, 4 (1951-52), 65-85. (int; 12-16, 303-6, 767-69, 3074-75)

1975   ———. "Four Cruxes in *Beowulf*." In *Schlauch* pp. 413-30. (ana, hst, int, lng, nam, wrd; 1316-20, 1687-98, 1931-33, 2032-35)

1976   ———. "The Making of *Beowulf*." Inaugural lecture 18 May 1961. Durham, 1961. (ana, com, unt)
        Review: R. M. Wilson, *YWES*, 42 (1961), 57

1977   SMITHSON, George Arnold. *The Old English Christian Epic. A Study in the Plot Technique of the "Juliana," the "Elene," the "Andreas," and the "Christ," in Comparison with the "Beowulf" and with the Latin Literature of the Middle Ages.* Univ. of Calif. Publications in Modern Philology, I, no. 4. Berkeley, 1910. (ana, com, epc, rel, src, stl, str, tec)
        Review: H. L. Creek, *JEGP*, 10 (1911), 640-42

1978   SMYSER, H. M. "Ibn Fadlān's Account of the Rūs with Some Commentary and Some Allusions to *Beowulf*." In *Magoun*, 92-119. (ana, hst, mth, rel)

1979   SNELL, F. J. *The Age of Alfred.* London, 1912. (gen)

†   SOCIN, Adolf, see [815].

?1980 SOENS, E. "*Beowulf.*" *Dietsche Warande*, 11 (1898), 240–50.

1981   SOKOLL, Eduard. "Zur Technik des altgermanischen Alliterations-verses." *Beiträge zur neueren Philologie, Jakob Schipper dargebracht.* Vienna and Leipzig, 1902. pp. 321–65. (mtr)

1982   SONNEFELD, Gottfried. *Stilistisches und Wortschatz im "Béowulf": Ein Beitrag zur Kritik des Epos.* Strasbourg diss., Würzburg, 1892. (dct, stl)

1983   SONNENSCHEIN, William Swan. *The Best Books.* 3d ed., London, 1931. Vol. V, pp. 3277–78. (bbl, Fnb)

1984   SOUTHWARD, Elaine C. "The Knight Yder and the *Beowulf* Legend." *MAE*, 15 (1946), 1–47. (ana, mth, src)
       Reviews:
            1   M. Daunt, *YWES*, 27 (1946), 61
            2   G. D. Willcock, *YWES*, 27 (1946), 88–89

1985   SOWA, Hosei. "*Beowulf* no Ingeld Episode ni tsuite." [The Ingeld Episode in *Beowulf*]. *Acta Litterarum: Kenkyu Ronshu (Nagoya Univ.),* (1965), 223–42. (int) In Japanese.

1986   SPAETH, John Duncan. "Beowulf." In Henry S. Pancoast and J. D. Spaeth, eds., *Early English Poems.* N.Y., 1911. pp. 5–29, 389–403. (nts, trl) Translates into English alliterative verse 2087 lines.
       Repr. in his *Old English Poetry: Translation into Alliterative Verse, with Introduction and Notes.* Princeton, 1921.
       Reviews:
            1   *The Bookman,* 56 (1922–23), 103
            2   *The Dial,* 73 (1922), 458
            3   *The Nation,* 115 (5 July 1922), 23
            4   *The Nation–Athenaeum,* 31 (26 Aug. 1922), 715–16
            5   *New Statesman,* 20 (7 Oct. 1922), 20
            6   *N&Q,* 143 (1922), 79–80
            7   *SR,* 30 (1922), 381
            8   *The Springfield Republican,* 29 April 1922, p. 10
            9   *TLS,* 13 July 1922, p. 12
           10   L. Bacon, *Literary Review,* 16 (21 Oct. 1922), 125–26
           11   R. H., *New Republic,* 31 (2 Aug. 1922) 288
           12   A. D. McKillop, *JEGP,* 24 (1925), 279–81
       Repr. in J. D. McCallum, ed., *English Literature: The Beginnings to 1500.* N.Y., 1929. pp. 1–68.
       Partially repr. in William H. Davenport, ed., *Dominant Types in British and American Literature.* N.Y., 1949. pp. 11–24

1987   SPALDING, William. *The History of English Literature with an Outline of the Origin and Growth of the English Language.* N.Y., 1859. pp. 39–40. (gen)

1988   Item canceled.

1989   SPENCE, Lewis. "Beowulf." *Dictionary of Medieval Romance and Romance Writers.* London and N.Y., 1913. pp. 30–31. (gen)
Repr. N.Y., 1962

1990   SPENCER, R. A. *The Story of Beowulf and Grendel Retold in Modern English Prose.* London and Edinburgh, [1923]. (par) Paraphrases lines 1–1250.

1991   SPINNER, K. *Die Ausdrücke für Sinnesempfindungen in der ags. Poesie verglichen mit den Bezeichnungen für Sinnesempfindungen in der altnord., altsächs., und althochdeutschen Dichtung.* Halle diss., 1924. (dct).

1992   SPLITTER, Henry Winfred. "Note on a *Beowulf* Passage." *MLN*, 63 (1948), 118–21. (int, txt; 745–49)
Review: R. M. Wilson, *YWES*, 29 (1948), 59

1993   ——. "The Relation of Germanic Folk Custom and Ritual to *Ealuscerwen* (*Beowulf* 769)." *MLN*, 67 (1952), 255–58. (hst, img, int, txt, wrd; 769a)
Review: R. M. Wilson, *YWES*, 33 (1952), 41

   †   STALLYBRASS, James Steven, see [687].

1994   STANDOP, Ewald. "Zum Tempus der Ingeld-Episode im *Beowulf*." *Archiv*, 197 (1961), 298–301. (lng, txt; 2032–68)

1994.1 STANLEY, Eric Gerald. "Beowulf." In his *Continuations and Beginnings: Studies in Old English Literature.* London, 1966. pp. 104–41. (ana, dct, for, mns, str, tec, thm, var; 864–86)
Review: *Speculum*, 42 (1967), 572

1995   ——. "Hæ þenra Hyht in *Beowulf*." In *Brodeur*, pp. 136–51. (int, rel; 179a)
Review: R. M. Wilson, *YWES*, 44 (1963), 73

1996   ——. "Old English Poetic Diction and the Interpretation of the *Wanderer*, the *Seafarer*, and the *Penitent's Prayer*." *Anglia*, 73 (1956), 413–66. (dct, img, smb; 33)

1997   ——. "The Search for Anglo–Saxon Paganism." *N&Q*, 119 (1964), 204–9, 242–50, 282–87, 324–31, 455–63; 120 (1965), 9–17, 203–7, 285–93, 322–27. (hst, mth, rel, sch)

1998   STARR, H. W. "*Beowulf* in the Eighteenth Century." *MLN*, 63 (1948), 60. (sch) On an anachronism in William Vaughan Wilkin's *Being Met Together.* N.Y., 1944. p. 82.

1999   STEADMAN, J. M., Jr. "The Ingeld-Episode in *Beowulf:*
        History or Prophecy?" *MLN*, 45 (1930), 522–25. (hst, int,
        lng) Continued by Huppé [930].
        Review: M. Daunt, *YWES*, 11 (1930), 53–54

2000   STEDMAN, Douglas. "Some Points of Resemblance be-
        tween *Beowulf* and the *Grettla* (or *Grettis Saga*)." *Saga Book*, 8
        (1913), 6–28. (ana)

2001   STEFANOVIĆ, Svetislav. "Ein Beitrag zur angelsäch-
        sischen Offa-Sage." *Anglia*, 35 (1912), 483–525. (hst, mth)
        Continued in his [2003]; rewritten as [2002].

2002   ——. "Epizoda o Ofl i Dridi u *Beowulfu.*" *Strani Pregled*,
        (1927). (hst, mth) Rewritten from his [2001].
        Review: F. Holthausen, *Beibl*, 42 (1931), 341

2003   ——. "Zur Offa-Thryðo-Episode im *Beowulf.*" *ESt*, 69
        (1934), 15–31. (ana, hst, mth) Continues his [2001].
        Review: M. Serjeantson, *YWES*, 15 (1934), 65–66

2004   STEINECK, H. "*Beowulf.*" In his *Altenglische Dichtungen in
        Wortgetreuer Übersetzung.* Leipzig, 1898. pp. 1–102. (trl)
        Translates into literal German prose, based on Heyne [815].
        Reviews:
            1   G. Binz, *Beibl*, 9 (1899), 220–22
            2   F. Holthausen, *Archiv*, 103 (1899), 376–78
            ?3 E. Nader, *Zeitschrift für deutsches Realschulwesen*, 24
        (1899), 9
            4   R. Wülker, *Beibl*, 9 (1899), 1–2

2005   STENTON, Frank M. *Anglo–Saxon England.* Oxford, 1943.
        (hst)
        Reviews:
            1   *TLS*, 5 Feb. 1944, p. 66 and 67
            2   O. G. S. C[rawford], *Antiquity*, 20 (1946), 47–49
            3   W. A. Morris, *AHR*, 50 (1944), 108–10
            4   D. Whitelock, *MLR*, 39 (1944), 293–95
            5   ——, *YWES*, 24 (1943), 28

2006   STÉPHANI, K. G. *Der älteste deutsche Wohnbau und seine
        Einrichtung.* Leipzig, 1902–3. Vol. I, pp. 388–433. (arc,
        hst)

2007   STEPHENS, George. *The Old Northern Runic Monuments in
        Scandinavia.* London, 1867. Folio I, pp. xiv–xv. (hst, lng)

2008   STERN, Gustav. "Old English *Fuslic* and *Fus.*" *ESt*, 68
        (1933), 161–73. (wrd; 232, 324, 1241, 1422, 2613)
        Review: D. E. M. Clarke, *YWES*, 14 (1933), 83–84

2009   STEVENS, C. H. "The Treatment of Death in Anglo–
        Saxon Poetry." Unpub. Ph.D. diss., Univ. of California at
        Berkeley, 1925. (epc, img, int, mth, thm)

2010 STEVICK, Robert D. "Christian Elements and the Genesis of *Beowulf.*" *MP*, 61 (1963), 79–89. (chr, com, for, int, rel) Review: R. M. Wilson, *YWES*, 44 (1963), 72

2011 ——. "Emendation of Old English Poetic Texts: *Beowulf* 2523." *MLQ*, 20 (1959), 339–43. (mtr, txt; 2523) Defends Pope [1660] against Orrick [1603]. Review: R. M. Wilson, *YWES*, 40 (1959), 61

2012 ——. "The Oral-formulaic Analyses of Old English Verse." *Speculum*, 37 (1962), 382–89. (dct, for) Reply to Creed [412].

2013 Item canceled.

2014 STEWART, Hugh Fraser. *Boethius, an Essay.* London and Edinburgh, 1891. pp. 163–64. (rel, src; 1059–62) Attacked by H. R. Patch. *The Tradition of Boethius.* N.Y., 1935. p. 135.

2015 STIVERS, E. B. "Women of *Beowulf.*" *High School Teacher*, 8 (1932), 177. (chr)

2016 STJERNA, Knut. "Arkeologiska anteckningar till *Beovulf.*" *Kungl. Vitterhets Akademiens Månadsblad*, (1907), 436–51. (hst)

2017 ——. "Drakskatten i *Beovulf.*" *Fornvännen*, 1 (1906), 119–44. (arc)

2018 ——. *Essays on Questions Connected with the Old English Poem of "Beowulf."* Trans. and ed. by J. R. C. Hall. Viking Club Publications, extra series 3. Coventry, 1912. (arc, hst) Contains translations of his [2021–23].
Reviews:
    1 *Athenaeum*, 1 (1913), 459–60
    2 *Nation*, 95 (1912), 386b–87a
    3 A. Brandl, *Archiv*, 132 (1914), 238–39
    4 F. Klaeber, *JEGP*, 13 (1914), 167–73 [1073]
    5 E. T. Leeds, *EHR*, 28 (1913), 148–51
    6 A. Mawer, *MLR*, 8 (1913), 242–43
    7 E. Mogk, *Historische Vierteljahrsschrift*, 18 (1921), 196–97
    8 A. Olrik, *NT*, 44 (1915), II, 127
    9 G. Schütte, *ANF*, 33 (1917), 64–96

2019 ——. "Fasta fornlämningar i *Beovulf.*" *ATS*, 18 (1908), 4. (lng)

2020 ——. "Hjälmar och svärd i *Beovulf.*" In *Studier tillägnade O. Montelius.* Stockholm, 1903. pp. 99–120. (arc, hst)

2021 ——. "Skölds hädanfärd." In *Studier tillägnade Henrik Schück.* Stockholm, 1905. pp. 110–34. (chr, hst, mth) Trans. in his [2018].

2022 ——. "Svear och Götar under folkvandringstiden." *Svenska*

Förnminnesforeningens Tidskrift, 12 (1905), 339–60. (hst)
Trans. in his [2018].

2023 ———. "Vendel och Vendelkråka." *ANF*, 21 (1904), 71–80.
(hst; 2939–41)
Trans. in his [2018].

2024 STOCK, Rudolph. *Die Verstärkung der Alliteration im Beowulf-liede.* Königsberg diss., 1921. (mtr) Summary in *Inaug. Diss. d. phil. Fak. Königsberg*, 1921.

2025 STORMS, Gotfrid. "Compounded Names of Peoples in *Beowulf*, a Study in the Diction of a Great Poet." Utrecht-Nijmegen, 1957. (dct, for, hst, int, nam)
Reviews:
    1 K. Malone, *ES*, 41 (1960), 200–205 [1401]
    2 H. C. Matthes, *Anglia*, 80 (1962), 168–70
    3 R. M. Wilson, *YWES*, 38 (1957), 75

2026 ———. "The Figure of Beowulf in the O.E. Epic." *ES*, 40 (1959), 3–13. (chr, hst, mth, tec, thm)
Review: R. M. Wilson, *YWES*, 40 (1959), 60

2027 ———. "The Subjectivity of the Style of *Beowulf*." In *Brodeur*, pp. 171–86. (dct, stl, tec, wrd; 1399–1417)
Review: R. M. Wilson, *YWES*, 44 (1963), 74

2028 STROEBE, Klara. "Altgermanische Grussformen." *Beitr*, 37 (1911–12), 173–212. (hst)

2029 STROEBE, Lilly L. *Die altenglischen Kleidernamen.* Heidelberg diss., Leipzig, 1904. (hst, wrd)

2030 STRÖMHOLM, D. "Försök över Beowulfdikten och Ynglingasagan." *Edda*, 25 (1926), 233–49. (ana, chr, hst)
On Ingeld.
Review: M. Daunt, *YWES*, 7 (1926), 62–63

2031 STRONG, Archibald Thomas. *"Beowulf" Translated into Modern English Verse.* London, 1925. Foreword by R. W. Chambers [308]. (com, gen, hst, mns, mth, mtr, nts, stl, trl)
Reviews:
    1 E. Blackman, *RES*, 3 (1927), 115–16
    2 S. J. Crawford, *MLR*, 22 (1927), 325–27
    3 E. V. Gordon, *YWES*, 6 (1925), 72–74
    4 F. Klaeber, *Beibl*, 37 (1926), 257–60
    5 A. Pompen, *ES*, 9 (1927), 115–17
    6 M. B. Ruud, *MLN*, 43 (1928), 54–55

2032 STUMPFL, Robert. *Kultspiele der Germanen als Ursprung des mittelalterlichen Dramas.* Berlin, 1939. (chr, src)

2033 SUCHIER, Hermann. "Ueber die Sage von Offa und Þryðo." *Beitr*, 4 (1877), 500–21. (Ana, hst)

2034 SULLIVAN, M. Ancilla. "Passion Motives in Old English Poetry." Unpub. Ph.D. diss., Fordham Univ., 1939. *DDABAU*, 1938–39, no. 6, 94. (thm)

2035 SUTHERLAND, Raymond Carter. *The Celibate Beowulf, the Gospels, and the Liturgy.* Atlanta, 1964. Georgia State College School of Arts and Sciences Research Papers, no. 2. (img, rel)

2036 ——. "The Meaning of *Eorlscipe* in *Beowulf.*" *PMLA*, 70 (1955), 1133–42. (hst, int, lng, thm)
Review: R. M. Wilson, *YWES*, 36 (1955), 61

2037 SVENNUNG, J. *Scadinavia und Scandia, Lateinisch-Nordische Namenstudien.* Acta Societatis Litterarum Humaniorum Regiae Upsaliensis, 44: 1. Uppsala and Wiesbaden, 1963. (hst, nam; 1686)
Review: N. Hasselmo, *YWMLS*, 24 (1962), 463–64

2038 SWEET, Henry. *An Anglo–Saxon Reader.* Oxford, 1876. (edt, nts) Lines 1251–1650, based on Grein text [677].
Review: K. Körner, *ESt*, 1 (1877), 500 [1128]
2d ed., 1879; 3d ed., 1881; 4th ed., 1884; 5th ed., 1886; 6th ed., 1888; 7th ed., 1891; 8th ed., 1894; repr. 1899, 1904, 1908, 1912, 1918, 1921
9th ed , rev. by C. T. Onions, 1922; repr. 1924, 1927, 1933, 1940, 1943
10th ed., 1946
Review: M. Daunt, *YWES*, 27 (1946), 59
11th ed., 1948; 12th ed., 1950; 13th ed., 1954; 14th ed., 1959; repr. 1962
15th ed., rev. by D. Whitelock, 1967

2039 ——. *First Steps in Anglo–Saxon.* Oxford, 1897. (par) Part I paraphrased in Old English prose!
Review: F. Klaeber, *MLN*, 13 (1898), 93–94

2040 ——. "Old English Etymologies: I. *Beóhata.*" *ESt*, 2 (1879), 312–14. (chr, mth, nam)

2041 ——. "Sketch of the History of Anglo–Saxon Poetry." In Thomas Warton's *History of English Poetry*, ed. by W. C. Hazlitt. London, 1871. Vol. II, pp. 3–19. (Fnb, gen, trl) Translates into English prose 1357–76, 1724b–68, 3156–82.

2042 SWERINGEN, Grace Fleming van. "The Main Literary Types of Men in the Germanic Hero-Sagas." *JEGP*, 14 (1915), 212–25. (chr)

2043 ——. "Old Norse *bauni.*" *MLN*, 20 (1905), 64. (int)

2044 SWIGGETT, Glen Levin. "Notes on the *Finnsburg Fragment.*" *MLN*, 20 (1905), 169–71. (epc, Fnb, int, lng)

2045   SYDOW, Carl Wilhelm von.   "Beowulf och Bjarki."
       SSLSN, 14 (1923), no. 3.   (ana, chr, mth, src)
       Reviews:
           1   H. Hecht, *Beibl*, 35 (1924), 218–19 [769]
           2   A. Heusler, *AfdA*, 43 (1924), 52–54
           3   F. Holthausen, *Beibl*, 34 (1923), 357–58
           4   S. B. Liljegren, *Neophilologus*, 10 (1924), 73–74
           5   K. Malone, *JEGP*, 23 (1924), 458–60

2046   ——— .   "Beowulfskalden och nordisk tradition."   *Yearbook of
       the New Society of Letters at Lund, Årsbok*, 1923, p. 77–91.   (com,
       epc, mth, src)
       Reviews:
           1   H. Hecht, *Beibl*, 35 (1924), 218–19
           2   F. Liebermann, *Archiv*, 148 (1925), 95

?2047 ——— .   "Draken som skattevaktare."   *Danmarks Folkeminder*,
       17 (1917–18), 103ff.

2048   ——— .   "Grendel i anglosaxiska ortnamn."   *NB*, 2 (1914),
       160–64.   (ana, mth, nam, src)

2049   ——— .   "Hur mytforskningen tolkat Beowulfdikten."   *Folk-
       minnen och Folktankar*, 11 (1924), 97–134.   (mth)

2050   ——— .   "Irisches in *Beowulf*."   *Verhandlungen der 52. Ver-
       sammlung deutscher Philologen und Schulmänner in Marburg, 1913*.
       Leipzig, 1914.   pp. 177–80.   (ana, mth, src)

2051   ——— .   "Scyld Scefing."   *NB*, 12 (1924), 63–95.   (int, mth,
       nam; 4–52)

2052   ——— .   (Untitled review of Panzer [1618]).   *AfdA*, 35 (1911),
       123–31.   (ana, mth)

2053   SYKES, Egerton.   "Beowulf."   In his *Everyman's Dictionary
       of Non-Classical Mythology*.   London and N.Y., 1952.   pp. 33ff.
       (mth)

2054   SYMONS, B.   *Heldensage*.   *PGrdr*, IIa (1893), paragraphs
       17–18.   (epc, hst, mth)
       2d ed., 1900.   Vol. III, paragraphs 23–25

2055   SZÖVERFFY, Franz.   "From *Beowulf* to the *Arabian Knights*
       (Preliminary Notes on Aarne-Thompson 301)."   *Midwest
       Folklore*, 6 (1956), 89–124.   (mth)

†   TABUSA, Takemitsu, see [1219].

2056   TAGLICHT, Josef.   "*Beowulf* and Old English Verse
       Rhythm."   *RES*, 12 (1961), 341–51.   (mtr)
       Reviews:
           1   *AES*, 5 (1963), 654
           2   R. M. Wilson, *YWES*, 42 (1963), 56

2057 TAINE, Hippolyte. *Histoire de la littérature anglaise.* Paris, 1863–64. (gen)
2d ed., 1868; 3d ed., 1870; 4th ed., 1878; 5th ed., 1881; 6th ed., 1886; 7th ed., 1891
Trans. into English by H. van Laun. Edinburgh and N.Y., 1871, 1873, 1874
Other eds. of this translation: N.Y., 1872, 1876, 1877, 1878, 1879, 1886, 1891, 1895, 1900; Philadelphia, 1896, 1912; London, 1877, 1878, 1885, 1886

2058 TAKAYANAGI, Shunichi. "*Beowulf* and Christian Tradition." *SELJ*, 37 (1961), 149–63. (rel)
Review: T. S. Dorsch, *YWES*, 43 (1962), 14

2059 TATLOCK, John S. P. "Epic Formulas, Especially in Layamon." *PMLA*, 38 (1923), 494–529. (dct, epc)

2060 ——. "Layamon's Poetic Style and Its Relation." In *Manly*, pp. 3–11. (dct, epc, stl)

2061 TAYLOR, A. R. "Two Notes on *Beowulf.*" *LSE*, 7 (1952), 5–17. (ana, int, mth; 2444–71) On *Grettissaga.*
Review: R. M. Wilson, *YWES*, 33 (1952), 41

2062 TAYLOR, Henry Osborn. *The Medieval Mind: A History of the Development of Thought and Emotion in the Middle Ages.* N.Y., 1911. (gen)
2d ed., 1914; 3d ed., reprint only; 4th ed., N.Y. and Cambridge, Mass., 1925

2063 TAYLOR, Paul Beekman. "*Heofon Riece Swealg:* A Sign of Beowulf's State of Grace." *PQ*, 42 (1963), 257–59. (ana, dct, rel, tec; 3155b)
Review: R. M. Wilson, *YWES*, 44 (1963), 75

2064 ——. "Heorot, Earth, and Asgard: Christian Poetry and Pagan Myth." *TSL*, 11 (1966), 119–30. (mth, nam, rel)

2065 ——. "O E *Eoletes* Again." *Lingua*, 13 (1964–65), 196–97. (int, txt, wrd; 224a) Answer to Salus [1755]; answer by Salus [1756].

2066 ——. "Snorri's Analogue to Beowulf's Funeral." *Archiv*, 201 (1965), 349–51. (ana, hst, smb)
Review: R. M. Wilson, *YWES*, 45 (1964), 60

2067 [TAYLOR, William?] (Untitled review of Thorkelin [2080]). *Monthly Review*, 81 (1816), 516–23. (chr, hst, nam, trl) Some translations into English. Identification based on Cooley [386].
Repr. in his *Historic Survey of German Poetry, Interspersed with Various Translations.* London, 1828. Vol. I, pp. 78–90
2d ed., 1830

† TEN BRINK, see BRINK.

2068   THOMAS, Antoine. "Un manuscript inutilisé du *Liber Monstrorum.*" *Bulletin Du Cange*, 1 (1924), 232–45. (hst, mth, src, txt; 2420)

2069   THOMAS, Percy Goronwy. "*Beowulf* and *Daniel A.*" *MLR*, 8 (1913), 537–39. (ana, com, src)

2070   ——. "*Beowulf*, ll. 1604–5, 2085–91." *MLR*, 17 (1922), 63–64. (txt, wrd; 1604–5, 2085–91)

2071   ——. *English Literature before Chaucer.* London, 1924. (gen)

2072   ——. "Further Notes on *Beowulf.*" *MLR*, 22 (1927), 70–73. (int, txt; 358–59, 804, 937–39, 970–72, 1231, 1537, 1798, 1880, 2394, 2691–92) On Wyatt/Chambers [2267].
        Review: M. Daunt, *YWES*, 8 (1927), 83–84

2073   Item canceled.

2074   ——. "Notes on the Language of *Beowulf.*" *MLR*, 1 (1906), 202–7. (lng) On dialects.

2075   ——. (Untitled review of Sedgefield [1892]). *MLR*, 6 (1911), 266–68. (int, lng, txt; 24, 204, 207–9, 459, 749, 870, 1072, 1363, 1512, 1537, 1541, 1781, 1797, 1936, 2029, 2035)

2076   THOMAS, R. "On Translations of *Beowulf.*" *N&Q*, 108 (1903), 83. (about trl) Reply by H. P. L., *N&Q*, 108 (1903), 198

2077   THOMAS, W. "*Beowulf* et les premiers fragments épiques anglo-saxons: Étude critique et traduction." *Revue de l'enseignement des langues vivantes*, 30 (1913), 586–92, 645–48; 31 (1914), 142–49; 33 (1916), 11–16, 97–102, 353–58, 446–54; 34 (1917), 212–16, 249–57, 304–12, 343–49, 441–54. (Fnb, gen, nts, trl) Translates into literal French 1–490, 710–3182. Separate ed., Paris, 1919

  †   THOMPSON, Stith, see [560].

2078   THOMSON, Clara L. *The Adventures of Beowulf.* London, 1899. (par) Selected English prose paraphrase.
        Review: *N&Q*, 100 (1899), 509
        2d ed., 1904

2079   THOMSON, R. L. "Three Etymological Notes." *EPS*, 6 (1957), 79–91. (lng, wrd; 224)
        Review: R. M. Wilson, *YWES*, 38 (1957), 55

2080   THORKELIN, Grímur Jónsson. *De Danorum Rebus Gestis Secul. III et IV. Poema Danicum Dialecto Anglosaxonica. Ex Bibliotheca Cottoniana Musaei Britannici.* Copenhagen, 1815. (com, edt, trl) First ed., with trans. into Latin prose.
        Reviews:
        1   *Dansk-Litteratur-Tidende*, 1815, pp. 401–32, 437–46, 461–62 [27]

2 *Iduna*, 7 (1817), 133–59 [28]

3 N. F. S. [Grundtvig], *GGA*, 1818, pp. 41–48 [713]

4 N. F. S. Grundtvig, *Nyeste Skilderie af Kjöbenhavn*, no. 60 (1815), cols. 945, 998, 1009, 1025, 1030, 1045 [708]

5 N. Outzen, *Kieler Blätter*, 1816, III, 307–27 [1609]

?6 "Pia," *Jenaische Literatur-Zeitung*, 1816, Ergänzungsblätter, pp. 353–65 [1648]

7 [W. Taylor], *Monthly Review*, 81 (1816), 516–23 [2067]

2081 ———. *Poema Anglosaxonicum de Rebus Gestis Danorum ex Membrana Bibliothecae Cottonianae . . . Fecit Exscribi Londini A.D. 1787 Grimus Johannis Thorkelin, L. L. D.* Now in Great Royal Library, Copenhagen. (edt, mns) Often called "Transcript A," the work of a copyist hired by Thorkelin. Malone [1386] is a facsimile.

2082 ———. *Poema Anglosaxonicum . . . Exscripsit Grimus Johannis Thorkelin L. L. D. Londini Anno 1787.* Now in Great Royal Library, Copenhagen. (edt, mns) Often called "Transcript B," the work of Thorkelin himself. Malone [1386] is a facsimile.

2083 ———. (Untitled note). *Nyeste Skilderie af Kjöbenhavn*, 12 (1815), cols. 1057, 1073. (txt) Reply to Grundtvig [708].

2084 THORPE, Benjamin. *The Anglo-Saxon Poems of "Beowulf," "The Scop" or "Gleeman's Tale," and the "Fight at Finnesburg."* Oxford, 1855. (edt, Fnb, list, mns, nts, trl) Literal and complete English translation in prose.
2d ed., 1875; 3d ed., 1889
Repr. as *"Beowulf" Together with "Widsith" and the "Fight at Finnesburg" in the Benjamin Thorpe Transcription and Word-for-Word Translation.* Great Neck, N.Y., 1963. Introduction by Vincent F. Hopper.
Review: R. M. Wilson, *YWES*, 43 (1962), 55

† ———, see [1179] and [1688].

2085 THURNAM, John. "On Ancient British Barrows, Especially Those of Wiltshire and the Adjoining Counties." *Archaeologia*, 42 (1869), 161–244. (arc; 34–37)

2086 TILLYARD, Eustace Mandeville Wetenhall. *The English Epic and Its Background.* London and N.Y., 1954. (epc) Repr. Galaxy paperback no. GB 167, 1966

2087 TIMMER, Benno Johan. "*Beowulf*: The Poem and the Poet." *Neophilologus*, 32 (1948), 122–26. (com, epc, tec, thm)
Review: R. M. Wilson, *YWES*, 29 (1948), 58–59

2088 ———. "Irony in Old English Poetry." *ES*, 24 (1942), 171–75. (rht, stl, tec)

2089   ——— . "A Note on *Beowulf*, ll. 2526b–2527a and ll. 2295."
        ES, 40 (1959), 49–52. (int, lng, txt, var; 2295, 2468, 2526–27)
        Review: R. M. Wilson, *YWES*, 40 (1959), 61

2090   ——— . "*Wyrd* in Anglo–Saxon Prose and Poetry." *Neo-*
        philologus, 26 (1940–41), 24–33, 213–28. (mth, rel, thm)

  †   ——— , see [2151].

2091   TINKER, Chauncey Brewster. *Beowulf: Translated Out of the*
        Old English. N.Y., 1902. (nts, trl)   Trans. into English
        prose; based on Wyatt [2267], 2d ed.
        Reviews:
            1   J. M. Garnett, *PMLA*, 18 (1903), 445–51, 455–58
            2   F. Holthausen, *Beibl*, 14 (1903), 7–8
            3   F. Klaeber, *JEGP*, 5 (1903–5), 91–93
        2d ed., 1910
        Selections in A. S. Cook and C. B. Tinker, eds., *Translations*
        from Old English Poetry.   Boston, 1902.   Lines 26–52, 89b–98,
        499–606,   710–836,   1345–79a,   2232b–70,   2711b–2820,
        3137–82
        Rev. ed., 1926
        Reviews:
            1   F. P. Magoun, *Speculum*, 1 (1926), 460–61
            2   K. Malone, *MLN*, 41 (1926), 488

2092   ——— . "Notes on *Beowulf*." *MLN*, 23 (1908), 239–40. (int,
        txt, wrd; 166ff, 311, 760, 783ff)

2093   ——— . "The Translations of *Beowulf*: A Critical Bib-
        liography." Ph.D. diss., Yale Univ., 1903. (bbl, mns, about
        trl)   Pub., same title, N.Y., 1903.   Yale Studies in English,
        16.
        Reviews:
            1   G. Binz, *Beibl*, 16 (1905), 291–92
            2   F. Klaeber, *JEGP*, 5 (1903), 116–18

2094   TODT, August. "Die Wortstellung im *Beowulf*." *Anglia*, 16
        (1894), 226–60. (lng)

2095   TOLKIEN, John Ronald Renel. "*Beowulf*: The Monsters
        and the Critics." *PBA*, 22 (1936), 245–95. (chr, dct, epc,
        img, int, rel, smb, str, tec, thm, unt)   See Bonjour [161],
        Gang [603], Van Meurs [2135].
        Reviews:
            1   R. W. Chambers, *MLR*, 33 (1938), 272–73
            2   F. Klaeber, *Beibl*, 48 (1937), 321–23
            3   H. R. Patch, *MLN*, 54 (1939), 217–18
        Separate repr., London, 1937, 1958, 1960; repr. in Nicholson
        [1560], pp. 51–103

2096   ——. "Prefatory Remarks on Prose Translation of *Beowulf.*"
        In Hall [740], 1940 ed., pp. ix–xliii. (dct, mtr, str, about trl,
        var) Translates 210–28 into English alliterative verse.

2097   ——. "Sigelwara land." *MAE*, 1 (1932), 183–96; 3 (1934),
        95–111. (wrd; 1966)
        Reviews:
            1   M. Daunt, *YWES*, 13 (1932), 69–70
            2   M. Serjeantson, *YWES*, 15 (1934), 81

2098   TOLLER, T. Northcote. "The Oldest English Poetry." A
        lecture delivered in the Owens College at the opening of the
        season 1880–1881. Manchester, n.d. (gen)

2099   TOLMAN, Albert H. "The Style of Anglo–Saxon Poetry."
        PMLA, 3 (1887), 17–47. (dct, img, mtr, smb, stl, trl, var)
        Translates various lines into English verse.
        Repr. in his *The Views about Hamlet and Other Essays.* Boston
        and N.Y., 1904. pp. 337–82

2100   TOUSTER, Eva K. "Formal Aspects of the Meter of
        Beowulf." Unpub. Ph.D. diss., Vanderbilt Univ., 1951. *DA*,
        12 (1952), 623. (mtr, stl, str) Abstract in *Bulletin of Vander-
        bilt Univ.*, 51 (1951), 28–29.

2101   ——. "Metrical Variation as a Poetic Device in *Beowulf.*"
        Anglia, 73 (1955), 115–26. (com, epc, mtr, stl, str)
        Review: R. M. Wilson, *YWES*, 36 (1955), 60

2102   ——. "Phonological Aspects of the Meter of *Beowulf.*" In
        Curry, pp. 27–38. (lng, mtr)
        Review: R. M. Wilson, *YWES*, 36 (1955), 14

2103   TRAILL, H. D. *Social England.* London, 1893. (hst)
        2d ed., London and N.Y., 1894
        Illustrated ed., by Traill and J. S. Mann, 1901–4
        Repr. 1909, 1912

2104   TRAUTMANN, Moritz. "Auch zum *Beowulf:* Ein Gruss
        an Herrn Eduard Sievers." *BB*, 17 (1905), 143–74. (txt)
        Reply to Sievers [1943].
        Review: F. Klaeber, *MLN*, 22 (1907), col. 252

2105   ——. "Beiträge zu einem künftigen 'Sprachschatz der
        altenglischen Dichter.'" *Anglia*, 33 (1910), 276–79. (wrd;
        756) On *gedraeg*.

2106   ——. *Das Beowulflied: Als Anhang das Finn-Bruchstück und
        Waldhere-Bruchstücke.* Bonn, 1904. *BB*, 16. (edt, Fnb, trl)
        Translates into literal German prose.
        Reviews:
            1   A. J. Barnouw, *Museum*, 14 (1907), 96–98
            2   E. Eckhardt, *ESt*, 37 (1907), 401–3

       3 H. Jantzen, *NRs*, 24 (1905), 549–50

       4 F. Klaeber, *MLN*, 20 (1905), 83–87 [1074]

       5 L. L. Schücking, *Archiv*, 115 (1905), 417–21 [1859]

       6 F. Tupper, *PMLA*, 25 (1910), 164–81

2107   ——. *Berichtigungen, Vermutungen und Erklärungen zum "Beowulf": Erste Hälfte.* BB, 2 (1899), 121–92. (int, txt; 1–1215)
Reviews:

       1 *Athenaeum*, no. 3730 (1899), 494

       2 G. Binz, *Beibl*, 14 (1903), 358–60 [107]

       3 F. Holthausen, *LGRP*, 21 (1900), 62–64 [886]

       4 H. Jantzen, *NS*, 8 (1900–1901), 379

       5 E. Sievers, *Beitr*, 27 (1902), 572 [1935]

       6 ——, *Beitr*, 28 (1903), 271–72 [1942]

       7 ——, *Beitr*, 29 (1904), 305–31 [1943]

2108   ——. "Cynewulfs Werke." BB, 1 (1898), 23–42. (lng, mtr, src)

2109   ——. "Finn und Hildebrand." BB, 7 (1903), 1–64. (edt, Fnb, int, trl, txt; Fep) Text and trans. of fragment and episode into German. See his [2110].
Reviews:

       1 G. Binz, *ZDP*, 37 (1905), 529–36 [110]

       2 H. Jantzen, *NRs*, 22 (1903), 619–21

       3 ——, *NS*, 11 (1903–4), 543–48

2110   ——. "Nachträgliches zu Finn und Hildebrand." BB, 17 (1905), 122. (Fnb, int, txt; Fep) Addition to his [2109]

2111   ——. "Die neuste Beowulfausgabe und die altenglische Verslehre." BB, 17 (1905), 175–91. (mtr) On Holthausen [845]
Review: F. Klaeber, *MLN*, 22 (1907), col. 252

2112   ——. *Verhandlungen der 50: Versammlung deutscher Philologen und Schulmänner (Graz, 1909).* Leipzig, 1910. pp. 15–19. (mtr)

2113   ——. "Zum altenglischen Versbau." *ESt*, 44 (1912), 303–42. (dct, lng, mtr)

2114   ——. "Zur alt- und mittelenglischen Verslehre." *Anglia*, 5 (1882), Anzeiger, 111–30. (dct, lng, mtr)

2115   ——. "Zur Berichtigung und Erklärung der *Waldhere-Bruchstücke.*" BB, 5 (1900), 162–91. (about trl)

2116   ——. "Zur Kenntnis des altgermanischen Verses, vornehmlich des Altenglischen." *Beibl*, 5 (1894–95), 87–96. (dct, mtr)

2117   ——. (Untitled review of Heyne [815], 6th ed.; Wyatt [2267], 2d ed.; Holder [834], 2d ed.) *Beibl*, 10 (1899–1900), 257–62. (hst, int, mtr, txt)

2118   ——— . (Untitled review of Gummere [720])   *Beibl*, 21 (1910),
        353–60. (mtr, about trl)

2119   TRAVER, Hope. *"Beowulf* 648–649 Once More."   *Archiv*,
        167 (1935), 253–56. (int, txt, wrd; 648–49)
        Review: D. E. M. Clarke, *YWES*, 16 (1935), 80–81

2120   TRENEER, Anne. *The Sea in English Literature from "Beo-
        wulf" to Donne*. London and Liverpool, 1926. (img, thm)
        Review: M. Daunt, *YWES*, 7 (1926), 65–66

2121   TRNKA, Bohumil. "Dnešní stav badání o Beowulfovi."
        Časopis pro moderní filologii, 12 (1925–26), 35–48, 124–36,
        247–54. (Title translated: Present State of the *Beowulf*
        Problem) (sch)

2122   TROSS, L. *Epistola ad Iulium Fleutelot*. Hammone, 1844.
        (ana, chr, hst) On Huncglacus of *Liber Monstrorum*.

2123   TURK, Milton Haigh. *An Anglo–Saxon Reader*. N.Y., 1927.
        (edt) Lines 1–52, 194–331a, 702b–836
        Review: G. T. Flom, *JEGP*, 27 (1928), 107–09

2124   TURNER, F. A. *Beowulf*. London, 1894. (par) Popular
        paraphrase.

2125   TURNER, Sharon. *The History of the Manners, Landed Prop-
        erty, Government, Laws, Poetry, Literature, Religion, and Language
        of the Anglo–Saxons*. London, 1799–1805. Vol. IV, pp. 398–
        408. (epc, hst, mns, rel, trl) Translates into English verse
        lines 18–40, 47–83a, 199b–279, 320–24, 333–36, 499–517a.
        Review: *British Critic*, 26 (1807), 387–88
        2d ed., 1807; Vol. II, pp. 294–303; translates in addition
        lines 1–17, 41–46, 83b–114, 189–99a, 387–497, 522–28
        3d ed., 1820; translates in addition lines 529–31, 535–58,
        607–46, 671–74, 720–38, 991–96, 1013–42, 1060b–68a,
        1159b–65a, 1168b–80a, 1215b–26a, 1240b–46a
        4th ed., 1823; 5th ed., 1827; 6th ed., 1836
        Repr., Paris, 1840; Philadelphia, 1841
        7th ed., 1852

2126   TURVILLE-PETRE, Joan Blomfield. "The Style and
        Structure of *Beowulf*."   *RES*, 14 (1938), 396–403. (rel, stl,
        str, tec, var)

   †   TYLER, Moses Coit, see [1476].

2127   UHLAND, Ludwig. "Zur deutschen Heldensage:
        I. Sigemund und Sigeferd."   *Germania*, 2 (1857), 344–63.
        (Fnb, hst, mth, smb, trl) Prose translation of *Finnsburh* into
        German.
        Repr. in his *Schriften zur Geschichte der Dichtung und Sage*, 8
        (1873), 479–504

2128   UHLENBECK, C. C. "Elias Wessén: Forntida
        Gudsdyrkan I Östergötland–Minnen af Forntida
        Gudsdyrkan I Mellan–Sveriges Ortnamn–Studier till
        Sveriges Hedna Mytologi och Fornhistoria." *APS*, 3 (1928–
        29), 172–75. (hst, nam, wrd; 2910)   Review of Wessén
        [2189].

2129   ———. "Het *Beowulf*-Epos als Geschiedbron." *TNTL*, 20
        (1901), 169–96. (hst)

2130   UHLER, Karl. *Die Bedeutungsgleichheit der altenglischen Ad-
        jektiva und Adverbia mit und ohne-lic(e)*. Heidelberg, 1926.
        (lng)
        Review: M. Daunt, *YWES*, 7 (1926), 66–67

2131   UNWERTH, Wolf von. "Fiolnir." *ANF*, 33 (1917), 320–
        35. (chr, hst, mth, nam)   On "Beow."

2132   ———. "Eine schwedische Heldensage als deutsches
        Volksepos." *ANF*, 35 (1918–19), 113–37. (ana)   On
        Biterolf, Þ*ídrekssaga*, and *Herbot ûz Tenelant*.

2133   UTLEY, Francis Lee. "Folklore, Myth, and Ritual." In
        Dorothy Bethurum, ed., *Critical Approaches to Medieval Litera-
        ture*. London and N.Y., 1960. pp. 83–109. (mth, smb)
        Repr. 1965

2134   VAN DRAAT, P. Vijn. "The Cursus in Old English
        Poetry." *Anglia*, 38 (1914), 377–404. (mtr)

2135   VAN MEURS, J. C. "*Beowulf* and Literary Criticism."
        Neophilologus, 39 (1955), 114–30. (hst, str, unt)   Opposes
        Bonjour [159] and Tolkien [2095].
        Review: R. M. Wilson, *YWES*, 36 (1955), 59

2136   VAPEREAU, Gustave. "Beowulf." In his *Dictionnaire
        universel des Littératures*. Paris, 1876. pp. 233–34. (bbl,
        Fnb, gen)

2137   VETTER, Ferdinand. "*Beowulf* und das altdeutsche
        Heldenzeitalter in England." *Deutschland*, 3 (1904), 558–71,
        767. (epc, gen, thm)

2138   ———. *Über die germanische Alliterationspoesie*. Vienna, 1872.
        (mtr, txt; 89, 1404, 2165, 2174)   Opposes Schubert [1833].

2139   ———. *Zum Muspilli und zur germanischen Alliterationspoesie*.
        Vienna, 1872. (mtr)
        Review: T. Schmitz, *Anglia*, 33 (1910), 175

2140   VIGFÚSSON, Gudbrand, and POWELL, F. York. "Ex-
        cursus III: On the Traces of Old Heroic Poems to Be Found
        in the Icelandic Family Tales (*Islendinga Sögur*). 1. Gretti and

Beowulf." In their *Corpus Poeticum Boreale.* Oxford, 1883.
Vol. II, pp. 501–3. (ana, mth)
Repr. N.Y., 1965

2141 ——. *Icelandic Prose Reader.* Oxford, 1879. pp. 209, 404. (ana, mth)

2142 ——. *Sturlunga Saga.* Oxford, 1878. (ana, mth, src) On *Grettissaga.*

2143 VISSER, F. T. "*Beowulf* 991–992." *ES*, 35 (1954), 116–20. (lng, txt; 991–92)
Review: R. M. Wilson, *YWES*, 35 (1954), 40

2144 VOGEL, W. "Schiff (und seine Teile)." *RL*, 4 (1918–19), 94–114. (hst)

2145 VOGT, Paul. *Beowulf: Altenglisches Heldengedicht.* Halle a.S., 1905. (com, Fnb, gen, str, trl) Translates *Beowulf* into German verse, abridged and rearranged; also translates *Finnsburh*, Möller text [1460].
Reviews:
  1 G. Binz, *Beibl*, 21 (1910), 289–91
  2 A. Eichler, *ZOG*, 57 (1907), 908–10
  3 H. Jantzen, *LitCbl*, 27 (1906), 257–58
  4 F. Klaeber, *Archiv*, 117 (1906), 408–10

2146 VOGT, Walther Heinrich. "Altgermanische Druck– 'Metrik.'" *Beitr*, 64 (1940), 124–64. (mtr)

2147 ——. "Der frühgermanische Kultredner." *APS*, 2 (1928), 250–63. (chr, hst, wrd) On the þyle.

2148 ——. *Stilgeschichte der eddischen Wissensdichtung: I. Der Kultredner (þulr).* Kiel Schriften der Baltischen Kommission zu Kiel, 4. Breslau and Kiel, 1927. (chr, hst, wrd) On þyle.
Reviews:
  1 H. de Boor, *AfdA*, 48 (1929), 9–14
  2 L. M. Hollander, *JEGP*, 28 (1929), 414–15
  3 K. Malone, *MLN*, 44 (1929), 129–30
  4 E. Mogk, *Beibl*, 39 (1928), 254–56

† VON names, see under next element of the name.

2149 VRIES, Jan de. *Altgermanische Religionsgeschichte.* Berlin, 1935–37. *PGrdr* 12.1 and 12.2. (mth, rel)

2150 ——. "Die beiden Hengeste." *ZDP*, 72 (1953), 125–43. (chr, Fnb, hst; Fep)

2151 ——. *Heldenlied en Heldensage.* Utrecht and Antwerp, 1959. (com, epc, Fnb, hst, mth, tec)
Trans. into German as *Heldenlied und Heldensage.* Bern, 1961.
Review: W. T. H. Jackson, *Speculum*, 39 (1964), 136–37

Trans. into English by B. J. Timmer as *Heroic Song and Heroic Legend*. London, N.Y., and Toronto, 1963: Oxford paperback 69.
Review: R. M. Wilson, *YWES*, 44 (1963), 70

2152   ——. "Die Starkadsage." *GRM*, 36 (1955), 281–97.   (ana, epc, hst, int, mth)

2153   WACKERBARTH, A. Diedrich.   *Beowulf: An Epic Poem Translated from the Anglo–Saxon into English Verse*. London, 1849.   (trl)   Translates into English ballad measure in imitation of Scott, based on Kemble [989].

2154   WADSTEIN, Elis.   "*Beowulf*, Etymologie und Sinn des Namens." In *Sievers*, pp. 323–26.   (chr, mth, nam)

2155   ——. "The *Beowulf* Poem as an English National Epos." *APS*, 8 (1933–34), 273–91.   (com, epc, hst)

2156   ——. "Norden och Västeuropa i gammal tid."   *Populärt vetenskapliga föreläsningar vid Göteborgs Högskola*, n.s. 22 (1925), 10–32, 159–67.   (com, hst)   Reply by Malone [1344].
Review: C. C. Uhlenbeck, *APS*, 2 (1927–28), 287–88

2157   ——. *On the Origin of the English*. Uppsala, n.d. (1927).   (hst, nam)
Review: M. Daunt, *YWES*, 8 (1927), 77–78

2158   WAGNER, Reinhard.   *Die Syntax des Superlativs im Gotischen, Altniederdeutschen, Althochdeutschen, Frühmittelhochdeutschen, im "Beowulf" und in der älteren Edda*. Berlin, 1910.   Palaestra 91.   (lng)
Reviews:
   1   E. A. Kock, *ANF*, 28 (1912), 347–49
   2   J. Schatz, *DLZ*, 31 (1910), 2848–49

2159   WÄGNER, W.   "Beowulf."   In his *Deutsche Heldensagen für Schule und Haus*. Leipzig, 1881.   (par)   German prose paraphrase.
Trans. into English as "The Legend of Beowulf."   In W. S. W. Anson, ed., *Epics and Romances of the Middle Ages*. London and Philadelphia, 1883.   pp. 347–64.
2d ed., 1884; 3d ed., 1884; 4th ed., 1886; 5th ed., 1888; 6th ed., 1890; 7th ed., 1893; 8th ed., 1896
Latter reissued as *Romances and Epics of our Northern Ancestors: Norse, Celt, and Teuton*.   Trans. by M. W. MacDowall. Norroena 12.   London, Stockholm, Copenhagen, Berlin, and N.Y., 1907.   pp. 266–85.

2160   WAHBA, Yousef Magdi Mourad.   *Qudamā' al-Injilīz wamalhamat Biyulf*.   Cairo, 1964.   In Arabic; title translates as

A Study of "Beowulf." (ana, chr, epc, for, gen, hst, int, lng, mth, mtr, nam, rel, smb, tec, thm, trl, txt, unt, wrd) First Arabic translation.

† WAKELIN, Martyn F., see [1696.1].

2161 WALKER, Louise J. "Beowulf in 1941 American." English Journal, 30 (1941), 773. (sch) Experiment with students.

2162 WALKER, Warren S. "The 'Brunecg' Sword." MLN, 67 (1952), 516–20. (int, txt; 1546)

2163 WANLEY, Humphrey. Antiquae literaturae Septentrionalis Liber Alter: Seu Humphredi Wanleii Librorum Vett. Septentrionalium, qui in Angliae Bibliothecis extant, nec non multorum Vett. Codd. Septentrionalium alibi extantium Catalogus Historico-Criticus. Oxford, 1705. Book II or Vol. III of Hickes [818]. pp. 218–19, 266–69. (edt, Fnb, mns) First mention of poem, transcribes lines 1–19, 53–73. See Langebek [1175].

2164 WARD, Gordon Reginald. "Hengest." Archaeologica Cantiana, 61 (1949), 77–135. (chr, epc, Fnb, hst, thm)
Repr. as Hengest: An Historical Study of His Danish Origins and of His Campaigns in Frisia and in South-East England. London, 1949.
Review: TLS, 10 March, 1950, p. 158

2165 ——. "The Name Hygelac." N&Q, 156 (1929), 263. (chr, nam)
Review: M. Daunt, YWES, 10 (1929), 92

2166 WARD, Harry Leigh Douglas. "Beowulf." Catalogue of Romances in the Department of Manuscripts in the British Museum. London, 1893–1919. Vol. II, pp. 1–15, 741–43. (mns)
Repr. 1962

2167 WARDALE, Edith E. "Anglo-Saxon Studies." YWES, 1 (1919–20), 32–38. (sch)

2167.1 ——. Ibid., 2 (1920–21), 33–40. (sch)

2167.2 ——. Ibid., 3 (1922), 25–31. (sch)

2167.3 ——. Ibid., 4 (1923), 38–44. (sch)

2168 ——. "Beowulf, ll. 848ff." MLR, 24 (1929), 62–63. (int, lng, txt; 850a)
Review: M. Daunt, YWES, 10 (1949), 92

2169 ——. "Beowulf: The Nationality of Ecgðeow." MLR, 24 (1929), 322. (hst, nam) Ecgðeow a Swede.
Review: M. Daunt, YWES, 10 (1949), 91

2170 ——. Chapters on Old English Literature. London, 1935. (epc, mth)
Reviews:
1 TLS, 8 Aug. 1935, p. 499

2   D. E. M. Clarke, *YWES*, 16 (1935), 66–68
3   K. Malone, *ES*, 18 (1936), 121–22
4   W. J. S., *MLR*, 31 (1936), 126

2171   WARREN, Kate M. *A Treasury of English Literature.* London, 1906. Introd. by S. A. Brooke. (Fnb, trl) Selected translations of *Finnsburh* and *Beowulf* into English prose.

2172   WASHBURN, Emelyn W. *Studies in Early English Literature.* N.Y., 1882. (gen)
2d ed., 1884

2173   WATERHOUSE, Mary E. *"Beowulf" in Modern English: A Translation into Blank Verse.* Cambridge, 1949. (trl)
Reviews:
    1   *TLS*, 17 Mar. 1950, p. 175
    2   R. M. Lumiansky, *JEGP*, 50 (1951), 247–48
    3   S. Rypins, *Speculum*, 26 (1951), 420–21
    4   G. Storms, *ES*, 32 (1951), 141
    5   J. N. Swannell, *MLR*, 46 (1951), 300–301
    6   R. M. Wilson, *YWES*, 30 (1949), 40

2174   WATSON, George. *Concise Cambridge Bibliography of English Literature: 600–1950.* Cambridge, 1958. (bbl)
Review: T. S. Dorsch, *YWES*, 39 (1958), 10

2175   WATTS, Ann Chalmers. "Swutol Sang Scopes: A Study of Oral Tradition in Old English Poetry." Unpub. Ph.D. diss., Yale Univ., 1965. *DA*, 26 (1965), 2194. (com, dct, for, str)

2176   WEBER, Edmund. "Der Germanenglaube im *Beowulf.*" *Germania*, 6 (1934), 273–77. (mth, thm)

2177   ——. "Die Halle Heorot als Schlafsaal." *Archiv*, 162 (1932), 114–16. (ana, hst)
Review: M. Daunt, *YWES*, 13 (1932), 74

2178   ——. "Seelenmörder oder Unholdtöter?" *NMs*, 2 (1931), 293–95. (int, smb; 171–79)

2179   ——. "Zur gemeingermanischen Ritterlichkeit im Beowulfslied." *NMs*, 10 (1940), 201–4. (hst, thm)

2180   WEBER, Henry William. "On the Teutonic Romances." In his *Illustrations of Northern Antiquities from the Earlier Teutonic and Scandinavian Romances, Being an Abstract of the Book of Heroes and the Nibelungen Lay; with Translation of Metrical Tales from the Old German, Danish, Swedish and Icelandic Languages, with Notes and Dissertations.* Edinburgh and London, 1814. (gen, sch) Mentions Thorkelin [2080] as forthcoming.
Review: *Edinburgh Review*, 26 (1816), 181–83

2181   WEBSTER, A. Blyth. "Translation from Old English: A Note and an Experiment." *E&S*, 5 (1914), 153–71. (trl) Translates 4–52.

2182 WEGNER, Richard. *Die Angriffswaffen der Angelsachsen.*
      Königsberg diss., 1899. (hst) On spears.

2183 WEIBULLS, Curt. "Om det svenska och det danska rikets
      uppkomst." *Historisk Tidskrift för Skåneland*, 7 (1917-21),
      300-360. (hst) On Geats and Jutes.

2184 WEINHOLD, K. "Die Riesen des germanischen Mythus."
      Sitzungsberichte der K. Akademie, Wien, Phil.-Hist. Classe, 26
      (1858), 225-306. (chr, mth) On Grendel and his mother.

2185 ——. *Spicilegium Formularum.* Halle, 1847. (mtr, stl)

2186 WENDE, Fritz. *Über die nachgestellten Präpositionen im Angel-
      sächsischen.* Palaestra 70. Berlin, 1915. (lng)
      Reviews:
          1   E. Björkman, *Archiv*, 135 (1916), 437-39
          2   A. Eichler, *Beibl*, 29 (1918), 99-102
          3   W. Franz, *ESt*, 51 (1917-18), 81-82
          4   J. Ries, *LGRP*, 37 (1916), 116-18
          5   A. Schröer, *DLZ*, 37 (1916), cols. 1455-60

2187 WESSÉN, Elias. "De Nordiska folkstammarna i *Beowulf.*"
      KVHAA, 36:2. Stockholm, 1927. (hst, nam) Opposed by
      Schütte [1870].
      Reviews:
          1   M. Daunt, *YWES*, 8 (1927), 79-80
          2   F. Holthausen, *Beibl*, 39 (1928), 303-6
          3   K. Malone, *Speculum*, 5 (1930), 134-35 [1406]
          4   R. E. Zachrisson, *SN*, 1 (1928), 87-88

2188 ——. "Nordiska namnstudier." *UUA*, 1927, pp. 1-118.
      (hst, mth, nam)
      Review: R. E. Zachrisson, *SN*, 1 (1928), 85-87

2189 ——. *Studier til Sveriges hedna mytologi och fornhistoria. UUA*,
      (1924). (hst, mth)
      Review: C. C. Uhlenbeck, *APS*, 3 (1928-29), 172-75 [2128]

2190 WEYHE, Hans. "König Ongentheow's Fall." *ESt*, 39
      (1908), 14-39. (ana, hst, mth) Danish parallels.

2191 WHALLON, William. "The Christianity of *Beowulf.*" *MP*,
      60 (1962), 81-94. (com, rel, smb, thm, unt)
      Review: R. M. Wilson, *YWES*, 44 (1963), 72

2192 ——. "The Diction of *Beowulf.*" *PMLA*, 76 (1961), 309-19.
      (dct, for, ken) Amplified by his [2193]; answer by Greenfield
      [669].
      Review: R. M. Wilson, *YWES*, 42 (1963), 57

2193 ——. "Formulas for Heroes in the *Iliad* and in *Beowulf.*"
      MP, 63 (1965), 95-104. (dct, for) Amplifies his [2192];
      answer by Greenfield [669].

2194 ——. "The Idea of God in *Beowulf.*" *PMLA*, 80 (1965),
      19-23. (ana, dct, for, rel, src, thm, wrd)

2195   WHEATON, Henry. *History of the Northmen, or Danes and Normans, from the Earliest Times to the Conquest of England by William of Normandy.* London, 1831. (gen, hst)

2196   WHITBREAD, L. "*Beowulf* and Archaeology: Two Footnotes." *NM*, 68 (1967), 28–35. (arc, int; 2088, 3159)

2197   ——. "Beowulf and Grendel's Mother: Two Minor Parallels from Folklore." *MLN*, 57 (1942), 281–82. (ana, mth) Polynesian tales.
        Review: D. Whitelock, *YWES*, 23 (1942), 38

2198   ——. "Beowulfiana." *MLR*, 37 (1942), 480–84. (ana, int, txt, wrd; 1604, 1608, 1700–84, 2246–47) Notes on Klaeber [1026], 2d ed.
        Review: D. Whitelock, *YWES*, 23 (1942), 35

2199   ——. "Grendel's Abode: an Illustrative Note." *ES*, 22 (1940), 64–66. (ana; 1137–39, 1361–65, 1405–10) Old Irish *Fís Adamnáin.*

2200   ——. "The Hand of Æschere: A Note on *Beowulf* 1343." *RES*, 25 (1949), 339–42. (int, str, tec; 1343)
        Review: R. M. Wilson, *YWES*, 30 (1949), 42

2201   ——. "Three *Beowulf* Allusions." *N&Q*, 189 (1945), 207–09. (ana, int, smb, src; 244, 544–48, 569–72, 579–81, 1609, 2247)
        Review: M. Daunt, *YWES*, 26 (1945), 40–41

2202   WHITE, Anne Terry. *The Golden Treasury of Myths and Legends.* N.Y., 1962. pp. 68–81. Illustrated by Alice and Martin Provensen. (par) Children's paraphrase.

2203   WHITEHEAD, Guy. "The Heroic Tradition in Anglo–Saxon Life and Poetry." Unpub. Ph.D. diss., Vanderbilt Univ., 1955–56. *DA*, 16 (1956), 1909–10. (hst, int, thm)

2204   WHITELOCK, Dorothy. "Anglo–Saxon Poetry and the Historian." *Transactions of the Royal Historical Society*, 4th series, 31 (1949), 75–94. (com, hst, rel, sch)
        Review: R. M. Wilson, *YWES*, 30 (1949), 39–40

2205   ——. *The Audience of "Beowulf."* Oxford, 1951. (ana, com, hst, int, mns, rel)
        Reviews:
            1   *TLS*, 9 Dec. 1951, p. 790
            2   N. Davis, *RES*, 3 (1952), 376–77
            3   G. Kane, *MLR*, 47 (1952), 567–68
            4   F. Mossé, *EA*, 6 (1953), 147
            5   T. F. Mustanoja, *NM*, 53 (1952), 434–37
            6   J. C. Pope, *MLN*, 67 (1952), 353–54
            7   S. Potter, *MAE*, 21 (1952), 49–51

    8 G. Storms, *ES*, 33 (1952), 262–64
    9 H. B. Woolf, *MLQ*, 15 (1954), 182
Corrected ed., 1958.
Repr. 1964

2205.1 ——. *The Beginnings of English Society.* Pelican History of England, 2. London and Baltimore, (gen, hst)
Repr. 1954, 1956, 1959

2206   ——. *"Beowulf* 2444–2471." *MAE*, 8 (1939), 198–204. (hst, int, trl; 2444–71)
Review: G. N. Garmonsway, *YWES*, 20 (1939), 28

2207   ——. *"Changing Currents in Anglo–Saxon Studies."* Cambridge, 1958. (sch)
Reviews:
    1 F. M. Stenton, *EHR*, 74 (1959), 519–20
    2 R. W. Zandvoort, *ES*, 41 (1960), 61–62

2208   ——. "Old English." *YWES*, 23 (1942), 32–49. (sch)
2208.1 ——. *Ibid.*, 24 (1943), 28–40. (sch)
    † ——, see [2039].

2209   WHITESELL, J. Edwin. "Intentional Ambiguities in *Beowulf.*" *TSL*, 11 (1966), 145–49. (dct, stl, tec)

    † ——, see [33].

2210   WICKBERG, Rudolf. *"Beowulf,"* en fornengelsk hjältedikt *översatt.* Westernik Programm, 1889. (hst, trl) First Swedish translation, in verse, based on his own readings of manuscript.
2d ed., Uppsala, 1914
Review: E. A. Kock, *ANF*, 32 (1916), 223–24

2211   WIERSMA, Stanley Martin. "A Linguistic Analysis of Words Referring to Monsters in *Beowulf.*" Unpub. Ph.D. diss., Univ. of Wisconsin, 1961. *DA*, 22 (1961), 570. (chr, dct, lng, wrd)

2212   WILBUR, Richard. "Notes on Heroes (I–IV). I. First Forth Gewat. II. Beowulf." *Wake*, 6 (1948), 80–81. (trl) Translates 210–24a into alliterative verse. Part II is an original poem.
Part II repr. in his *Ceremony and Other Poems.* London and N.Y., 1948–50. pp. 36–37.
Part II repr. in *The Poems of Richard Wilbur.* N.Y., 1963: Harvest paperback. pp. 148–49.

2213   WILD, Friedrich. "Beowulf und die Waegmundinge." *Die Moderne Sprache, Marburg, Schriftenreihe*, 6. Vienna, 1961. (chr, hst, nam)

?2214 ——. *"Beowulf* und Phokas." *AION-SG*, 3 (1960), 1–16.

2215   ——— . *Drachen im Beowulf und andere Drachen: Mit einem Anhang Drachenfeldzeichen, Drachenwappen und St. Georg.* *SÖAW*, 238, Vol. 5 (1962). (chr, mth)
Reviews:
    1   F. R. Schröder, *GRM*, 44 (1963), 216–17
    2   R. W. Zandvoort, *ES*, 44 (1963), 73

†   WILKINS, William Vaughan, see [1998].

2216   WILLARD, Rudolph. "*Beowulf* 2672b: līg ȳðum fōr." *MLN*, 76 (1961), 290–93. (int, txt, wrd; 2672b)
Review: R. M. Wilson, *YWES*, 42 (1963), 58

2217   ——— , and CLEMONS, Elinor D. "Bliss's Light Verses in the *Beowulf.*" *JEGP*, 66 (1967), 230–44. (mtr)   On Bliss [130].

2218   WILLIAMS, Blanche Colton. *Gnomic Poetry in Anglo–Saxon.* Columbia Univ. Studies in English and Comparative Literature, 49. N.Y., 1914. pp. 29–42. (rel, thm; 20–25, 183b–88, 287b–89, 440b–41, 455b, 572b–73, 931b–32, 1003b–4, 1058b–63, 1385b–90, 1535b–37, 1664b–65a, 1839b–40, 1941b–44, 2030b–32, 2167b–70a, 2292–94a, 2601b–2, 2765b–67, 2891b–92, 3063b–66, 3078–79, 3176b–79)

†   ——— , see [16].

2219   WILLIAMS, Margaret. *Word-Hoard.* N.Y., 1940. (Fnb, gen, trl)   Translation of *Finnsburh* into verse.

2220   WILLIAMS, R. A. "*Beowulf*, ll. 1086–1088." *MLR*, 22 (1927), 310–13. (int, txt; 1086–88)
Review: M. Daunt, *YWES*, 8 (1927), 82–83

2221   ——— . *The Finn Episode in Beowulf: An Essay in Interpretation.* Cambridge, 1924. (ana, Fnb, hst, int; Fep)
Reviews:
    1   *N&Q*, 149 (1925), 89
    2   *TLS*, 19 Mar. 1925, p. 182
    3   E. Blackman, *RES*, 1 (1925), 228–31
    4   H. M. Flasdieck, *LGRP*, 47 (1926), 156–64
    5   E. V. Gordon, *YWES*, 5 (1924), 72–74
    6   H. Hecht, *AfdA*, 44 (1925), 121–25
    7   J. Kindervater, *LitCbl*, 76 (1925), 1744
    8   F. Klaeber, *Beibl*, 37 (1926), 5–9; reply by Williams [2222]; apology by Klaeber, *Beibl*, 38 (1927), 160
    9   K. Malone, *JEGP*, 25 (1926), 114–17 [1402]
    10   H. Schreuder, *Neophilologus*, 11 (1926), 294–97
    11   W. J. Sedgefield, *MLR*, 20 (1925), 338–39

2222   ——— . "Zur Erwiderung an Fr. Klaeber." *Beibl*, 38 (1927), 61–63. (int; Fep)   Reply to F. Klaeber, *Beibl*, 37 (1926), 5–9; see also Klaeber's apology, *Beibl*, 38 (1927), 160.

2223   WILLMS, J. E. *Untersuchung über den Gebrauch der Farbenbezeichnungen in der Poesie Altenglands.* Münster diss., 1902. (dct, img, wrd)

2224   WILSON, David M. "From the Vigorous North: The Norsemen and Their Forerunners." In David Talbot Rice, ed., *The Dawn of European Civilization: The Dark Ages.* N.Y., Toronto, and London, 1965. pp. 219–40.   (hst, trl) Translates 32–42 into literal English prose.

2225   WILSON, R. M. "Old English." *YWES*, 28 (1947), 56–66. (sch)

2225.1   ——. *Ibid.*, 29 (1948), 54–67. (sch)

2225.2   ——. *Ibid.*, 30 (1949), 38–51. (sch)

2225.3   ——. *Ibid.*, 31 (1950), 42–52. (sch)

2225.4   ——. *Ibid.*, 32 (1951), 45–56. (sch)

2225.5   ——. *Ibid.*, 33 (1952), 36–48. (sch)

2225.6   ——. *Ibid.*, 34 (1953), 42–56. (sch)

2225.7   ——. *Ibid.*, 35 (1954), 38–44. (sch)

2226   ——. "Old English Literature." *YWES*, 36 (1955), 56–64. (sch)

2226.1   ——. *Ibid.*, 37 (1956), 69–75. (sch)

2226.2   ——. *Ibid.*, 38 (1957), 71–79. (sch)

2226.3   ——. *Ibid.*, 39 (1958), 69–75. (sch)

2226.4   ——. *Ibid.*, 40 (1959), 54–65. (sch)

2226.5   ——. *Ibid.*, 41 (1960), 51–60. (sch)

2226.6   ——. *Ibid.*, 42 (1961), 54–62. (sch)

2226.7   ——. *Ibid.*, 43 (1962), 52–64. (sch)

2226.8   ——. *Ibid.*, 44 (1963), 67–79. (sch)

2226.9   ——. *Ibid.*, 45 (1964), 56–65. (sch)

2227   WITKE, Charles. "*Béowulf* 2069b–2199: A Variant." *NM*, 67 (1966), 113–17.   (for, str, unt; 2069b–2199) Answer to Magoun [1295].

2228   WOLF, Alfred. *Die Bezeichnungen für Schicksal in der angelsächsischen Dichtersprache.* Breslau diss., 1919. (dct, thm, wrd)

2229   WOLFF, Ludwig. "Über den Stil der altgermanischen Poesie." *DVLG*, 1 (1923), 214–29. (stl)

2230   WOLZOGEN, Hans von. *Beovulf (Bärwelf): Das älteste deutsche Heldengedicht aus dem Angelsächsischen.* Leipzig, [1872]. (trl)   Translates into German alliterative verse, based on Grein [677].

2231   WOOD, Cecil. "*Nis þaet seldguma: Beowulf* 249." *PMLA*,

75 (1960), 481–84. (ana, int, rht; 249b)
Review: R. M. Wilson, *YWES*, 41 (1960), 55

2232   WOODWARD, Robert H. W.   *"Swanrad in Beowulf."*
MLN, 69 (1954), 544–46. (int, ken, wrd; 200) Continues
Brady [188].
Review: R. M. Wilson, *YWES*, 35 (1954), 40

2233   WOOLF, Henry Bosley.   "Beowulf and Grendel: An
Analogue from Burma." *MLN*, 62 (1947), 261–62. (ana)
Review: R. M. Wilson, *YWES*, 28 (1947), 61

2234   ——. "Hrothgar." *Louisiana State Univ. Studies, Humanities
Series*, 5 (1954), 39–54. (chr, epc, nam)

2235   ——. "The Name of Beowulf." *ESt*, 72 (1937), 7–9. (chr,
nam; 2604) = Aelfhere. See Malone [1346] and [1353].
Review: C. L. Wrenn, *YWES*, 19 (1938), 51

2236   ——. "The Naming of Women in Old English Times."
MP, 36 (1938), 113–20. (mtr, nam, var; 62)
Review: C. L. Wrenn, *YWES*, 19 (1938), 45–46

2237   ——. "A Note on the Hoard in *Beowulf*." *MLN*, 58 (1943),
113–15. (epc, hst, int; 2247–49, 2764–66, 3166–68)
Review: D. Whitelock, *YWES*, 24 (1943), 33

2238   ——. "On the Characterization of Beowulf." *ELH*, 15
(1948), 85–92. (chr, int, tec, txt; 457)
Review: R. M. Wilson, *YWES*, 29 (1948), 58

2239   ——. "Subject-Verb Agreement in *Beowulf*." *MLQ*, 4
(1943), 49–55. (lng; 1408)
Review: D. Whitelock, *YWES*, 24 (1943), 30

2240   ——. "Unferth." *MLQ*, 10 (1949), 145–52. (chr, int, tec)
Review: R. M. Wilson, *YWES*, 30 (1949), 40–41

2241   WORK, James A. "Odyssean Influences on the *Beowulf*."
PQ, 9 (1930), 399–402. (ana, chr, epc) Unferth and
Euryalus.
Review: M. Daunt, *YWES*, 11 (1930), 56

2242   WORKMAN, Rhea Thomas.   "The Concept of Hell in
Anglo–Saxon Poetry before A.D. 850." Unpub. Ph.D. diss.,
Univ. of South Carolina, 1958. *DA*, 19 (1959), 1746–47.
(img, lng, rel, thm)

†   WORSTER, William, see [701].

2243   WRENN, Charles L.   "Anglo–Saxon Poetry and the
Amateur Archaeologist."   Chambers Memorial Lecture,
University College, London, 12 March 1962. London, 1962.
(arc, int, wrd; 326, 725, 2105–10)
Review: P. M. Vermeer, *ES*, 44 (1963), 448–49

2244   ——. *"Beowulf": With the "Finnesburg Fragment."* London and Boston, 1953.   (bbl, com, dct, edt, Fnb, hst, mns, mth, mtr, nam, nts, src, stl, str)

Reviews:

   1   *TLS*, 7 May 1953, p. 298

   2   K. R. Brooks, *MLR*, 49 (1954), 487–88

   3   K. Brunner, *Anglia*, 72 (1954), 467–68

   4   W. Clemen, *Anglia*, 71 (1953), 346–48

   5   E. Ekwall, *ES*, 35 (1954), 75–81

   6   R. Girvan, *RES*, 5 (1954), 75–79

   7   R. Willard, *JEGP*, 53 (1954), 617–23

   8   R. M. Wilson, *YWES*, 34 (1953), 45–46

2d ed., London, 1958

Review: R. M. Wilson, *YWES*, 39 (1958), 71

Repr. 1959, 1961, 1963, 1964

2245   ——. "Magic in an Anglo–Saxon Cemetery." In *Tolkien*, pp. 306–20. (arc, hst, mth, txt; 204, 326)

2246   ——. "Old English." *YWES*, 19 (1938), 39–60. (sch)

2247   ——. "Saxons and Celts in South-West Britain." *THSC*, 1959, pp. 38–75. (hst)

2247.1   ——. *A Study of Old English Literature*. N.Y., 1967. (ana, com, epc, Fnb, lng, mns, str)

2248   ——. "Sutton Hoo and *Beowulf*." In *Mossé*, pp. 495–507. (arc, com)

Review: R. M. Wilson, *YWES*, 40 (1959), 60

Repr. in Nicholson [1560], pp. 311–30

2249   ——. "Two Anglo–Saxon Harps." *CL*, 14 (1962), 118–28. (arc, for, hst, smb) Also in *Brodeur*, pp. 118–28.

†   ——, see [307] and [740].

2250   WRIGHT, C. E. *The Cultivation of Saga in Anglo–Saxon England*. Edinburgh, 1939. (com, hst, tec)

Reviews:

   1   *DUJ*, 1 (1940), 239–40

   2   *TLS*, 30 Mar 1940, p. 163

   3   A. G. Brodeur, *AJF*, 54 (1941), 88–90

   4   H. R. Ellis (Davidson), *RES*, 16 (1940), 458–60

   5   G. N. Garmonsway, *YWES*, 21 (1940), 44–45

   6   K. Malone, *ES*, 23 (1941), 110–12

2251   WRIGHT, David. *Beowulf: A Prose Translation with an Introduction*. London and Baltimore, 1957: Penguin Classics 1–70. (arc, bbl, gen, hst, mns, nam, nts, trl)

Reviews:

   1   K. Amis, *Spectator*, 198 (5 April 1957), 445 [10]

   2   *TLS*, 16 Aug. 1957, p. 492

3   R. M. Wilson, *YWES*, 38 (1957), 74

4   E. Zeeman, *Cambridge Review*, 78 (1956–57), 651, 653

2252   WRIGHT, Elizabeth M.   "*Beowulf* l. 1363." *ESt*, 30 (1902), 341–43. (int, txt, wrd; 1363)   Reply by Holthausen [847].

2253   WRIGHT, Herbert G.   "Good and Evil; Light and Darkness; Joy and Sorrow in *Beowulf*." *RES*, n.s. 8 (1957), 1–11. (smb, str, tec, thm)   Opposes Gang [603].
Review: R. M. Wilson, *YWES*, 38 (1957), 74–75
Repr. in Nicholson [1560], pp. 257–67, abridged

2254   Item canceled.

2255   WRIGHT, Thomas.   *Biographia Britannica Literaria; or Biography of Literary Characters of Great Britain and Ireland Arranged in Chronological Order: Vol. I. Anglo–Saxon Period.* London, 1842. (ana, Fnb, gen, trl)   Prints and translates lines 89b–98, 149b–51a, 264–65a, 320–24, 405–6, 496b–97a, 565–67a, 816b–18a, 867b–72, 1063–68, 1321–31a, 1343b–44, 2262b–63a, 3156–58.

2256   ——— .   *The Celt, the Roman and the Saxon.*   London, 1852. (hst)
2d ed., 1865; 3d ed., 1875; 4th ed., 1885

2257   ——— .   *Essays on Subjects Connected with the Literature, Popular Superstitions, and History of England in the Middle Ages.*   London, 1846. (src)

2258   [———].   "On Anglo–Saxon Poetry."   *Fraser's Magazine*, 12 (1835), 76–92. (edt, par)   Summary of 499–606.

2259   WÜLKER, Richard Paul.   *Beowulf: Text nach der Handschrift.* In his revision of Grein's *Bibliothek der angelsächsischen Poesie.* Kassel, 1881.   Vol. I, pp. 18–148.   (edt, Fnb, mns)   Diplomatic ed.
Review: E. Kölbing, *ESt*, 5 (1882), 239–41 [1124]; 7 (1884), 482–89 [1124.1]

2260   ——— .   *Das Beowulfslied, nebst den kleineren epischen, lyrischen, didaktischen und geschichtlichen stücken.*   In his revision of Grein's *Bibliothek der angelsächsischen Poesie.*   Kassel, 1883.   Vol. I, pp. 149–277.   (edt, Fnb, nts)
Review: E. Kölbing, *ESt*, 7 (1884), 482–89 [1124.1]
Repr. Hamburg, 1922

2261   ——— .   "Besprechung der Beowulfübersetzungen, im Anschluss an *Beowulf, an Old English Poem, Translated into Modern Rhymes by Lieut. Colonel H. W. Lumsden*."   *Anglia*, 4 (1881), Anz., 69–78. (bbl, about trl)   Survey of translations and review of Lumsden [1278]; reply by Harrison [757].

2262   ——— . *Geschichte der englischen Litteratur von den ältesten Zeiten bis zur Gegenwart.* Leipzig, 1896. (gen)
Review: E. Kölbing, *ESt*, 23 (1897), 306 [1125]
2d ed., Leipzig and Vienna, 1906–7
Review: G. Binz, *Beibl*, 20 (1909), 65–73

2263   ——— . *Grundriss zur Geschichte der angelsächsischen Litteratur mit einer Übersicht der angelsächsischen Sprachwissenschaft.* Leipzig, 1884–85. (bbl, Fnb, gen) Supersedes Krüger [1165].
Review: E. Einenkel, *Anglia*, 8 (1885), Anz., 157–58

2264   ——— . *Kleinere angelsächsische Dichtungen.* Halle and Leipzig, 1879. (edt of Fnb)

2265   ——— . (Untitled review of Arnold [36]) *Anglia*, 1 (1877), 177–86. (com, int)

2266   WYATT, Alfred J.   *An Anglo–Saxon Reader.* Cambridge, 1919. (edt) Edits lines 1–52, 499–606, 1251–1309, 1572b–1676, 1866–1919, 2270b–2344; interspersed with summaries by Morris [1483].
Reviews:
        1   G. Hübener, *Beibl*, 32 (1921), 79–80
        2   A. E. H. Swaen, *ESt*, 56 (1922), 422–24
        3   E. E. Wardale, *YWES*, 1 (1919–20), 34
Repr. 1922, 1925, 1930, 1939, 1947, 1948, 1953, 1959, 1962, 1965

2267   ——— . *Beowulf: Edited with Textual Foot-Notes, Index of Proper Names, and Alphabetical Glossary.* Cambridge, 1894. (edt, Fnb, nam, nts, txt)
Reviews:
        1   H. Bradley, *Academy*, 46 (1894), 69–70
        2   O. Brenner, *ESt*, 20 (1895), 296
        3   R. Wülker, *Beibl*, 5 (1894–95), 65–67
        4   J. Zupitza, *Archiv*, 94 (1894), 326–29
2d ed., 1898.
Reviews:
        1   G. Sarrazin, *ESt*, 28 (1900), 407–08
        2   M. Trautmann, *Beibl*, 10 (1899–1900), 257–62 [2117]
Repr. 1901, 1908
Rev. ed. by R. W. Chambers.   *"Beowulf," with the "Finnsburg Fragment."* Cambridge, 1914. (edt, Fnb, mns, nam, nts, txt)
Reviews:
        1   J. W. Bright, *MLN*, 31 (1916), 188–89
        2   J. D. Jones, *MLR*, 11 (1916), 230–31
        3   W. W. Lawrence, *JEGP*, 14 (1915), 611–13
2d ed., 1920

Reviews:
1   O. L. Jiriczek, *NS*, 29 (1921), 67–69
2   H. Patch, *MLN*, 37 (1922), 418–27
3   L. L. Schücking, *ESt*, 55 (1921), 88–100 [1862]
Repr. 1925, 1933, 1943, 1948, 1952

2268   Item canceled.

2269   ——. *The Threshold of Anglo–Saxon.* Cambridge, 1926.
(edt)   600 normalized lines with Morris's summaries [1483].
Reviews:
1   *N&Q*, 151 (1926), 144
2   G. T. Flom, *JEGP*, 26 (1927), 600
3   K. Malone, *MLN*, 42 (1927), 60–61

†   ——, see [1482].

2270   WYLD, Henry Cecil. "Diction and Imagery in Anglo–
Saxon Poetry." *E&S*, 11 (1925), 49–91. (dct, img, wrd)
Reviews:
1   A. Eichler, *Beibl*, 37 (1926), 232–33
2   E. V. Gordon, *YWES*, 6 (1925), 68–70

2271   ——. "Experiments in Translating *Beowulf.*" In *Klaeber*,
pp. 217–31. (trl)   Translates 26–52, 611–38, 1345–76,
2794–2820.
Review: M. Daunt, *YWES*, 10 (1929), 81–82

2272   [——]. "Gothique." *Oxford Magazine*, 12 Mar. 1925. (trl)
Parody by "Mr. Beach"; identification by R. W. Chambers.

†   YOUNG, Jean, see [1880].

2273   ZACHRISSON, Robert Eugen. "Grendel in *Beowulf* and in
Local Names." In *Jespersen*, pp. 39–44. (chr, hst, int, lng,
mth, nam, wrd)
Review: M. Daunt, *YWES*, 11 (1930), 61

2274   ——. "Notes on Early Germanic Personal Names." *SN*, 1
(1928), 74–77. (int, nam)

2275   ZAPPERT, G. "Virgil's Fortleben im Mittelalter."
Denkschriften der k. Akademie Wien, Phil.-Hist. Classe, 2 (1851),
17–70. (ana)

2276   ZESMER, David M. *Guide to English Literature from Beowulf
through Chaucer and Medieval Drama.* N.Y., 1961: College
Outline Series 53.   Bibliography by Stanley B. Greenfield.
(bbl, Fnb, gen, nam, rel, stl, str)
Reviews:
1   A. C. Cawley, *MLR*, 58 (1963), 621–22

 2 R. P. Creed, *CE*, 23 (1961), 162

 3 J. Turville-Petre, *SN*, 33 (1962), 335–36

 4 R. M. Wilson, *YWES*, 42 (1963), 56

?2277 ZINSSER, G. *Der Kampf Beowulfs mit Grendel als Prober, eine metrische Uebersetzung des angelsächsischen Epos "Beówulf."* Program der Realschule zu Forbach, 448. Saarbrücken, 1881. (trl) Translates 1–836 into German verse, based on Heyne [815].

Reviews:

 1 B. Hölscher, *Archiv*, 68 (1882), 446

 2 T. Krüger, *ESt*, 7 (1884), 370–72

2278 ZUPITZA, Julius. *Beowulf: Autotypes of the Unique Cotton MS. Vitellius A. XV in the British Museum, with a Transliteration.* London, 1882. EETS, o.s. 77. (edt, mns, txt) Facsimile of [226]. Collated with Thorkelin [2081–82].

Reviews:

 1 E. Kölbing, *ESt*, 7 (1884), 482–89 [1124.1]

 2 M. Rödiger, *Literatur Zeitung*, 1883, p. 1030

 3 E. Sievers, *LitCbl*, 35 (1884), 124

 4 G. Stephens, *Athenaeum*, 1883, II, 499, 567

 5 M. Trautmann, *Anglia*, 7 (1884), Anzeiger, 41

 6 H. Varnhagen, *AfdA*, 10 (1884), 304

2d ed., with introd. by Norman Davis. London, 1958. EETS 245. Collotypes from same negatives as Malone [1371]. Retains Zupitza's transcription.

Reviews:

 1 P. H. Blair, *RES*, 12 (1961), 326

 2 O. Funke, *ES*, 42 (1961), 94–95

 3 E. van Schaubert, *Anglia*, 79 (1961), 72–76

 4 R. M. Wilson, *MLR*, 56 (1961), 139–40

 5 R. M. Wilson, *YWES*, 40 (1959), 59

2279 ———. *Verbesserungen zu den Drachenkämpfen.* Oppeln diss., 1867. (epc, gen)

2280 ———. "Zu *Beowulf* 850." *Archiv*, 84 (1890), 124–25. (int, txt; 850)

Indexes

Subject Classifications[1]

Read down

alg	246	379	734	1177	1519	1803	2177	1253	403
	260	387	744	1181	1521	1814	2190	1254	473
131	261	404	756	1188	1522	1817	2194	1255	480
156	263	405	766	1189	1532	1823	2197	1256	481
1716	264	406	772	1202	1547	1825	2198	1311	507
	267	406.1	777	1203	1548	1827	2199	1553	540
	268	407	785	1205	1550	1837	2201	1554	559
ana	270	415	791	1209	1556	1867	2205	1556	606
	281	446	810	1210	1576	1869	2221	1585	614
12	283	447	813	1225	1580	1878	2231	1586	615
29	287.1	463	819	1237	1591	1879	2233	1636	656
39	290	465	821.1	1248	1592	1892	2241	1638	700
65	291	468	824	1263	1596	1902	2247.1	1644	730
77	297	471	840	1265	1597	1920	2255	1821	740
82	300	474	848	1283	1609	1930	2275	1916	845
83	301	494	891	1286	1612	1934		2006	931
87	306	498	899	1288	1617	1964		2017	953
92	307	499	913	1295	1618	1972	arc	2018	995
94	309	500	932	1297	1632	1973		2020	997
101	310	501	951	1299	1633	1975	32	2085	1000
106	312	518	965	1300	1645	1976	70	2196	1026
109	313	537	966	1303	1649	1977	103	2243	1037
116	314	565	985	1304	1666	1978	128	2245	1055
134	318	575	988	1318	1669	1984	236	2248	1188
138	320	578	997	1331	1671	1994.1	250	2249	1251
139	330	589	998	1332	1677	2000	251	2251	1311
141	334	600	1013	1336	1680	2003	252		1477
142	339	604	1017	1343	1696	2030	253		1582
145	345	620	1024	1346	1698	2033	335		1625
147	348	627	1026	1350	1703	2045	339	bbl	1673
150	359	631	1028	1361	1712	2048	402		1696.1
156	361	637	1032	1382	1716	2050	444	12	1725
175	362	642	1033	1384	1737	2052	445	13	1868
187	363	643	1041	1391	1747	2061	461	14	1881
191	364	646	1046	1394	1758	2063	589	44	1892
195	365	648	1047	1395	1768	2066	664	71	1983
201	366	689	1049	1434	1769	2069	789	86	2093
202	368	696	1081	1439	1772	2122	827	103	2136
203	370	704	1092	1441	1773	2132	981	166	2174
205	371	706	1127	1458	1775	2140	983	170	2244
227	372	714	1134	1465	1779	2141	1073	189	2251
238	374	726	1139	1472	1784.1	2142	1108	235	2261
240	375	729	1140	1501	1794	2152	1217	238	2263
243	377	730	1142	1502	1802	2160	1218	307	2276

[1]General and line notes are not indexed here.

1026	136	822	2046	2222	551	989	1405	2127	1186
1078	144	924	2054		559	996	1421	2136	1219
1080	146	942	2059	Fnb	560	997	1424	2145	1263
1123	153	976	2060	3	588.1	998	1443	2150	1264
1224	164	977	2086	12	589	1000	1445	2151	1265
1228	168	997	2087	36	590	1002	1460	2163	1298
1289	169	998	2095	44	614	1003	1462	2164	1306
1296	171	1047	2101	45	619	1020	1463	2171	1310
1307	177	1168	2125	47	624	1026	1477	2219	1312
1371	182	1188	2137	48	626	1027	1501	2221	1313
1443	189	1189	2151	78	637	1028	1504	2244	1401
1460	191	1214	2152	79	649	1034	1506	2247.1	1404
1468	201	1225	2155	99	653	1035	1511	2255	1531
1486	206	1240	2160	106	663	1038	1512	2259	1562
1516	238	1241	2164	110	664	1043	1541	2260	1563
1542	244	1248	2170	128	670	1050	1542	2263	1599
1630	254	1264	2234	141	675	1051	1581	2264	1625
1650	287.1	1265	2237	177	676	1061	1613	2267	1627
1688	291	1523	2241	178	678	1063	1633	2276	1664
1705	292	1525	2247.1	182	679	1076	1650		1675
1761	302	1533	2279	189	700	1078	1673		1684
1787	307	1545		196	704	1080	1684	for	1696
1851	331	1546		222	707	1098	1696.1		1725
1891	354	1567	Fep	225	720	1100	1705	101	1728.1
1892	380	1580		230	737	1110	1708	154	1744
1948	388	1587	48	231	740	1115	1709	163	1784
1971	487	1588	141	238	741	1118	1752	229	1962
2038	520	1589	159	239	744	1119	1770	254	1994.1
2080	525	1590	222	261	747	1175	1787	262	2010
2081	533	1608	225	272	754	1183	1795	287.1	2012
2082	536	1616	230	273	763	1184	1796	294	2025
2084	565	1624	231	274	774	1188	1811	332	2160
2106	582	1631	273	300	785	1190	1813	397	2175
2109	603	1673	663	304	794	1208	1822	409	2192
2123	604	1677	744	307	803	1223	1847	410	2193
2163	644	1692	936	315	804	1230	1851	412	2194
2244	656	1695	937	316	806	1261	1879	414	2249
2258	668	1740	967	322	814	1271	1886	415	
2259	670	1742	1051	355	815	1278	1891	416	
2260	671	1780	1184	356	818	1289	1892	417	hst
2264	673	1804	1190	384	820	1290	1897	421	2
2266	711	1811	1326	400	831	1292	1921	525	5
2267	713	1823	1327	403	842	1294	1951	574	6
2269	715	1871	1338	408	845	1296	1952	588.1	6.1
2278	729	1877	1421	420	862	1307	1960	589	9
	730	1878	1443	430	878	1310	1961	590	12
	750	1883	1460	449	880	1312	1983	591	15
epc	762	1914	1708	475	889	1326	2041	622	32
	802	1915	1795	479	896	1328	2044	669	36
31	803	1920	1894	480	931	1329	2077	670	40
34	804	1951	2109	481	936	1338	2084	672	44
45	806	1977	2110	507	945	1353	2106	820	47
59	809	2009	2150	548	949	1375	2109	941	50
104	821.1	2044	2221	550	967	1376	2110	988	51

63	239	480	726	1027	1311	1506	1733	1955	2183
87	248	483	727	1042	1318	1509	1739	1962	2187
90	249	492	731	1043	1320	1511	1745	1975	2188
93	254	498	732	1061	1321	1514	1766	1978	2189
94	257	499	737	1079	1330	1522	1771	1993	2190
95	258	500	740	1081	1331	1523	1772	1997	2195
98	259	501	744	1083	1335	1524	1773	1999	2203
100	259.1	505	756	1088	1337	1526	1774	2001	2204
101	259.2	506	764	1090	1339	1530	1775	2002	2205
106	261	511	765	1091	1340	1531	1777	2003	2205.1
111	266	516	766	1108	1343	1534	1780	2005	2206
114	268	518	777	1115	1344	1540	1790	2006	2210
116	269	521	783	1116	1345	1543	1793	2007	2213
117	270	547	787	1120	1346	1544	1794	2016	2221
118	273	548	788	1127	1348	1545	1795	2018	2224
119	296	554	790	1138	1349	1547	1803	2020	2237
120	298	555	792	1139	1350	1549	1812	2021	2244
121	300	556	793	1141	1353	1550	1816	2022	2245
122	302	557	796	1142	1358	1552	1820	2023	2247
123	303	562	797	1146	1361	1553	1821	2025	2249
124	306	565	801	1162	1381	1554	1822	2026	2251
128	307	566	806	1176	1384	1555	1825	2028	2256
129	308	578	808	1177	1390	1556	1826	2029	2273
133	311	584	809	1181	1391	1575	1829	2030	
137	315	589	816	1182	1393	1576	1835	2031	
139	317	604	817	1184	1394	1580	1836	2033	
140	320	606	820	1187	1395	1582	1837	2036	img
142	339	619	824	1188	1401	1584	1838	2037	
144	342	631	827	1200	1402	1585	1845	2054	
150.1	360	636	837	1211	1404	1586	1852	2066	89
153	371	652	838	1214	1405	1587	1856	2067	105
159	374	655	900	1217	1406	1588	1865	2068	135
173	377	657	901	1218	1410	1591	1870	2084	154
174	378	666	904	1226	1421	1594	1873	2117	156
176	384	673	914	1229	1422	1598	1874	2122	162
177	392	678	921	1237	1425	1609	1875	2125	213
180	393	687	930	1246	1443	1611	1876	2127	232
187	394	688	931	1247	1444	1616	1877	2128	239
189	395	690	936	1249	1448	1617	1878	2129	247
189.1	409	694	950	1250	1449	1621	1880	2131	277
190	418	696	951	1251	1453	1627	1883	2135	279
191	428	698	954	1252	1461	1635	1890	2144	284
192	429	699	958	1253	1463	1636	1891	2147	292
198	432	700	975	1255	1465	1638	1892	2148	331
199	445	701	978	1256	1466	1642	1894	2150	334
202	449	707	989	1257	1472	1650	1900	2151	402
209	462	708	991	1258	1477	1673	1905	2152	414
215	463	709	992	1259	1480	1674	1910	2155	446
225	464	711	997	1274	1490	1699	1911	2157	488
228	465	714	998	1297	1491	1703	1916	2160	491
231	466	718	1003	1301	1500	1707	1930	2164	523
233	467	719	1006	1302	1503	1720	1937	2169	537
234	468	721	1017	1304	1504	1727	1950	2179	565
236	475	722	1026	1305	1505	1728	1951	2182	672

685	inf	346	678	901	1104	1354	1672	2044	490
717		349	680	904	1106	1355	1695	2051	656
731	433	360	681	910	1107	1356	1708	2061	725
746	1519	373	685	912	1108	1358	1718	2065	820
756		376	713	914	1118	1362	1719	2072	825
765		397	741	919	1119	1364	1734	2075	897
786	int	402	750	930	1120	1365	1735	2089	943
829		404	759	932	1121	1366	1736	2092	989
897	2	407	760	934	1122	1367	1755	2095	1028
910	22	415	769	936	1125	1368	1756	2107	1030
927	33	418	781	937	1126	1369	1760	2109	1145
943	41	461	784	940	1127	1370	1780	2110	1222
1009	44	475	823	942	1128	1372	1781	2117	1347
1028	48	477	832	947	1132	1373	1788	2119	1366
1178	51	484	837	948	1135	1377	1789	2152	1403
1202	78	486	838	949	1136	1384	1795	2160	1413
1253	81	489	847	954	1151	1388	1796	2162	1414
1260	82	490	851	958	1152	1389	1804	2168	1429
1309	99	491	852	976	1153	1397	1830	2178	1459
1312	104	495	853	977	1154	1398	1840	2196	1531
1328	110	508	854	980	1155	1399	1853	2198	1664
1332	125	510	855	998	1156	1400	1857	2200	1665
1431	127	519	857	1016	1158	1401	1859	2201	1687
1436	132	520	858	1018	1160	1402	1860	2203	1717
1448	157	522	859	1022	1164	1404	1861	2205	1725
1473	158	523	860	1023	1166	1405	1862	2206	1818
1485	164	524	861	1024	1169	1407	1871	2216	2192
1526	168	530	863	1025	1184	1411	1872	2220	2232
1602	169	534	864	1028	1190	1413	1883	2221	
1623	177	536	865	1029	1201	1426	1886	2222	
1649	181	537	866	1034	1202	1445	1894	2231	lng
1684	189	547	867	1035	1206	1449	1898	2232	
1685	189.1	552	868	1042	1207	1450	1899	2237	1
1687	190	564	869	1043	1214	1460	1904	2238	18
1696	212	572	870	1044	1221	1466	1911	2240	19
1712	222	573	872	1045	1223	1470	1919	2243	20
1725	225	582	873	1051	1243	1545	1923	2252	21
1737	229	585	874	1052	1247	1580	1931	2265	26
1746	230	587	875	1059	1275	1602	1935	2273	30
1775	234	588	876	1069	1281	1603	1947	2274	36
1791	243	597	884	1070	1288	1614	1957	2280	52
1818	245	598	885	1071	1291	1621	1962		61
1841	259	602	886	1072	1292	1622	1974		62
1900	259.1	606	887	1074	1293	1623	1975	ken	80
1957	259.2	607	888	1075	1298	1625	1985		87
1993	273	628	889	1076	1303	1627	1992	78	88
1996	278	637	890	1095	1318	1629	1993	135	107
2035	279	639	891	1096	1324	1640	1995	188	108
2095	284	641	892	1097	1326	1652	1999	207	125
2099	288	645	893	1098	1327	1657	2009	265	130
2120	295	646	894	1099	1328	1659	2010	334	176
2223	312	662	896	1101	1338	1663	2025	353	180
2242	317	667	898	1102	1341	1664	2036	389	181
2270	321	671	900	1103	1346	1667	2043	418	189

193	543	866	1056	1372	1779	2108	997	2267	303
200	544	867	1056.1	1373	1780	2113	1000	2278	306
209	545	868	1062	1374	1781	2114	1026		307
211	553	869	1069	1377	1788	2130	1027	mth	309
212	567	870	1070	1381	1789	2143	1076		310
219	568	871	1071	1388	1791	2158	1123	45	319
223	574	873	1072	1392	1792	2160	1124	46	336
230	579	875	1075	1398	1795	2168	1124.1	58	345
255	581	880.1	1077	1400	1805	2186	1173	84	348
256	588	884	1082	1416	1806	2211	1174	90	372
275	598	885	1085	1420	1815	2239	1213	93	384
276	605	886	1086	1422	1819	2242	1270	94	387
285	622	887	1089	1435	1828	2247.1	1371	106	395
286	636	888	1092	1446	1834	2273	1378	109	397
287	640	898	1093	1453	1840		1380	111	405
294	641	899	1104	1454	1846		1385	113	444
307	652	905	1105	1461	1847	mns	1386	115	447
321	654	909	1106	1484	1854		1387	116	450
324	656	911	1108	1488	1855	12	1479.1	117	451
329	657	918	1112	1489	1859	18	1527	120	452
332	661	920	1117	1527	1860	36	1570	121	463
333	667	922	1126	1531	1861	98	1572	124	464
340	682	926	1128	1535	1863	127	1601	129	465
344	683	937	1135	1536	1886	128	1655	139	468
347	690.1	938	1136	1537	1892	186	1662	141	478
366	691	939	1147	1538	1898	223	1670	144	484
373	692	940	1148	1551	1899	226	1676	145	487
390	695	943	1149	1568	1904	239	1696.1	146	492
397	702	946	1150	1570	1906	254	1748	147	498
408	703	950	1152	1601	1914	307	1749	150	499
425	736	960	1154	1602	1917	312	1750	177	500
426	738	973	1156	1606	1918	321	1751	180	508
427	740	983	1158	1622	1919	356	1861	189	516
429.1	755	990	1161	1626	1923	357	1892	193	529
441	758	995	1164	1627	1925	399	1951	198	558
442	759	1004	1166	1647	1929	441	1954	199	561
443	760	1005	1167	1650	1933	442	1956	204	564
453	770	1014	1221	1656	1950	480	1958	205	566
454	776	1019	1223	1676	1956	481	1961	206	573
455	812	1022	1244	1701	1958	532	1970	215	575
456	825	1024	1266	1702	1960	577	1994.1	222	578
457	826	1025	1267	1710	1975	670	2031	225	585
458	828	1026	1269	1713	1994	704	2081	238	599
459	847	1028	1271	1717	1999	751	2082	239	600
462	849	1031	1280	1736	2007	756	2084	261	620
470	850	1033	1317	1749	2019	761.1	2093	263	627
477	851	1035	1328	1750	2036	833	2125	264	631
513	856	1039	1351	1751	2044	895	2163	270	636
514	857	1044	1354	1754	2074	923	2166	271	642
517	858	1045	1360	1755	2075	931	2205	273	643
526	859	1046	1363	1756	2079	984	2244	282	647
530	860	1048	1365	1765	2089	986	2247.1	283	648
533	861	1049	1368	1770	2094	989	2251	289	655
542	863	1053	1370	1777	2102	993	2259	291	670

671	1142	1564	1891	2215	674	1375	1945	119	787
687	1157	1565	1892	2244	682	1418	1946	121	788
689	1162	1582	1902	2245	716	1419	1951	122	802
696	1171	1587	1921	2273	740	1474	1965	123	811
697	1172	1588	1930	mtr	768	1481	1969	124	820
700	1187	1593	1932		771	1484	1981	136	837
726	1188	1596	1937	15	795	1513	2011	150.1	856
727	1200	1597	1951	17	798	1558	2024	177	916
734	1201	1618	1955	18	803	1562	2031	181	926
737	1202	1623	1966	36	807	1563	2056	193	950
756	1203	1625	1967	74	812	1566	2096	198	974
777	1205	1628	1978	75	820	1570	2099	199	983
778	1206	1629	1984	77	825	1579	2100	206	992
783	1207	1642	1997	101	830	1582	2101	208	1006
787	1209	1643	2001	130	876	1603	2102	215	1028
792	1210	1656	2002	138	904	1619	2108	221	1034
793	1211	1657	2003	143	921	1625	2111	239	1038
797	1214	1666	2009	148	922	1650	2112	257	1040
801	1216	1671	2021	149	943	1651	2113	258	1088
811	1220	1680	2026	174	962	1660	2114	273	1089
813	1226	1685	2031	210	963	1661	2116	297	1090
819	1229	1690	2040	216	968	1662	2117	307	1091
824	1237	1693	2045	221	969	1675	2118	315	1109
831	1264	1700	2046	222	971	1686	2134	394	1112
848	1268	1708	2048	224	972	1702	2138	406	1157
912	1271	1731	2049	225	979	1704	2139	406.1	1174
913	1315	1733	2050	277	1026	1706	2146	449	1175
914	1331	1739	2051	287.1	1028	1738	2160	472	1177
915	1353	1742	2052	321	1064	1741	2185	511	1184
916	1397	1743	2053	333	1069	1754	2217	512	1211
917	1428	1746	2054	341	1085	1763	2236	518	1237
925	1438	1747	2055	343	1103	1797	2244	525	1245
950	1439	1766	2061	356	1143	1798		541	1246
952	1440	1770	2064	363	1165	1799		561	1250
954	1456	1771	2068	409	1185	1807	nam	571	1257
955	1457	1772	2090	410	1219	1809		579	1258
961	1458	1773	2127	411	1222	1828	29	585	1259
965	1463	1774	2131	413	1231	1833	30	614	1301
989	1466	1775	2133	429.1	1232	1846	31	618	1309
991	1470	1780	2140	440	1233	1884	36	623	1314
992	1472	1786	2141	469	1234	1887	45	652	1320
997	1477	1794	2142	515	1235	1888	48	656	1321
998	1501	1802	2149	531	1236	1889	82	726	1322
1026	1502	1813	2151	563	1239	1892	84	734	1323
1040	1503	1814	2152	564	1264	1899	87	735	1325
1081	1504	1817	2154	580	1270	1903	95	736	1330
1083	1508	1824	2160	583	1272	1904	106	737	1336
1109	1509	1827	2170	593	1272.1	1909	110	738	1337
1110	1512	1836	2176	595	1273	1924	111	743	1340
1112	1515	1852	2184	606	1298	1926	113	744	1341
1127	1532	1865	2188	618	1347	1927	114	758	1342
1139	1540	1866	2189	649	1352	1936	116	769	1343
1140	1548	1869	2190	656	1359	1938	117	777	1344
1141	1550	1875	2197	659	1363	1939	118	783	1350

1358	1961	1615	406.1	1625	839	693	2226.3	1653	802
1366	1966	1681	409	1629	1056	738	2226.4	1685	805
1369	1975	1714	472	1632	1137	752	2226.5	1690	821.1
1379	2025	1762	480	1646	1238	757	2226.6	1716	823
1381	2037	1912	483	1649	1673	779	2226.7	1824	904
1390	2040	1990	484	1654	1919	780	2226.8	1996	929
1393	2048	2078	489	1657	2088	925	2226.9	2066	936
1394	2051	2124	492	1673	2231	1028	2246	2095	998
1395	2064	2159	497	1716		1163		2099	1013
1398	2067	2202	509	1732	sch	1165	smb	2127	1015
1401	2128	2258	528	1739	1	1175		2133	1017
1445	2131		529	1740	11	1188	98	2160	1032
1472	2154		549	1746	14	1271	101	2178	1134
1475	2157	ref	558	1785	138	1333	131	2191	1189
1491	2160		565	1852	163	1334	154	2201	1211
1510	2165	367	636	1865	181	1335	156	2249	1260
1511	2169	835	638	1951	189	1385	157	2253	1263
1540	2187	1219	644	1962	197	1412	161		1271
1557	2188	1262	645	1968	289	1451	234		1297
1575	2213	1294	646	1977	304	1487	254	src	1331
1577	2234	1453	656	1978	307	1518	397		1415
1586	2235	1915	658	1995	323	1604	488	73	1456
1656	2236		700.1	1997	337	1610	492	97	1519
1673	2244		707	2010	337.1	1668	547	112	1528
1678	2251		742	2014	338	1721	565	178	1532
1683	2267	rel	745	2035	338.1	1722	575	189	1591
1698	2273		756	2058	357	1723	603	201	1592
1707	2274	37	787	2063	382	1782	618	223	1629
1731	2276	67	820	2064	383	1907	641	240	1632
1760		69	821.1	2090	384	1907.1	644	268	1645
1767		126	925	2095	385	1997	645	287.1	1649
1773	par	131	950	2125	386	1998	646	290	1687
1775		132	975	2126	401	2121	699	300	1693
1795	25	156	982	2149	435	2161	707	307	1698
1816	35	158	997	2160	436	2167	742	318	1699
1820	47	177	998	2191	437	2167.1	765	345	1732
1824	67	179	1011	2194	438	2167.2	823	358	1765
1826	293	180	1026	2205	438.1	2167.3	974	359	1770
1827	326	193	1030	2218	438.2	2180	1109	362	1775
1835	356	206	1115	2242	438.3	2204	1142	363	1794
1870	398	207	1189	2276	438.4	2207	1171	365	1813
1872	430	229	1214		439	2208	1260	368	1823
1876	502	239	1316		460	2208.1	1316	371	1852
1877	570	254	1332		473	2225	1383	377	1853
1879	624	261	1428	rht	476	2225.1	1436	446	1869
1880	632	281	1455		564	2225.2	1438	520	1955
1886	656	289	1459	18	599	2225.3	1439	585	1968
1890	710	300	1470	55	609	2225.4	1455	625	1977
1892	907	307	1532	64	610	2225.5	1485	627	1984
1894	956	308	1533	78	611	2225.6	1526	645	2014
1911	957	319	1564	99	650	2225.7	1532	690.1	2032
1921	1229	346	1582	183	651	2226	1561	729	2045
1932	1417	397	1584	184	691	2226.1	1623	734	2046
1955	1483	406	1623	419	692	2226.2	1625	791	2048

2050	829	str	806	2096	673	2088	910	2034	548
2068	830		820	2100	731	2095	921	2036	586
2069	839	12	822	2101	733	2126	941	2087	596
2108	899	64	825	2126	756	2151	942	2090	614
2142	941	91	904	2145	761.1	2160	959	2095	626
2194	943	92	924	2175	762	2200	975	2120	629
2201	1010	97	955	2200	785	2209	976	2137	630
2244	1026	126	959	2227	799	2238	1009	2160	653
2257	1028	129	975	2244	821	2240	1178	2164	660
	1039	155	976	2247.1	822	2250	1243	2176	677
	1110	159	998	2253	854	2253	1277	2179	696
stl	1131	160	1024	2276	924		1279	2191	700
	1137	161	1026		927		1312	2194	707
18	1170	165	1028		940	thm	1396	2203	712
21	1219	189	1043	tec	941		1411	2218	719
34	1235	229	1113		942	100	1425	2228	720
64	1271	231	1114	56	1003	105	1431	2242	723
69	1375	232	1188	64	1238	152	1439	2253	737
73	1410	233	1238	69	1240	154	1470		738
78	1427	234	1243	99	1243	167	1473		739
96	1432	238	1295	129	1276	193	1485	trl	740
97	1442	239	1298	154	1288	231	1531		747
99	1566	254	1316	157	1316	233	1533	7	814
135	1570	261	1319	159	1319	261	1600	12	820
144	1582	262	1407	160	1356	265	1605	27	831
167	1607	307	1411	165	1397	319	1607	28	889
182	1673	332	1460	167	1408	331	1625	36	931
183	1728	381	14/0	182	1436	373	1627	72	967
184	1738	421	1507	229	1471	388	1646	85	989
222	1742	422	1561	231	1529	390	1658	112	996
225	1770	423	1570	232	1574	419	1673	128	997
257	1792	424	1571	254	1580	424	1684	151	998
277	1846	434	1574	261	1605	492	1692	174	999
284	1848	492	1584	281	1607	496	1695	196	1008
370	1849	496	1600	331	1652	525	1698	213	1028
414	1850	535	1607	332	1664	536	1715	225	1078
470	1882	536	1684	397	1675	565	1717	235	1133
492	1919	549	1694	412	1684	588.1	1732	238	1183
524	1957	565	1696	415	1694	601	1745	239	1224
535	1977	590	1728	416	1696	603	1785	241	1230
539	1982	603	1730	421	1715	645	1804	242	1231
546	2027	618	1737	422	1725	646	1808	299	1234
668	2031	621	1742	423	1737	649	1841	305	1251
686	2060	644	1743	434	1743	656	1848	316	1261
717	2088	649	1759	496	1792	670	1849	322	1278
733	2099	656	1792	520	1850	672	1850	351	1326
746	2100	663	1801	522	1957	673	1852	355	1329
773	2101	670	1810	535	1968	699	1871	356	1409
774	2126	706	1836	588.1	1977	746	1878	403	1462
775	2185	728	1892	590	1994.1	750	1883	420	1475
782	2209	740	1962	637	2026	777	1973	475	1477
799	2229	761.1	1977	663	2027	811	1994.1	479	1482
803	2244	762	1994.1	667	2063	812	2009	485	1517
810	2276	774	2095	670	2087	820	2026	501	1539

1541	385	218	834	1056	1321	1735	2143	943	407
1559	527	219	836	1056.1	1323	1736	2160	1010	408
1581	559	220	841	1057	1324	1760	2162	1028	418
1582	592	241	842	1058	1326	1788	2168	1030	477
1625	594	242	843	1061	1347	1795	2198	1056	487
1630	615	245	844	1062	1355	1796	2216	1074	489
1650	616	246	856	1063	1356	1805	2220	1110	510
1678	617	256	857	1065	1357	1830	2238	1143	519
1726	708	272	864	1066	1358	1843	2245	1531	522
1752	709	273	865	1067	1359	1859	2252	1613	567
1758	724	274	867	1070	1360	1862	2267	1664	568
1761	757	276	872	1071	1363	1863	2278	1725	602
1787	1068	278	874	1074	1364	1892	2280	1792	605
1951	1334	280	875	1075	1369	1893		1917	608
1952	1679	288	876	1076	1370	1895		1959	623
1972	1689	295	877	1082	1371	1897	unt	1994.1	633
1986	1711	312	878	1084	1376	1898		2089	634
2004	1800	321	879	1094	1378	1904	155	2096	635
2031	1901	349	880	1095	1380	1928	159	2099	639
2041	1903	352	881	1096	1382	1929	161	2126	641
2067	1919	356	882	1097	1385	1935	196	2236	657
2077	2076	376	883	1098	1387	1940	233		667
2080	2093	390	888	1099	1388	1941	234		671
2084	2096	391	889	1100	1389	1942	261	wrd	681
2091	2115	405	893	1101	1400	1943	346		699
2099	2118	408	898	1102	1402	1944	492	5	756
2106	2261	411	901	1104	1407	1947	496	26	758
2109		462	902	1106	1413	1949	535	30	784
2125		477	903	1107	1422	1951	603	41	849
2127	txt	482	932	1108	1424	1953	649	52	850
2145		486	933	1120	1433	1957	707	60	851
2153	2	487	935	1121	1447	1958	728	88	852
2160	22	501	936	1122	1449	1961	1411	110	870
2171	27	519	937	1125	1467	1964	1531	129	873
2173	30	525	938	1128	1469	1970	1584	162	890
2181	41	530	947	1129	1474	1992	1654	176	891
2206	57	550	948	1132	1522	1993	1673	181	892
2210	58	564	949	1166	1566	1994	1728	188	893
2212	62	572	973	1168	1572	2011	1892	211	898
2219	104	597	980	1174	1582	2065	1976	212	902
2224	107	602	987	1184	1602	2068	2095	219	911
2230	110	628	993	1206	1603	2070	2135	247	934
2251	125	639	1007	1208	1620	2072	2160	265	939
2255	127	679	1016	1221	1640	2075	2191	278	950
2271	129	682	1020	1223	1652	2083	2227	288	983
2272	132	700	1026	1251	1659	2089		292	985
2277	141	707	1027	1269	1660	2092	var	296	989
	168	708	1028	1289	1662	2104		306	1004
	177	709	1036	1291	1663	2107	59	324	1024
about	181	738	1042	1292	1708	2109	135	340	1025
trl	211	776	1043	1293	1709	2110	162	349	1028
	212	812	1045	1296	1719	2117	223	366	1052
323	215	824	1050	1303	1724	2119	229	376	1056
325	217	831	1054	1317	1734	2138	265	405	1056.1

1060	1147	1159	1372	1622	1733	1816	1975	2097	2211
1067	1148	1160	1373	1625	1734	1818	1993	2105	2216
1071	1149	1208	1374	1626	1736	1819	2008	2119	2223
1072	1150	1220	1377	1667	1737	1840	2027	2128	2228
1074	1151	1267	1388	1672	1755	1854	2029	2147	2232
1076	1152	1269	1396	1691	1756	1855	2065	2148	2243
1077	1153	1351	1445	1712	1781	1899	2070	2160	2252
1125	1154	1363	1448	1725	1785	1923	2079	2194	2270
1135	1158	1365	1614	1728	1805	1964	2092	2198	2273

Derivative Works	Recordings
10.1	102
43	749
79	1308
172	
327	
749	
1285	
1998?	

Line Numbers
Beowulf

Line	Item	Line	Item	Line	Item
1–3	333	35	876	93	542, 543
1–52	8, 723	44	1097, 1860	94	1067
1–62	215	46	217	99	1097
1–121	539	48ff	1942	100	1706
1–1215	2107	49	288, 459,	101	1324
4–5	1324		1691	104	876
4–52	2051	51	1363	106	1363, 1840,
5	1107	53	321		1923
6	876, 1095,	53–114	1688	106–107	1027
	1107, 1911,	54	1097	107–108	1014
	1944	58	876	107ff	1011
7	876	59–63	1422	112	898, 1084,
9–10	1324	61	1043, 1961		1149, 1150,
11	1425	61–62	1081		1159
12–16	1974	62	81, 259,	115ff	1028
14–15	1108, 1860		259.1,	120	1407
14ff	1027		259.2, 399,	121	876
15	180, 1324		1022, 1321,	126	876
16ff	1097		1324, 2236	126–133	776
19	605	62ff	1035	129–130	1028
20–25	2218	63	876, 1082	130	255, 784
20ff	1027	63–64	1097	133	1028
21	180, 1447	67	1097	138	1067
22	1097	67–70	1724	139	399
22–24	1027	69–70	219	142	519
23	1098	69ff	903	143	1860
24	2075	70	1036, 1956	149	1860
26	1027	71	691	150	1904
26–53	242	73	519	152	1961
28	1136	75ff	876	154–156	1098
28–31	1788	76–77	1027	156	1028
29	1620	78	591, 1027	159–163	359
30	220, 321	78ff	522	161	1028
31	399, 1084,	81ff	1108	162	387, 1027
	1860, 1898	82	892	163–164	296
31–32	947	82–83	1029, 1300	166ff	2092
32	1893	82–84	1336	168	489
32–33	1097	82–85	876	168–169	317, 404,
33	836, 869,	83ff	1028		519, 547,
	1153, 1220,	84	1156		759, 910,
	1893, 1935,	86–98	346		942, 1027,
	1996	89	2138		1121, 1657,
34–37	2085	89–100	369		1664

Finnsburh

Line	Item	Line	Item	Line	Item
1–7	1310	5	1050, 1118	6–8	1445
4–5	1119	6	1035	8	1020
16	78, 1035	34	862, 1223,	36	862
18	1208		1424	39	1376
33	78	35	1290, 1897	40	1290, 1897